This Book is Presented to
The Clayton Community Library
by the

Clayton Valley Sunrise Rotary Club
in Honor of our Guest Speaker

7/28/05
date

E.O. James was Professor Emeritus of the History and Philosophy of Religion in the University of London. He was educated at Exeter College, Oxford, and at University College, London, where he was a student of Sir Flinders Petrie. In a long and distinguished career he held numerous posts, among them, Professor of History and Philosophy of Religion at the University of Leeds, Lecturer at the University of Amsterdam, and Wilde Lecturer in the University of Oxford. Among his many published works are *Myths and Ritual in the Ancient Near East*, *Prehistoric Religion*, and *Primitive Ritual and Belief*.

The
Ancient Gods

The History and Diffusion of Religion in the
Ancient Near East and the Eastern Mediterranean

E. O. JAMES

*Professor Emeritus of the History of Religion in
the University of London. Fellow of University
College and Fellow of King's College, London*

CASTLE
BOOKS

This edition published in 2004 by
CASTLE BOOKS ®
A division of BOOK SALES, INC.
114 Northfield Avenue
Edison, NJ 08837

This book is reprinted by arrangement with
Orion Publishing Group Ltd.
Orion House, 5 Upper St. Martin's Lane, London WC2H 9EA

First published in Great Britain
by Weidenfeld & Nicolson in 1960
Paperback edition published in 1999 by Phoenix,
an imprint of Orion Books Ltd.

A CIP catalogue record for this book
is available from the British Library.

ISBN 0-7858-1833-2

Printed in the United States of America

CONTENTS

CONTENTS

LIST OF ILLUSTRATIONS

7

LINE ILLUSTRATIONS IN THE TEXT

The illustrations which appear between pages 176 and 177 are referred to in the text as Figs. 1 to 85. The line illustrations are referred to as figs. 1 to 11.

PREFACE

It is appropriate that the first two volumes in a new series on the history of religion should deal, one with religion in prehistoric times, and the other (the present volume) with its development and diffusion in the Near East, from Western Asia to India, and from North Africa and the eastern Mediterranean to the Aegean and the Graeco-Roman world. As Professor Albright has recently remarked, 'archaeological research has established beyond doubt that there is no focus of civilization in the earth that can begin to compete in antiquity and activity with the basin of the eastern Mediterranean and the region immediately to the east of it—Breasted's Fertile Crescent. Other civilizations in the Old World were all derived from this cultural centre or were strongly influenced by it; only the New World was entirely independent. In tracing our civilization of the West to its earliest home we are, accordingly, restricted to the Egypto-Mesopotamian area.' (*From the Stone Age to Christianity*, 1948, p. 6.) Hence the importance of the attention that is now being paid by archaeologists to the Near East, and the significance of the results of these investigations for the history of religion.

To deal in detail with this vital region from first-hand knowledge of each area would require a team of experts in the several cultures confining their attention to their own highly specialized field of research. In the present series, which is to be devoted mainly to the higher living religions, this, however regrettable, was not a practical proposition. Since all that could be attempted here was an overall survey related to the requirements of the prescribed scheme as a whole, a specialist in one region quite naturally would be inclined to concentrate upon his own domain and he would hardly be in a position to view it in relation to the other volumes in the series. Therefore, I undertook to write the book myself as I happened to have had some first-hand acquaintance with Near Eastern and the adjacent religions, and the relevant archaeological data, over a number of years since, after having been trained as an anthropologist, I first worked in this field under the guidance of Sir Flinders Petrie in the earlier part of the century. It was not without some misgivings, however, as my equipment does not include an ability to read the texts in their original scripts. So, like many other interpreters of the documentary evidence, I have had to rely upon the renderings of those engaged in their decipherment and translation. For these comparative purposes it is unfortunate that the linguistic experts are by no means always agreed among themselves about one another's findings and interpretations of the literary material, which often is in a very fragmentary condition. Where I have had occasion to use the texts in this volume I have consulted the most authoritative sources available, such as those of Albright, Driver, Ginsberg, Goetze, Gordon, Güterbrock, Gurney, Heidel, Jacobsen, Kramer, Virolleaud and Wilson, to mention but a few outstanding names. While I have not hesitated to exercise independent judgment in the light of my own wider inquiries in this field and in the history and comparative study of religion, I have at least gone to the most reliable sources of information and made an impartial selection of the data available. The textual evidence, however, has been only one aspect of the investigation.

Since the successive phases and complementary manifestations of religion in this region have been very largely a product of the environment, to place the discipline in its proper setting a brief introductory survey has been made of the rise and development of civilization in the area. Against this general background the emergence of religion has been then reviewed, particularly in relation to the three most critical and perplexing situations in the environment in which it arose—those connected with birth and fertility, the food supply and the seasonal sequence, death and the afterlife—and out of which the ancient gods assumed their several forms and functions. From these foundations the subsequent course of development and diffusion has been traced and the interconnexions and correspondence between the various elements in this complex and widespread structure of faith and practice have been determined.

Since it was in this vital cradleland of civilization that most of the higher living religions arose, and at the present juncture of events it has again become the dynamic centre of world affairs in which religion is still playing a very important role, an objective investigation of the historical situation and its antecedents is of more than academic interest and concern. Because the entire region from beyond the Caspian Sea and the Persian Gulf to North Africa, the Aegean and Crete, with outposts in the Indus valley and northern Europe, has been so interrelated, it provides the essential basis of history, be it that of religion, or of any other aspect of culture. It also readily becomes the happy hunting-ground for ideological and doctrinaire propaganda, not least in the field of religion and politics. In this volume care has been taken to avoid these pitfalls and to present and interpret the archaeological and documentary data, and the systems and movements brought under review, historically and in a scientific manner, leaving it to the reader to draw his own conclusions for his specific purposes.

The public for which this series is designed is the intelligent reader anxious to become better acquainted with the history, beliefs, practices and characteristic features of the ancient and living religions, though not necessarily equipped with an expert or a specialized knowledge of the particular discipline. For such a purpose it would have been inappropriate to attempt to produce a work of specialized and localized scholarship covering so wide a subject. Therefore, so far as possible technicalities have been avoided, and an endeavour has been made to render the subject generally comprehensible at a scholarly level, without it is hoped diminishing its usefulness for other workers in this field of research. Thus, references have been supplied in the footnotes to the most important relevant literature and to first-hand sources where additional information can be obtained, together with a selective bibliography appended to each chapter confined for the most part to relatively recent and accessible books.

It is to those who by the spade or the textual tablets have revealed the hidden secrets of the past that I owe a great debt for without the resources they have made available this volume could not have been written. I am also most grateful to all who have helped in various ways in the preparation of the manuscript, and to my friend, Professor S. G. F. Brandon of the University of Manchester, for reading the entire typescript and making most useful criticisms from his wide knowledge of the field of inquiry.

Oxford.   E. O. JAMES

CHAPTER ONE

THE RISE OF CIVILIZATION
IN THE ANCIENT NEAR EAST

Earliest Neolithic agricultural settlements: Jericho, Qalat Jarmo, Hassuna, Halaf culture, Mesopotamia, Sumerian urban and literary civilization—Iranian civilization: Sialk, Susa and Elam—Western Indian civilization: Baluchistan, Harappan civilization, Mohenjo-daro and Harappa—Valley of the Nile: Badarian and Amratian prehistoric cultures, Gerzean period, Dynastic period—Asia Minor: Hittites and Hurrians, Ugarit-Ras Shamra, Hebrews in Palestine—Eastern Mediterranean: Aegean civilization, Minoan-Mycenaean civilization, Achaeans and the Dorian invasion

THE WEALTH of new material recovered in recent years from the Ancient Near East by archaeological excavation and investigation and the discovery, decipherment and translation of a number of texts hitherto unknown, has made possible a clearer knowledge and understanding of the religion of this crucial region from prehistoric times to the end of the Bronze Age, and of all that has emerged from it in the higher faiths of mankind. It may be confidently affirmed, indeed, that it was here that the birth of civilization occurred with its revolutionary effects upon the development of religion. It is true the transition from hunting, fishing, and collecting edible roots and fruits to cattle breeding, the cultivation of the soil and its products, and mixed agriculture, was a gradual process slowly adopted and localized in certain places. And doubtless it occurred more than once in different regions. Nevertheless, the claims of the Middle East to be the cradleland of ancient civilization are overwhelming, though in which of the several possible centres the emergence first took place is still in debate.

THE EARLIEST NEOLITHIC AGRICULTURAL SETTLEMENTS

If the discovery and development of agriculture be taken as the criterion, Sir Mortimer Wheeler probably is right in arguing in favour of settled communities engaged in the cultivation of the soil and with public works and needs implying an organized and durable administration, originating in fertile oases like Jericho in the Kingdom of Jordan rather than in the great river valleys of the Nile, the Euphrates and the Tigris, the Indus, or further afield the Huang Ho, which were always liable to serious flooding.[1] Thus, Miss Kathleen Kenyon has now

unearthed at Tell es-Sultan in the mound of ancient Jericho the remains
of a very early pre-pottery Neolithic settlement, dated between 8000
and 6000 BC, containing mortars and grinding stones for milling corn
in the lowest levels. Although no potsherds have been found, these very
early Neolithic herdsmen practised agriculture and had acquired a
highly developed unified culture with an elaborate architecture, communal buildings, domestic houses, town walls, rock-cut ditches, shrines,
cult objects and remarkable plastered human skulls. Within the fortified
enclosure is a spring said to produce a thousand gallons of water a
minute, which still supports the town and irrigates the luxuriant oasis.[2]
It must always have been the symbol of the life it so lavishly bestows
in the midst of an arid plain, throwing into relief the mysterious forces
of vegetation and stimulating the practice of agriculture in the earliest
farming community that has as yet been discovered by archaeological
excavation.

Jericho, Qalat Jarmo and Hassuna

In northern Iraq at Qalat Jarmo on the Kurdish foothills to the north-
east of the Tigris where wild grains grow abundantly, a similar pre-
pottery Neolithic site has been revealed, dated by Carbon 14 analysis
of radio-active organic material (snail-shells and charcoal) at about
4750 BC. Here it would seem, if the Jericho dating is correct,[3] that a
thousand years or so later there was a parallel development on a smaller
scale in the second half of the fifth millennium BC, with agriculture
preceding pottery-making. At Tell Hassuna near Mosul in Assyria,
west of the Tigris, on the other hand, the art of pottery-making is
shown to have been practised in each of the succession of stratified
settlements of farming communities. In the lowest and earliest level
the soil was tilled with stone hoes, the grain was ground with stone
pestles and mortars and the flour stored in coarse jars, some of which
were also used for infant burials. In the next deposit rectangular houses
appear, divided into several rooms furnished with ovens and grouped
round a court in which were also round clay bread ovens. The pottery
was tempered, incised and painted in two or more colours. In the higher
levels a steady advance in agriculture and the arts is shown. Animal
bones include those of the sheep, ox, ass, goat, gazelle, hare and pig,
mixed farming having become the means of subsistence. Indeed, as
Dr Seton Lloyd says, farming people of one race or another have lived
and worked at Hassuna almost without interruption for close on seven
millenniums, many of the original methods and their magico-religious
cultus having hardly changed in all these thousands of years.[4]

The Halaf culture

In the transitional phase from the late Neolithic to the Chalcolithic period, when artefacts were hammered in malleable copper, a stable, well organized culture was beginning to take shape in the Ancient Near East in the fourth millennium BC (c. 3800), characterized by fine painted pottery, a more general use of copper, permanent houses, and a definite religious cult. The type station of this culture is Tell Halaf on the upper Khabur river in eastern Syria on the Anatolian border, but its wide distribution through northern Mesopotamia, Iran and Kurdistan, shows that it was firmly established throughout the region.[5] Besides the excellent well-fired pottery elaborately decorated and glazed, clay figurines, seal pendants, spindle whorls, amulets in limestone and shell, and small beads of metallic copper were in abundance. Emmer wheat and barley were cultivated, and sheep, cattle, goats and pigs were domesticated to supplement a hunting economy. Apart from houses, ten peculiar circular stone structures known as *tholoi* with a domed roof and in some cases having a rectangular passage or chamber attached to them, as in the Mycenaean beehive tombs in the Aegean, are generally thought to have been used for ritual purposes, though there are no traces of burials in them. The importance of the culture, however, for the elucidation of Near Eastern religion is very considerable, especially in relation to the cult of the Mother-goddess. Its origin is not easy to determine. The most probable source is either the Mosul region of northern Iraq or the Khabur of eastern Syria, with Armenia as a possible alternative (e.g., Tilki Tepe). There is much to be said in favour of northern Iraq,[6] and it would seem to have been in Assyria that it became most fully developed, until it was replaced by a somewhat inferior ceramic technique named after Al Ubaid in Sumer, when the delta in the south became habitable.

Mesopotamia

The pottery of the earliest settlers in southern Mesopotamia indicates that they came from Persia and having established themselves in the lower reaches of the Tigris and Euphrates they succeeded in cultivating the marshland, tilling the fields on the shallow islands and reclaimed land with stone hoes. In addition to erecting well-planned houses built of stone or mud-brick in their villages, they constructed temples with a long central hall flanked on either side with smaller rooms and approached by an entrance porch. In the oblong sanctuary stood an altar and a table of offerings. The plan, in fact, was the prototype of the later Sumerian temples. At Eridu, for instance, the great sanctuary of the city-god Enki in the third millennium BC was super-imposed on a succession of sacred edifices which go back to the small square temple standing on a platform and built of mud-brick in the late Ubaid period.[7]

The Sumerian urban and literary civilization
The Al Ubaid settlement, however, seems to have been short-lived by comparison with the period of occupation at Ur before the great Flood in the valley of the Tigris somewhere about 3000 BC that swept over several Sumerian cities, the recollections of which survive in the King-lists and the legend of Enki and Ziusudra (Utnapishtim), the Sumerian prototype of the biblical Noah in the Hebrew version of the event.[8] At Ur the sterile layer of water-worn sand was reached in an ancient cemetery beneath the succession of Jemdet Nasr, Uruk and Ubaid levels. But at Shuruppak (Fara) and Warka, traces of another flood occur above the latest remains of the Jemdet Nasr period, named after a site in northern Mesopotamia near Babylon dated in the fourth quarter of the fourth millennium BC, or possibly in the very beginning of the third millennium. It was doubtless one or the other of these catastrophes that gave rise to the tradition in the early Dynastic period immortalized in the deluge legends, and regarded as making a definite break in the history of the Sumerian kingship as a divine institution. In fact, however, although the Dynastic period was distinguished by its exceptional wealth and prosperity, actually there were very few visible changes in or additions to the buildings, graves and other remains in the archaeological sites to differentiate it from the Jemdet Nasr, Al Ubaid and other pre-flood cultures.

Nevertheless, the way was now open for the development of an urban civilization with new techniques, monumental architecture in temples and other structures, and all that resulted from the invention of writing. In Babylonia this epoch-making discovery assumed the form of the cuneiform script inscribed on clay tablets that gradually was adopted throughout western Asia for the keeping of documentary records, the making of religious texts, and the practical purposes of commerce and administration. Indeed, so important was the achievement that Gordon Childe has regarded it as symptomatic of 'a quite novel socio-economic structure—the city'. It was, he thinks, the essential element in the 'Urban Revolution', centred in communities comprising a large pro-portion of rulers, officials, priests, artisans and merchants who lived on the surplus produced by farmers and fishermen outside the city.[9] This no doubt to some extent may be true, as writing unquestionably was an essential condition of civic organization, but civilization was well on its way to being an accomplished fact in the pre-literate agricultural cultures in the Near East.

In Mesopotamia, it is true, the earliest written documents were primarily concerned with the organization of the city-states, contracts, accounts, legal procedure, excerpts from political events and business memoranda, rather than in Egypt where the hieroglyphic inscriptions and texts were concentrated upon the magico-religious control of the food supply, the cult of the dead and the gods and their Enneads. Nevertheless, as the representations in Mesopotamian art were predominantly religious, so the cuneiform tablets were the product of the temple communities and included lists of kings with divine descent, incantations, ritual and omen-texts, legends, lamentations and hymns, from which much information may be derived about current belief and practice from about 3000 BC when the wedge-shaped script emerged from the early pictographic signs, of which the limestone tablet from Kish in the Ashmolean Museum in Oxford, and its successors from Jemdet Nasr, Fara, and Uruk are the archetypes.[10]

Thus, in the vast collection of these texts in the royal library at Nineveh, founded by Ashurbanipal during the last days of the Assyrian Empire (668-626 BC), almost every aspect of Sumerian and Babylonian sacred learning and knowledge is to be found, going back to a very early period. Priests and scribes were commissioned by their royal patrons to collect, revise and catalogue the extant texts, and to make a thorough search of the oldest temple archives throughout the country. The bulk of this material was of a religious character, the product of the temple schools, and among the most important tablets recovered were the fragments of the Gilgamesh heroic epic, one of the finest literary productions of Babylonia, the earliest Akkadian version of which belongs to about 2000 BC with still earlier material on the tablets. Again, the seals in the form of stone cylinders with engraved designs, used for marking merchandise and documents, were also essentially religious symbols depicting gods and goddesses and the performance of ritual acts like the scenes on vases, in temple friezes, and other representations of decorative art. But although every city was under the dominion of its own deity and the temple was the administrative centre, the nation as a whole was never, as in Egypt, a theocracy unified in a single god as the head of the state.

Behind the achievements of the Sumerian civilization lay a long history prior to the pre-Flood Early Dynasties. Indeed, in some of its aspects the Ubaid culture can be regarded as Sumerian,[11] while in those sections of the Al Ubaid site known as Uruk, associated with immigrations from Anatolia or Trans-Caucasia, engraved cylinder-seals, writing on clay, sculpture in the round, and stone-built temples occur. The term 'Sumerian', it has to be remembered, is really a linguistic designation of the cuneiform script invented to express its sounds, probably not later than the fifth millennium BC when the people who introduced the original civilization into Mesopotamia descended from the Elamite mountains into the valleys of the Tigris and Euphrates, bringing with them a distinctive social and religious organization as well as their agglutinative language and its signs and syllabary. But as a cultural heritage the Sumerian civilization constituted a blending of traditions derived from a variety of sources which, notably about 3000 BC, marked a new epoch in the colonization of Mesopotamia.

That the innovation introduced by Al Ubaid and Uruk folk, taken in conjunction with the earlier Hassuna and Halaf phases, were constituent elements in this cultural emergence seems clear. However, of the language of the people we know nothing, and unless and until new light is thrown on their manner of speech the name 'Sumerian' can be attached to this hybrid culture only in the sense that it represents the first colonization of Sumer. Where it arose is also conjectural. The pottery of Al Ubaid is indicative of the Persian highlands, though it was influenced by the Halaf culture,[12] while the temples show many features reproduced in Sumerian and Babylonian architecture suggestive of the Flood period about 3000 BC.

THE IRANIAN CIVILIZATION

The highlands of Iran which extend north of Babylonia through Armenia to the Caucasus, Syria and Palestine, lack the homogeneity of the river valleys. In these steppe-lands a much more loosely organized life was inevitable, free from the complex commercial and industrial undertakings, social submissions, planning and mechanization of the settled urban communities. The principal enemy was drought and the constant struggle with the vagaries of the climate was largely responsible for driving the nomadic wanderers to seek greater security in the oases and river valleys when circumstances permitted.

Sialk

From the fifth millennium BC, however, settlements which have revealed a wide assortment of painted pottery were established in the lower levels of Tepe Sialk, near Kashan in western Iran.[13] The earliest consisted probably of little more than temporary dwellings until in the higher levels permanent houses were constructed in mud-brick, as a semi-nomadic hunting and fishing economy gave place to a more settled life lived in villages. Copper gradually was introduced to supplement the polished stone axes and hoes and sickles with flint teeth set in rib-bones of animals of Natufian type. The hand-made ware at first was coarse and either dark-faced, red buff, or occasionally black, and the slipped ware often was decorated with basketry patterns. As the technique developed decoration with geometric animal and plant designs was introduced, and ring bases or pedestals were added to vases. Carving on bone was abandoned, but copper gradually came into more general use, though it was hammered into the required shape like flint or stone. The appearance of turquoise and carnelian indicates an extension of commercial activities, and in Sialk II connexions with the parallel site at Anau in Transcaspia, on the border of the plateau, are suggested. In the third stage at Sialk there are indications of a break in the tradition and new features and improved techniques appear which in all probability were first made in the Persian highlands before they were introduced into Mesopotamia. Anyway, the Copper Age was now definitely established and in the next stage, in the fourth millennium BC, a proto-Elamite script and cylinder seals engraved in the Jemdet Nasr Mesopotamian style were introduced, as well as other features characteristic of the first city of Susa and of the Jemdet Nasr phase.

Susa and Elam

In Elam where at Susa in the lowest level of the famous site first excavated by de Morgan in 1887, a peasant culture flourished contemporary with that in Sumer, its distinguishing features seem to be only the reflexes of a civilization developed in a more easterly region on the Iranian plateau.[14] The earliest settlement is known almost exclusively from its cemetery and there the grave goods are in advance of those in the Ubaid burials, and the funerary pottery is of a very high quality and ornamented with magico-religious designs.[15] In the succeeding higher levels, corresponding to Uruk, Jemdet Nasr and Early Dynastic phases, the cultural development is maintained. In the third stage (Susa C) proto-Elamite tablets first make their appearance with seals of the Jemdet Nasr period, with which and with that of Uruk the pictographic script has affinities. All these tablets are based on the same original invention of writing current in the fourth millennium BC. Therefore Sumer and Susa both shared in this significant discovery, however much the respective scripts may have differed in their pictographic signs. In fact the proto-Elamite script remained in use until the Sargonic Dynasty of Agade.[16]

From the Early Dynastic period in Sumer a fairly uniform culture seems to have persisted in the Zagros mountains from Susa to Giyan, the divergencies being most marked in the north and south. That Dynastic influences predominated scarcely can be doubted, and in the Musyan area on the Mesopotamian border the tombs and their contents conform to Sumerian types in relation to the royal cultus. Indeed, in both regions the divine kingship seems to have become an established institution, and by providing a unifying dynamic it tended to produce a common culture pattern which found expression in similar techniques as well as in ritual and social organizations. In which of the two areas the dynasty first arose is a matter of conjecture.

The Iranian highlands geographically represent the natural position for a common home of the whole range of cultural achievements in the Ancient East in the fourth millennium BC. If it was the source of the first civilization of Elam it may well have been the centre from which similar movements and influences radiated across the Zagros mountains into Mesopotamia, through Baluchistan and the Himalayas to India, and over the Mongolian plain to North and West China, where traces of an identical ancient agricultural culture have been detected. In western Turkistan at Anau, east of the Caspian Sea, the series of settlements unearthed by Pumpelly in 1904 have revealed further evidence of another outpost of the same civilization on the alluvial land of Transcaspia, while in Baluchistan Indian pottery has been found in association with wares having Persian affinities. There, despite local peculiarities, the same broad distinction recurs between buff wares in the south and east and red ware in the north and west, with corresponding differences in the clay figurines.[17] In form, technique and decoration there are striking resemblances to the pottery of the first period of Hissar in northern Iran, as, for example, in the stylized rendering of animals.

WESTERN INDIAN CIVILIZATION

Baluchistan

In the present state of the data available it is not possible to determine precisely the course of events in Baluchistan before 3000 BC, but it would seem to be among these small farming communities that the sources of Indian civilization must be sought. Thus, while Baluchistan villages would appear to have behind them the earlier Iranian settlements, such as Sialk and Giyan, they in their turn made their contribution to the urban culture of Mohenjo-daro and Chanhu-daro on the

Indus and Harappa on the Ravi, the three great ruined cities of the Punjab which flourished in the third millennium BC. These villages were, in fact, the connecting link between the Indus civilization and that of the Fertile Crescent and western Iran.

In their secluded mountain valleys in Baluchistan they developed the local characteristics reflected in their pottery at Quetta, Nal, Kolwa and the Zhob valley and at Amru in Sind.[18] If these tells can be described as centres of distinctive 'cultures', since the techniques of the ware that has been discovered in them do not conform strictly to a specific type as in Mesopotamia at Hassuna, Halaf and El Ubaid, they reveal a considerable measure of uniformity. Black on red pottery, for instance, predominated in the Zhob valley in the north and black on buff at Nal, Amri, Quetta and Kulli in the south. Therefore, they would seem to represent the remains of large settled self-contained peasant communities in which agriculture, pottery-making with the aid of the wheel, metallurgy and other crafts flourished, and opened the way for commercial intercourse with the cities that were rising in North-west India. This is indicated by traces of exchange of goods between the villages of Baluchistan and Sind and the towns of the Indus valley and Harappan civilization.

The Harappan civilization

Since in 1922 excavations were begun by Rai Bahsdur Daya Ram Sahni at Harappa, and by R. D. Banerji, M. S. Vats, K. N. Dikshit, E. Mackay and Sir John Marshall at Mohenjo-daro, four hundred miles to the south-west, a remarkably homogeneous urban culture has been revealed. Originally it must have occupied a very much larger area than either that of Egypt or Sumer, and a number of sites of large towns in the Bahawalpur State await exploration, presupposing a very considerable agricultural population and surplus of goods for export and exchange. Like the deltas of the Nile and of the Tigris and Euphrates, the broad fertile plains of Lärkäna, between the Indus and the Kohisthan or Kirthar hills, depended upon the annual inundation for their irrigation, and in the absence of artificial canals in prehistoric times they were subject to extensive floods when the snow at the source of the Indus melted rapidly in the summer, or the rainfall was exceptionally heavy, as it seems to have been on occasions, judging from the elaborate drainage systems in the ruined cities. Indeed, at Mohenjo-daro some of the buildings were raised on platforms and artificial hills, presumably to place them out of reach of the flood water. Sind, instead of being the desert it has become, before the south-western monsoon shifted eastwards was a rich grain-growing region, and as the records of Alexander the Great indicate, in the fourth century BC it was still a fertile country (cf. Strabo XVc. 693). Here and in the Punjab a complex civilization developed from the middle of the third millennium BC until it came to an end abruptly about a thousand years later (i.e. probably before 1500 BC) never to be resuscitated. While it lasted it was a remarkable achievement in urban organization and unification which also allowed scope for individualization in its material products and techniques, as is shown by its self-conscious ceramic and glyptic creations. The cities probably were unified under a central government with a common culture, religion, language and script, which, as will be seen, was destined to play an important role in the subsequent development of Hindu India and not least of its syncretistic faith.

Mohenjo-daro and Harappa
The material prosperity with its high standard of comfort was derived from farming, manufactures and commerce, and gave rise to a brisk and extensive trade with the rest of the centres in the Ancient East. The cities were well-planned and their construction and activities required co-operative effort on the part of their builders and citizens. The governors lived in the citadels beneath which at Harappa were small working-class dwellings similar to the group of bare red brick two-roomed cottages at Mohenjo-daro, each 20 feet by 12 feet internally. They were devoid of any semblance of ornament and bore every indication of a 'utility' motive. Arranged in parallel rows along one of the many straight streets aligned from east to west, and crossed by others at right angles from north to south, the lay-out at Mohenjo-daro suggests that it was an industrial city, likened by Sir John Marshall to the ruins of a modern cotton town in Lancashire,[19] and by Professor Piggott to contemporary coolie-lines,[20] a view he thinks which receives confirmation from the more explicit Harappa evidence.

In the more spacious thoroughfares several wheeled carts drawn by oxen (models of which have been found in pottery) could pass the broadest street so far cleared, since it is over 30 feet wide. The straight streets, in fact, seem to have been constructed to facilitate mobility and ventilation, the prevailing winds coming from the west to the south. Along the main street are the remains of shops and booths, and at the corners of some of the streets buildings with paved floors, having depressions to hold large jars of liquids, have been thought to have been restaurants where communal meals were served.[21] Some of the houses seem to have been a combination of a shop and a dwelling.

While most of the private houses were small there were also larger residences grouped round a courtyard with staircases, bathrooms, rubbish-shoots and drains, though very few had fireplaces and lavatories. The bathroom generally was situated on the street side to facilitate the removal of the water, and when latrines were provided they were added between the bath and the street wall. In addition to these private bathrooms, to the west of the highest mound, now surmounted by a small Buddhist *stupa* and monastery, a great bath was the most imposing structure of all the excavations at Mohenjo-daro, described by Sir John Marshall as 'a vast hydropathic establishment',[22] consisting of a large swimming bath in an open quadrangle built of burnt brick entered by a staircase. To the north are the remains of small bathrooms with paved floors and a stairway leading presumably to an upper storey, containing, it is thought, the cells of the priests engaged in a water cult of which the great bath was the central sanctuary. Here it would seem is the prototype of the ritual bathing which became such a prominent feature in the sacred streams in Vedic India and in modern Hinduism.

To the south of the *stupa* mound stood a spacious hall some 85 feet square, with paved aisles and unpaved strips about $3\frac{1}{2}$ feet wide between them which Marshall believes contained stone benches comparable to those on which Buddhist monks sat in their rock-cut temples. If this interpretation is correct the building must have been used for religious gatherings, but in contrast to most settlements of this nature in the Ancient Near East, there is no conclusive evidence of temples or palaces. The great bath is the most imposing structure in the city, and there is a large straggling edifice which may have been the governor's residence and administrative centre. Some of the other more pretentious erections may have been shrines of the Great Mother, though they cannot be detected with any degree of certainty in the ruins today, notwithstanding the abundant evidence of the cult in the terracotta figurines and carved seals.

Before it was established in its Indian area of characterization the civilization had a long period of development behind it in western Asia. If in Sind and the Punjab it was static, it was superior in urban organization to that in Sumer and Elam. In the lowest levels at Mohenjo-daro bronze and copper have been found without any indication of a Neolithic substratum. Therefore, if it became deeply rooted in Indian soil, pre-Aryan and non-Aryan, its cradleland lay elsewhere. The convergence of the three great civilizations of the Ancient East—those of Elam, Mesopotamia and North-west India—in the third millennium BC suggests that they were differentiated from a common stock, the origins of which would be expected to be situated somewhere between Sumer and India. Ultimately the source of the Indus-Harappan culture could hardly have been other than the Fertile Crescent and the Iranian highlands, and it was apparently merchants of the Kulli culture in southern Baluchistan who fostered commercial relations with Sumer,[23] until by 2500 BC an independent static civilization had been established in the Indus cities which continued with little or no change until, in the middle of the second millennium before 1500 BC, they were deserted and left in ruins.

At the western extremity of the Fertile Crescent, although the Delta of the Nile resembled southern Mesopotamia with its marshes and jungle-like swamps of papyrus and forest of reeds, the annual inundation of the valley at regular intervals was in marked contrast to the unpredictable behaviour of the Tigris and Euphrates. In Egypt the higher fertile ridges on the banks of the Nile built up by the deposits of silt attracted settlers not later than 5000 BC who, like the dwellers in Mesopotamia, engaged in primitive forms of agriculture and erected settlements at Deir Tasa and other sites on the more habitable spurs of the desert near the east bank of the Nile in Middle Egypt. Here Dr Brunton claims to have detected a less developed semi-nomadic cultural phase known as Tasian, in which hunting and fishing were combined with the cultivation of emmer wheat and barley, though they did not live in a settled community.[24] They were, he thinks, contemporary with a very early group of people at Merimde Benisalame, west of the Rosetta branch of the Nile, who had hardly emerged from Mesolithic conditions. About this, however, there is some doubt, as the Tasian graves were found in the same cemeteries as those of the more settled agricultural Badarians who were in a Chalcolithic state of culture.

The Badarian and Amratian prehistoric culture
The settlers at Badari, twenty miles south of Asyut on the east bank of the Nile, were so wedded to the soil that they made mud-lined storage bins for the emmer wheat they cultivated, and they may have tried to drain the swampy banks of the river to increase the productivity of the parched ground in the immediate neighbourhood of their settlements. While they engaged extensively in hunting and fishing they also domesticated cattle and sheep and apparently carried on a brisk trade with their neighbours. They clothed themselves in skins and cloth of

vegetable fibre, painted their eyes with malachite, ornamented them-selves with quartz beads, ivory combs and necklaces of shells from the Red Sea, and buried their dead, similarly adorned, in small and scattered groups dug in the soft sandy gravel or limestone detritus on the spur of the desert.[25]

In the First Predynastic or Amratian culture of Upper Egypt, Getulan or Libyan strains from the margins of the desert began to be apparent in the latter part of the fifth millennium, or soon after 4000 BC. This mixed population lived a composite life in villages composed of round huts on the fertile banks of the Nile, cultivating their crops and tending their flocks and herds, though still engaging in hunting and fishing. As they had animal clan symbols they may have been organized on a totemic basis. There is, in fact, good reason to suppose that in Predynastic times Egypt was divided into 'nomes' or 'counties', each of which had a sacred animal as its supernatural ally and with which the group regarded itself as *en rapport*, very much as in primitive society today where this socio-religious organization prevails. The Badarian industries still flourished, but copper was more extensively used for tool-making. The reeds which grew in the swamps were plaited into boots, mats and baskets, and the Nile mud was utilized in making pots, plates and dishes, though the technique and design hardly compares favourably with the best Badarian ware. Malachite was still used for painting the eyes, the body was tattooed, and necklaces adorned the dead just as they were worn as amulets by the living.

The Gerzean period

In the fourth millennium in the Gerzean or Naqada II Middle Pre-dynastic period, Asiatic influences began to make their way in Lower Egypt and gave rise to a more advanced metallurgy in copper, new types of vases, weapons, ornaments and painted pottery designs. There were also changes in dress and in toilet articles in funerary furniture in the graves. Villages became larger and the administration centralized as they developed into towns like Hierakonpolis, Abydos and Naqada. The increase in the population led to the cutting of irrigation canals involving a very heavy drain on the available manpower. The person responsible for carrying out this very essential and enterprising work no doubt acquired immense power and prestige, and eventually in all probability a divine status. In addition to having been a great benefactor he was in a position to regulate and cut off the water supplies which would have far-reaching effects on the towns, villages and the crops. Not only would he be able to impose a tariff on all who used the canals, but in course of time he might easily rise to the dignity of a local chieftain. It would then only remain for the small states or nomes to be consolidated into a province for the most powerful of these irrigation-chiefs to attain sovereignty over the whole district. Then the way would be open for the establishment of the union of the 'Two Lands' of Upper and Lower Egypt under a single ruler. Therefore it is significant that in a very early representation of a Pharaoh the king is depicted in the act of inaugurating an irrigation canal with a hoe.[26]

The Dynastic period
Be this as it may, the unification is held to have been effected towards the end of the fourth millennium when the traditional founder of the Egyptian dynasty, Menes, having become identified with Horus, the god of the Falcon clan, is alleged to have conquered the Delta and set up a single line of kings with a centralized administration. That the Nile valley for some considerable time had been the scene of internal strife and foreign invasions is shown by the designs on the Predynastic ivories, as, for example, on the Gebel el-Arak knife-handle where a battle is displayed in which Nilotic papyrus boats are engaged in an action with vessels having Mesopotamian features, and on the reverse side a hero, clad in a Sumerian or Semitic garment and cap, is standing in Mesopotamian fashion above two dogs (Figs. 1, 2).[27]

In the reproduction of this scene on the walls of a tomb at Hierakon-polis, the Predynastic centre of the Horus cult and of the Falcon clan in Upper Egypt, the victory of the southern nomes over the northern clans and foreigners was commemorated and amplified in a series of portrayals on palettes and mace-heads.[28] On the palette of Nar-Mer, Menes is represented attended by a sandal-bearer inspecting the bodies of his northern enemies who had been slain in the battle, while the falcon has seized a semi-human figure symbolic of Lower Egypt. Above are the heads of Hathor the cow-goddess, typifying apparently the union of the Two Lands (Fig. 4). The conquest of the north is further illustrated on the great mace-heads of Hierakonpolis in the Ashmolean Museum in Oxford, where the king is shown seated on a throne in a shrine approached by nine steps and wearing the white crown of Upper Egypt and a long robe, and holding in his hand a scourge.[29] Thus, he is identified with the god as the living Horus, in which capacity he has conquered the nomes of Lower Egypt and their foreign allies. More-over, he is depicted inaugurating ceremonially an irrigation canal by cutting the first sod to symbolize his bestowal of beneficence on the soil (Fig. 3), while the combination of the White Crown of Upper

Egypt and the Red Crown of the north on two sides of a large palette[30] shows that his sovereignty over the entire country was an accomplished fact.

The Horus symbol of the Pharaoh being the nar-fish, his name has been read as Nar-Mer. It was either this king, or one Aha, whose name also occurs on a very early tomb at Nagada and at Abydos, who has been equated with the traditional Menes, though he may have been the personification in a single individual of the conquest of Lower Egypt by the Horus clans in the north. When the 'Two Lands' were united as a single nation under one ruler, the Pharaoh attained divine status as the incarnation of the Falcon-Sky-God Horus, and subsequently by the Fifth Dynasty (c. 2500 BC) he had acquired a filial relationship with the Sun-god Re under the influence of the Heliopolitan priesthood. Once this was accomplished the deification of the occupant of the throne became the unifying dynamic and cohesive centre of the nation, giving to Egypt its remarkable stability.

As Dr Jacobsen has pointed out, in the Nile valley civilization arose in 'a compact country where village lay reassuringly close to village, the whole ringed round and isolated by protecting mountain barriers'. Over this sheltered world passed every day a dependable, never-failing sun, calling Egypt back to life and activity after the darkness of night; here arose every year the trusty Nile to fertilize and revivify the Egyptian soil. It is almost as though Nature had deliberately restrained herself, as though she had set this secure valley apart so that man could disport himself unhindered.[31] Into this situation the monarchy with its divine foundations and significance fitted perfectly as the consolidating centre of a static order. In Mesopotamia, on the other hand, the prevailing conditions were those of uncertainty. Unlike the Nile, the Tigris and Euphrates are unpredictable in their rise and fall, and floods have always been a terrifying menace rather than a beneficent inundation. Nevertheless, although the dwellers in Mesopotamia viewed the cosmos with misgivings and were alive to the vagaries of Nature, as early as the fifth millennium BC they set to work to conquer their environment and cultivate their soil in the sweat of their brow. Their vitality was such that it stimulated to even greater efforts the vigorous civilization of Egypt in the proto-dynastic phase of its remarkable development (c. 2900-2700 BC).[32]

ASIA MINOR

The Hittites and the Hurrians
By two routes the oriental civilizations converged upon the eastern

Mediterranean. The first and earliest way was by sea from Egypt; the second by land through Asia Minor from Mesopotamia and Iran. Thus, the Aegean islands on the one hand and the peninsula of Asia Minor on the other became the connecting links between Asia and Europe. On the high plateau which rises from the Aegean coast in the west to the mountains of Armenia in the east in 'the Land of Hatti' to the north-east of Anatolia, the Hittite Empire flourished in the second millennium BC within the circuit of the Halys River (Kizil Irmak), where its capital at Boghazköy stands. In the Middle Bronze Age the pre-Hittite Anatolian princes had established a stable civilization in this mountain stronghold, and recent excavations in 1954 and 1956 at Kültepe (Kanesh) near Kayseri have brought to light public buildings in one of which was an inscription on a bronze spearhead bearing the words 'Palace of Anittas, the King'. His name occurs on three tablets in cuneiform Hittite as a historical character who controlled apparently the greater part of the plateau shortly before it was absorbed into the Hittite kingdom, residing himself at Kussara. From him the royal Hittite line may have descended, though in fact it was from the ancient ruler Labarnas that the Hittite kings traced their lineage.[33] Assyrian merchants having forced their way into the Anatolian plateau at the end of the third millennium BC and united under one rule the small principalities, the way was opened for the rise of the dynasty of Labarnas, an early Hittite king who claimed to have conquered and destroyed Arzawa, the administrative centre of the earlier state. By about 1380 BC the kingdom had been established by Suppiluliumas, King of Hatti, who conquered and incorporated into his empire the Mesopotamian kingdoms of Mitanni and the Hussilands, and sent armies into Syria and Palestine, making Lebanon his frontier (*c.* 1370 BC).

In the second half of the third millennium BC the Hurrians (the biblical Horites), an Armenoid people who spread gradually southwards and westwards from their cradleland in the mountainous region south of the Caucasus, made their first appearance in history about 2400 BC in the Zagros area. From the Kurdish mountains they swarmed into northern Mesopotamia east of the Tigris, and during the second millennium BC they became a dominant element throughout the Middle East. Adopting the principal gods and the myths of the Sumero-Akkadians which they combined with their own pantheon and its mythology, they produced a great number of ritual texts in the clay tablets that have been recovered from Boghazköy, Tell Hariri (the ancient Mari) on the Middle Euphrates, Ras Shamra in Syria and

Mitanni, dating from about 2400 to 1500 BC. At Nuzi near Kirkuk in eastern Mesopotamia thousands of these tablets belonging mainly to the fifteenth century BC have been found, written by Hurrian scribes in the Babylonian language but including numerous Hurrian words. As the texts are largely of a religious character, their decipherment has been of the greatest value for the study of Near Eastern religion, as well as for the information they give about the life and transactions of the people.[34] A letter from the king of Mitanni, Tushratta, to the Egyptian Pharaoh Amenhotep III about 1400 BC, discovered at Tell el Amarna, is of particular value for transliteration owing to its state of preservation.[35]

It is only in recent years that the full significance of Hurrian and Hittite culture and religion has become apparent, as a result of the recovery and decipherment of these important inscriptions and texts written in this particular form of cuneiform script from 2400 to 1100 BC. Hrozný led the way by publishing the first attempt at a Hittite grammar in 1915. Although this was not an outstanding success it has now become possible to translate a very considerable number of tablets which have thrown much light upon the life and beliefs of this syncretistic Anatolian civilization occupying a key position in Asia Minor. Thus, it is now apparent from the Cappadocian tablets that from the beginning of the second millennium BC until about 1200 BC the Hittites and the Hurrians constituted the dominant influence in the region. Under Mursilis I the Hittite kingdom expanded to North Syria and Babylon, probably about 1600 BC. Aleppo was captured and the Amorite kingdom subdued. This brought the First Dynasty to an end, but it was only a temporary occupation of southern Mesopotamia, the Hurrians soon gaining control. About 1520 BC Telipinu, who had usurped the throne, recovered Hittite domination in Asia Minor, consolidating the Hittite state and keeping the invaders at bay to the north and east of the capital. But no attempt was made to reconquer Syria, and a treaty was concluded with Mitannia, which under the leadership of an Indo-European dynasty had risen to supremacy in western Asia in the fifteenth century. In 1380 BC, however, when Suppiluliumas came to the throne, Hittite control over Aleppo, Carchemish and other cities in northern Syria was established, Mitanni was reduced to a tributary state, and the tablets discovered at Tell el Amarna in Middle Egypt from the palace of Amenhotep IV (Ikhnaton) inscribed in Akkadian cuneiform reveal that it was the dominant influence in the fourteenth century. With the revival of Egyptian power in the Nineteenth Dynasty Egyptian sovereignty over Syria was restored, and although a concordat was established between the two nations, effected by the customary royal marriage, barbarian invasions in which the Phrygians may have played an important part suddenly brought the Hittite Empire to an end about 1230 BC.

Ugarit-Ras Shamra

Meanwhile in Syria and Palestine where, as we have seen, a Neolithic agricultural civilization arose at Jericho perhaps as early as 7000 BC, the cultural movements of the Chalcolithic period and the Bronze Age were adapted to local conditions. In North Syria, being on the great land route from Asia to Egypt, the painted pottery associated with Tell Halaf and all that this signified, flourished in the highlands as well as in the Jordan valley and in Transjordan.[36] Imperceptibly the Chalcolithic passed into the Early Bronze Age in the third millennium BC, and in such centres as Megiddo, Beth Shan, Khirbet Kerak (Beth Yerah) near Tiberias, Jericho, Hazor, Byblos and elsewhere, a high level was attained in these strategic sites by their mainly Amorite inhabitants. It was these western Semites who were largely responsible for the collapse of the Babylonian Empire in the Middle Bronze Age about 1800 BC, and from the vast collection of clay tablets written in cuneiform script recently recovered from their capital Mari on the Middle Euphrates, numbering some twenty thousand, we are left in no doubt about their importance, cultural achievements, and elaborate civic administration.[37]

About this time many languages were written down in cuneiform characters, which originated in Mesopotamia and were employed to inscribe Canaanite, Phoenician and early Hebrew as well as Hurrian, Hittite and Akkadian. Thus, at Ras Shamra, the site of the ancient Ugarit on the northern coast of Syria near the modern town of Latakia, a north Canaanite script and literature, written in a previously unknown archaic cuneiform alphabet, have come to light since 1929 and been deciphered. In fact two languages are represented on these tablets, the one an ancient Canaanite dialect akin to very early Hebrew, the other a Hurrian dialect. Both of them date from about the fifteenth and early fourteenth centuries BC and are mainly concerned with three mythological epics connected with the death and resurrection of the vegetation god Aleyan-Baal, the legend of Keret, a demi-god, and the heroic figure Danel (Daniel). At present the texts are too fragmentary and the decipherment too incomplete to be able to arrive at very definite conclusions about the precise details of their contents. But it is clear, nevertheless, that early Canaanite myth and ritual conformed in general outline and basic structure to that of the rest of the Near East, despite local variations as elsewhere.[38]

Like the Babylonian tablets those of Ugarit appear to be part of the archives of the local temple, having been housed in a building situated between the two great temples in the city, one dedicated to Baal, the other to Dagon. Variant examples of the same Semitic alphabet script have been found at Beth Shemesh and Mount Tabor. This Canaanite-Hurrian dialectal adaptation of cuneiform being mainly suitable for use on clay tablets, it was of short duration, because in Palestine writing with ink or incised on parchment, papyrus or potsherds was adopted by the Hebrews from the ninth and eighth centuries BC, as is shown by the ostraca recovered from Samaria which Albright dates in the reign of Jeroboam II in the first quarter of the eighth century BC[39] and by the large collection of 'letters' written on potsherds found at Lachish in 1935, recording a correspondence in Hebrew writing in the ancient Phoenician script between a certain Hoshaiah to a high commanding officer Jaosh, when Nebuchadnezzar was about to besiege the city in 588 BC.[40] The earliest inscriptions in Phoenician-Hebrew go back to the ninth century BC, in that on the Moabite Stone discovered in 1868, and to about 1100 BC on the sarcophagus of Ahiram of Byblos.

The Hebrews in Palestine

It was not, in fact, until the beginning of the Early Iron Age (*c.* 1200-900 BC) that the traditional Hebrew invasion of Palestine began, and it is by no means easy to determine the historical situation that lies behind the Israelite tradition preserved in the Old Testament narratives. That nomadic tribes entered Palestine from north-western Mesopotamia is supported by the course of events there in the third millennium BC and at the beginning of the second millennium, as described in the Mari tablets, though there is no archaeological confirmation of the alleged Abrahamic migration from Ur to Harran, sixty miles west of Tell Halaf (Gen. xi, 28–30; xii, 1–3; xiv, 13; xv, 7). If, however, the story has a historical foundation, the destruction of Ur by the Elamites about 1950 BC would afford an excellent reason for the departure of the Hebrew ancestors to the safer and flourishing city (Harran) in the north-west. Below it in the Balikh valley, Nahor, the traditional home of Rebekah, often occurs in the Mari documents as Nakhur, and like Harran it was ruled by Amorite princes.[41]

Whether the ancient Hebrews are to be equated with a widely dispersed people in Mesopotamia designated Habiru in inscriptions from the time of Rim-Sin, from whom Hammurabi wrested the mastery of Sumer, is still in debate. The name in cuneiform in the various documents in which it occurs (Babylonian, Nuzian, Hittite and Amarna) from the nineteenth to the fourteenth centuries BC, is difficult to determine at all precisely, except that it was applied to intruders and raiders and outsiders, but linguistically and phonetically it would seem to be identical with 'Hebrew'.[42] If the equation is correct the ancestral Hebrews may be regarded as a group within this widely dispersed nomadic composite people, roving about with their flocks and herds between Mesopotamia and Syria from 1720 to 1570 BC in the wake of the Hyksos infiltrations from the north, while others remained in Palestine.[43]

Unquestionably the traditional account of the events and incidents in the quasi-legendary patriarchal period in the book of Genesis, and the final Hebrew settlement in Palestine in and after the middle of the second millennium BC, is largely mythical. Nevertheless, behind and within the aetiological stories there lies a hard core of fact, however much it may have been distorted by and embellished with legendary interpretations in terms of later religious beliefs and practices, of ethnological situations, and of place-names and sacred sites. When due allowance has been made for all this romanticism, and for the absence of an agreed chronology concerning the Hebrew tribes' entrance and exodus from the Nile valley, it seems reasonably certain that the migration bore some relation to the movement into the northeastern Delta of the heterogeneous collection of Asiatics called the 'Hyksos', with their horses and chariots. This occurred about 1720 BC and their régime continued until the rise of the New Kingdom in 1570 BC.

The obvious time for the Hebrew sojourn would be during their occupation, in view of their ethnological affinities, and for the change in the fortunes of the dwellers in Goshen to be explained as a result of a new king arising 'who knew not Joseph' (Exod. i, 8). But the equation of the Pharaoh of the oppression with Ahmose I of Thebes, who expelled the Hyksos in the Seventeenth Dynasty, and his successors, the Thutmoses, in the great Eighteenth Dynasty (c. 1546–1450 BC), conflicts with the statement in the Bible that the Israelite slaves were assigned the task of building the store-cities Pithom and Rameses.[44] This would seem to make Ramesses II (c. 1299–1232 BC) the oppressor rather than Ahmose I and the Thutmoses, and to suggest that the Exodus was effected at the accession of Merenptah (c. 1232–1221 BC) who we know from a stele discovered in Thebes in 1896 had to quell revolts in Palestine.[45] On this interpretation of the event, which now holds the field, the enslavement coincided with the extensive building operations in the Delta in the second half of the thirteenth century, more than two hundred years after the dating of those who assigned the Exodus to the accession of Amenhotep II in 1477, notwithstanding the fact that this earlier dating seemed to confirm the biblical chronology of 1. Kings vi. 1 alleging that the building of the temple of Solomon was begun 480 years after the Exodus.[46]

From these conflicting conjectures it is clear that the problem is one of such complexity that no simple solution is possible. Indeed, as Professor Rowley says, there is no feature of the reconstruction of the date of the Exodus, the route followed to the Holy Mountain, its location, the duration of the sojourn in the desert, or which among the Hebrew tribes were involved in the conquest of Palestine, that has not been challenged in recent years.[47] So far as the Exodus is concerned, every theory encounters almost insuperable difficulties in trying to reconcile the biblical traditions with the archaeological data, yet the sojourn in Egypt and the eventual escape are so vital a part of Israelite historical tradition that they cannot be lightly eliminated. Similarly, the date and details of the conquest and occupation of Palestine are very obscure, and we cannot be sure who the Hyksos really were, or what exactly was their relation to and with the Hebrews. The narratives for the most part have assumed the form of aetiological myths drawn up to explain or give a reason for the events described and separated from the actual occurrences by not less than five hundred years, when the documents in their present form were first compiled between 850 and 750 BC. But, nevertheless, they are based on historical situations, outstanding personalities and significant events, which have become an integral part of the national history in its religious setting. Some of the complications may have arisen from there having been more than one entry of the tribes into Palestine, perhaps those claiming descent from Joseph having migrated into Egypt while the rest remained in Canaan.

In the book of Joshua the conquest of Palestine was represented by the writers and editors in the southern kingdom of Judah as a single event under the leadership of Joshua, the successor of Moses. The campaign, according to this account, was as ruthless as it was complete in the extermination of the indigenous Canaanite population, and the enslavement of all the other peoples in the land. The compilers of this narrative, under the influence of the Deuteronomic contention of the absolute domination of the chosen nation by divine decree,[48] made the invasion a triumphant march to total victory, largely in the form of aetiological stories.[49] This, however, is not confirmed by the record in the book of Judges or by the extra-biblical evidence. In fact the penetration of the invading nomadic tribes was a very gradual process resulting in a fusion which produced a composite culture and cultus.

The part played by Joshua in the conquest of Canaan is very difficult to determine, in view of the uncertainty about the date of the capture of Jericho and whether or not it can be attributed to his efforts. The biblical story has so many legendary elements, and despite the conjecture of Garstang,[50] the excavations have thrown no light on the alleged destruction of the city by the Israelites, as the Middle Bronze Age defences have not survived.[51] Moreover, if Miss Kenyon is correct in placing the destruction of the city by the Israelites in the third quarter of the fourteenth century BC, it cannot be equated with either the later or the earlier dating for their entry into Palestine.

Similarly, no historical connexion can be established between the Hebrew invasion under Joshua and the inroads of the Habiru in the south and the tribes called Sa-Gaz coming from the north, as Garstang and others have contended.[52] The troubled situation in Palestine described in the Amarna Letters in the first half of the fourteenth century BC cannot be regarded as reflecting the condition portrayed in the books of Joshua and Judges, as has been supposed. Apart from the problem of chronology, the insurrections to which reference was made in these documents were minor maraudings in which particular towns or territories were involved, requiring only very small forces of up to fifty men to suppress.[53] The names of the kings mentioned in the biblical narratives (e.g. Adonibezek, Haram, and Jabin) are also very different from those in the Amarna texts (e.g. Abdi-hiba, Yapahi and Abdi-tirshi). It seems, therefore, that the Amarna Age can be dismissed as the setting of the conquest, in spite of the attempts of Albright and Meek to connect some of the incidents in the Israelite settlement with this period.[54]

So far as the historical campaigns of Joshua are concerned, they appear to have been confined mainly to the central highlands where his own tribe of Ephraim was located, and whither he may have led the Joseph tribes across the Jordan. Whether or not he attacked and destroyed Jericho, he would seem to have functioned on the ridge north-east of Mizpah on which Bethel and the enigmatical Ai were situated.[55] As Ai was already in ruins the story of its capture and the Akan incident may have been transferred to Joshua and interpreted in relation to his campaign as a sequel to the miraculous destruction of Jericho, unless Ai was confused with Bethel, the fall of which occurred probably in the first half of the thirteenth century BC. Lachish was captured later in this century,[56] and while there are references in the Amarna Letters to the city giving help to the Habiru, the first mention of its destruction is in the Joshua narrative. Therefore, although behind the biblical tradition in its composite form there lies a background of historical fact, the correlation with the archaeological evidence again is beset with almost insuperable difficulties, because the account of the events leading up to and culminating in the invasion of Canaan has been so drastically transformed and recast to serve the purposes of later theological interpretation.

Nevertheless, the settlement of the tribes in the fertile oasis of the Jordan was accomplished at the beginning of the Iron Age (1200–900 BC) at a time when Egypt, Babylonia and Anatolia were in a state of temporary decline, and the Eastern Mediterranean littoral was being subjected to constant attack by the raiding people of the sea—the Philistines—perhaps of Cretan origin. The subsequent history of Israel and Judah reflects the vicissitudes of this part of the Near East under the domination of the reviving rival empires of Mesopotamia and Egypt in Iron Age II (900–650 BC), until at the end of the Exile of the southern kingdom of Judah, the Neo-Babylonian Empire was brought to an end by Cyrus the Persian after the fall of Babylon in 539 BC. If the conqueror attributed his victory to the god of the city, Marduk, the Hebrew prophet commonly called the Deutero-Isaiah did not hesitate to regard Cyrus as the anointed instrument of Yahweh,[57] raised up to bring about the restoration of the exiled Jews to their own land and the establishment of the post-exilic community in and around Jerusalem. Thus, by restoring Israel to Palestine, the Persians were instrumental in preserving and transmitting the great legacy of religious thought and practice which Judaism bestowed upon the Graeco-Roman world and Western civilization.

THE EASTERN MEDITERRANEAN

Aegean civilization

Before they settled in their respective cradlelands, the Hebrews and the Iranians were both descended from nomadic shepherd ancestors who drove their flocks and herds from pasture to pasture, the Hebrews making their way into Palestine on the western edge of the desert, the Iranians to the plateau on its eastern border. From the same great reservoirs of unsettled populations in the Near East continually leaving the grasslands on the margin of the desert in search of a settled abode, came the Indo-Europeans speaking one and the same Aryan language from which were descended the Latin, Sanskrit, Celtic and Teutonic tongues. It would appear that their original home was on the steppe in the region east and north-east of the Caspian Sea, whence the western section was dispersed through southern Russia and along the Danube until eventually, about 2000 BC, some of them reached the pastures of Thessaly from the Balkans. The eastern tribes having pastured their herds among the earliest agriculturists on the steppes and the lands eastwards to the Caspian Sea, exercised pressure in Mesopotamia, and the entire northern boundary of the Fertile Crescent, early in the second millennium. A new dynasty was established under the Kassites from the eastern mountains whose rulers had Indo-European names, as was also the case among the influential rulers in Mitanni at the head of the Khabur river, who dominated western Asia for a time, and about 1380 BC concluded a treaty with the Hittite king Suppiluliumas Hittite. Inscriptions and documents, in fact, indicate Aryan literary influences in Anatolia soon after the beginning of the second millennium BC.

In its south-western diffusion the Indo-European group of languages moved over the steppes and plains of Europe and towards the Mediterranean, cutting across the earlier route from Anatolia to Greece and Italy, and coinciding with the advances of the Chalcolithic warrior cultures with their battle-axes, corded pottery and single graves. Those who spoke these Aryan dialects had behind them the impact of Near Eastern influences which they imposed on the indigenous cultures they encountered and dominated, notably in south-eastern and in central Europe.

Greece, therefore, being closer than anywhere else in the Aegean to the Nile Valley, the Levant and the cradles of Neolithic farming communities in the Fertile Crescent, was where this process of adaptation was most likely to occur. Linked to the Anatolian *massif* by 'island chains', it was the natural route across the plateau from central and western Asia,[58] just as the Danube was the natural corridor for the diffusion of culture from the region around the Black Sea and the Balkans to Central Europe. In the south the Mediterranean was the channel along which in the closing years of the third millennium BC maritime trade and its associated influences, spiritual and material, passed from Egypt and western Asia by way of Cyprus, Crete and the Cyclades to the Aegean, southern Italy, Malta and the Iberian coast and its islands. Indeed, the Aegean world from east Crete to western Greece, where the impact was most strongly felt, was 'a sort of cultural confederacy, bound together in a growing intercourse by maritime trade' with a unity in religious ideas no less than in material culture.[59]

The Minoan-Mycenaean civilization

When the Indo-Europeans reached the pastures of Thessaly from southern Russia and the Balkans about 2000 BC and settled under the shadow of Mount Olympus, they brought with them their own sacred traditions and the gods whom they installed on the misty Olympian heights under the leadership of Zeus. Having taken up their abode on the peninsula, they encountered the earlier inhabitants who had long been established not only in Greece but throughout the Aegean and its islands in the eastern Mediterranean.

Crete with its succession of winds and currents making it accessible from the Delta of the Nile and Syria as well as from the Anatolian mainland and Cilicia, had become the natural centre of new cultural influences since late Neolithic times, when the impact on the indigenous substratum gave rise to a new civilization, known as Minoan, about 3000 BC. It was this which Sir Arthur Evans displayed in all its magnificence when in 1900 he began the systematic excavation of the Palace of Minos at Knossos on the northern coast of the island.[60] Inland from the southern shore stood a second palace at Phaestos. These have been described, not very aptly, respectively as 'the Windsor and Balmoral of a Cretan potentate', since in fact they were the sacred and administrative centres of priest-kings, ruling city-states and engaged in extensive commercial enterprises, whose palaces were equipped with a logia-shrine, ceremonial double axes, baetyls, doves and other emblems of the Mother-goddess, and all the outward signs of sacred symbolism and regal splendour befitting a divine monarch.

If at first the mainland lagged behind the islands, though probably less so than was formerly supposed, this was because Crete and the Cyclades were in regular communication with Egypt, Asia Minor and the rest of the Mediterranean from Syria to Sicily, Malta, Sardinia and North Africa, while the presence of shells from the Indian Ocean may suggest still wider intercourse. But the fleets of Crete and Egypt maintained commercial relations with the coast of Greece and by the middle of the second millennium BC a new dynasty had come to power in the Peloponnese, and massive strongholds arose at Mycenae and Tiryns with heavy stone foundations, walls and gateways (Fig. 63). It now appears, however, that the urban civilization, first consummated at Mycenae, situated on a direct line of communication between the southeast and the north-west, although not founded by Minoans, as was at one time suggested, was in close touch with Crete. This doubtless the Indo-European invaders perceived when on reaching the Mycenaean region they looked across the waters of the Aegean and saw the white sails of the boats plying their trade on their lawful occasions between the islands and the mainland.

The bearded Mycenaeans, however, unlike the clean-shaven Minoan princes, were essentially warriors, and their cities were strongly fortified and reasonably secure from attack. In Crete, on the other hand, the palaces and towns (Knossos, Phaestos, Gournia) were unprotected by fortifications and until the second phase of the Late Minoan period (*c.* 1580–1400 BC) when armour began to appear, there were no indications of the arts of war. Swords were mainly rapiers, better adapted to fencing than fighting, and beyond putting down piracy, in her capacity of a sea-power Crete was well content to keep clear of hostile disputes and campaigns among her neighbours and concentrate upon her commercial relations with Asia, Egypt, Libya and the Cyclades. But at the beginning of the second half of the second millennium BC, the Minoan civilization, having reached its zenith, was suddenly overtaken with disaster. The precise cause of the final collapse is uncertain. Earthquakes may have played some part, but the Mycenaean bid for the mastery of the Aegean can hardly be ruled out, since as the rising power it was penetrating into regions hitherto regarded as Cretan preserves. In any case, the fall of Knossos came in 1400 BC with tragic suddenness, and apparently without any assistance from her Egyptian ally under Amenhotep III.

Whether or not it was the people called by Homer Acheans who are to be identified with the Mycenaeans and made responsible for the onslaught, the fall of Knossos was a turning point in European Bronze Age civilization, establishing Mycenaean supremacy in the Aegean against the inroads from the Orient. The triumph, it is true, was short-lived. Nevertheless, for some two hundred years it endured, extending its influence throughout the Peloponnese, controlling the mountain trade-routes leading to the west and north from the east and the south, and engaging in an active overseas expansion which embraced Egypt as well as the Aegean islands, Cyprus and the coasts of Palestine and Syria. Westwards Sicily and southern Italy became outposts, and from Minoan-Mycenaean sources came the cult of the axe that has now been detected at Stonehenge and in Brittany. Trade was maintained also with Troy and Cilicia, until in the twelfth century peaceful commercial enterprise was brought to an end by the Trojan war and the subsequent Dorian invasion, shortly before 1100 BC, when Mycenae was destroyed.

Thus, the Greeks of classical antiquity were of very mixed origin, partly Aegean, partly Achaean, partly Dorian, but these question-begging designations are to be interpreted ethnologically and linguistically. That an Indo-European strain was deeply laid in the nation is beyond doubt, and gradually a feeling of racial unity was acquired among the very diverse group isolated in loosely organized communities in narrow valleys, separated by mountain ranges and long gulfs from their neighbours except by sea communications. Protected by these natural barriers, they developed a number of small city-states which never became united in a single nation or empire as in Egypt, the Fertile Crescent and Persia. Each was a sovereign state in itself and developed a rich and varied culture and an intense local patriotism, until by the seventh century BC they were conscious of being an entity in spite of their composite origin and widespread provenance. Therefore, just as the Hebrew tribes regarded themselves as the descendants of their eponymous ancestor Jacob (Israel), so the Greeks adopted the title 'Hellenes' in the belief that they were descended from a single mythical ancestor, Hellen, the son of Deucalion. Those who were not Hellenes were 'barbarians', and the remnant of the earlier population who spoke their language was Pelasgian.

It is now becoming apparent that the Greek language is older than has been generally assumed, since the Linear B simplified script of Knossos, recently deciphered by Ventris and Chadwick, has been shown to be an early Greek dialect identical with that current in Mycenaean Greece. It is suggested, in fact, that Linear B was designated for a language which originated in the Aegean and that it represents the general idiom of Mycenaean Greece as distinct from the older Linear A script, with signs resembling Egyptian hieroglyphs in the earlier Minoan sites in Crete.[61] Thus, some six hundred tablets in Linear B were found by Blegen at Pylos in the Palace of Nestor, a Mycenaean building of about 1200 BC,[62] two hundred years after the sack of Knossos. Similarly, A. B. Wace has discovered a few more at Mycenae dated about 1275 BC.[63] If the language was an early form of Greek which survived in Arcadia and was taken over by the Achaeans from the Minoans, as has been suggested, or from Near Eastern sources, and imperfectly adapted to Greek from the conventions of a very different language, Greek must have been in vogue in Crete before the destruction of Knossos. It is possible, indeed, that before the Aegean hegemony passed to the mainland it may have been established already in the Palace of Minos on the island, coinciding with the introduction of the Linear B script.

The Achaeans and the Dorian invasion

It has long been recognized that before the Dorian invasion from north-central Greece about 1100 BC, an Achaean population inhabited the Peloponnese and the southern islands, but these brown-haired (Xanthoi) conquerors under their Zeus-born kings of the Homeric tradition certainly did not introduce the higher civilization into Greece. They found the culture already established on the Aegean mainland and ruled over the dark-skinned, black-haired people as a feudal aristocracy from the fifteenth to the twelfth centuries BC, when the Mycenaean Age came to an end. In Greece the Bronze Age culture known as Helladic pursued its own course of development, as did the corresponding phases in the Cyclades, where independent commercial enterprises established contacts with the Black Sea, southern Russia, Italy and Sicily. In Thessaly the earliest pottery was quite distinct from that of the Minoan-Cycladic tradition, and although it was copied from metal models, metal was not actually in use. It would seem, therefore, that the hand-made burnished ware with its basketry designs came into the Thessalian plain in the fourth millennium from a region in which bronze was known and worked, situated probably in the south-east of Europe.

In Macedonia with its thick forests and cold winters, a Neolithic culture developed having affinities with the second Thessalian period. The peasants cultivated wheat, millet, and fig-trees, bred sheep, goats, cattle and pigs, tilled the land with their 'shoe-last celts' (i.e. stone hoes) and decorated their black polished wares with fluting, spirals and other geometric patterns. Parallel to the contemporary Aegean migration came people from Asia Minor attracted thither by the copper, gold and silver ores, though the use of metal was very limited in the region. The commercial centre being the second city of Troy, it was with this important port occupying a key position on the Helles-pont that trade was maintained, rather than with the Aegean.

In the Middle Macedonian period (c. 2000–1630 BC) Anatolian influences appear to have ceased, and as the Early Macedonians penetrated into Thessaly another wave of people spread rapidly into Greece bringing with them a smooth well-turned wheel-made yellow or grey pottery with polished surface. As this ware was first discovered at Orchomenos in Boeotia, the legendary home of the Minyai, it has been named 'Minyan', though it is by no means confined to this area. On the contrary, it is a characteristic feature of the Middle Helladic period, and its immediate affinities are with the Troad. It is possible that these so-called Minyans were Indo-Europeans who came from the direction of northern Iran and by 1800 BC had dominated the central and western regions of Greece, without making any attempt to destroy the older inhabitants. While their influence extended to the Peloponnese, it did not eliminate that of Minoan Crete which at Mycenae and elsewhere fused with the Helladic culture to produce the composite Minoan-Mycenaean civilization of the Middle and Late Bronze Age.

This in its turn was broken up by the Dorians and their associates from the north-west of Greece shortly before 1100 BC, who overran the whole of the peninsula except Attica and Arcadia. Eventually (i.e. by about 900 BC) it was divided between the Aeolians, who occupied the north, the Ionians the centre and the Dorians the south, with their new city Argos taking the place of Mycenae. The Mycenaean civilization, however, survived the onslaught to some extent, partly by fusion of the two elements in the population, as in the case of the Canaanites and Hebrews in Palestine, and also by penetration to Cyprus and the coast of Asia Minor. Thus, the widespread disturbance in the eastern Mediterranean in the twelfth century brought a wave of Aegean settlers into the western half of Cyprus, and introduced a mixed culture in which Mycenaean elements were superimposed on and fused with the indigenous tradition. It is now becoming apparent that the Cypriot syllabary was in fact based on a Mycenaean prototype in which were incorporated some elements of the Linear B script. At Enkomi near Famagusta a clay tablet from a Mycenaean settlement was discovered in 1953 inscribed with what is believed to be a Cypro-Minoan script and in association with painted sherds in Mycenaean IIIc style of the end of the thirteenth century.[64] It is not improbable, therefore, that the dialect may have been descended from Mycenaean Greek.

These Greek settlements in Cyprus remained the easternmost outpost of the Hellenic world, though the Mycenaeans are known to have come into contact with the Hittites, and to have been located sporadically along the southern and western coasts of Asia Minor, notably at Miletus, and in Syria, Cilicia and Pamphylia. To the south Hellenic influence penetrated the Delta of the Nile, and west of it eventually Cyrene was founded. In short, the fusion of the Aegean and the Ancient Near East by this two-way traffic was such that for the purposes of our present inquiry the entire region must be regarded as constituting an integrated whole.

CHAPTER TWO

THE EMERGENCE OF RELIGION
IN THE ANCIENT NEAR EAST

Fertility female figurines: Jericho, Iraq, Anatolia, Iran and Elam, Transcaspia, Baluchistan, Sind and the Punjab, Egypt, eastern Mediterranean—Cult of the Dead: cult of skulls, plastered skulls at Jericho, treatment of the head in Ancient Egypt, substitute heads and masks, grave equipment and disposal of the body, Mesopotamian sepultures, royal tombs of Ur, Indus valley, eastern Mediterranean—Concept of Deity: Sky-gods in Egypt, Babylonian Triad, Indo-European Sky-gods

It has been necessary to examine in broad outline the rise of civilization in the Near East and the Aegean, because the cultus was so essentially a product of its environment at a critical juncture in the transition from hunting and food gathering to agriculture and herding, with antecedents going back into the Palaeolithic. This is particularly apparent in the ritual and its symbolism centred in the various aspects of fecundity, which became a recurrent phenomenon and dominating influence throughout the region. This at first found expression in an exaggeration of the organs of maternity, in the conditions of pregnancy and occasionally of childbirth, the life-producing mother being the personification of fertility. Around her a network of emotions and sentiments collected which gave a sacred significance to the female principle and all its attributes, particularly those connected with birth and the food supply. Generation, in fact, was linked with the conservation of the means of subsistence as far back into the prehistoric past as the evidence takes us. Thus, while the Magdalenians at the end of the Palaeolithic concentrated upon the maintenance and control of the chase, their Aurignacian predecessors, now called Gravettians, were primarily interested apparently in the maternal aspect of birth.

FERTILITY FEMALE FIGURINES

It was they who introduced into Europe the 'Venus' female figurines in ivory, bone, stone and bas-relief, and since these life-giving amulets are most abundant in their west Asiatic sites on the Russian steppes and in the valley of the Don, it is generally agreed that the southern Eurasian loess plain was in all probability the original diffusion centre of the cult.[1] Moreover, it was in this region that it became most highly developed and firmly established in the religion of the Ancient Near East, with the rise of agriculture in the Neolithic civilization in and after the fifth millennium BC. This has become very apparent at Arpachiyah near Nineveh in Mesopotamia where the squatting female figurines are in direct line with the Palaeolithic examples in central and western Europe, especially those from Lespugne, Wisternitz and Willendorf.[2] Whether or not they were emblematic of the Mother-goddess as such, they certainly suggest the veneration of maternity as a divine principle. Some are naturalistically modelled in the round, others are flat and hardly more than a stump with no attempt to fashion the face or head. But they all emphasize the breasts, the navel and the vulva region, and almost always they are represented in a squatting position, this being a normal attitude adopted in child-birth in the Middle East. Therefore, although it is debatable whether they portray the actual Goddess, the figurines unquestionably symbolize her functions and attributes.[3] The tendency towards conventionalization suggests that they were used as amulets rather than images and their abundance shows the popularity of the cult (Figs. 7, 8).

Jericho

At Jericho Miss Kenyon has now carried the cult back to the pre-pottery Neolithic substratum which, as we have seen, may be as early as the seventh millennium BC. There she discovered two small headless female figurines in the typical attitude. One is clad in a long flowing robe gathered at the waist and with the hands placed beneath the breasts. The other is similar though less well-preserved. Associated with them were a number of animals, as at Arpachiyah, where doves, so often connected with the Mother-goddess, occurred. The Jericho examples could be children's toys, as Miss Kenyon recognizes,[4] but on the other hand, animal figures of this nature are a recurrent feature of and allied in purpose to fertility figurines in the promotion of the productivity of the soil and its crops.

Iraq

In the earliest Neolithic sites, however, apart from Tell Arpachiyah and Jericho, the cult was not very prominent in western Asia, and female figurines did not become abundant until the Chalcolithic culture arose in the Halafian Age about 3800 BC. At Tell Hassuna only a very few clay female statuettes have been recovered from the pre-Halaf stratum, whereas in the Halaf deposits they become prevalent everywhere from the Syrian coast to the Zagros mountains. At Tepe Gawra near Nineveh, north-west of Arpachiyah, on the caravan route to Iran, they are of common occurrence in the lower levels of the mound which belong to the Halaf period, often depicting women in a squatting posture and holding their breasts. The heads are merely pinched out of the clay, though sometimes the facial features are painted without any attempt at modelling. The eyes are drawn in black paint, and horizontal lines on the shoulders, arms and feet may represent some form of ornamentation, or possibly articles of clothing (Fig. 6). Painted terracotta types recur at Arpachiyah, and also at Tell Halaf and Chagar Bazar in north Syria, where the figures are seated on circular stools as if in parturition.[5] At Tepe Gawra a highly conventionalized torso shaped like a violin was found with the breasts and all the details of the lower part of the body strongly emphasized in contrast to those of the waist and hips. Below the navel a sexual triangle is marked by incised lines.[6]

At Tell Brak in the Khabur valley a number of figures with large eyes delineated have been found in abundance at a site excavated by Professor Mallowan, which he has called the Eye Temple, dated at about 3000 BC.[7] That they represent a female divinity is very probable,[8] (Fig. 9), and if this is so the temple may have been dedicated to the Mesopotamian Mother-goddess, Inanna-Ishtar, as Mallowan suggests, and the smaller figure with which she is sometimes accompanied in front of her body may be that of her son and consort, Dumuzi-Tammuz, the Young god.*

In southern Mesopotamia before the devastating flood of the Tigris and Euphrates in the third millennium BC, the first settlers at Ur of the Chaldees in the marshes of the Euphrates delta fashioned clay figurines with grotesque heads but well-modelled bodies, holding a child to the breast, or resting it on the hips. A few survived the catastrophe and became shapeless grotesques devoid of the technical skill displayed in the earlier sculptures. In the mound of Warka which marks the city of Erech, the ancient Uruk, the female statuettes resemble those of Ur in form and ornamentation, executed in black paint. One has a cylindrical body, a splayed base with the division between the legs marked by incision and wing-like arms. Nude women holding their breasts recur on rectangular reliefs, with almond eyes and rounded faces, their necks adorned with necklaces and their wrists with bracelets (Figs. 10, 11, 12). The hair is coiled round the head and locks frequently hang down on the shoulders.

*cf. Chap. III, pp 78f.–79f.

Anatolia

In Anatolia a number of pottery female figurines with pronounced sexual characteristics and conventionalized faces with exaggerated noses have been discovered in the mount of Alishar H iyük in the centre of the highland region some forty-five kilometres south-east of Yazgad. These were introduced by an intrusive group of people of a different racial type from that of the indigenous population, characterized by wheel-made pottery having Cappadocian affinities. Associated with the pottery statuettes was one of a woman made of lead and more elaborately constructed. The upper part is nude, and there are indications that the arms may have held the breasts (Fig. 13). In addition to an elaborate head-dress are five necklaces and disk-shaped ornaments. In some of the clay and pottery types the protruding abdomen suggests pregnancy, and the conical breasts are very prominent, in one case the mamilla being marked by a small depression. A lead figure shows pronounced breasts combined with a phallic elevation, indicative of a divine figure with male and female attributes.[9]

In the earlier Chalcolithic levels of an ancient mound, Yumuk Tepe, about four kilometres to the north-east of the small port of Mersin in Cicilia on the southern Turkish coast, situated on the direct route from east to west, a cruder goddess figurine has been recovered among the remains of the village community engaged in agriculture and stock-breeding (c. 4000 BC), prior to the Halaf culture.[10] Above this Chalcolithic horizon several stone and pottery female statuettes have been found in the Bronze Age levels, suggesting that the worship of the Mother-goddess was a permanent tradition in Anatolia.

Iran and Elam

In Persia the distribution of the cultus appears to have been more sporadic. There when food production began to supplement and supplant food-gathering in the south and south-west, it seems that a naked divinity was much in evidence at prehistoric transitional sites. At Tepe Giyan near Nihavend south of Hamadan, for example, rude figures occurred with painted hair and eyes but without excessive emphasis on the maternal organs. But in the north-east no traces of the cult have been detected.[11] At Susa in Elam in the earliest settlement in the parallel sites, figures of women modelled in clay with eyes and breasts rendered by dabs have come to light, the nose and brows indicated by thick rolls stuck on the flat slab, and on an incised sexual triangle. Later, in the first Elamite period (c. 2800 BC) a female statuette was found on the Acropolis with one of the splayed hands placed on the stomach and the other holding the breast. Others were incised with lines representing the eyes, bracelets and necklaces with a rosette pendant in the middle.[12]

Transcaspia

Similarly, in the mound at Anau in Transcaspia on the fertile border of the plateau to the north of the Ezburg Mountains, extending from the Caspian Sea to the Pamirs, naked figurines with the sexual organs emphasized in a realistic manner have been recovered from the middle strata of the south Kurgan. Here the cultural affinities are with those of Tepe Hissar near Damghan, south of the Caspian Sea, and in neither of these sites have figurines of this nature been discovered in the lowest strata containing the remains of the Neolithic villages similar to those of the mount of Sialk in north-west Iran, near Kashan, south-east of Teheran. (Map.) These very early agricultural communities (*c.* 5000 BC), so widely diffused from Iran to Anatolia and Egypt, probably were established rather later at Anau in Russian Turkistan than at Tepe Sialk in northern Persia. How long they survived is largely a matter of conjecture, as the dating of the deposits depends mainly on the height of ancient mounds and the contents of the several layers, which are variable quantities subject to many factors that cannot always be determined with any degree of accuracy. Nevertheless, all the indications now point to the Neolithic occupation in western Asia having been established before 5000 BC, prior to the Chalcolithic phase, when copper came into general use in most of the centres, not later than the fourth millennium BC.

At Anau and Tepe Hissar the marked change in pottery technique in the earlier and later settlements suggests an intrusion of new peoples into the area. Since it is in association with the new painted ware tradition and its Chalcolithic traits that the female figurines come into prominence, it would seem that the Goddess cult was introduced into Turkistan and northern Iran by these settlers. Moreover, there seems to have been contact between these early Iranian settlements on the edge of the Persian desert (Sialk, Giyan, Hissar), which were self-contained peasant communities with a uniform prehistoric culture but each having its own local distinguishing features, and those in the secluded mountains of Baluchistan on the borders of India.

Baluchistan

Thus, in the foothills in Makran in the Zhob valley small farming groups were established in villages before 3000 BC. There clay figurines

50

of women splayed at the waist on a flat-bottomed pedestal, with hands on the hips, were very numerous (fig. 1). The maternal organs, how-

Fig. 1. Clay female figurines from the Kulli culture of Western India, *c.* 2300 B.C.

ever, are not unduly exaggerated in these statuettes, and oval pendants resembling cowrie shells sometimes hang from three rows of necklaces. The faces are grotesque caricatures featured in clay, in spite of the hair having been elaborately dressed, except in the Zhob valley, north and north-east of Quetta, where they are hooded with a coif or shawl. Here the breasts are more prominent, the eyes are circular, the nose is owl-like and beak-shaped, and the mouth is indicated by a slit, producing collectively a grim appearance. As they came from the third occupation level in the sites in which they have been recorded (e.g. Dabar Kot, Periano Ghundai, Sur Jangal and Mogul Ghundai) they are assignable to the third millennium BC.[13] In style and features they are so uniform that Professor Piggott regards them as 'a grim embodiment of the Mother-goddess who is the guardian of the dead—an underworld deity concerned alike with the crops and the seed-corn buried beneath the earth.'[14] The carving of a phallus at the mound of Mogul Ghundrai near the left bank of the Zhob river, south-west of Fort Sandeman, and of a vulva depicted with great prominence at the neighbouring mound of Periano-Ghundai on the right bank of the river, shows that they had a fertility significance.[15]

Sind and the Punjab

That the cult flourished in the urban civilization in Sind and the Punjab from 2500 to 1500 BC is demonstrated by the quantities of terracotta female figurines unearthed by the excavations at Mohenjo-daro, Chanhu-daro and Harappa, and also in the neighbourhood of the Indus valley. Most of them are nude except for a small skirt round the loins, and in the higher levels little clay statuettes are roughly modelled in a seated posture, while others suggest that they were engaged in a ritual dance, like the figures on a faience plaque.[16] To enhance their life-giving properties most of them were painted over with a red slip or wash, and there can be little doubt, as Sir John Marshall said when he first brought them to light at Mohenjo-daro in 1922, that they represent 'a goddess with attributes very similar to those of the great Mother-goddess: Lady of Heaven, and a special patroness of women.'[17] It is not improbable that they were kept in the dwellings and streets of Mohenjo-daro and Harappa as tutelary divinities, very much as in India today the Mother-goddess is still the guardian of the house and village, presiding over childbirth and domestic affairs. In the ancient cities in the Indus valley these household deities seem to have been preserved in a niche in the wall in almost every house, and to have been held in the same veneration as are their successors among the illiterate population with their perennial struggle to bring forth and nurture their ever-increasing families.

The recurrence of nude male horned figures associated with the sacred *pipal* tree and cult animals, one of which represented a three-faced god in the *yoga* posture between four animals—the prototype of the Hindu Shiva as Lord of the Beasts and Prince of *yoga*[18]—suggests that as elsewhere in the Ancient Near East the Goddess may have had a male counterpart as a son or spouse. While they do often appear together in the iconography, limestone conical phallic emblems (*linga*) frequently are shown in conjunction with their female *yoni* rings.[19] Behind this symbolism unquestionably lay the mystery of birth, in which in the lowest levels the 'Goddess' was the most prominent figure, because at first attention was concentrated upon the feminine and maternal aspects of the process of generation. This is borne out by all the available evidence from the Indus valley to the Mediterranean in the third millennium BC., and it is confirmed by the Egyptian data.

Egypt
Thus, in the Nile valley three small statuettes of women have been recovered from the prehistoric cemeteries near Badari in Upper Egypt which cannot be later than about 4000 BC. One is very narrow-waisted and has a wide sexual triangle with horizontal lines. The breasts are small and pointed. The arms are folded in front and the buttocks are thickened. In the second example there is no suggestion of steatopyga, the waist is not prominent, the triangle is narrow with vertical lines, and the breasts are long and pendant. The third figure is very crudely fashioned without arms and legs, the buttocks are steatopygous, the head is small and has a string of beads in front of the neck, the waist is defined and the triangle is wide.[20] In prehistoric Egypt almost all the female figures are from the Early Pre-dynastic period, and do not recur until Proto-dynastic times when they become plentiful at Hierakonpolis and Abydos.[21] The pendant breast type is more prevalent than that showing thickening of the buttocks, a feature which Petrie maintained was characteristic of an earlier race continuing the Venus Palaeolithic tradition. As a matter of fact the so-called steatopygous and slim varieties constantly recur throughout the Near East and in the eastern Mediterranean where they tend to become highly conventionalized. This is apparent, for example, at the ancient towns of Thermi in Lesbos and the first two cities of Troy (*c*. 3000–2600 BC), which occupied key positions on the Hellespont as the meeting point of trade routes by land and sea from Mesopotamia to the Aegean, across the Anatolian plateau and up the straits. There the fiddle-shaped squatting figurines are combined with those in which the genitalia are emphasized.

The eastern Mediterranean
In Thessaly the affinities of the Neolithic female statuettes are with Thrace and the North rather than with the Troad, Anatolia, the Aegean Basin and Crete. It is possible, therefore, that they may represent an independent phase in the development and diffusion of the Goddess cult from the Near East, when generations of peaceful farming communities lived in relative isolation from their warlike neighbours until they were invaded by incursions from the Danube and the surrounding district. In Crete all the principal types of clay figurines have been recovered from the earliest Neolithic stratum in the Tell of

53

Knossos, where the earliest Asiatic influences were felt about 4000 BC. These included the Goddess emblems—the steatopygous figurines, squatting or sitting, clay 'idols', the double axe, and the dove—so prominent in the Middle East a thousand years before the cult was established in the eastern Mediterranean, where Crete was destined to become one of its most important centres. Indeed, later it was represented as the original home of the Phrygian Great Mother, Kybele,[22] and in Crete and the Aegean the Minoan Goddess assumed the guise of the Mountain-Mother, the Mistress of wild beasts, with outstretched or uplifted arms, often holding or encircled by snakes, clad in a skirt with flounces, wearing a high crown (Fig. 14). On some of the seals and signets she is represented as seated beneath a tree receiving offerings of the first-fruits of her bounty. Near her are such symbols as the double axe, sacral horns, a pillar, and her lions. These scenes belong to a later development of the cult, but, as Sir Arthur Evans says, it can scarcely be a coincidence that all the various centres from the Aegean to Elam in which these female figures and their emblems occur, became the centres of the worship of a series of goddesses who often combined ideas of motherhood and virginity, and eventually of the worship of the Great Mother herself.[23]

At first they may have been symbolic of the maternal attributes and functions of womanhood without any very specific personification in an all-embracing goddess of fecundity, or in that of separate and independent fertility divinities. Nevertheless, they seem to be the antecedents of the cult centred in the mystery of birth and generation, of fertility and generation, which was so conspicuous a feature in Ancient Near Eastern religion everywhere, and was eventually diffused to India in the East and to Crete, the Aegean, Sicily and Malta, before it passed westwards to the Iberian Peninsula. Thence it spread along the Atlantic littoral to Brittany and the British Isles, and from the Pyrenees to the Seine-Oise-Marne region in the Paris Basin.

THE CULT OF THE DEAD

The extension of the life-giving process to the dead, which has been one of the earliest features of prehistoric religion, could hardly fail to bring the mystery of birth and fertility into relation with that of death. It is not surprising, therefore, that the Goddess cult very early acquired a funerary and chthonian significance when her dominion was made to embrace the land of the dead. Thus, many of the female figurines discussed in the foregoing pages have been found in tombs and cemeteries, and scenes portraying the cult have a mortuary setting, as, for instance, those depicted on a Late Minoan sarcophagus at Hagia Triada in Crete.[24] But although in the Near East Mother-Earth was regarded as the ultimate source of life both for the living and the dead, the earliest indications of the idea of immortality appear to have been associated with the head as the seat of soul-substance and vitality.

The cult of skulls

That particular sanctity was attached to the cranium from very early times is shown by the careful preservation and ritual treatment of human skulls. Thus, in the Dragon-bone hill caves at Chou-kou-tien near Peking in deposits dated by Professor Zeuner 'in the neighbour-hood of 500,000 years',[25] the skeletal remains of a number of bodies had been decapitated after death, buried until the flesh had decomposed, and the crania then carefully preserved and broken open in order to extract the brain from them. Again, in Java, the skulls at Nyandoeng seem to have been treated in the same manner and used apparently as drinking vessels, very much as some primitive people today drink from the skull of a warrior to acquire his strength. In Europe in a grotto at Monte Circeo on the Tyrrhenian coast of the Pomptine Fields, a Neanderthal skull was found in 1939 in a small chamber within a circle of stones resting on two metacarpals of an ox and a deer. The foramen magnum connecting the brain with the spinal cord had been cut away after death, and the brain would appear to have been extracted and eaten sacramentally to imbibe its life-giving qualities. In the same way head-hunters in Indonesia collect human heads to increase the fertility of their crops by planting them in the fields or suspending them on the barns, because soul-substance as a vitalizing agent is thought to reside in them. In the Upper Palaeolithic, about twenty thousand years ago, drinking cups made from the upper part of the vault of human skulls have been found in the Solutrean and Magdalenian levels of a cave at Placard, Charente. The two nests of skulls embedded in red ochre found at Ofnet in the Jura had been deliberately cut off after death and ceremonially preserved, ornamented with shells and necklaces, and orientated in a westerly direction.

Plastered skulls at Jericho

Miss Kenyon has now produced remarkable confirmatory evidence from the pre-pottery Neolithic levels at Jericho. Apart from the skull of an elderly man carefully set in the angle of a room beneath the floor, at the end of the second season's excavation in 1952, in the centre of the west side of the mound, a skull was extracted from a trench which had the features moulded in plaster with eyes inset with shells. Deeper in the section lay two other crania similarly plastered, with three more behind them, and then a seventh. Upon examination it seemed that they were remarkably realistic portraits, probably of members of a family group. The crown had been left uncovered, but the rest of the skull had been completely encased in plaster. The features were delicately modelled, and in six of them the eyes had been composed of two segments of shell with vertical slits to indicate the pupils. In one case (viz., the seventh) the shells were cowries. The interior of the head had been filled with earth or clay, and this could have been done only after the soft tissues had decayed[26] (Fig. 16). Ten of these heads have now been found, the last a product of the 1957–58 excavations.

In these Neolithic portrait-skulls we have the earliest known example of naturalistic portraiture, dated by the Carbon 14 method not later than 6250 BC, which reached such heights later in Mesopotamian, Egyptian and in Greek art. The treatment was similar to that in New Guinea, where masks of venerated ancestors or powerful enemies have been constructed in the same manner, and there can be little doubt that seven thousand years ago at Jericho these plastered trophies were the object of veneration. That the practice was a common one is suggested by the discovery of two more examples in 1956 very near the rest, beneath the floor of the house, while decapitated skeletons were of frequent occurrence in this area of the excavation, usually below the several floors of superimposed dwellings. Now yet another has been reported from the last season's work (1957–58), as has been mentioned, making the total up to ten. Indeed, so prevalent was the practice that it seems not at all unlikely that the heads were preserved as the relics of the deceased members of the family for cult purposes, based on the belief that the head was the seat of spiritual power. Therefore, it became the centre of a ritual technique for the benefit and protection of succeeding generations, as well as to render to the dead the respect and service which was their due.

Moreover, in the later Neolithic phase the cult of skulls continued to prevail, the crania then being arranged in groups, either in a circle looking inwards, or in three sets orientated in the same direction. Indications of child sacrifice, so very common in Palestine, also began to appear. Thus, beside one infant burial was a collection of infant skulls with the cervical vertebrae attached, showing that the heads had been systematically cut off.[27] Burial beneath floors continued to be the normal practice, at any rate in the case of the more respected, venerated or feared members of the family and of the community. The rest may have been disposed of in any convenient manner, as, for instance, in disused passages which were found to have been filled with skeletons.

In the next occupation at Jericho, about 3200 BC, the newcomers buried their dead in cemeteries in shaft graves sunk into the rock, instead of beneath the floors of houses. The larger tombs contained so many skeletons that they can only be explained as secondary interments after the flesh had decayed. The bones were then collected and burnt on a funeral pyre around which the skulls were placed during the cremation, suggesting that particular significance was attached to the head, requiring it to be preserved for ritual purposes at the final ceremony For this reason the skulls were detached from the rest of the skeletal remains in the cremation pile of charred bones in the centre of the tombs, and the pots containing the offerings were inserted after the cremation before the tomb was filled in with the débris.

Treatment of the head in Ancient Egypt

In Ancient Egypt where the cult of the dead assumed such gigantic proportions and became the characteristic feature of this remarkable civilization, the skull in prehistoric times was severed from the body and buried separately. Thus at Nagada in five graves the cranium was set up on a pile of stones as at Monte Circeo, and in one case on a brick. In other graves the body was inside a recess with the neck against the wall, without any skull.[28] The practice ceased when mummification was introduced in and after the Fifth Dynasty, but references to it continued in the later literature. For example, in The Book of the Dead it is stated, 'I am a Prince, son of a prince . . . whose head is restored to him after it has been cut off.'[29] Or again in the Osiris myth, it is alleged that when his body was dismembered by Seth his head was preserved and buried at Abydos, having been placed in a coffer surmounted by two plumes and mounted on a staff. This was the most treasured possession and symbol of the city and made the sanctuary the holiest in the land.[30]

While many of the Predynastic graves contained entire skeletons, often the head was separated from the rest of the body. Sometimes it remained attached to the vertebrae of the neck, though it was not in its normal position in respect of them. The mutilated or dismembered remains may have been intrusive burials introduced by foreigners, as in the oldest prehistoric interments the corpses had been buried whole and intact. But before the brain was extracted through the nose in the process of mummification, the head was cut off and filled with spices and unguents to preserve it.[31] Extreme care was taken to make quite certain that it was then restored to its rightful owner, as it was believed to contain his soul-substance, and like the restored body of Osiris, it must be complete with all its members when its youth was renewed in the hereafter.[32] Indeed, long after the practice of decapitation had ceased, the formula was retained in the Theban Recension of The Book of the Dead, in which reference was made to the head of Osiris not having been taken away, in a context that suggests that its loss would be fatal to the attainment of eternal life.

Substitute heads and masks

Among the neighbouring African tribes secondary burial and the preservation of the skull was widely adopted, especially in the case of chiefs and powerful medicine men whose wisdom and divine powers were thought to reside therein. Therefore, they were kept for magical purposes and duly venerated, the Baganda, for instance, having kept those of their kings for a thousand years.[33] In Egypt, as in Jericho, the head was covered with stucco-plaster, and the face was carefully modelled, unless it was painted on the linen-enveloped head to enhance its lifelike appearance[34] (Fig. 17). In the Pyramid Age, in the Fourth Dynasty, a life-sized simulacrum of the deceased was made by modelling his head in limestone or mud and placing it in the burial chamber with the mummy, to secure the continuance of his existence if and when his mortal remains decayed or became unrecognizable.[35] About the same time plaster death-masks were introduced, an example of which was that discovered by J. E. Quibell at Sakkara belonging to this period,[36] and thought to have been taken directly from the face of the Pharaoh Teta immediately after his death.

The head being regarded as the most vital part of the body, containing the soul-substance and the organs of sight, hearing, taste and smell, as well as showing the likeness of the individual, its preservation was essential for the attainment of immortality. Therefore, a permanent simulacrum was produced in stucco, resin, or similar durable materials in the form of a plaster-covered head, a mask or substitute head (Figs. 15 to 18) to take the place of the body when it decayed, thereby preparing the way for the full-scale portrait statues which were inserted in the chamber, called the *serdab* or 'statue-house', of the mastaba tomb. With the establishment of the First Dynasty soon after 3000 BC under the rule of a single Pharaoh, significant changes in tomb construction were effected. The simple Predynastic pit-graves continued to be the normal mode of sepulture for the mass of the people, but with the elevation of the sovereign ruler to divine status the royal tombs underwent a corresponding elaboration in construction, contents and cultus, and in the treatment of the corpse, as befitted his unique position in the nation.

Grave equipment and the disposal of the body

In late prehistoric times prior to the rise of the Dynasty, graves often were plastered with mud or lined with brick, while the bodies sometimes were wrapped in matting or occasionally enclosed in wooden coffins and buried in the contracted position orientated towards the west, if they were not dismembered or decapitated. Grave furniture became more plentiful, and the ornamentation of the bodies more elaborate, with stones, shells, carnelian, turquoise, lapis lazuli, and steatite bead necklaces and ivory bracelets. The female equipment included ceremonial slate palettes on which malachite was ground for painting the eyes, while in a cemetery at Hierakonpolis, the Predynastic (i.e. Gerzean) centre of the Horus cult of Upper Egypt, a brick-lined tomb was decorated with coloured hunting scenes, combats and ships painted on the surface and coated with yellow ochre.[37] Thus, the normal method of disposal of the dead in Neolithic times in the Nile valley was by interment, usually in the contracted position, in cemeteries near the settlements. Only at Merimde on the western marshes of the Delta, west of the Rosetta branch of the Nile, were they buried among or within the huts, close to the fireplace, without any grave goods. Since the bodies invariably were orientated towards the west, an occidental land of the dead is suggested, until in the Dynastic Pyramid Age the hereafter was placed in the east, though sometimes it was located in the Elysian Fields among the circumpolar stars in the northern sky.

With the increase in the funerary furniture, the grave pit was undercut on one side at the bottom to make room for the equipment, and as this became deeper and deeper rock steps were required to gain access to the subterranean chamber. This development became most apparent in the royal tombs at Abydos where the houses or palaces of the Pharaohs were reproduced below ground,[38] with a large chamber under the superstructure in the centre and smaller tombs grouped round it to contain the offerings, which included courtiers and servants sacrificed at the royal obsequies. The mastaba tomb, in fact, arose as a vast rectangular brick creation over a series of chambers and a shaft leading to the grave, the outside walls becoming ornamented with a series of vertical recesses and projections. In the Third Dynasty stone was substituted for brick to make the tomb 'an everlasting habitation' for the occupant. Thus, that of Zoser was a huge stone oblong construction made up of five mastabas superimposed on each other in steps of decreasing height and size in the form of a pyramid. Subsequently the steps were filled in with stones, the sides were straightened and brought to a point at the top (fig. 2 and Fig. 19). These vast royal pyramids

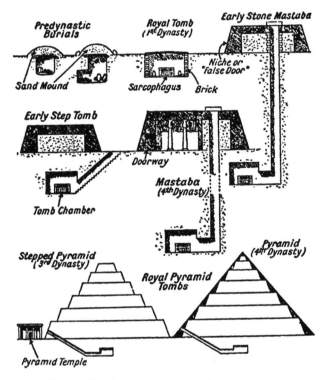

Fig. 2. The development of the Mastaba tomb

reached their climax about 2900 BC in those erected at Gizeh for Cheops, Khafra and Menkaura, with smaller stepped pyramids of royal relatives, courtiers and officials arranged in rows at a respectable distance.[39]

Access to the rock-cut burial chamber was by means of a passage entered in the northern side of the pyramid, and on the east front stood the temple containing provisions for the deceased with his portrait statue placed before the table of offerings. There, as in the group of chambers forming the tomb-chapel in the mastaba, known as the 'ka-house', the ka or guardian alter ego guiding the fortunes of the individual through his life as well as after death, partook of the offerings and beheld the mortuary rites performed in it.[40] Originally, in fact, the reanimation ceremony seems to have been held not in connexion with the mummy but with the statue, the sculptor being called 'he who makes to live' ($s'n_a^h$) just as the mortuary priest who supplied the needs of the deceased in the hereafter was known as 'the servant of the *ka*'.[41]

The mummy was too inaccessible, and also at first always liable to disintegrate, to be the recipient of the libations, lustrations, censings, and the food and drink presented in the cultus. These rites, therefore, were held before the statue as the simulacrum of the dead man after it had been 'brought to life' by an elaborate process of restoring the bodily functions and attributes one by one. Thus, in the ancient texts this 'Opening of the Mouth' ceremony is mentioned in association with the fashioning of the statue,[42] and may have been performed in the workshop which was called 'the House of Gold'—at first perhaps a chamber in the pyramids. The earliest mention of this observance is in the Fourth Dynasty in the sculptured tomb of Methen. Therefore, although The Book of 'The Opening of the Mouth' was not compiled until the Nineteenth Dynasty (*c.* 1318 BC), the rites are very ancient, some of them in all probability going back to Predynastic times[43] as a reanimation and purification rite, before becoming a repetition of what was alleged to have been said and done by the sons of Horus for their father Osiris, when they restored him to life by the aid of the eye which Horus lost in his fight with his uncle Seth (Fig. 20).

In Egypt the ancient belief that the dead lived in or at the tomb, which in consequence had to be adequately equipped and supplied with grave goods and offerings, persisted until at length it acquired the vast dimensions of the great monumental structures which have remained throughout the ages the most impressive expression of this conception of the hereafter in the ancient world. Even after the Fifteenth Dynasty, when the mortuary ritual and the cult of the dead became crystallized in their final form, the sojourn in the tomb persisted side by side with the belief in a blessed immortality in remote celestial realms and Elysian Fields. In the Pyramid Age this hope was reserved for the Pharaohs, and in some measure for the nobility, who moved away their tombs from the royal cemeteries to their own domains to seek their own eternity in their own right when they joined their *kas* beyond the grave. When every Egyptian in due course was destined to become an Osiris and attain eternal blessedness, the earlier belief in a continued existence as a 'glorified personality' (*akh*) in which the head played a very significant part, found expression in an ever-developing mortuary ritual and a growing complexity in the conception of the nature and destiny of man. How rapidly the cult of the dead developed in the Nile valley is shown by the simple grave with its sand heap surrounded by a circle of stones assuming the gigantic proportions of the mighty pyramids in the course of a few centuries from about 3200 to 2900 BC, the greatest of which covers thirteen acres and contains over two million blocks of limestone, each weighing on an average two and a half tons, and stands nearly five hundred feet high. That a hundred thousand men were involved in its construction, as an ancient tradition quoted by Herodotus affirms, may not be a very great exaggeration.

Mesopotamian sepultures

In the Nile valley climatic and geographical conditions appear to have played their part in the preservation of the dead buried in the sand of the desert, and in 'the proud pyramids of stone proclaiming man's sense of sovereign power in his triumph over material forces'. Indeed, it may have been because originally corpses were naturally desiccated by the hot dry sand and so were preserved indefinitely, that in Egypt attention came to be concentrated to such a marked degree upon human survival. This led to the adoption of increasingly elaborate methods to preserve the tissues from decay by evisceration and embalmment, and to the attainment of the same end by the creation of masks and portrait statues as substitutes for the immortal mummy, when burial in stone-lined tombs removed the corpse from direct contact with the desiccating sand. In Mesopotamia, on the other hand, the position was very different. Neither the natural desiccation nor the regularity of the rise and fall of the Nile prevailed. This unpredictability of the Tigris and Euphrates, always liable to cause disastrous floods, and the absence of preservative properties in the soil, were reflected in the Babylonian cult of the dead, alike in the precarious condition of the hereafter and in the dearth of great cemeteries, elaborate mortuary equipment, or of any indications of mummification, enduring pyramids, or a cult of skulls, substitute heads and portrait statues.

In Sumer the normal procedure was for the body to be wrapped in a mat or in a linen winding sheet, clad in its ordinary clothes, in the flexed position with the head on a cushion. With a bowl of water and a few personal belongings it was then enclosed in a wicker or pottery coffin (*larnake*), or in two large pottery jars with their open ends together in the form of a *pithos*, and placed in a simple earth grave, or in a small brick-built vault. In towns the interment was often under the pavement of one of the rooms in the house in which the deceased had lived. After the funeral rites were over, the flooring was relaid and the occupation of the house by the surviving members of the household was resumed in the customary manner. At Hassuna, west of the Tigris, in the earliest known Neolithic settlement in Mesopotamia, the bodies of infants in painted and incised jars occurred, and beneath the floor of a room above these burials was an undisturbed interment in the fully contracted position with the head to the north, but no grave furniture was found. At a higher level two skeletons had been flung into a grain bin, and a skull into a rubbish pit,[44] so that no uniformity of burial seems to have been adopted. Relatively few cemeteries have been discovered anywhere in Mesopotamia, and cremation was not systematically practised in the historic period, notwithstanding traces of burning in the upper part of the body in some of the early graves at Ur (c. 3500 BC).

In Assyria at Tepe Gawra near Nineveh circular stone structures (tholoi) with a domed roof, sometimes having a rectangular chamber attached to them, were used for ritual purposes, and associated with them were graves numbering in all nearly five hundred tombs. But as throughout its history the mound was used as a burial ground, from 5000 BC to the Bronze Age, this must represent a very small proportion of the population. The more elaborate tombs roofed with mud-brick, matting, stone or wood, and containing a rich collection of burial furnishings, were confined to a limited period in its history (strata IX), whereas the simpler graves occur at all levels. Therefore, they represent the normal mode of disposal of the dead.[45] In most of them the bodies were flexed, though a few of the skeletons were in the extended position as they were in the narrow rectangular troughs isolated from the rest of the cemetery at Tell Al'Ubaid in Sumer. This, however, was an unusual practice which may have been due to chance or carelessness, though the extended burials in the brick graves probably mark a different cultus or a foreign intrusion in the population.[46] That such changes in mortuary ritual were effected through diffusion is shown in the closely allied cemetery belonging to the Al'Ubaid period (c. 3500 BC) at Arpachiyah in Assyria, where parts only of the skeleton were buried (i.e. the head, legs, arms or ribs were missing). This custom of 'fractional burial' seems to have originated in an Iranian centre and to have spread eastwards through Baluchistan to the Indus valley and westwards to Arpachiyah.[47] Nevertheless, in Mesopotamia and the Iranian Highlands there were no strict rules governing the disposal of the dead though flexing was a very widely adopted mode of sepulture.

In the great cemetery outside the walls of the renowned city of Ur, the traditional home of Abraham, situated between Baghdad and the upper head of the Persian Gulf, about ten miles west of the Euphrates, two types of burials have been discovered since the systematic excavation of the mounds called by the Arabs 'Tel al Muqayyar' was begun by the joint expedition of the British Museum and the University of

Pennsylvania under the direction of Sir Leonard Woolley in 1922. Near the surface lie the graves of the commoners at varying levels and in great profusion, enclosing the corpse wrapped in matting or in a coffin of clay, wood or basket-work, and lying on its side slightly flexed. With it were a few personal belongings—a knife or dagger, a pin, beads, and perhaps a cylinder seal—together with offerings of food and drink, weapons and implements, for use in the hereafter, and to mark his position in society.

The royal tombs of Ur

The royal tombs, now dated about 2250 BC,[48] differ from the simple graves of their subjects in that they consisted of one or more chambers constructed in stone or brick, roofed with domes, with a pit for offerings and additional burials. The grave goods were immense and included a fine head of a bull in gold with eyes of lapis lazuli, exquisitely fashioned stags, gazelles, bulls and goats in gold, with clusters of pomegranates and branches of trees with stems and fruits of gold and carnelian, silver and gold bowls and stone vessels, clay jars, silver tables and offerings, harps and lyres, an inlaid gaming-board, the statue of a ram on its hind legs with its front legs bound to the branches of a tree with silver chains, a wooden chariot decorated with mosaic and golden heads of cows and bulls and cockle-shells containing green paint (Fig. 22). With such a galaxy of priceless objects it is not surprising that the tombs have been rifled, so that the total wealth in them cannot be estimated, but it must have been colossal, and the offerings were not confined to the grave goods as the mortuary ritual also involved human sacrifice on the grand scale. Thus, with them were the richly clad and ornamented bodies of courtiers, maids of honour and guards, who, faithful unto death, had been buried so magnificently in order to continue the royal service they had rendered so loyally in this life.

In the chamber were soldiers in two ranks with copper spears by their sides, and court ladies wearing a gala head-dress of lapis and carnelian beads, golden pendants of beech leaves, ear-rings, gold necklaces and a wooden harp on top of their bodies, with the head of a bull in gold and copper respectively.

This, in fact, appears to have been the tomb of a ruler named A-bar-gi, according to the inscription found in it on a cylinder seal, and behind it was a similar second chamber in which apparently his queen Shub-ad had been buried. Although the king's chamber had been plundered traces of retinue survived, together with two model boats, and in that of the queen, her body, enveloped in a mass of costly beads,

64

lay on a wooden bier with a gold cup near her hand. The remains of an elaborate head-dress covered her crushed skull, fortified with a lapis amulet on each end, one shaped as a seated bull and the other as a calf (Fig. 21). By the side of the body was a second head-dress containing thousands of lapis lazuli beads, with some figures of gazelles, stags, bulls and goats in gold, and the mortal remains of two women attendants against the bier, one at the head and the other at the foot. Inside the entrance stood the wooden chariot used as a hearse and around the interments were the remains of fires and a funeral feast.

Whatever may have been the funerary rites performed, there are no indications of any kind of struggle or of a violent death. Arrayed in their courtly finery and regalia, the attendants were adorned in their full glory to accompany the sovereign and his consort to the next life. As they walked to their appointed places in the chamber, it is not improbable that they drank some fatal potion such as hashish or opium from the little clay or metal cups each carried, and then having lost consciousness they were placed in position before the filling up of the shaft was begun.[49] So ended the sacrifice on behalf of the divine rulers, doubtless made gladly and voluntarily by his entourage in hope of retaining their status and of continuing their service under new conditions in their final abode.

These royal tombs and their ritual, however, appear to have been quite unique in Mesopotamia, there being nothing in the Sumerian texts or the archaeological data to indicate the practice of human sacrifice in this connexion as a general custom. Indeed, it has been suggested that they represented the annual offerings of a substitute for the divine king in the Spring Festival to renew the processes of vegetation, as a fertility rite. But for such a purpose the sixteen Ur graves seem to be quite inadequate, and there are no indications of these sacrifices being part of the sacred marriage ceremonial. On the contrary, the names of two of the royal occupants of the tombs have been discovered and all the circumstances of the elaborate interment suggest that the occasions were the obsequies of the local deified city-kings at the rise of the Dynasty of Ur. In that case, however, it would seem that the royal tomb ritual at Ur approximated more to the Egyptian cult of the dead than to the gloomy and uninspiring 'Land of No-return' current later in Babylonia, where rulers and commoners alike dwelt in darkness and dust, unless, of course, it was to escape this fate that the select company assembled in the chambers arrayed in all their splendour to defy the sinister predictions that were beginning to arise and became dominant after the Third Dynasty (c. 2100 BC).

E

The Indus valley

A similar situation seems to have obtained in Baluchistan and in the Harappan civilization in India, where coupled with the scant attention paid to the disposal of the dead in the so-called 'fractional burials', the pottery vessels, copper axes, beads, mirrors, necklaces and red pigment in the graves indicate a continued existence requiring provision for the well-being of the deceased. In the secluded valleys of Baluchistan the cemeteries of the self-contained peasant communities have revealed that 'fractional burial' was practised in the third millennium BC, suggestive of secondary interment after exposure elsewhere. Moreover, the graves contained the customary furniture and in some of the funerary vessels red ferruginous earth occurred, so widely employed as a life-giving agent in the cult of the dead. At Mohenjo-daro no traces of a cemetery have been discovered, and the few skeletal remains in the houses and pits appear to have been those of victims of raiders when the city was destroyed, probably in the middle of the second millennium BC.[50] As some of the bones show signs of charring, partial cremation may have been adopted, and this may explain to some extent the absence of burials and grave goods.

On the outskirts of the ancient city of Harappa in the Punjab what may have been an ossuary has been found, containing skulls, long bones, animal remains and pottery, and in the corner of a house a possible fractional burial.[51] This, however, may have been a modern interment, possibly, as Sir Mortimer Wheeler suggests, after a plague or battle when vultures had done their grim work on the bodies.[52] In the cemetery known as R 37 to the south of the citadel mound, large quantities of pottery had been placed at the head, the feet, and along the sides of the corpses which had been adorned with personal ornaments and toilet objects, together with a copper mirror, a shell spoon, antimony, and mother-of-pearl. In one grave a body, probably of a girl, had been wrapped in a shroud of reeds and placed in a wooden coffin with thirty-seven pots, mostly near the head of the coffin,[53] reminiscent of similar burials in Sumer in the Early Dynastic period (*c.* 2800 BC).[54]

Thus, throughout the Ancient East, from Egypt and the Fertile Crescent to the Indus valley, the funerary ritual underwent singularly little change from the beginning of the Neolithic to the establishment (and in India the break-up) of the urban cultures. This uniformity suggests the solidarity of the area as a cultural unity, in which in spite of the marked differences in climatic and economic conditions and in the social and religious structures, the procedure followed a common pattern. In the Indus valley the evidence is meagre, and no tombs have been discovered at all comparable to those in Ancient Egypt or at Ur. Cremation may have been partly responsible, but in this respect the evidence is by no means conclusive, though we know it was widely adopted in Vedic India.

The eastern Mediterranean

In the western extension of the cult of the dead in the second half of the fourth millennium BC (i.e. from *c.* 3500–3000 BC), as it made its way through the eastern Mediterranean and along the Danube from the Middle East and Egypt, it came under the influence of the worship of the Mother-goddess, which, as we have seen, followed much the same course of diffusion. Therefore, her emblems were of frequent occurrence in the tombs and in the mortuary ritual throughout the region. Collective interment in tholoi was widely adopted in the eastern Mediterranean, just as rock-cut and chamber tombs, combined with corbelled tholoi, abounded in the Iberian area in the west where the megalithic tradition predominated, notably in Almeria. At Khirokitia, one of the earliest settlements in Cyprus (*c.* 4000–3500 BC), where very close links with the cities of South Anatolia were apparent, remains of tholoi occur similar to those of the Tell Halaf period at Arpachiyah near Nineveh. Towards the end of the transition from the Chalcolithic to the Bronze Age (3500–3000 BC), female figurines appeared in graves, suggesting that the Goddess cult had been introduced from western Asia.[55] Further to the west in the last centuries of the third millennium, Malta seems to have become the sacred isle of the Asiatic Mother, colonized by people whose traditions were very deeply rooted in Anatolia, notwithstanding evidence of Cycladic, Siculan and Minoan-Mycenaean influences. But the temples, mortuary ritual and rotund female figures were essentially Asiatic, and the polished grey ware is reminiscent of Syria and Palestine,[56] while the sanctuaries had affinities with Arpachiyah.

In Crete the vaulted tombs never attained the magnificence they reached on the mainland in the great beehives, like the so-called Treasury of Atreus at Mycenae (Fig. 64) and the Treasury of Munyas at Orchomenos. The Minoan funerary ritual appears to have been relatively simple, consisting in placing the body in the burial chamber unburnt, though fires were lighted in the tholoi for some ceremonial purpose and the offerings were deposited in annexes to the circular tombs, unless they were votive offerings. Sometimes libations were poured out within a special enclosure, and at Knossos in the Tomb of the Double Axes, vessels had been placed before a sacred pillar against an inner wall evidently as an offering to the Minoan Mother-goddess on behalf of the dead.[57] On a Late Minoan sarcophagus at Hagia Triada, as will be considered later,* offerings may have been made to Mother-Earth on behalf of the deceased interred, therein suggesting that the Cretan Goddess had her place in the mortuary ritual.

The widespread adoption of cremation in the Middle Bronze Age in the Near East and its extension in the eastern Mediterranean, and subsequently in central and northern Europe, had a significant effect upon the conception of the nature and destiny of man, especially as it coincided with a greater emphasis on an extra-mundane celestial divine order controlling for good or ill human affairs and natural events, and involving sometimes a spiritualized conception of creation (e.g. in the Egyptian Memphite Theology). Earth and Sky then tended to become the primeval pair from whom all things emanated, though not infrequently it was either the Earth-Mother or the Sky-Father who ultimately was responsible for beginning the creative process. When the dead were interred in 'mother earth' doubtless they were thought in the first instance to return whence they had come. But as the more obscure figure of a transcendent Creator in the sky came into greater prominence and was given clearer definition, he was regarded as the begetter, breathing into man the breath of life. Therefore, since when the life left the body it was thought very frequently to go back to the god who had bestowed it and given it a body, it was to the celestial realms that it returned. The practice of cremation was calculated to emphasize this interpretation of the hereafter and to facilitate the transition to a sky-world. But the correlation of this mode of disposal of the body and the belief in a heavenly spirit world is too sporadic to warrant the assumption that the one necessarily depended upon the other.

In Greece, for example, cremation was introduced by the Dorian invasion without any marked change regarding the nether regions, except that the emphasis was then placed on the liberation of the soul and of the immortal element in the grave goods. Moreover, as cremation was reserved for rulers and the more distinguished section of the community, it tended to be related to the divine Elysian realms. In the Tyrian version of the legend of Herakles, the hero is said to have ascended to the sky in the smoke of his own funeral pyre.[58] In Brahmanic mortuary ritual, sacred fires were kindled to assist the soul in its celestial ascent,[59] while the infant son of the archon of Eleusis was bathed in the fire by Demeter to render him immortal.[60]

*cf. Chap. III, p. 100.

68

THE CONCEPT OF DEITY

In Mesopotamia the highest of the gods was Anu, whose name meant 'sky' and who was recognized in and behind the various phenomena of nature. In fact, he owed his prominent position to the dominant role the sky played in the universe, while the earth as the source of the life-giving waters also had a male connotation (Enki) as well as a maternal function (Ninhursaga), at once the begetter and producer of vitality, together exercising the greatest influence on creation in all its aspects and attributes. But the awesomeness of the vast all-encircling sky could hardly fail to arouse a numinous reaction which gave a special significance to the hierarchy of superior gods who reigned therein in transcendent majesty and splendour, and bestowed their gifts or meted out their wrath upon mankind. Rivalling in power and glory the all-encompassing heavens was the sun, rising anew every morning and passing into oblivion in the underworld in the evening, giving life and light to the living and the dead, and becoming incarnate in the occupant of the Egyptian throne. Sometimes the moon was his satellite, or the order might be reversed, the moon taking precedence of the sun. But whatever status was accorded to them, the various members of the polytheistic hierarchy were regarded to some extent as departmentalized deities with localized functions.

Nevertheless, the development of the concept of Deity cannot be interpreted in an evolutionary sequence from animism, a belief in innumerable spiritual beings animating natural phenomena, through a polytheistic hierarchy of gods, each concerned with his or her own particular functions, to one single sovereign Lord and Creator of heaven and earth, as was formerly conjectured.[61] This neat and tidy theoretical interpretation of a very complex development cannot be sustained, because so far from animism and polytheism having passed into monotheism as a result of abstraction and generalization, simplification and unification, speculation about nature and its processes and the constitution of man in a body-soul relationship appears to have led to the peopling of natural phenomena with a multiplicity of spirits, departmental gods, ancestors and culture heroes in such profusion that the Sky-god or Supreme Being often has tended to retire into the background. He has, however, usually retained a transcendental status with a greater and wider significance, if a less clearly defined sphere of influence than that exercised by lesser secondary divinities. Thus, among the Nuer people in Nilotic East Africa, Professor Evans-Pritchard has recently recorded that God (*Kwoth*) is regarded as a Being of pure spirit, and because he is like the wind or air 'he is everywhere and being everywhere he is here now'. He is far away in the sky yet present on the earth which he created and sustains. 'Everything in nature, in culture, in society and in men is as it is because God made it so.' Although he is ubiquitous and invisible he sees and hears all that happens, and as he is responsive to the supplications of those who call upon him, prayers are addressed to him and sacrifices offered to avoid misfortunes. Since God can be angry he can and does punish wrong-doing, and suffering is accepted with resignation because it is his will, and, therefore, beyond human control. But the consequences of wrong-doing can be stayed or mitigated by contrition and reparation, prayer and sacrifice.[62]

Such a conception of deity is a religious response to the notion of Providence more fundamental than any gradual development from plurality to unity. It is rather a spontaneous purposive functioning of an inherent type of thought and emotion; an evaluation of the ultimate moral value of the universe; an awareness of the *mysterium tremendum* transcending all things, rather than speculation about natural processes and spiritual beings. Indeed, when the human mind has reflected upon the animation of nature and arrived at conceptual ideas about spirits and organized pantheons, the Supreme Deity not infrequently has become obscure and even otiose.

The Sky-gods in Egypt
So deeply rooted and firmly established in the religions of the Near East from Neolithic times onwards was this belief in an extra-mundane Power as the source of universal creative activity centred in the god of the sky, that it may well go back to a very early period prior to the rise of civilization in the Fertile Crescent, western Asia and the eastern Mediterranean. Everywhere the same linguistic root connects the heavens, the clouds and the rain with their personifications in the Sky-god and his manifestations in the revivification of nature, the thunder and the storm. As Zeus or Dyaus Pitar among the Indo-Europeans was primarily the god of the sky and the weather, known under a variety of names, before he assumed the functions of the various gods whom he assimilated, so in Egypt the Falcon-god Horus is represented in the Pyramid Texts as the source of life and death, of rain and of celestial fire. As the cult of the hawk was one of the oldest and most widespread in the proto-historic period in the Nile valley, in all probability originally there were many Falcon-gods who eventually were absorbed in the royal god, Horus the Elder, to form a compound deity, as theological speculation developed. (Figs 23, 24.) Among his various titles 'lord of the heaven' (*nb-p. t.*) was the commonest, and as the personification of

the power of the sky he was the Sky-god *par excellence* in his different manifestations. When his followers conquered Upper Egypt he, as Horus of Edfu, assumed the symbol of the solar disk, but by representing it as the outspread wings of a falcon he retained his earlier designation.[63]

The many forms in which the Sun-god and Horus were represented in the Egyptian texts doubtless are survivals of an earlier cult of the omniscient Sky-god brought into conjunction with the all-prevailing solar worship in its many manifestations. As Breasted has pointed out, 'the all-enveloping glory and power of the Egyptian sun is the most insistent fact in the Nile valley',[64] and it is hardly surprising that the ancient Egyptians saw the solar deity in different aspects and local forms. Flying across the heavens like a falcon in his daily course he was known as Harakhte, the 'Horus of the Horizon', who with three other local Horuses constituted the Four Horuses of the eastern sky, represented as four youths with curly hair sitting on the east side of the sky. In the morning he came forth as Khepera, a winged scarab beetle rising in the east, and then flew across the sky as Harakhte in the form of a hawk with outstretched wings, the red solar disk on his head identified with Re, until in the evening he tottered down to the west as an aged man, Atum, having run his course.

As the head of the pantheon Re represented the sun in the fullness of his strength, combining all the forces of nature. Before the First Dynasty at Heliopolis he was the sun in the sky personified and worshipped in the solar disk and identified with the primordial Father of the gods Atum.[65] In this capacity he was thought to be self-produced, having arisen out of the primeval waters, Nun,[66] though in other theophanies he was regarded as the son of Geb and Nut, or else born from a lotus flower, or from an egg by Ptah, the self-created great god of Memphis. Horus became the son of Re, and as the solar cult developed and predominated after the unification of Upper and Lower Egypt by the victorious Horus-kings, when they came under Heliopolitan influence, Re was made supreme among the gods, absolute in his control of the Nile valley, the ally and protector of the throne. Thus, in addition to his being the source of life and increase, he was the primordial great god, Re-Atum, the self-created Creator, Re-Harakhte the youthful god on the eastern horizon, and eventually at Thebes he became Amon-Re, the 'king of the gods', worshipped with great magnificence at Karnak and Luxor (Figs. 81, 82).

Among the most ancient of the Egyptian gods was Min of Koptos who was both a sky and a fertility deity closely related to Amon, the Egyptian Zeus, and as early as the Gerzean phase of the proto-historic period having as his emblem the thunderbolt, the weapon of the Sky-god.[67] Later he became a son of Re, and of Osiris and Isis, and of Shu, but before he was incorporated in the pantheons of the great gods he was a prehistoric Supreme Being represented as an ithyphallic bearded man concerned essentially with sexual reproduction, and as a storm-god wielding his thunderbolt. From archaic times to the New Kingdom in the form of his bull, he presided over the ceremonial reaping of the new corn by the Pharaoh, and over the hoeing festival to ensure the fruitfulness of the earth and the well-being of the country and its people. Throughout the ages he survived in his full vigour. At a very early period he was equated with the falcon as a symbol of heaven and so became identified with Horus the Elder as a Sky-god, associated sometimes with the moon, thereby making him the equivalent of Pan.

It would seem, however, that Seth was the god most widely worshipped among the indigenous population in Upper Egypt, the eastern Delta and Libya in prehistoric and early dynastic times. Genealogically he was the son of Geb and Nut, the Earth-god and the Sky-goddess, and before his followers were confined to the south by the Asiatic invaders, probably he held sway in Lower Egypt as well as in Upper Egypt, Libya and the adjacent desert region. At first his followers appear to have been on friendly terms with the worshippers of Osiris and Horus, their respective gods being related to each other as members of one and the same family.*[68] It was not until later that strife broke out among them, represented mythologically as Seth killing Osiris and engaging in mortal combat with Horus. He then became the malevolent incarnation of evil (Typhon) in perpetual conflict with the beneficent forces personified in Osiris, the author and giver of life. Seth, on the other hand, was a Storm-god and Rain-god originally personifying the sky and the weather, and when Osiris was equated with the life-giving waters of the Inundation (the Nile), he had to be suppressed as a serious rival of the Osirian cultus, which was firmly established by the Twelfth Dynasty. During the Hyksos period his popularity was restored, being the counterpart of the Semitic Baal, but despite sporadic revivals in the Nineteenth Dynasty, during the reigns of Seti II and Rameses I and II, his worship declined in the Twenty-second Dynasty until in the Saite period (c. 663–525 BC) he was identified with Apophis or Typhon, the Egyptian devil. Therefore, in spite of his great antiquity and his status as a Sky-god and Weather-god, Seth was destined to play a declining role, the Nile valley depending on the inundation of the great Osirian

---

*In the Pyramid Texts Seth was the brother of Osiris and uncle of Horus, suggesting that their respective human groups were in close contact with each other.

river for its fertility and rain being regarded with intense disfavour as the scourge of a malign power.

Although Egyptian religion remained essentially polytheistic, a latent conception of a universal God can be detected underlying the persistent polytheistic tradition. Thus, in due course the various aspects of Re, together with Ptah, the 'Great One' of Memphis, were blended not into a single monotheistic deity but into three independent divinities with the same nature. The abortive attempt of Amenhotep IV (Ikhnaton) to establish a solar monotheism centred in Aton as the sole God of heaven and earth failed, because it was primarily a royal cultus confined to the Pharaoh and his family, divorced from human affairs in general and the fundamental needs of mankind at large expressed in an accessible efficacious cultus. To fulfil these requirements the Sky-gods and goddesses of the Egyptian solar cycle were brought into relation with the Earth-gods and Weather-gods of the Osiris cycle, so that the beneficence of the celestial realms through their agency might be bestowed upon the earth in fruitful seasons with abundance of corn and wine, destroying the forces of evil, giving health and strength to the living and immortality to the dead.

The Babylonian Triad

In Mesopotamia the assembly of gods in the sky constituted the highest authority in the universe, determining the course of events on earth. Under the leadership of Anu, the god of heaven, whose name means 'sky', 'shining', 'bright',[69] the cosmic order was established out of primeval chaos as an organized whole. He was, in fact, the personification of the sky and the most potent force in the cosmos, older than all the other gods, and the ultimate source of all existence. As 'God' *par excellence* he occupied an independent position, and from the time of Gudea, the priest-king of Lagash (*c.* 2060–2042 BC) (Fig. 30) he became supreme. Even after his cult had fallen into obscurity, like that of so many Supreme Beings, his supremacy was affirmed and maintained, and in the later theological lists of gods he always stood at the head. In his celestial abode he kept the bread and water of immortal life, and it was he who gave the divine authority exercised by kings on earth.

Next to Anu was Enlil, the Storm-god, the second member of the Great Triad, who was also described as 'King of the gods' as well as 'Lord of the winds'. Being less obscure than the remote Anu, he became the great Sumerian deity, the leader of the pantheon during the greater part of the third millennium BC. His power was manifest in the violence of the storms he personified and produced, but he was also the beneficent bestower of the rains and brought forth from his celestial abode in the northern constellation trees and grain in abundance for the well-being of mankind—'the way of Enlil'. He was held responsible for the destruction of Ur by the Elamites, interpreted in terms of a devastating storm,[70] and it was under his sanction that the Sumerian ruler Umma, Lugal-zaggisi, attacked and subdued Lagash at the end of the Early Dynastic period and introduced the new title 'King of the Land'.[71] Enlil, therefore, was potentially active and often malevolent in human affairs, employing all the forces under his control to his own ends and purposes. If Anu was the ultimate divine authority in the sky, Enlil was the executor of divine power on earth from time immemorial.

The third of the Triad was Enki, or Ea (Fig. 26) as he was called in the later texts, 'the Lord of the watery deep', whose dwelling was in the Apsu (i.e. the abyss or subterranean ocean) upon which the world rested, and who was the personification of divine wisdom and the source of all esoteric knowledge. He was therefore invoked in incantations, and was alleged to have taught mankind the art of writing and geometry, how to build cities and temples, and to cultivate the soil. In short, he was held to have been responsible for the introduction of civilization after the Flood in the third millennium BC, his cult-centre being located at Eridu at the head of the Persian Gulf. There stood his temple with its sacred tree where the 'sweet waters' of the rivers mingled with the salt or 'bitter waters' of the sea, as in the primeval watery chaos when the Apsu blended with Tiamat. There too the human race was fashioned from clay by Anu and all creatures were endowed with the breath of life by Ea, who was at once the god of the Tigris and Euphrates, of rivers and fountains, the giver of life, the patron of the arts and the 'creator of fates' who determined the destinies of all human beings.

Notwithstanding the power exercised by these three leaders of the cosmic state over natural phenomena and the affairs of men, neither Anu, Enlil nor Enki occupied the unique position of the Sun-god and his earthly incarnation the Pharaoh in Egypt. In the Sumerian heavenly pantheon, although Anu was a shadowy figure with the form and appearance of a Supreme Being, Enlil also was hardly less exalted, while Enki (Ea) was 'Lord of the earth'. Moreover, the earlier Triad were eclipsed in great measure by the rise of the next generation of younger gods—Sin the Moon-god, Shamash the Sun-god and Adad the Storm-god, with whom Ishtar (Fig. 36) was associated—and when Marduk became predominant and was accredited with the conquest of Tiamat and her malign forces, he inherited the status, attributes and functions of Enlil as head of the pantheon. They continued to rule over the three divisions of the universe—the heavens, the air and the waters—but it was only in a very restrictive sense that their divine prerogatives were maintained and executed. Anu, Enlil and Marduk never were regarded as Creators and the source of all the other gods like Re or Ptah in Egypt, and although 'kingship came down from heaven', both the gods and the rulers whom they established in their respective cities on earth were regarded as subject to the vicissitudes of the hegemonies over which they presided in a turbulent world.[72] Even when Hammurabi unified the State into an Empire and made Babylon the capital with Marduk as its chief god, it was only a temporary stability that was attained, though the gods had conferred upon Marduk their collective power.[73]

The Indo-European Sky-gods

In the Indo-European cradleland and between the Oxus and the Danube the gods of the sky, the sun, the wind and the storm were deified, with Varuna, the head of the pantheon, becoming the all-encompassing heavens when the Aryans made their way into north-west India. His Sanskrit name meaning 'sky' may be equated with the Greek 'Ouranos', while as the heavenly monarch living in a golden celestial abode he was identified with his twin brother Mitra, a solar god of light, regarded as two aspects of the Eternal Light. The mighty warrior Indra, the god of the thunder, had his headquarters in the atmosphere, between the sky and the earth, and Agni, the god of fire, was all-pervading as the wind. Behind all these celestial gods was the ancient Indo-European Dyaus Pitar, the counterpart of the Greek Zeus and the Roman Jupiter (Fig. 54), the Sky-god and Weather-god who eventually found a home on the Capitoline hill in Rome, in the temple open to the sky in which a boundary-stone had been venerated from time immemorial. As the personification of the heavens Dyaus Pitar was the source of the fertilizing rain and thunder, and like the Anatolian Teshub and the Weather-god of Hatti, he was the supreme Deity, though in the Rigveda he was vaguely conceived, having been displaced by the nature gods and goddesses. Similarly, in Iran it was the all-encompassing Varuna who eventually emerged as the omniscient governor of the universe and of the actions of mankind, in the capacity of Ahura Mazda, the Wise-Lord of the Avesta.

When the Indo-Europeans migrated from their Eurasian grasslands in a westerly direction and settled on the pastures of Thessaly, they brought with them their great Sky-god whom they worshipped under a variety of names derived from the same root 'to shine', and who finally was known as Zeus, 'the sky'. On the misty heights of Mount Olympus

75

he was 'the cloud-gatherer' sending the rain and manifesting his presence in the lightning and thunder, but his original abode was in the heavens with which he was identified and whence he controlled the weather. Although in his Olympian aspect he was represented in the Homeric tradition as a glorified Nordic chieftain, in an age of chivalry he was regarded as the permanent overlord of his retainers, each of whom controlled his own realm in a feudal manner, be it that of nature or of human affairs. But Zeus was essentially the supreme deity.

His proper home, and that of the rest of the Olympians, being in the sky, it was in the celestial realms that he ruled as 'the father of gods and men'. Instead of becoming an obscure figure like so many high gods, he was a composite divine being absorbing the features and attributes of the other gods who fell into the background, or were made subordinate to him. Moreover, legends grew up around him which had little or nothing to do with his original nature, such as the Cretan story of his birth. In this myth rather than being the Sky-god *par excellence* he was the son of Rhea (the consort of Kronos and the counterpart of the Anatolian goddess Kybele) born in a cave in Crete and suckled by a goat. Here he was represented as a very primitive figure having no resemblance to the Indo-European Sky-god and venerable ruler of the universe. But in spite of his syncretisms he remained the head of the pantheon and took over a number of offices and aspects beyond the range of his original nature as Sky-god and Weather-god, the cloud-gatherer, the rain-giver, the thunderer, and the chief of the Olympians.

CHAPTER THREE

THE MOTHER-GODDESS
AND THE YOUNG GOD

Mesopotamian Mother-goddesses, Inanna-Ishtar and Dumuzi-Tammuz, Ninlil and Enlil—Isis and Horus, Hathor, Neith, Nut, The Goddess of many names—Anat, Asherah and Baal in Syria, Yahweh and the Queen of Heaven in Israel—Sun-goddess of Arinna, Hannahanna the 'Grandmother'—Idaean Mother in Phrygia, Attis and Kybele—Rhea, great Minoan Goddess, Mountain-mother, Mistress of the Beasts, The Goddess and the Young god

ALTHOUGH the hierarchy of higher gods who reigned in heavenly splendour in the celestial realms and sent down rain to nourish the earth, or manifested their displeasure in thunderstorms and hurricanes, were conceived anthropomorphically as 'glorified non-natural men', it was, as we have seen, the life-producing mother who was the dominant figure in ancient Near Eastern religion. With the establishment of husbandry and domestication, however, the function of the male in the process of generation became more apparent and vital, and the Mother-goddess then was assigned a spouse to play his role as the begetter, even though, as in Mesopotamia for example, he was her youthful son-lover or her servant. From India to the Mediterranean, in fact, she reigned supreme, often appearing as the unmarried goddess.

Mesopotamian Mother-goddesses

In Mesopotamia, as Langdon has pointed out, whereas 'the intensity of the worship of other gods depended somewhat upon the political importance of the cities where their chief cult existed, before the orders of the gods of nature arose, before the complex theology of emanations supplied the religion with a vast pantheon, in which the masculine element predominated, the productive powers of the earth had supplied in prehistoric times a divinity in which the female element predominated'.[1]

When the birth cult was brought into relation with the seasonal cycle and its vegetation ritual in agricultural communities such as those of the Tigris and Euphrates valley, the Earth-goddess was conceived as the generative power in nature as a whole, and so she became responsible for the periodic renewal of life in the spring after the blight of winter or the summer drought. She therefore assumed the form of a many-sided goddess, both mother and bride, destined to be known by many names and epithets, such as Ninhursaga, Mah, Ninmah, Inanna-Ishtar, Nintu or Aruru. Thus, in Sumerian mythology Ninhursaga, 'the mother of the land', was called Ninsikil-la, 'the pure (i.e. virgin) lady', until she was approached by Enki, the Water-god of wisdom, and gave birth painlessly to a number of deities after nine days of pregnancy. Then she became Nintu-ama-Kalamma, 'the lady who gives birth', 'the mother of the land', and as his wife she was Dam-gal-nunna, 'the great spouse of the prince'. Having conceived as the fertile soil and given birth to vegetation she was known as Nin-hur-sag-ga, 'the lady of the mountain', where nature manifested its powers of fecundity in the spring in luxuriant vegetation on its lush slopes. Since the name gives expression to its underlying reality, these several connotations represent the Goddess in her different roles occasioned by the events to which they refer in her matrimonial vicissitudes, related to their consequences in nature.[2]

Inanna-Ishtar and Dumuzi-Tammuz

In Mesopotamia 'Mother Earth' was the inexhaustible source of new life. Consequently, the power manifest in fertility in all its forms was personified in the Goddess who was the incarnation of the reproductive forces. It was she who renewed vegetation, prompted the growth of the crops, and the propagation of man and beast. As Inanna, the Sumerian counterpart of the Assyrian Ishtar, her marriage with the shepherd-god Dumuzi (i.e. Tammuz) (Figs. 27, 28), who incarnated the creative powers of spring, was held to symbolize and effect the renewal of life at the turn of the year, delivering the earth from the blight of sterility. Her nuptials were celebrated annually at the spring festival in Isin, to arouse the vital forces in the dormant soil and the processes of fecundity everywhere at this season, because her marriage with Dumuzi gave expression to the vegetation cycle.

As 'the faithful son of the waters that came forth from the earth' he was the youthful suffering god who died annually in the rotation of the seasons and passed into the nether regions from which normally there was no return. Inanna, however, having become queen of heaven as the wife of Anu by one of her many matrimonial alliances, seems to have gone to the underworld to secure his release, if the Sumerian version of her descent was the prototype of the Semitic myth. Arraying herself in all her regalia and equipped with the appropriate divine decrees, she set forth on her perilous quest, instructing her messenger Ninshubur to raise the alarm in the assembly hall of the gods and in their principal cities should she not return within three days. Arriving at the gate of the grim abode, she gained admittance on false pretences, but having been recognized she was led through its seven gates, losing at each of them part of her robes and jewels until on reaching the temple of Ereshkigal, the queen of the underworld, she was stark naked and turned into a corpse. By the fourth day Ninshubur followed his instructions and Enki devised a plan to restore her to life. To this end he fashioned two sexless creatures and sent them to the nether regions with the food and water of life to sprinkle on her body. This accomplished she revived, and accompanied by shades, demons and harpies, she left the land of the dead and ascended to the earth where with her ghostly companions she wandered from city to city in Sumer.

Here the Sumerian version of the myth breaks off, but it follows so closely the Semitic 'Descent of Ishtar to the Nether Regions' inscribed on Akkadian tablets dating from the first millennium BC, that it can hardly be other than its prototype. Although Dumuzi is not actually mentioned, the story and its sequel almost certainly represents an earlier account of the same mythological incident. From some recently discovered new material it seems that Inanna on her return did bring Dumuzi with her from the underworld but because he did not show signs of mourning for her descent to rescue him, 'seating himself on a high seat', she handed him over to the demons, presumably to carry him back whence he came. But here, again, the text breaks off at the critical point.[3] Nevertheless, although it is not stated that her mission was to rescue the shepherd-god Dumuzi-Tammuz, there is good reason to think that this was the purpose of her visit to the nether regions, with all that it involved. As the embodiment of the creative spring, she stood in the same relation to Dumuzi as did Ishtar to Tammuz, the Young god who personified the autumnal decline in the seasonal cycle. Therefore, their joint return brought to an end the blight that had fallen upon the land during their absence, enabling the barren ground to blossom as the rose, and mankind to be fruitful and replenish the earth. Indeed, the death and resurrection of the vegetation goddess and the Young god became the archetype of all deaths and resurrections in whatever plane they might occur.

It was, however, the Goddess in Mesopotamia who was the dominant force in this act of renewal, whatever form it took. The Young god died annually in the rotation of the seasons and had to be rescued and restored from the land of the dead by his mother-lover. It was she who resuscitated him, and by so doing brought about the revival of life in nature and in mankind. So in the last analysis Inanna-Ishtar was the ultimate and constant source of regeneration, Dumuzi-Tammuz being only instrumental in the process as her agent. She was the embodiment of creative power in all its fullness; he was the personification of the decline and revival of vegetation and of all generative force.

Ishtar and her Sumerian equivalent Inanna assumed the role assigned to Earth-goddesses in the Ancient Near East, and as the controller of vegetation and fertility as she moved downwards from one stage to another, change and decay took place in the upper world, vegetation languished and died, and all signs of life ceased. With her return there was a corresponding emergence in nature from its death-like sleep, and a revival of vitality. Thus, Ishtar personified this ceaseless sequence of the seasons—life emerging from the soil, coming to fruition, and then drooping and perishing in the drought of summer, until it was again restored in the spring. So regarded, she was inevitably identified with Mother-Earth, brought into relation with the seasonal cycle, being the source and embodiment of fecundity symbolized in the fertile soil.

Ninlil and Enlil

Behind all the distaff goddesses lay the inexhaustible creative activity of motherhood. Thus, in the early lists of gods, drawn up in the middle of the third millennium BC, the Earth-goddess known under a variety of names as Aruru, Nintu, Ninmah, Ningal (Fig. 29) and Ninhursag (who may have been identified with Ki, the Earth-mother of the land) was associated with the first Great Triad, Anu, Enlil and Enki. Ninlil was herself in all probability an Earth-divinity before her husband Enlil acquired this status and function as a result of cohabiting with her in the manner related in a Sumerian myth, explaining how her mother Nunbarshegunu, the ancient goddess of Nippur, showed her how to secure the love of Enlil[4] and become the mother of Nanna, the Moon-god and a succession of underworld deities. The Earth-goddess, in fact, was primarily concerned with childbirth and maternal functions, while Allatu, the goddess of the nether regions, was another aspect of the Earth-mother in her chthonian capacity.

In Mesopotamia all life was conceived as proceeding from a union of earth, air and water, personified as goddesses. Thus, Nammu, the controller of the primeval waters, gave birth to Anu and Ki as the bi-sexual combination of heaven and earth. They then produced Enlil, the Storm-god and Air-god, the second member of the Triad, who separated them as male and female—the Heaven-god and the Earth-goddess—with their respective capacities and functions. By union with his mother Ninhursag (i.e. Ki, the earth) Enlil with the help of Enki produced vegetable and animal life on earth, while mankind was the result of the combined efforts of the goddess Nammu, the primeval sea, and the goddess Ninmah, perhaps identified with Ki, and the Water-god Enki. Although the goddess represented as the mother of the various divine personifications bore different names throughout this succession of creative alliances, they appear to have been merely several designations of one and the same creatrix, whether she is called Ki, Ninhursag, Ninmah or Nammu. Originally doubtless she was the embodiment of the generative process as a whole, until as more clearly defined goddesses and their male partners emerged the pantheon assumed its later form with its departmentalized nature and agricultural deities. But she always retained to some extent her earlier predominance. Thus, in the Tammuz liturgies and in the myth and ritual of the Annual Festival, it was she who released and restored her 'resurrected child', with reciprocal effects on vegetation and the well-being of the human race. Throughout she took the initiative, the Young god and the king being the agents she employed to bestow her gifts.

Isis and Horus in Egypt

In Egypt, on the other hand, the position was reversed. When the official priesthood systematized theological speculation and organized the local cults on the basis of the unified rule of the 'Two Lands' under one Pharaoh, the king became from the Fifth Dynasty (c. 2580 BC) the incarnation and physical son of Re, the Sun-god, at Heliopolis, and later of Amon at Thebes, reigning as Horus, the son of Osiris and the earthly embodiment of the gods he embraced, all of whom were males. Unlike the Babylonian monarchs, the Pharaohs were divine in their own right and the gods they incarnated were dominant in their own spheres. Neither were secondary and subservient to the Goddess. Thus, although Isis eventually became the syncretistic 'Goddess of many names' she was not in her essential nature a mother-goddess, rather she was the 'throne woman' personifying the sacred coronation stool charged with the mysterious power of kingship.[5] To this extent she was the source of vitality before she became the prototype of the faithful wife and of motherhood, representing the female creative principle.

According to the Heliopolitan genealogy she was the daughter of Geb and Nut, the earth and the heavens, and became the wife of her brother Osiris (Fig. 56), whom she taught the secrets of agriculture. After his assassination by Seth she collected his dismembered body, and caused it to be mummified by Anubis. She then conceived Horus from her dead husband,[6] and as the Young god he revived his father by the gift of the eye he lost in his combat with his uncle Seth. But although she was, therefore, ultimately responsible for the restoration of Osiris, he remained the dead god living in his son and the Pharaoh, in spite of the exalted position he attained as the judge and 'king of the dead', and when his cult had been solarized, 'lord of the sky'. Neither he nor Horus was subservient to Isis, and in the great Judgment scene on the papyrus of Ani of the Nineteenth Dynasty, Isis and her sister Nephthys are represented standing behind him (Fig. 56).

Hathor
Nevertheless, such was the popularity of Isis that she was identified with almost all Egyptian goddesses in some capacity, and as 'queen of all gods and goddesses' and 'mother of heaven', she was associated especially with Hathor 'the heavenly cow', Nut the Sky-goddess and Neith of the Sais in the western Delta, all of whom shared the same attributes. It was Hathor, however, who was the Mother-goddess *par excellence.* As Sky-goddess she was the daughter of Nut and Re, or according to the Heliopolitan tradition the wife of Re and mother of Horus the Elder. She was also the nurse of Horus, the son of Isis, in her role of the Cow-goddess, but she was never the spouse of Osiris or the mother of his son Horus. It was not until all reproductive goddesses became identified with her that Isis incorporated her horns in her symbolism. Originally Hathor, who was one of the oldest of the Egyptian deities, was worshipped under the form of a cow, an animal that had acquired a fertility significance from time immemorial. Her name, however, means 'the House of Horus', represented in a compound hieroglyph as a temple containing a falcon, depicting the Sun-god in his heavenly abode in the eastern portion of the sky, where he was born afresh daily. She was, therefore, the star-bespangled celestial cow adorned with the plumes of Re, the father, and the solar disk encircled with a cobra, the emblem of the Mother-goddess.[7]

In this capacity of the Sky-goddess and Cow-goddess she exercised her maternal functions from the Gerzean phase of the Predynastic epoch to the beginning of the Roman period, in due course becoming identified with all the local goddesses and the heavens in their entirety, at once the mother and wife of Re and Horus, the 'mistress of the stars', the 'lady of the West' and of the underworld, the goddess of love, of music and the sacred dance. In the Greek period she was the patroness of women, who became 'Hathors' at their death just as men became

Fig. 3. The Cow-goddess Hathor, adorned with the plumes of Re

Osiris. In the Pyramid Texts her male counterpart was the Bull of Re[8] with his four horns at the cardinal points of the compass, while she symbolized the reproductive forces in nature. She was the protectress, midwife and nurse of pregnant women, and as wife, mother and daughter she embodied all that was best in womanhood. Similarly, the dead looked to her for sustenance during their mummification and when their hearts were weighed in the Judgment Hall and sought her aid in the opening of their eyes and in the attainment of joy and felicity hereafter; such was her power among the gods of the underworld. She was also connected with the annual rise of the Inundation, and all the blessings this brought to the Nile valley. In fact, she was the great mother of the world, the personification of creative power in nature, and the mother of every god and goddess in heaven and on earth, all of whom were regarded as her forms though they might be worshipped under a variety of names.[9] At Denderah seven Hathors were represented as young and beautiful women with cows' horns, solar disks and vulture head-dresses, carrying tambourines in their hands. They comprised the Hathor of Thebes, of Heliopolis, of Aphroditopolis, of the peninsula of Sinai, of Memphis, of Herakleopolis, and of Keset. So great was her

83

influence that she had shrines not only throughout Egypt but also in Sinai, Nubia and at Byblos in Syria.

Neith

Another very ancient goddess was Neith (Fig. 34) of Sais in the western Delta in the fifth nome of Lower Egypt. She was originally connected with the chase like the Greek Diana, but although she was represented with bows and arrows she also appeared as a Cow-goddess with the head of a lioness. She too was the virgin mother of the Sun-god, having given birth to Re as the great cow, and was identified with Isis as the wife of Osiris, later becoming one of the forms of Hathor. Indeed, she was 'the Great Goddess, the mother of all the gods'. Two queens of the First Dynasty adopted her name as Neit-Hotep and Meryt-Neit, and sixteen out of the seventy of the stelae round the tomb of Zer bore names compounded with Neith.[10] Having started as a goddess of hunting and the mistress of the cow, in which form she gave birth to Re, she became equated with the primeval watery chaos like Nut, with whom probably she was identified if her name Net or Neith was akin in meaning to Nut, as Brugsch has suggested. In any case she was regarded as the personification of the sky and so was brought into relation with Nut.

As early as the Fourth Dynasty she was thought, as the mother and daughter of Re, to conceive and give birth to the Sun-god daily.[11] Since she was called 'the opener of the ways' she was a kind of female counterpart of Anubis and protectress of the dead, giving rebirth to them in the next world.[12] As the 'Lady of Heaven' and 'Mistress of all the gods' she occupied a position in the pantheon comparable to that of Re or Ptah, or of Hathor as the supreme goddess. In fact, she was identified with most of the goddesses in turns until by the Twenty-sixth Dynasty (655 BC) she rose to the position of pre-eminence, when the Pharaohs of Sais were at the height of their power and she became the State deity. Then she was regarded as the divine Being *par excellence*, the creative and ruling Power of heaven, earth and the underworld, and of every creature and thing in them. She was eternal, self-existing, self-sustaining and all-pervading, personifying the female principle from very early times. She was believed to have brought forth the transcendent Sun-god without the aid of a male partner, very much as in the Memphite Theology Ptah created all things virtually *ex nihilo* by thinking as the 'heart' and commanding as the 'tongue'. As the universal Mother she 'made the germ of gods and men', and having raised up Atum in primeval times 'she existed when nothing else had being and created that which existed after she had come into being'.[13] Though after the fall of the Dynasty in 525 BC she lost this exalted status, the late Greek writers attributed to her remarkable powers,[14] and the Persian ruler Cambyses worshipped in her temple in Sais and brought offerings to Neith as the Mother of the gods.

Nut

While no organized cultus appears to have been associated with the Sky-goddess Nut (Fig. 35), as the celestial counterpart of Nun, the abyss, the daughter of Shu and Tefnut and the wife of Geb, the Earth-god, the 'bull of Nut', she was 'lady of heaven', 'mistress of the Two Lands', and the mother of Isis and Osiris and of Nephthys and Seth. Like Neith of Sais she had connexions with the underworld as well as with the heavens and the clouds, and appeared in the guise of a great cow whose legs formed the four cardinal points. She absorbed the attributes of many goddesses whose functions were allied to her own, and eventually she adopted the horns and solar disk of Hathor and also uraei, standing in a sycamore tree pouring water from a vase on behalf of the souls of the dead. The hawk of Horus was among her emblems[15] too, representing the rising or the setting sun, Nut being regarded as giving birth to the Sun-god daily when he had passed through her body during the night and sailed over her back in the day before he entered the boat of Re at noon. In Thebes she was identified with Isis and alleged to have given birth to Osiris: and such were her forms, offices and attributes that she was one of the types of the Mother of the gods.

The Goddess of many names

Her daughter Isis, however, remained the most popular and important of all these maternal goddesses. She unquestionably was the greatest and most beneficent female deity, personifying all that was most vital in motherhood. Therefore, she became 'the Goddess of many names', until eventually she was equated with the Magna Mater of western Asia, Greece and Rome, as well as with Hathor, Neith and Nun in Egypt. It was her worship that spread so rapidly in the Hellenistic period until it became a predominant element in the welter of religions in the Roman Empire before and after the beginning of the Christian era. The readiness to identify one deity with another made it possible to evolve some kind of unity out of this jumble of cults. Thus, the Cow-goddesses had so much in common, centred in their maternal attributes and functions, that they readily were resolved into a syncretistic deity.

All of them were concerned with motherhood as their principal feature, giving birth to gods and men, suckling kings, and bestowing life and fecundity in the natural order. Therefore, they were treated as more or less synonymous divine figures so that Hathor and Isis, Nut and Neith, were never clearly differentiated.

Isis as 'she of many names' is the most outstanding example of this syncretism, and in association with the Memphite cult of Serapis at Alexandria (Fig. 84), the cult spread rapidly in the Hellenistic Age, until it became the predominant element with sanctuaries in the Campus Martius in Rome, at Pompeii, at Titheres and Philae, to mention but a few of its centres in the Graeco-Egyptian world. In spite of official opposition it attracted more and more votaries during the first century BC from Athens, the Aegean and the adjacent islands to North Africa and Asia Minor. The hymn to her in the Oxyrhynchus papyrus contains a long list of epithets applied to her and the goddesses with whom she was identified,[16] her mysteries having affinities with the Eleusinian Demeter rites. In the process, however, so many Greek and Asiatic features were absorbed that it is difficult to determine to what extent the later Byblite versions in the classical sources can be regarded as representative of the Egyptian uncontaminated goddess and her worship. In the third century BC she was fused with the Semitic Astarte in the form of Atargatis, the Syrian goddess of Hierapolis, in which capacity she shared a temple with Zeus, Hera and Kore at Oxyrhynchus in the third century AD.[17] Similarly, the Babylonian Nanna in combination with Isis became Namaia, while the Hesis, the hellenized sacred cow of Hathor, was after death Isis.

In all these various aspects and forms of the Goddess pagan thought was moving more and more towards the conception of one universal Magna Mater in her several manifestations under a variety of names. It was, however, in western Asia that this became most apparent. There the worship of a nature goddess in whom the productive powers of the earth were personified, culminated in that of the Great Mother who combined within herself all the local aspects of this all-embracing divinity. Among the Sumerians and Babylonians, as we have seen, she had been known as Inanna-Ishtar, while in Syria and Palestine she appeared as Asherah, Astarte (Fig. 37) and Anat, corresponding to Hera, Aphrodite and Artemis of the Greeks, representing the three main aspects of womanhood as wife and mother, as lover and mistress, and as a chaste and beautiful virgin full of youthful charm and vigour, often confused one with the other. It was with this goddess that Anat was mingled in Egypt, when Semitic influences were strongly felt in the

New Kingdom, especially at Memphis, in the guise of Anata, 'the Mistress of the Sky', 'Lady of the gods', the daughter of Ptah or Re. In her many syncretisms she was identified with Isis and Hathor as a Mothergoddess, with Sekhmet the wife of Ptah, and Ramesses III called his favourite daughter *Bent anta*, 'daughter of Anta'. In the treaty with the Hittites she was represented with Astarte as the national goddess of the Syrian Kheta. Besides her martial functions which included her being 'mistress of horses, lady of chariots' and 'shield of the king against his enemies,' she was the goddess of love who 'conceives but never brings forth,' like Aphrodite. Although her attributes were virtually indistinguishable from those of Astarte, the two divinities actually were distinct entities in Egypt.

Anat, Asherah and Baal in Syria

This was also true of Anat (Fig. 38), Asherah and Astarte in Syria, all of whom had much in common and yet were independent personalities. Although the evidence, apart from figurines, plaques and amulets, is very fragmentary in this region, derived as it is mainly from the Ugaritic texts first discovered in 1929 at Ras Shamra (Ugarit) on the north coast of Syria, there is every indication that originally they were all Earthgoddesses associated with a corn cultus. Thus, in the texts, which belong to the later part of the fourteenth century (*c.* 1400–1350 BC), the vegetation theme is pre-eminent, the two goddesses Anat and Asherah playing the leading roles. As the rival aspirants for supremacy, they both sought to become the consorts of the Storm-god and Weather-god Aleyan-Baal, the bestower of the fructifying rain, giving life to the earth as 'the Lord over the furrows of the field'. When Asherah originally was the wife of the old supreme Deity, El, she was the adversary of Baal, but later she joined forces with Anat, Baal's sister and wife, in furthering his cause and fighting his battles, after he had eclipsed the shadowy El.

In the Ugaritic literature Aleyan-Baal (Fig. 40) occupied a position similar to that of Marduk in Babylonia, when as the Young god he replaced Anu and Enlil at the head of the pantheon. Established as the dynamic personification of the storm, the wind and the clouds, and the controller of the rainfall and the growth of the crops, he was the counterpart of Tammuz, the fertility god of vegetation whose descent into the nether regions caused the languishing of the earth. In the Baal-Anat cycle of myths, however, in which the glorification of Baal is the central theme, so far as the details can be made out on the seven fragmentary tablets, the story assumes a form peculiar to the Ugaritic tradition. Baal is said to have planned to build a house and plotted to secure the consort of his father El, the Supreme God (Fig. 41). Having engaged in a successful encounter with the dragon, Yam, Lord of the Sea, he achieved his objective and installed himself in his heavenly palace, but he refused to have any windows in it, perhaps as a precautionary measure against attack by his adversary Yam or Mot, the ruler of the underworld. Eventually he was persuaded to insert lattices, presumably to enable rain to fall on the earth,[18] as this seems to have been the underlying purpose of the episode. It may, in fact, have been a mythological interpretation of a rain-making ceremony at the autumnal festival.[19] In any case, Baal was 'the Rider of the clouds', and in Syria rain was the primary source of fertility rather than a river like the Nile in Egypt or the Euphrates in Mesopotamia. Therefore, because he was equated with the rainfall he was 'Lord over the furrows of the field' and 'Lord of the earth'.[20] In the house-building project Baal and Anat sought the help of Asherah, bribing her with silver and gold to intervene with El on their behalf. To this extent she recognized his claims to pre-eminence, referring to him as 'our king', 'our judge', asserting that 'none is above him'.[21]

When, for a reason which is not specified, his adversary Mot, the god of sterility and death, contrived to cause him to descend to the nether regions, all vegetation ceased in the customary manner amid universal lamentation.[22] To remedy this devastating state of affairs his sister-consort Anat with the help of the Sun-goddess, Shapsh, went in search of Baal, hunting every mountain in the land, lamenting as bitterly as Demeter or Adonis grieved for Kore or Attis, 'desiring him as a cow her calf or a ewe her lamb'[23]—a symbolism true to type in the Goddess cult. Exactly what transpired cannot be determined in the fragmentary state of the tablets, but it appears that he was found dead in the pastures of Shlmmt. Although his death removed the rival of El, the ancient Supreme God joined in the mourning for his loss, and under the name of Ltpn, god of mercy, he left his exalted throne in heaven and sat on the earth in sackcloth and ashes, lacerating himself and crying 'Baal is dead'. This refrain was repeated by Anat when she found his body[24] and took it to the heights of Sapan, his former abode, and there buried him.[25] She then poured out her complaint to El and forestalled Asherah, who rejoiced at Baal's demise and endeavoured to get her son Attar appointed to the vacant throne. After a violent discussion Attar was made to recognize his incapacity to succeed to the office.[26]

Knowing that Mot was responsible for her lover's death, Anat continued her search for him. When at length she found him she seized him, ripped his garments and demanded her brother-husband. He admitted that he had killed him, making him like a lamb in his mouth and crushing him in his jaws like a kid. Anat thereupon clave Mot with a ritual sickle (*harpé*), winnowed him in a sieve, scorched him, ground him in a mill, scattered his flesh over the fields like the dismembered body of Osiris, and gave it to the birds to eat.[27] In short, she treated him as the reaped grain. This is an anomaly in view of Mot having been represented as the god of death and sterility whose abode was the underworld. But consistency is never a characteristic feature of mythological traditions of this nature, and in seasonal folklore the corn spirit so often has been treated as Mot was and equated with death.[28]

In the Ugaritic vegetation theme Mot was the god of aridity and drought, 'wandering over every mountain to the heart of the earth, every hill to the earth's very bowels', turning them into desolation by robbing all living things of the breath of life.[29] When Anat treated him as the harvested grain, she was repeating the ritual slaying of the corn spirit at the ingathering of harvest, ushering in the season of sterility which would continue until Baal was released from the nether regions, whither he had taken the rain-producing clouds. When this was accomplished then would 'the heavens rain oil and the wadis run with honey'.[30] But as the theme was the perennial struggle in nature between growth and aridity, be it an annual or a septennial occurrence, neither of the contending forces could be ultimately destroyed. Therefore, notwithstanding Anat's drastic treatment of Mot, he survived to continue the conflict when Baal had been restored to life and vigour. But whereas in their earlier encounter Baal had been paralysed with fear at the approach of his enemy and ready to surrender without resistance[31]—typifying the decline in vitality in the dry season—now he engaged in an energetic battle with Mot, because he (Baal) personified the urge of life at its full strength after the return of the rains. Realizing that Baal's turn had now come to bring life out of the earth, El 'overturned Mot's throne and broke the sceptre of his dominion', forcing him to surrender and acknowledge the kingship of Baal.[32] The drought ended and fertility was re-established, the efforts of Anat on behalf of her brother-husband having prevailed.

Being herself the goddess of war and slaughter, wallowing in blood, as well as of love and fertility, she furthered his cause with all her furious violence, once she had transferred her allegiance from El to the young and virile Baal.[33] She was now content to be regarded primarily as the daughter of the older head of the pantheon (El),[34] and like Isis to be the wife of her brother (Baal). But notwithstanding her prominence in the Anat-Baal Texts, Anat never occupied the position of Inanna-Ishtar in Mesopotamia. She was always overshadowed by her august husband who was predominantly the virile giver of life, and with whom she had passionate rather than conventional marital intercourse. It was he who was the supreme figure dwarfing all the other divinities, male and female alike, though in the beginning El and Anat may have together dominated the scene. Her original character and status, however, are very obscure, though she seems to have been primarily a virgin goddess conceiving but not bearing, in contrast to Asherah who was the 'creatrix of the gods' rather than their 'progenitress', bringing forth her brood of seventy deities.[35]

Asherah appears to have occupied much the same position as Anat as the consort and daughter of El, but her relations with Baal are by no means clear. She is represented as at once his mother consort and bitter antagonist, giving birth to 'devourers' to destroy him,[36] rejoicing at his death and endeavouring to make one of her offspring king in his stead.[37] Yet she proved to be capable of being bribed to intervene with El on his behalf at the behest of Anat, and even to assert his supremacy.[38] It would seem, in fact, that the two goddesses were both struggling to attain the status of the wife of Baal when he rose to supremacy, but that neither of them was able to displace the other. Therefore, they had to remain in joint possession of one and the same office, in which fertility and war were combined without completely merging and developing into the 'goddess of many names'. Nevertheless, it is by no means improbable that they represented one and the same divinity in the beginning, since they were so inextricably interrelated and brought into juxtaposition in these very imperfectly preserved texts. Thus, Anat watched over Baal like a genuine Mother-goddess, and when he escaped from her vigilant eye and left the security of his mountain-home on Sapan to hunt on the plains below, it was she who went in search of him and with the help of the Sun-goddess brought back his mortal remains. The position of Asherah was anomalous, and in the struggle to become the consort of the most potent figure in the pantheon—the Young virile Weather-god—counsels were divided and rivalries rampant. But underlying all the contradictory episodes the vegetation theme remained constant and conformed to the customary pattern.

Yahweh and the Queen of Heaven in Israel
After the Hebrew settlement in Palestine in the first millennium BC,

the seasonal cultus and its vegetation divinities were strenuously opposed by the staunch adherents of the desert tradition centred in the worship of Yahweh as the only legitimate God of Israel. In the reign of Ahab, however, Baal (later known as Melkart) and Asherah were the chief deities of Tyre, of whom Jezebel, the wife of Ahab, was an ardent devotee. Hence arose the grim struggle between Elijah, the *nabi* or seer of Yahweh, and the Queen's priests of Baal, which appears to have reached its climax in the ritual contest on Mount Carmel, probably an ancient sanctuary of the Canaanite Storm-god and Weather-god (Aleyan-Baal), served apparently by some four hundred and fifty prophets and four hundred priestesses.[39] Although Elijah's crusade is represented as having triumphed in a spectacular manner, Baalism continued to flourish. The vindication of Yahweh, according to the narrative, was followed by a reaction. The altars of the god of Israel were thrown down, his prophets were massacred, and Elijah himself fled in terror to Horeb, believing that he alone remained alive.[40] This may have been too sinister a view of the situation, but, nevertheless, while the Carmel incident may mark the dominance of Yahweh in Israel, so deeply ingrained was the vegetation and goddess cult in Palestine that it survived all attempts at drastic reformation by the pre-exilic mono-Yahwists until the end of the monarchy.

Thus, in the southern kingdom of Judah, after the Josiah reformation in 620 BC, Jeremiah lamented that he encountered children gathering wood in the streets of Jerusalem and in other cities for the fires to be kindled by their fathers for the worship of the Queen of Heaven, while the women kneaded dough to make sacrificial cakes on which her image was inscribed.[41] When after the Exile he again upbraided the remnant in Egypt that survived the catastrophe, they declared that they would certainly not cease from burning incense and pouring out drink offerings to her as the kings and princes always had done because then food was in abundance and the people knew no evil.[42] Since Josiah had suppressed the cult nothing but misfortune had befallen them, they affirmed. Jehoahaz had been deported to Egypt, Jehoiachin and the cream of the nation had been carried away into captivity in Mesopotamia, Jerusalem had been captured and destroyed, Zedekiah had had his eyes put out, and they, the remnant, had had to flee into Egypt to escape Chaldaean retaliation for the murder of Gedaliah. Confronted with this series of mishaps attributed to the neglect of the worship of the Queen of Heaven, the prophet only could reply that they were the result of their apostasy from Yahwism.[43]

In the Northern Kingdom of Israel a similar situation obtained, and in the middle of the eighth century Amos and Hosea were not less scathing in their denunciations of the cultus practised in their day at Bethel, Gilgal and Beersheba than was Jeremiah in Judah in the succeeding centuries.[44] Indeed, there can be little doubt that refugees from Bethel developed the syncretistic cult in the Jewish colony at Elephantine (Yeb) near Assuan in Upper Egypt in the sixth and fifth centuries BC.[45] From the numerous figurines and plaques recovered from Gezer, Bethshan, Shechem, Megiddo, Tell Beit, Mirsim, Gerar and other Late Bronze Age and Early Iron Age sites,[46] Astarte appears to have been as much at home in this region as at Ugarit, or Beth-Anat, or Denderah, though they are not conspicuous in the Israelite deposits in central Palestine. On the wall at Mizpeh (Tell en-Nasbah), north of Jerusalem, temples of Asherah and Yahweh appear to have stood side by side in the ninth century BC, and to have survived until the city was destroyed. The equipment suggests that the Astarte sanctuary was the centre of the Goddess cult with which it would seem the worship of Yahweh was closely associated.[47] If this were so, goddesses with Canaanite names such as Anath-Yahu, comparable to Yo-Elat in the Ugaritic texts, and assigned to Yahweh at Elephantine, can hardly have been an innovation.

This is borne out by the practice of ritual prostitution in connexion with Israelite shrines at Shiloh,[48] condemned by Amos who inveighed against those who profaned Yahweh by having congress with *zonah* (i.e. ritual prostitutes) at sacrificial feasts, 'drinking the wine of the raped'.[49] As Hosea makes it abundantly clear, these priestesses continued to exercise their functions with undiminished zeal in his day (750–735 BC), in spite of the efforts of Amos and other reformers like Asa to eliminate them.[50] In Judah the Deuteronomic legislation was equally unsuccessful in suppressing male and female hierodouloi,[51] the practice going back in Hebrew tradition to Patriarchal times[52] in spite of the attempts of the later narrators to transform *zonah* and *qadeshah* into common harlots, and of Hosea to give a loftier interpretation of the marriage of Israel to Yahweh.[53] The symbolism he employed to this end was that of the Goddess vegetation ritual brought into conjunction with the covenant of the nation with its god, which allowed no place for alien deities, male or female, or of sacred prostitutes. This, however, was not accomplished until Yahwism was re-established in the post-exilic Jewish community after the return of the exiles in 538 BC, when most of the Canaanite and Mesopotamian accretions were either eliminated once and for all or transformed into uncompromisingly monotheistic Yahwist institutions.

The Anatolian Goddess and the Weather-god of Hatti

In the neighbouring 'Land of Hatti' to the north-east of the Anatolian plateau, closely connected culturally as well as geographically with Syria and Palestine, the Mother-goddess and the Young god occupied a position in the cultus not very different from that in the rest of Asia Minor and the Near East (Fig. 48). Here, again, the Storm-god and Weather-god and his female partner were conspicuous figures with whom the king was intimately related, as will be considered later.[54*] Although the male Weather-god was the principal Hittite deity, the Goddess was often given precedence over her husband, and in the Hurrian pantheon Hebat (or Hepit), the consort of the Weather-god Teshub, was not infrequently accorded the same worship and status as her spouse.

Thus, in the great rock-sanctuary of Yazilikaya, about two miles from Boghazköy (Hattusas), the Hittite capital, she is depicted in the badly weathered bas-reliefs inscribed on the walls opposite the entrance, bearing the name Hepatu in the hieroglyphic script, clad in a full-sleeved robe with a pleated skirt, wearing a tiara and standing on a panther or lioness, holding a staff in her left hand; her right hand is stretched out to greet a male figure approaching her, to whom she proffers her gifts in the form of symbolic or hieroglyphic signs (Figs. 42, 43). Behind her in the procession, also mounted on a lioness or panther, is a smaller beardless youth with a pigtail, wearing a short tunic, upturned shoes and a conical fluted hat. He too clasps a staff with his outstretched right hand, and in his left hand he holds a double axe. From his belt hangs a short dagger, and representing the symbol denoting his name are a pair of human legs of a small figure clad in the same manner. Since this is the sign of the god Sharruma or Sharma, the son of Teshub and Hebat, it is not at all improbable that the youthful figure is that of the son of the Goddess. Behind him are two goddesses vested like Hebat (Hepatu) at the head of the procession and making the same gestures but standing on a single double-headed eagle with outstretched wings—perhaps the daughter and grand-daughter of the Sun-goddess of Arinna. In the background opposite to her on the left walls, a bearded male divinity bearing symbols meaning 'the Weather-god of Hatti', doubtless Teshub, is represented wearing a horned mitre, clad in a kilt and carrying a mace or club in his right hand, leading the male gods in procession.[54]

In the smaller gallery at the side of the main shrine, guarded by two winged figures at the entrance to the inner sanctuary, is a remarkable sculpture of the 'dirk-god' enveloped in lion-skins. A huge figure appears

*Chap. IV, p. 127f.

93

to be that of Sharruma holding King Tudhaliyas IV in his embrace. It is curiously carved to represent a youthful deity with a human head wearing a conical cap, and the body is composed of four crouching lions, two facing downwards and two upwards, back to back (Fig. 44). Below the knees the legs taper to the point of a sword. To the right are two figures, the larger similarly clad, who resembles the youth on the panther in the outer sanctuary, and has his left arm round the neck of the smaller figure of a beardless priest-king in a cloak from which the hilt of a sword projects. His right wrist is grasped by the god's left hand, and a *lituus* is held in his right hand.[55] In the palace of Alaja Hüyük (Euyuk) some twenty miles to the north-east of Boghazköy, a similar figure is shown followed by a priestess, each with one hand raised, approaching the image of a bull on a pedestal with an altar before it. On another relief the priest, followed by a priestess, is shown moving towards a seated goddess and pouring a libation at her feet.[56]

That these sculptures were part of the symbolic representation of the Goddess cult and the Young god is highly probable, and it is by no means unlikely that the outer recess of the Yazilikaya sanctuary was devoted to the rites connected with the Mother-goddess, and the inner chamber was used for the performance of those of her son, the Young god. If at the spring festival their sacred marriage was celebrated, as has been suggested,[57] it may very well have been at this great shrine that the nuptial rites were performed in which the king and queen played their respective roles that the earth should be fertile and the grain be plentiful during the forthcoming season. Thus, a recently published tablet contains a reference to 'the mighty festival of the beginning of the year' when 'all the gods have gathered and come to the house of the Weather-god' to 'eat, drink and be satisfied and pronounce the life of the king and the queen', and 'the life of heaven and earth'.[58] The scene is laid in the celestial realms, it is true, but Yazilikaya was the most likely place for its ritual observance in the Land of Hatti at the New Year Festival at the vernal equinox, as in the case of the *Akitu* at Babylon.

Garstang, in fact, has conjectured that it was the scene of the union of the Hurrian Teshub with Hebat accompanied by their retinue on the occasion of the marriage of Hattusilis III to the high-priestess of the Sun-goddess of Arinna, Puduhepa, the daughter of the priest of Ishtar of Lawazantiya.[59] While this is not indicated in the Hittite texts, in the Egyptian version of the treaty between Hattusilis and Ramesses II the Hittite queen Puduhepa appears on the royal seal embracing the Sun-goddess of Arinna.[60] The converging processions suggest the perambulations that were a characteristic feature of New Year rites and the sacred marriage, while the bull as the symbol of vital force was so very intimately connected with the Weather-god in his fertility aspects. In Hurrian iconography and mythology, for example, Teshub was associated with the two bulls Seri and Hurri, 'Day' and 'Night', attached to his chariot. He was frequently depicted standing on a bull. Its appearance round the legs of the Weather-god and his consort at Yazilikaya indicates the nature of the ritual performed at the sanctuary.

The Sun-goddess of Arinna

While there can be little doubt about the equation of the Hurrian goddess with the Hittite Weather-god, her relation, however, to the Hittite goddess is more difficult to determine, as is the position of the Sun-goddess of Arinna. There in proto-hattic under the name of Wurusemu or Arinitti she was the principal deity, the Weather-god as her consort taking second place to her. In the state religion she was 'the queen of the Land of Hatti, Heaven and Earth, Mistress of the kings and queens of the Land of Hatti, directing the government of the King and Queen of Hatti', but unlike her husband and the Hurrian Hebat she was essentially a solar deity.[61]

At Kummanni (probably the classical Comana Cappadociae) in the Taurus region, where some of the oldest sanctuaries were situated, Hebat as the prototype of MA, the chief Mother-goddess of Asia Minor, later identified with Kybele, became possessed of the essential attributes of the Sun-goddess of Arinna. Like her Semitic counterparts Ishtar and Anat she developed martial characteristics, and among the Romans she became Ma-Bellona, thereby following the familiar transformation of a fertility-goddess into a war-goddess. Her image on the coins of the Roman period at Comana is indistinguishable from that of the Hittite Sun-goddess of Arinna, and the cults practised at Comana and Arinna appear to have had much in common.[62]

As the principal figure in the pantheon and the supreme patron of the Hittite state and its monarchy, the Sun-goddess of Arinna eclipsed all other deities, male and female, and so insignificant was the part played by the Sun-god that the Goddess was herself addressed in masculine terms as 'the Sun-god of heaven, shepherd of mankind', rising from the sea and sitting in judgment daily upon man and beast.[63] This may indicate that the Sun-god Istanu was not indigenous to the Hittite pantheon, and that it was only after he had been introduced into Anatolia that his attributes and functions expressed in Akkadian hymns were transferred to the Goddess. In the official theology, however, the husband of the Sun-goddess of Arinna remained the Weather-god of

Hatti who was responsible for the fertilization of the earth, she being herself 'the Lady of the land' and the source of fecundity.

When, however, the Hittite Empire came under Hurrian influence and its goddess (Hebat) was identified with the Sun-goddess of Arinna,[64] she does not appear to have acquired any solar characteristics. The Anatolian goddesses were primarily Earth-mothers, a rule to which the Sun-goddess of Arinna does not appear to have been an exception at first. When eventually she became the Supreme Goddess with whom the life and cultus of the state were bound up, she absorbed through a process of syncretization almost all of the features of the local goddesses and sun-gods of a similar type, largely as a result of political fusion. So numerous in fact were her functions and those of her spouse, that they tended to be treated virtually as localized independent goddesses and gods. She was at once the Sun-goddess of Arinna in Hatti and Hebat in the 'land of the Cedar' (i.e. Hurri),[65] and was regarded as a duality in unity. As the gods and goddesses multiplied and were grouped in pantheons, the Supreme Goddess assumed a number of distinct divine personalities, each exercising her own particular role in the Hittite economy.

Hannahanna, the 'Grandmother'

In this syncretistic process Shaushka, the sister of Teshub, the Anatolian counterpart of the Babylonian Ishtar, combined belligerent qualities with those of sexuality and love, and had her attendants Ninatta and Kalitta, and other local 'Ishtars' under Anatolian names at Samuha and elsewhere in south-east Anatolia.[66] It was, however, Hannahanna, the 'Grandmother', whose name was written with the ideogram of the Sumerian Mother-goddess Nintud, who was really the Anatolian equivalent of the Phrygian Magna Mater. Thus, in the Telipinu myth recording the disappearance of Telipinu, the son of the Weather-god, bringing all life to a standstill, it was to Hannahanna that appeal was made to intervene in the desperate situation that threatened the extinction of every living thing. On her advice a bee was eventually sent out to discover the whereabouts of Telipinu and sting him, but although this device failed she was finally successful in securing his return and the restoration of fertility.[67]

In this very incomplete Hittite version of the Tammuz theme the effects of the disappearance of the god of fertility were the same as those produced when Dumuzi-Tammuz descended into the nether regions, though no indication is given that Telipinu died and was restored to life. Again, while Hannahanna was instrumental in rectifying the situation she is not represented as his consort or mother. Nevertheless, she brought about a renewal of fecundity, the story being a ritual myth, in all probability associated with a vegetation cult drama like its Babylonian counterpart, if not actually with a seasonal festival. Closely connected with it is a combat story recited at the *Purulli* festival, which may have been held in the spring in honour of the Weather-god of Hatti who slew a dragon, Illuyankas, personifying the forces of evil, with the help of the goddess Inaras.[68]

Thus, throughout western Asia the Goddess cult in association with the Young god had the same characteristic features, centred in the rhythm of the seasons in which she was the embodiment of generation and procreation in perpetuity, and her youthful male partner personified the transitory life of the ever-changing sequence of the cosmic cycle, each taking on its own autonomous significance. Originally it was a nature cult, in the first instance derived from the productivity of the soil capable of self-reproduction as the Universal Mother. In due course it incorporated the Young god as a satellite of the Goddess. From the fertile plains of Mesopotamia it was introduced into Asia Minor through the influence of Hittite peoples, the Goddess appearing as Anat and Asherah in Syria, Hebat, Shaushka, the Sun-goddess of Arinna, and Hannahanna in Anatolia, MA in Comana, Artemis in Ephesus, and Kybele in Phrygia, in association with her youthful consort, Baal, the Weather-god of Hatti, Teshub, Adonis and Attis, whose virility was necessary to complete her maternity in its several aspects, and her other qualities.

The Idaean Mother in Phrygia
In her Phrygian cradleland she was primarily the goddess of fertility, mistress of wild life in nature, responsible for the health and well-being of man and the animals, the protector of her people in war, and the recipient of orgiastic ecstatic worship in her chief sanctuary at Pessinus. With her youthful lover Attis, the god of vegetation, she was the guardian of the dead, like most Earth-mothers, while she was also the 'Lady of Ida', the *Mater Idaea*, and the *Dea domine Dindymone* (Μήτηρ 'ορεία), the goddess of the mountain in her Asiatic home. Later she acquired astral and celestial features, and, attended by her Phrygian daemonic Korybantes, she became a Dionysian Bacchic figure.

Attis and Kybele
Attis stood in much the same relation to the *Mater Idaea* in Phrygia and Lydia as did Adonis to Astarte in Syria. Both are said to have castrated themselves, and Agdistis, the hermaphrodite monster, was afterwards deprived of his male organs by the gods. From these genitals Attis was

conceived by his virgin mother Nana.[69] To prevent his marrying Ia the king's daughter, Agdistis, who had fallen in love with him, struck him with madness and caused him to emasculate himself under a pine-tree, where he bled to death.*[70] Ia mourned over the body and then killed herself, and Kybele and Agdistis wildly lamented Attis concealing the fatal pine in her cave. At Pessinus the corpse remained undecayed, and orgiastic rites were instituted to be held there annually in her honour.

The wild savage nature of this Thraco-Phrygian cultus with its ecstatic revels, mutilations, barbaric music and frantic dances, reminiscent of the Dionysian orgies, was indicative of its antiquity and original character and significance, its purpose being to establish an emotional communion with the Goddess and her paramour. The *gallos*, or mutilated priest, was called *kubebos* because he was regarded as the male embodiment of Kybele, and the high priest at Pessinus was himself Attis when he performed the ecstatic ceremonies.[71] The votaries underwent a process of regeneration during the course of their initiation which seems to have included eating from a timbrel (drum) and drinking from a cymbal.[72] A more drastic method of securing rebirth was the grim rite known as the Taurobolium which was said to have been efficacious for at least twenty years, and in one case the effect was declared to have been *in aeternum renatum*. This involved the neophyte standing in a pit beneath a grating over which a bull was stabbed to death, saturating him with its blood.[73] Its origin is very obscure, but like the rest of the Attis-Kybele cult it was an importation into the Roman world from the Near East. The priests were Asiatics, and no Roman citizen was allowed to take any part in the alien rites when they were first introduced in the Empire.

The cradleland of the Magna Mater and her worship was undoubtedly Phrygia, just as that of Ma-Bellona was Cappadocia,[74] and of Atargatis was Syria.[75] The Phrygian pipes and cap, the eunuch *galli*, the chariot drawn by lions containing the image of the Goddess, the sacrifice of the bull or ram, the ecstatic dances and mutilations, are indicative of a western Asiatic source of the rites, as are the astragaloi attached to the scourges, the cymbals, tambourines, and pine-cones and pomegranates. But the Mother of the Gods was such a syncretistic figure that she can hardly be said to have any particular provenance, however much she may have been particularly localized in Asia Minor.

Rhea

Thus, she was identified in the fifth century BC with the Cretan-Aegean

*In the Lydian version of the story he was killed by a boar like Adonis.

Rhea, a somewhat nebulous goddess of many names and attributes, sometimes having and sometimes without a male partner, whose traditional home and cult-centre was situated in Crete. There she was worshipped with frantic dancing and wild music which may have given rise to the story of the daemons called Kuretes dancing round the infant Zeus and clattering their shields and spears to drown his cries when she concealed him in a cave on a mountain (called by Hesiod Aigaion) from the evil designs of his father Kronos who had devoured all the rest of her children.[76] This myth, as Strabo recognized,[77] was simply the orgiastic worship of the Asiatic Mother-goddess in a very ancient fertility cultus interpreted in terms of the rearing of Zeus, after a wave of Dionysian ecstasy had passed over the island in pre-Homeric times. Thus, on the very spot where Minoan fertility rites were performed, there stood from the seventh century BC, at least, a temple of the Dictaean Zeus, the ruins of which have now been discovered at Palaikastro on the east coast of Crete.[78]

As the mother of the Cretan Zeus by Kronos, who may well have been an ancient pre-Hellenic agricultural deity, perhaps as Nilsson suggests, a god of the harvest,[79] Rhea stood in the same vegetation tradition as Kybele and her counterparts elsewhere. She was often also indistinguishable from Ge, or Gaia, Mother-earth. Therefore, she was connected with the Great Mother of Asia Minor as the personification of the female principle and the source and embodiment of life and fertility in all their aspects, although, unlike the western Asiatic Goddess, she never attained the unique status of her son Zeus. She was essentially a syncretistic figure absorbing first one divinity and then another in this locality and in that, wherever her cult was diffused. Before she became identified with the Phrygian Magna Mater, her affinities in Crete were with the Great Minoan Goddess in her threefold capacity of Earth-Mother, chthonic divinity and Mountain-Mother, with which she combined the role of Mistress of the Trees, Lady of the Wild Beasts, and Guardian of the dead. On the Aegean mainland these functions and features were divided among a number of goddesses—Hera, Athena, Aphrodite, Artemis and Demeter—but in Crete they were combined in one and the same Minoan Goddess, Britomartis or Diktynnan.

The Great Minoan Goddess

Although female statuettes identical with those in the later Minoan sanctuaries go back in Crete to the middle Neolithic period (c. 3500 BC),[80] it was not until more than a thousand years later (i.e. in the Middle Minoan period, c. 2100–1700 BC) that the Goddess herself emerged as an individualized anthropomorphic figure on seal impressions, intaglios, sacred pillars and other cult objects and scenes (Fig. 49). These for the most part were of Asiatic origin, having been diffused from the Near East through Anatolia, or by way of Cyprus and the Cyclades, while others spread from Egypt, or the Troad and Thessaly, in the third millennium BC.

In the central shrine at Knossos she was clad in a richly embroidered bodice with a laced corsage and a skirt with a short double apron, made in faience. Her hair fell behind her neck and on to her shoulders and was adorned with a high tiara. Her eyes were black, her breasts bare, and coiled round her were three snakes with a fourth held in her right hand and curling round her arm behind her shoulders, with a tail ascending to her left arm and head. Round her waist and hips were two more snakes with another extending across her bodice to her ear and tiara.[81] Similar representations of the snake-goddess recur at Gournia in East Crete as the principal object of veneration in the public sanctuary,[82] and in a small chamber known as the Snake Room of a private house at Knossos were tubular vessels with snakes moulded in relief drinking from the cups, perhaps offerings of milk, venerated in the opinion of Sir Arthur Evans as 'the visible impersonation of the spirits of the household'.[83]

In this aspect of the cult, however, going back to the Early Minoan period (c. 2500 BC), since it was the venomous viper rather than the grass snake that was held by the Goddess, it may be, as Evans suggested, that she was here depicted in her destructive chthonic role.[84] At Gournia again, which was neither a house nor a palace shrine, she appears to have been the chthonic Earth-Mother, Mistress of the nether regions, as well as the goddess of fertility. Similarly, in the scene on the Late Minoan sarcophagus at Hagia Triada near Phaestos on the south coast of the island, it would seem that the cult had acquired a funerary significance in which the blood of a bull was poured on the ground sacrificially through a bottomless pail, on behalf of the deceased interred in the tomb.[85] (Fig. 49).

The most prominent embodiment of the Mother-goddess in Minoan Crete was the sacred tree and pillar connecting the sky, the earth and the nether regions. The life-giving attributes of the tree were manifested by its fruit and foliage sometimes spreading over a baetyl or cairn with attendants holding libation jars, or by its being placed in a stone enclosure representing a shrine. This symbolism is secondary only to that of sacred 'horns of consecration' and the double-axe, and recurs with great frequency on gems, seals and signet rings, often associated with cult animals (e.g. the dove, the bull, the lion, and mythical creatures) and the young male god, of whom the pillar was often the aniconic representation.[86] But in the cult scenes the Goddess is the most prominent figure, with her priestesses, child attendants and female votaries performing ritual actions in her honour, carrying on the very deeply laid 'Venus' tradition which assumed an anthropomorphic guise in the Middle Minoan period. But two stalagmites in the cave sanctuary at Amnisos, near Herakleion, the old harbour town of Knossos, were venerated as the aniconic embodiment of Eileithyria, the goddess of birth, and in the double cave of Psychro on Mount Dikte, when it was identified with the legendary birthplace of Zeus, stalactite columns appear to have been worshipped as emblems of Rhea.[87]

The Mountain-mother

This baetylic imagery also survived in sacred groves and in the palace cult, but on the seal engravings it was the figure of Britomartis or Diktynna that was represented with pines, palms, cypresses and fig-trees, and lions or genii as her attendants, standing on a mountain with her youthful male partner. On the gold signet-ring from Knossos an aniconic column is shown in a sacred enclosure, the entrance of which is overhung by a fig-tree, with a female figure before the pillar in an attitude of incantation. Suspended as it were in the air is a small male figure holding a staff or weapon who, as Evans suggested, may represent the Young god surmounted by his mother, the Minoan Goddess.[88] The stone terrace on which she seems to be standing may indicate a mountain, and a smaller pillar in the middle of the portal of the sanctuary has some affinity with the Cypriot female bactyl (Fig. 4).

Fig. 4. Female figure in an attitude of incantation before a sacred pillar, depicted on a signet ring from Knossos

On the mainland at Mycenae a Late Minoan signet has been
found, now in the Ashmolean Museum at Oxford, with the Goddess in
an attitude of grief, wearing a flounced skirt, bending over a large jar
with her left arm bent at the elbow, resting on the rim in an attitude of
mourning. Above her are the eye and ear symbols, and to the left a male
figure holding an object that looks like a bow. Below to the left is a
female figure who may be the Mother-goddess (fig. 5). On another seal

Fig. 5. The Minoan goddess bending over a jar apparently in an attitude of grief,
on a signet ring from Mycenae

the goddess is shown standing ready to receive the fruit of a sacred tree
in a small sanctuary equipped with a baetyl, a young male attendant
bending towards her whom Evans equated with the Cretan Zeus in a
Tammuz role.[89] If the enclosure represents a tomb containing a phallic
stone the scene is brought into line with the grave of Attis in Phrygia
and that of Zeus at Knossos.[90] The mourning episode, therefore, may be
a Minoan version of the suffering goddess theme in western Asia and the
vegetation cycle, the coming of spring being expressed in the budding
leaves and ripening fruit.

This is confirmed by a scene on a gold ring in the Museum at Candia,
showing a sacred tree with scanty foliage in an enclosure. The stem is
grasped with both hands by a woman in a flounced skirt and having
prominent breasts in Minoan fashion, and to her left is an identical
figure with her back to the tree and her arms extended to a third
woman clad in the same manner.[91] Here it would seem the barrenness
of winter is depicted giving place to the epiphany of the Goddess ushering in the spring, very much as on another ring from a cist in a small

tomb an orgiastic dance is portrayed in a field of lilies conducted by four female votaries in Minoan garments. In the centre above the chief worshipper is a small female figure apparently rapidly descending, and to the left a human eye, which may symbolize the Goddess regarding the ecstatic dance being performed in her honour at the renewal of life in the spring, of which the snake by the side of the central figure below the eye is an emblem.[92]

On the ring from the Vapheio tomb near Sparta a female figure of the same type stands beneath the overhanging branches of a fruit tree which is growing out of a large vessel unless, as Evans believed, the object represents a stone pillar.[93] Below are rocks which may signify a hill or mountain, and a naked male figure with sandals and a loin-cloth bends the branches presumably to enable the Goddess to pluck the fruit. A similar scene occurs on a ring from Mycenae in which an identical figure is shown looking towards a tree laden with fruit, and a male attendant is pulling down a branch apparently for the same purpose. Below it is a stone column on a high base in a shrine, and the group is placed on a terrace, indicative perhaps of an eminence, in attitudes suggestive of a ritual dance.[94] To the right of the central figure on the Vapheio ring is a symbolic device, apparently a modification of the Egyptian sign of life (the crux ansata), and its Hittite variety in the form of the double axe, together with two mysterious objects, possibly a pair of sacral knots,[95] though Nilsson not very convincingly interprets them as 'cuirasses',[96] the scene being essentially a symbolic representation of the Goddess cult.

The Mistress of the Beasts

In her lofty sanctuaries the Mountain-mother was worshipped with upraised hands and the libations of her votaries. The sacred tree and pillar occupied a prominent position, but the snake was not in evidence, being confined to the chthonic and household cult of the domestic Goddess. In her several aspects she appears on the seals everywhere in Crete and on the Cypro-Mycenaean cylinders, often guarded by her lions (fig. 6) and often in association with her male satellite. Sometimes she is shown holding a dove, and on faience reliefs the cow, the calf, the wild goat and horned sheep find a place in the scenes. On a Middle Minoan clay seal from Knossos she wears a high peaked cap, a short skirt, and holds a spear and shield with a lioness or dog at her side,[97] but there is no indication of a mountain or a sacred pillar. In the central court of the palace of Knossos, on the other hand, clay sealings made by a signet have been discovered on the cement floor of a recess showing the

Fig. 6. The Goddess between lions as the Mistress of the Beasts

Goddess standing on a rock with her two lions, her arm outstretched and holding a sceptre or lance. Behind her is a shrine with pillars and sacral horns, and in front of her a youthful male figure.[98]

As Mistress of the Beasts she was intimately connected with hunting and wild life, and both she and her male attendant were represented surrounded with a multiplicity of animals, real and fabulous, among which lions, doves, bulls, griffins and sphinxes predominated, sometimes in a hybrid form[99] (Fig. 39). Demons with the head of a horse and the body of a lion appeared on seal impressions at Knossos together with flying fish, satyrs, and monsters as her servants. The male god, when he appeared in these scenes, was usually a later edition and venerated in a subordinate capacity. He is most conspicuous on a lentoid bead-seal found near Canea, the site of the ancient Kydonia. There he is represented as the Master of the Animals standing between two sacral horns with a daemon to the left holding a libation jar. To his right is a winged goat with the tail and hindquarters of a lion.[100] On a Mycenaean gem from this site he reappears with outstretched arms and supported by lions on either side, but on the Ashmolean ring he is shown as a smaller figure holding a spear.

The Goddess and the Young god
On an electrum ring from a tomb in the upper town at Mycenae a similar nude youth with a spear in his left hand would seem to be in conversation with the Goddess, while the chryselephantine statuette of the Snake-goddess of Knossos wearing a peculiar tiara, now in the Boston Museum, holds out her hands towards a boy, the heads of

snakes protruding from them. This Evans thought depicted the adoration of the Minoan mother of the Young god[101] (Figs. 50, 51), like the scene on the signet ring from a tomb at Thisbe in Boeotia, showing the Goddess vested on a throne with a child on her knee holding out her left arm in response to two adoring male figures approaching her. In her right hand she holds a disk-shaped object with a central cup, while behind her a female attendant has a similar article believed by Evans to be a bronze cymbal, later an emblem of Kybele.[102] The Thisbe hoard, however, contains too many forgeries to be a reliable source of authentic information (e.g. the 'Ring of Nestor').

Nevertheless, there can be little doubt that a young male divinity was associated with the Goddess in Crete and the Aegean, though except as Master of the Animals he was seldom much in evidence, and when he did appear it was in a subordinate capacity. In one or other of her several roles, aid was sought from her for the promotion of fertility, the regularity of the seasons, the well-being of the natural order and the protection of the household. As a chthonic deity she was at once the ruler and guardian of the dead and of fertility, while as the Mountain-mother her dominion was extended to the upper regions. When she passed from Crete to the mainland in the Late Minoan period she acquired warrior qualities as an armed war-goddess with a large eight-shaped shield. In this guise she was depicted on the Acropolis at Mycenae,[103] the militant Mycenaeans, unlike the peaceful Minoans, requiring a goddess who would help them in the defence of their fortified cities. At Mycenae in all probability she was the forerunner of Athena, just as at Knossos she appeared as 'the Lady of the Sea' reposing on the waves that protected her island home.

Whether or not she was the one Great Goddess exercising all her manifold functions as a composite deity like the Magna Mater in the Graeco-oriental world, as Evans and others have maintained,[104] or a plurality of divinities from the beginning, as Nilsson has contended,[105] is a recurrent problem of the cult. In favour of regarding the Minoan Mother as a universal deity is the fact that in Crete she occupied virtually the same position as her counterparts in western Asia. She was the source of all vegetation and the mistress of all the earth produced, the goddess of nature in all its aspects, 'the star of the sea', the lady of the nether regions, and later acquired martial qualities, in all of which aspects she was comparable to her later manifestations. Her consort assumed the role of the youthful male god as her satellite, personifying the transitory seasonal sequence of vegetation like Adonis, Attis, Tammuz or Baal. Whether or not this can be described as 'a largely monotheistic cult', as Evans affirms, in which the female form of divinity held the supreme place,'[106] depends on how monotheism is defined. But, as he says, 'the medieval worship of the Madonna with varying attributes and emblems, in conformity with local cults, supplies a good analogy,'[107] except, of course, that unlike the Minoan and western Asiatic Mother-goddess, the Theotokos, though the dominating figure, was always on a lower level than her divine Son, being herself but the instrument of the Incarnation.

It is true that the Minoans had a number of lesser gods and spirits, and subsequently the Cretan Goddess crystallized into a variety of forms such as Artemis, Rhea, Athena, and Aphrodite, each separate and distinct as an independent personality with her own name, attributes and functions (Figs. 52, 55). But it is difficult to understand the identical representation of the Great Goddess in so many forms recurring over such a wide area from Syria and beyond to Crete, unless there was a fundamental underlying unity in the personification of the female principle. In Crete as elsewhere the various aspects and guises of the Goddess can hardly be differentiated as separate divinities. The syncretism and fusion were so complete that they can be explained only as several forms and names of one and the same all-embracing divine figure—the Mother-goddess in association with her subordinate satellite, the Young god.

CHAPTER FOUR

THE SACRAL KINGSHIP

Divinity of the Pharaohs in Egypt, birth and accession of Hatshepsut, coronation ceremony, toilet ceremonies and temple liturgy, Sed-festival, Pharaoh at the Festival of Min, worship of the Pharaoh and his ancestors—Sumerian kingship in Mesopotamia, Babylonian monarchy, sacred status and function of the kingship—Ugaritic kingship, sacral kingship in Israel, Hittite kingship, royal cult, role of king and queen—Minoan priest-kings, Mycenaean kings, Archon in the Greek city-states

NOTWITHSTANDING the predominance of the Goddess in the cultus in the Near East and the Aegean, it was, nevertheless, the king who stood in the most intimate relationship with the divine in everyday affairs. This is most conspicuous in the Nile valley, where the Pharaohs were accorded a quite unique status as at once a hierarchy of gods and the official intermediaries between the nation and its deities. Even before the unification of Upper and Lower Egypt and the establishment of the Pharaonic dynasty, traditionally attributed to Menes, about 3200 BC, each nome was thought to have been ruled by its local god as its king. These ancient god-kings were succeeded by the Dynastic human rulers, who were also regarded as the living embodiments of the gods whom they incarnated as the heirs of their predecessors. Thus, the Predynastic king Scorpion, who probably preceded Menes, was regarded as an incarnation of the Sky-god Horus and inherited his divine attributes. When his worshippers in the north conquered Upper Egypt their rulers reigned as Horus-kings, with Edfu (Behdet) as their cult-centre, and Horus the Behdetite became the divine ancestor of the royal line, whose divine nature was embodied in the Pharaohs upon whom he bestowed his Horus-name.[1]

The divinity of the Pharaohs in Egypt
This, however, was not the only source of Pharaonic divinity. In *The Book of the Dead* the Creator is made to declare:
I am Atum when he was alone in Nun (the primeval waters) :
I am Re in his (first) appearances, when he began to rule that
which he had made.
What does that mean?
This Re whom he made to rule that which he had made,
Means that Re began to appear as a King,

One who existed before Shu had (even) lifted (heaven from earth).[1]

So regarded, the Pharaohs were represented as the physical sons of the Sun-god Re who was identified with Atum, the god of Heliopolis, as another aspect of Re, having emerged from the primordial waters (Nun) in the form of a phoenix on the top of the primeval 'sandhill'.[2] Moreover, when an attempt was made to reconcile the Heliopolitan Ennead with the Memphite Theology between the Third and Fifth Dynasties it was Ptah who installed the gods in their temples and the Pharaohs on the throne. Indeed, for more than three thousand years the coronation was held at Memphis in a rite under the auspices of Ptah, without conflicting with the solar royal theogony in which the king issued out of the body of the Sun-god, and at death returned to him in the celestial realms. Thus, in the New Kingdom when Amon-Re became the head of the Theban pantheon, it was he who embodied himself in the king, and visited the queen in his divine majesty to beget an heir to the throne from his own loins.[3] Osiris, however, was also thought to have lived on earth as the first civilizing king of Egypt,[4] and to have perpetuated his reign in the monarchy, each Pharaoh being identified with him at death after having reigned as Horus (the posthumous son of Osiris) during his lifetime (Figs. 25, 33).

Therefore, after the incorporation of the Osiris myth in the solar cultus in the Sixth Dynasty, every Pharaoh was at once Horus the Elder, the son of Re, in his various manifestations (e.g. Atum-Re, Amon-Re), the son of Osiris (Fig. 68) and the incarnation of Ptah (Fig. 58). Such complications, however confusing they may appear to us, were accepted by the ancient Egyptians without question because they were the generally recognized way of expressing the totality of the divinity of kingship on earth, in heaven and in the underworld, Re, Osiris and Horus having been represented as the first rulers of Egypt, and to that extent the Pharaoh was the image of them all. He reigned as 'the shepherd of the land keeping the people alive', co-ordinating the natural and social forces under his control for the well-being of mankind, maintaining the divine order of society and championing justice (*Maat*) of which he was the source. In short, as was affirmed on the tomb of Rekhmi-Re, an Eighteenth Dynasty vizier at Thebes, 'the king of Upper and Lower Egypt is a god by whose dealings one lives, the father and mother of all men, alone by himself, without equal'.[5]

The monarchy, therefore, was the consolidating and stabilizing dynamic of the static civilization in the Nile valley, the cosmic centre of the divine order established at the creation, the Pharaoh being in fact the gods he embodied in their various manifestations and syncretisms. Indeed, he was virtually the embodiment of all the deities of the 'Two Lands', since as the living Horus he succeeded to all the divine preroga- tives conferred upon the son of Osiris when he was established in his throne by decree of the heavenly tribunal, as well as to those of the Creator Amon-Re in his cosmic aspects. As Khnum, the 'fashioner of men' and 'maker of the gods', he was 'the begetter who brings people into being'. He was Bast, the beneficent solar goddess who protected the Two Lands, and also Sekhmet the wife of Ptah, who represented the destructive powers of the sun, emitting flames against her enemies. He was Thoth, the god of wisdom, knowing everything, 'the goodly herdsman, watchful for all mankind whom their maker has placed under his supervision', giving food in abundance, creating and sustain- ing the entire land.[6]

It was this fullness of divinity that gave the throne its amazing strength, vitality and cohesive influence. The Pharaoh was a unique personality isolated from the rest of mankind in lonely seclusion and remoteness as the mediator between heaven and earth. In theory he alone was the officiant at every temple (Fig. 68), and while for practical purposes he was compelled to delegate his functions to the local priest- hoods, just as the civil and legal administration and the military opera- tions had to be conducted by those he appointed to carry out his duties, they acted merely as deputies performing their respective functions in his name and on his behalf. Although, therefore, in course of time these officials became very influential, so that the Theban priesthood, for example, was able to destroy the royal cult of Aton after the death of its instigator, Ikhnaton, and restore the worship of Amon-Re, they only effected a return to the normal type of solar religion, of which the Ikhnaton movement was a heretical variation on the part of an individualistically-minded Pharaoh. Atonism was certainly not one whit less Pharaonic, being essentially a royal prerogative, so that its founder did not hesitate to call himself 'the beautiful child of the Aton' (i.e. Ikhnaton), 'the lord of every land', known only to his devoted son. Therefore, his heresy did not nullify his right to the throne, but because it abandoned the former eschatology it had nothing to offer which gave assurance of a blessed hereafter, and so it was ignored by the masses as well as opposed by the Theban priesthood.[7] As soon as the king died a return to the orthodox faith was welcomed, and his deviations were execrated with all possible speed and thoroughness. The Dynasty then continued and the divine succession was maintained by hereditary sequence from father to son, unless particular circumstances arose which required the adoption of special devices, as had occurred on the occasion of the accession of Hatshepsut, the daughter of Thutmose I in the Eighteenth Dynasty.

The birth and accession of Hatshepsut

For a woman to succeed to the throne was clearly an anomaly which demanded justification and rectification. This was accomplished by the enactment of the fiction of divine birth through the intervention of Amon-Re in a sacred marriage with the queen-mother, for the express purpose of 'placing in her body' his daughter that she might 'exercise the beneficent kingship in this entire land'.[8] Khnum is said to have been commanded to fashion her body and *ka*, and his wife Heket gave her life.[9] Since the first kings of the Fifth Dynasty had been similarly accredited with divine paternity, this procedure did not appear to be without precedent, and to establish her legitimacy to the throne she caused a representation of the intercourse between the god and her mother to be engraved upon the walls of the middle terrace of her temple at Deir el-Bahari, to bear witness to her divine birth as described in the text inscribed round the scene containing the words attributed to Amon-Re at the moment of her conception: 'She who unites herself with Amon, the first of the beloved, behold such shall be the name of the daughter who shall open thy womb, since those are the words that have fallen from thy lips. She shall exercise a beneficial power over all this land, for my soul is hers, my will is hers, my crown is hers, verily, that she may govern the two lands and guide all the living doubles'.[10]

The accouchement is next portrayed on the bas-reliefs, showing the preparations for the delivery of the royal infant fashioned in surpassing beauty by Khnum, and her actual birth and presentation first to the protecting goddesses who breathe into her the breath of life. Meskhent, the presiding goddess, declares: 'I surround thee with protection like Re. Life and good fortune are given to thee more than to all mortals; I have destined thee for life, luck, health, excellence, affluence, joy, sustenance, food, victuals, and all other good things. Thou wilt appear as King of Upper and Lower Egypt for many *Sed*-festivals while thou art living, remaining fortunate—while thy heart is in joy with thy *ka* in these two lands on the throne of Horus for ever'.[11] Then follows the presentation to her heavenly father, Amon, who addresses her with words of welcome: 'Come, come in peace, daughter of my loins, whom I love, royal image, thou who wilt make real thy risings on the throne of the Horus of the living, for ever'[12] (Fig. 59).

Having been duly acknowledged and worshipped by the other gods, in spite of the rival claims of her husband, the son of Thutmose I by an inferior wife, if he was still alive, Hatshepsut, 'beautiful to look upon' and 'like unto a god', was duly crowned by her actual father, Thutmose I, at Heliopolis and seated upon his throne before Amon-Re in the presence of the nobles and state officials, who did homage to her.[13] The white crown of Lower Egypt was placed on her head as she entered the sanctuary by the priests impersonating Horus and Seth, followed by the red crown of Upper Egypt. She is shown wearing this double crown in the scenes seated on a throne between the two gods of the south and the north (Horus and Seth), who tie together the lotus flower and bunches of papyrus under her feet, the emblems of Lower and Upper Egypt, to symbolize the union of the Two Lands over which she rules. Finally, arrayed in her crown and mantle and holding the scourge and flail of Osiris in her hands, she is led in procession round the walls of the sanctuary, to indicate her taking possession of the domain of Horus and Seth, before the rites conclude with her being embraced by her celestial father who had installed her as his daughter in the throne of Horus[14] (Fig. 60).

On these reliefs the principal episodes of the coronation ceremony have been depicted as they were practised in the Nile valley from proto-historic times to those of the New Kingdom. Thus, after various preliminary purifications by priests impersonating Horus and Seth, or Horus and Thoth, the ancient custom is shown of the Pharaoh visiting the Dual shrines of Upper and Lower Egypt before being crowned with the two diadems of Horus and Seth, and then being embraced by the god of the temple and led round the walls. In short, there can be little doubt that the accession of Hatshepsut followed the normal procedure when the divine royal child came of age, emphasis being given to the events in order to make her ascendancy to the throne quite secure in spite of her sex. Thus, an enthronement ceremony appears to have followed, involving further purifications and presentations, first to Amon and the gods and then to the people, with the proclaiming of the official names of the new Pharaoh as the son of the Sun-god.

The coronation ceremony
So long as the succession was maintained through the maternal line of descent without any impediment, accession to the Egyptian throne was a perfectly normal procedure, the son inheriting the office and status from his father at dawn immediately after the death of the reigning sovereign. It was only when some hitch or invalidating cause occurred, as in the case of Hatshepsut, that particular devices or state fictions had

to be resorted to to regularize the position by demonstrating that, in fact, the usurper was the son and heir of the god.* But once the accession was duly recognized and accomplished, the new king exercised his functions until he came of age and then he was crowned and invested with the royal insignia. The information about the date and place of the coronation is very incomplete and uncertain, but the rites appear to have been held at the beginning of the three seasons, especially the fifth month (i.e. the first month of winter) because of the intimate connexion between the kingship and the sequence of events in the agricultural year.[15] For the same reason it was at the same times that every thirty years the occupant of the throne renewed his reign at the festival of *Sed*.

Precisely what took place on these occasions remains largely conjectural, but from the dramatic incidents recorded in 'The Mystery Play of the Succession' of Senusert, the second king of the Twelfth Dynasty,[16] it appears that before his coronation the Pharaoh visited a number of cities in the royal barge. At each town in the enactment of the installation rite he played the role of Horus for the purpose of establishing an efficacious relationship between the throne and the land over which he had assumed the rule in this capacity (i.e. as Horus). Among the scenes portrayed was the victory over Seth in the Osiris myth, described as Horus taking possession of the Eye (i.e. of the royal power located in the crown), and treading of barley by oxen on the threshing-floor, symbolizing the dismemberment of Osiris by Seth and his fellow-conspirators, in a vegetation setting, followed by his revival by his son Horus. The accession rites were then enacted in a series of scenes which included the investiture of the Pharaoh with the royal insignia, censings and distribution of half-loaves of bread as the symbol of life to those who made homage to him. 'The affixing of the crown' with its Predynastic two feathers is merely mentioned without any specific description, though the antiquity and northern origin of the drama is thereby indicated. After the singing of dirges by two women in the guise of Isis and Nephthys as a prologue to the burial rites of the corpse of Osiris, articles were offered by the priests impersonating Thoth suggestive of the 'Opening of the Mouth' ceremony, and the play concluded with a scene portraying the ascent of Osiris to the sky, and a banquet.

From other sources, which include a few extracts from the Pyramid Texts, inscriptions of the first two dynasties, the Palermo Stone and the inscription at the back of the statue of King Haremhab in the Turin

*For purposes of the succession Hatshepsut was regarded as virtually a 'son' of the Sun-god and a male heir in spite of her sex.

Museum indicating his doubtful claims at his coronation at Thebes in the New Kingdom, the ceremonial is shown to have included a succession of episodes, some of which are suggested in the Mystery Play.[17] The proceedings opened with the purification of the sovereign by two priests impersonating Horus and Thoth (or Seth), and by the gods of the four cardinal points wearing their masks. He was then taken to the Dual Shrines and the crowns of Upper and Lower Egypt were presented to him by Amon-Re as the divine officiant, and he was invested with the crook and flail. A sacrificial oblation was offered and eaten, and the new Pharaoh was endowed with the divine qualities of his sacral office by a priest in the guise of Yahes (I'bo) pouring water from vessels depicted as streams of the *crux ansata* with the words, 'I purify thee with the water of all life and good fortune, all stability, all health and happiness.'[18] After his presentation to the gods and the people, and the proclamation of his official names, which at Heliopolis were written on the leaves of the sacred *isd*-tree, the walls of the city were circumambulated to symbolize his taking possession of his kingdom.

The toilet ceremonies and the temple liturgy
Of such supreme significance were these accession rites that they had to be repeated daily in the toilet ceremonies when the Pharaoh performed his renewal ritual every morning. After a repetition of the asperges in the coronation purifications, he was censed to unite him with Horus, and then he was given balls of natron to chew to complete his rebirth. Finally, he ascended the stairs to the great window to behold his celestial father, symbolizing the rising of the morning sun from the waters, before being vested. As the Sun-god was purified and reborn every morning in 'the House beneath the Horizon', so his earthly incarnation had to undergo the same daily ritual process in the House of the Morning to identify himself with the lord and giver of life.[19]

These rites had their counterparts in the temple liturgy. Every morning at dawn the cult-image in the Heliopolitan solar temple was asperged, censed, anointed, vested and crowned with the royal diadem of Upper Egypt and presented with the flail and the crook and the sceptre. What had been done to the Sun-god and his incarnation on the throne had to be done to the image as their visible embodiment. All three virtually were one and the same and so had to receive identical treatment. When, however, the solar theology was Osirianized, under the influence of the Osiris myth the ritual was transformed to some extent. The god in the shrine now became regarded as the dead Osiris requiring revivification every morning. Therefore, the Pharaoh in his

Horus manifestation took the dead god in his arms and restored him to life. Then he performed the toilet of the image, made offerings to it, and replaced it in the shrine. In most of the reliefs the king himself is represented as the sole celebrant in this temple liturgy to obtain the favour of the gods concerned with his well-being. In fact, however, he only performed the rites in person on rare occasions, his place being taken by a priest as his deputy and his assistants, all of whom had to undergo the same purifications as the Pharaoh since they impersonated him.[20]

The Sed-*festival*
In addition to these daily renewal rites, the *Sed*-festival, traditionally assigned to the first day of the first month of winter, was held at specific intervals such as thirty years after the accession, and then repeated every three years. It is unfortunate that the details and precise significance of this important very ancient observance—going back to the First Dynasty—are so obscure and uncertain.[21] Its date usually coincided with that of the coronation and the raising of the *Djed*-column at the Khoiak festival when the inundation was subsiding.[22] Helck, in fact, conjectures that it constituted the accession and coronation of a new Pharaoh when his predecessor had been slain, having reigned his allotted span.[23] This, however, has yet to be proved in the absence of any evidence that the practice of killing kings was ever observed in ancient Egypt, and its tenability rests largely on the interpretation of the scene depicting the jubilee of Amenophis III in the tomb of Kheruef at Thebes.[24] Nevertheless, the *Sed*-festival hardly can have been other than a periodic rejuvenescence and reinvestiture of the reigning king for the purpose of renewing his beneficent rule as the mediator between heaven and earth.[25]

Accompanied by the leading officials, princes and royal kinsmen, he visited the shrines of the gods erected in the festival court of the temple in which the solemnities were held after the purifications had been duly performed, and made offerings to them. For several days he walked in the processions with the statues of the gods and their priesthoods, the standard of the royal placenta, fan-bearers and attendants, and received pledges of loyalty seated upon his throne. His feet were then ceremonially washed before he entered the robing room, or 'palace' as it was called, to re-vest. He then proceeded to a double throne, sitting alternatively upon each of them to symbolize his rule over Upper and Lower Egypt. To assert his power over the land, he crossed ceremonially the area of the temple court known as the 'field' (i.e. the whole of Egypt), and then he was carried on a litter preceded by the standard of the jackal-god Upuaut of Siut to the chapel of Horus of Libya to receive the sceptre, flail and crook. Wrapped in a cloak, he was proclaimed four times and received the homage of his subjects and the blessing of the gods. In return he made appropriate offerings to the gods, and then took off his cloak and ran four ritual courses clad only in a kilt with the tail of an animal, wearing the crown of Upper Egypt on his head, and carrying a short sceptre and whisk. He offered his insignia to Upuaut and the proceedings concluded with a visit to the chapels of Horus of Edfu and of Seth of Ombos, where he shot arrows of victory to the four cardinal points, just as he was enthroned four times facing the four cardinal directions.[26]

Since the purpose of the festival seems to have been the renewal of the occupant of the throne in the kingship rather than the establishment of the succession in the coronation rite, it is more likely that the Pharaoh impersonated Horus than that he was identified with Osiris. Nevertheless, as it was performed to strengthen his life and re-establish him in his sacred office, the Osirian theme doubtless was inherent in the observance, and the concluding ceremonies appear to be reminiscent of those in the coronation ritual. It is possible that the Pharaoh may have been invested with a bull's tail at the festival as a symbol of the renewed vigour bestowed upon him.[27] In any case it was declared: 'thou beginnest thy renewal, beginnest to flourish again like the infant god of the Moon, thou art young again year by year, like Nun at the beginning of the ages, thou art reborn by renewing thy festival of *Sed*.'[28]

The Pharaoh at the Festival of Min
That the kingship was very closely connected with agriculture and fertility is shown by the representation of a Pharaoh at the beginning of the Dynastic period hoeing the ground, and perhaps attending to the irrigation dykes, in the presence of Min of Koptos who personified the generative force in nature, and as a rain-god 'opened the clouds' to stimulate the life in vegetation. Near the king an attendant is depicted in what may be the act of scattering seeds on the ground at the beginning of the inundation, the festival being observed in the first month of summer (i.e. the ninth month of the year*)[29] (Fig. 3). It was also associated with the harvest, and the king and queen went in procession walking in front of the ithyphallic statue of Min, which was preceded by a white bull, the sacred animal of the god in which he was incarnate. On reaching the harvest fields a shrine was erected. In it

*In Egypt ploughing and sowing begin as soon as the sodden land emerges from the floods.

the image was installed on a throne under a canopy and offerings were made to it. The king reaped a sheaf of emmer which he offered to the white bull of Min as the culmination of the harvest festival.

In the sculptures of the temple of Medinet Habu, Ramesses III in the New Kingdom is represented holding a ceremonial sickle, and it is by no means improbable, as Professor Gardiner has maintained, that he was impersonating Horus 'reaping the barley for his father Osiris, and thereby vindicating his title to the kingship', manifesting his generative powers as 'Min-Horus the powerful'.[30] The four sons of Horus dispatch geese to the four points of the compass, as in the coronation rite, to announce that 'Horus son of Isis and Osiris has assumed the great crown of Upper and Lower Egypt'. The king and queen may then have engaged in ritual sexual intercourse, since a priest proclaimed, 'Hail to thee, Min, who impregnates his mother! How mysterious is that which thou hast done to her in the darkness.' If this was so, it may have been the occasion for an heir to the throne to have been begotten. At the Min festival, however, it was the assumption of the crown by the god through his union with the Pharaoh, symbolizing the harmonious interlocking of nature and society in the person of the sovereign, that was duly announced as an annual renewal of fecundity and of the virility of the king and of the prosperity of the country as a whole.

The worship of the Pharaoh and his ancestors

To what extent, if any, Egyptian kings were accorded worship in their own person during their lifetimes is a moot point upon which opinion is divided. Moret, for instance, has contended that the Pharaoh was worshipped from the moment of his coronation,[31] whereas Erman believed that at any rate prior to the New Kingdom it was only after his death that he was the recipient of formal worship with temples, offerings and priests.[32] It has now been demonstrated, however, that in the time of the Ramesses the dead king in the mortuary temple at Medinet Habu was identified with the local Amon as well as with Osiris,[33] and Dr Nelson has raised the question how far the Osiris king and the living monarch can be differentiated in this respect. The monarch who erected the temple in the necropolis, he suggests, was carrying on for himself as an Osiris a tradition of service that went back to the Pyramid temples at least.[34] It cannot be demonstrated that the Pharaoh himself officiated before a statue in his mortuary temple as though he were already deceased. Nevertheless, the service on behalf of the king when he joined his *ka* in the celestial realms of Re hereafter may have been begun during his lifetime, as soon as the temple was established.

From his birth and accession he was the son of his heavenly father long before he became Osiris at his decease. It is not improbable, therefore, that his final status was anticipated before his death. Indeed, it would be surprising if the living king, who was always treated as a god and reigned as Horus, the son of the dead Osiris, were not the recipient of worship prior to the Graeco-Roman period, even though it was not until he went to his *ka* beyond the grave that in this respect his deification was completed, and his image accorded full divine honours in his temple in the necropolis. Virtually every ritual act was in theory a royal ritual, whoever may have performed it, and it is difficult to imagine how so sublime a being as the Pharaoh, 'a god by whose dealings men live', could be treated other than were the Hellenistic kings of the Ptolemaic period. Thus, one of his principal functions was to maintain the mortuary cult of his predecessor, and it was a recurrent feature in the coronation ceremony and in the principal seasonal festivals.[35]

The Sumerian kingship in Mesopotamia
In Mesopotamia the kingship occupied a very different position from that which it held in the Nile valley. Geographically and climatically the country did not lend itself to a stable social structure, unified in a single ruler claiming absolute divine sovereignty as the dynamic centre of the nation and of the cosmic order. The unpredictable behaviour of the Tigris and Euphrates, as we have seen, was in striking contrast to the uniformity of the inundation of the Nile. Devastating drought in summer and torrential rainfall in winter concentrated attention on the local group, which lived under shifting and perennially precarious conditions in an insecure environment. As a result Mesopotamia was divided up into a conglomeration of city-states, loosely bound together to meet the practical needs of recurrent emergencies, governed by a secular ruler or king who in Sumer (covering roughly the lower half of modern Iraq) bore the title of '*lugal*' (i.e. 'great man'), or by the high-priest (*sangu mah*) and the local governor (*ensi*). These administrators, however, although engaged mainly in secular duties, actually were priests exercising their functions in temples under the direction of a number of different heads, each of whom was independent in his own sphere (i.e. in the conduct of civil, military, religious, economic and social affairs). The *ensi* or governor appears to have occupied a permanent position in the body politic, and the high-priest (*sangu mah*) had a similar status in the sacred organization.

In this complex structure the precise position of the 'king' is very difficult to determine. In times of crisis, which were of very frequent occurrence, certain members of a ruling house might claim the title and office of *lugal*, or 'chief man', rather than of *patesi* or *ensi*, though in fact only a few of the early dynastic rulers adopted this designation.[36] The first of these, Ur-Nina of Lagash (*c.* 2900 BC), seems to have been engaged chiefly in building temples, digging irrigation canals and fortifications, but his grandson Eannatum (who called himself *Ensi* of Lagash) waged war on the city of Umma to the north, and claimed to have conquered Ur, Erech, Kish, Mari, and even Elam, thereby becoming virtually lord of Sumer and Akkad. This achievement he attributed to his having been established in his office by Enlil, endowed with strength by Ningirsu, the city god of Lagash, and suckled by Ninhursaga, the goddess of the earth.[37]

Although in the traditional king-lists the kingship is said to have 'descended from heaven' before the Flood in the third millennium BC, and to have been bestowed upon Nippur by Enlil, no attempt was made to impose a suzerainty of Sumer and Akkad by divine decree. It passed from city to city by force of arms, and in spite of the favour said to have been shown by Enlil for Nippur, it was never the dynastic capital. Before the Flood royalty was conferred only on a very few Sumerian kings, who were alleged to have reigned by divine prerogative and selection and to have lived to fabulous ages like Methuselah in Hebrew tradition. With the exception of Dumuzi, they were all mortals and described as 'shepherds of the people'.[38] Only a remnant of the population, it was said, survived the deluge, and the kingship had to be started afresh by a second descent from heaven. Dumuzi alone continued the antediluvian régime in the legendary Second Dynasty of Erech, but the 'Shepherd' *par excellence* was the historical ruler of Umma, Lugal-zaggisi, who at the end of the Early Dynastic period, after he had attacked and subdued Lagash, introduced the new title 'King of the Land', under the sanction of Enlil. As the 'son born of Nisa-ba, fed by the holy milk of Ninhursaga', he assumed dominion over the entire country and prayed that he might fulfil his destiny and always be 'the Shepherd at the head of the flock'.[39]

Although the rulers of Ur, Kish and Lagash had all exercised a similar jurisdiction, on the authority of Enlil, Lugal-zaggisi went beyond his predecessors in claiming ascendance over all countries from 'the Lower Sea' (i.e. the Persian Gulf) to the 'Upper Sea' (the Mediterranean).[40] Therefore, when in due course he was defeated by Sargon of Akkad, his conqueror called himself 'the ruler of the Four Quarters', while the son of Sargon, Naram-Sin, assumed the title 'King of the Four Quarters', thereby adopting the designation of the gods Enlil,

Anu and Shamash.[41] While no attempt was made to equate the king with these supreme deities, the new title did carry the implication of universal rule on earth comparable with that of the heavenly counterparts of the king. But in Mesopotamia the suzerainty of the great gods was never more than that of *primus inter pares*. In fact, therefore, no Sumerian king was a cohesive force in the country as a whole. The city-state was the unit of the political organization, ruled over by the *patesi* who was 'the tenant-farmer' of the principal local god, renewing annually his office at the New Year Festival. He stood at the head of the civic administration as law-giver, judge and commander, assisted by a staff of officials with the *sangumah* having control of the temple revenues and its organization, and the *ensi* managing the temporal aspects of the god's estate and maintaining law and order. Not infrequently, however, the two offices were held by the same person. When the king was himself a priest he established his claim to rule as the *lugal* by assuming sacerdotal functions in a temple, like Lugal-zaggisi, who in addition to being the priest of Anu exercised the same office in relation to Enlil when he conquered Sumer and ruled in his name. Gilgamesh, who was two-thirds a divine being, is represented as the king of Erech (Uruk) in southern Mesopotamia, and Gudea, the *Ensi* of Lagash (c. 2400 BC) was the steward of the god Ninginsu whose temple he had been commissioned to build.

The Babylonian monarchy

It was not until Hammurabi at the beginning of the second millennium BC made the small city-state of Babylon the capital of southern Mesopotamia, that the administrative functions of Enlil were transferred to Marduk, who it was affirmed had been declared head of the divine assembly of Anu and Enlil. Its ruler Hammurabi then became Marduk's steward and was entrusted by him with supreme executive authority in Sumer and Akkad, 'to make righteousness prevail in the land'.[42] But neither Marduk nor Hammurabi ever occupied the position in Mesopotamia that Osiris and Re and the Pharaoh held in the Nile valley. The earlier triad of gods, Anu, Enlil, and Ea, were only partially eclipsed, and Hammurabi continued to recognize Enlil. Marduk was never regarded as the creator and source of all the other gods like Re or Ptah, and only in his role as Tammuz was he an Osirian figure 'causing the rain to spring up' and giving to the kingship its sacred character and significance.[43] He was essentially a syncretistic city-god, as Hammurabi was the ruler of a small city-state which he had raised to pre-eminence by subjugating its rivals and as a result himself became the head of an

Empire he had created. For this achievement he claimed divine authority, but this was by no means recognized by all his subjects.

The sacred status and function of the kingship
In Mesopotamia the rise and fall of city-gods and their stewards was a recurrent phenomenon. Although divine selection remained the foundation of kingship until the end of the Assyrian Empire, the favour of the gods could always be withdrawn on any pretext, and there were times when they appointed no human rulers at all. As Isin and its goddess Nininsina, and Nippur and its god Enlil, gave place to Babylon and Marduk, so the supremacy of Babylon passed to Ashur, the Assyrian counterpart of Marduk and Enlil. Therefore, the monarchy lacked the security it enjoyed in Egypt, never having attained a divine status at all comparable to that assigned to the Pharaohs as the pivot of the social structure. They were not themselves gods incarnate, though they might be endowed with divinity by virtue of their office (alleged to have descended from heaven in the beginning) and by its insignia in which sacred power was inherent.[44] This gave them a unique relationship to the gods and rendered them sacrosanct to a high degree, and imposed upon them exacting ritual observances and religious duties (e.g. incantations, prayers, the maintenance of the sanctuaries and their worship), leaving little time or opportunity for secular affairs.

As in Egypt, so complex and far-reaching were the demands made upon them that an elaborate hierarchy under a high-priest (*urigallu*), appointed by the king to act on his behalf, was required for the temple organization and the performance of the seasonal rituals, spells, incantations, exorcisms and the interpretation of omens. He himself officiated as the ritual expert *par excellence*, occupying the central position in the cultus on specific occasions, notably, as will be considered in the next chapter, at the Annual Festival. He was responsible, however, for the due performance of the daily ritual observances, as the executive officer of the gods, without being in any sense the dynamic centre of the cosmic order.

Although the monarchy appears to have been regarded as a divine institution in origin and each occupant of the local 'throne' was thought to have been selected by the gods through the agency of omens, rather than by hereditary succession or a mythological qualification of divine descent from a heavenly progenitor, these claims did not constitute actual deification. This status was believed to have come to an end once and for all when the heroic age ceased with the Isin Dynasty (*c.* 2072 BC). From the beginning of the First Dynasty at Babylon no attempt was made to revive it, except very sporadically, after the time of

Hammurabi. Frankfort has suggested that 'only those kings were deified who had been commanded by the Goddess to share her couch. In a general way the kings who use the divine determinative before their names belong to the same period as the texts mentioning the marriage of kings and goddesses; and some kings adopted the determinative not at the beginning but at a later stage of their reigns. If we assume that they did so on the strength of a divine command, we remain,' he affirmed, 'within the scope of Mesopotamian thought, while the view that a king should have presumed of his own accord to pass the barrier between the human and the divine conflicts with everything we know of Mesopotamian beliefs.'[45] In support of this contention he quotes a text known as 'The deification of Lipit-Ishtar' in which the king (Lipit-Ishtar) was deified as a preliminary to his sacred marriage with Ishtar by being fused with a fertility god Urash, as son of Enlil, in order to enable him to exercise his beneficent functions in the promotion of the prosperity of the land and to prolong his life.[46]

That Babylonian kings were on occasion invited to share the couch of the Goddess as her bridegroom has been demonstrated, and it was she who was the active partner in the sacred marriage, bringing him into her bower with its couch decorated with grass and plants at the New Year Festival, to promote the growth of the fruits of the earth, to ensure prosperity in the forthcoming year, and to raise the sovereign to her divine status.*[47] But to what extent this was a regular custom has not been determined, or whether or not only those kings claimed divinity who had engaged in the connubium. It was the city-god who bestowed kingship and his consort does not appear to have been an essential or the predominant figure in the process of giving the occupant of the throne divine status. Unquestionably the king was often regarded as subservient to the Goddess, and was represented as her instrument on earth, but in his vegetation capacity his sacredness and annual renewal were dependent upon a much wider relationship with the gods, especially the local deity of the state over which he ruled, and whose favour was essential for the exercise of his royal functions in their several aspects.

The Ugaritic kingship
Elsewhere in western Asia the kingship, although not a universal institution, was a recurrent feature in the Ancient Near East. Up to a point it assumed a similar pattern in its widespread distribution, but there were also marked differentiations as well as similarities in its

*cf. Chap. III, p. 79ff.

nature, purpose and functions. In Syria the Ras Shamra texts suggest that behind the Canaanite mythology lay much the same situation, except that very little is said about the relation of Aleyan Baal, the Storm-god and Rain-god, and Hadad the 'thunderer', with the Ugaritic king, apart from references in the Keret-text to the king sacrificing to Tor-El and Baal.[48] Baal, however, in his Tammuz role caused the languishing of the earth by his descent into the land of the dead, and Danel and Keret as divine kings exercised control over the crops.[49]

Although the drought in summer is nowhere said to have been an annual occurrence, the death of the god certainly seems to have been equated with aridity and the return of the fructifying rains with his victory over his adversaries; first with Yam, the god of the sea and rivers, in his attempt to become the viceroy of the Supreme God El, and then with Athtar, god of the springs and wells, his rival claimant.[50] Having somehow established himself as a king, his adversary Mot, the sinister power of sterility, contrived to get him into the subterranean land of the dead. How he met his fate there is not known as the tablet is broken at this point in the story, but it had the effect of causing vegetation to cease on the earth until Anat had destroyed Athtar, savagely attacked Mot and restored Baal to his home on Mount Sapan, sacrificing on his behalf sheep, oxen, bulls, deer, goats and asses, amid universal mourning. Ultimately she reinstated him on the throne to resume his life-giving functions.[51]

Here would seem to be a reflection of the seasonal sequence of the agricultural year along the lines generally adopted in Near Eastern mythology. It may be true, as Gordon has contended,[52] that in Syria the summer was not a season of fertility, but even so the return of the refreshing rains was eagerly awaited, rain in Canaan being the primary source of fertility. It was to this recurrent phenomenon in the various phases of the Syrian year that the theme and its seasonal ritual were related, both annually and sabbatically. Mot was throughout the antithesis of Baal in a vegetation setting, regarded, as we have seen, as responsible for sterility and aridity, and yet treated as the reaped grain in the guise of the slain corn-spirit dying at the ingathering of harvest.

As the struggle between life and death in nature was perennial, neither of the contending forces could be ultimately destroyed. Baal, we are told, was king, and when his reign was restored fertility returned with him. But no indication is given of what, if any, effect this had on the Ugaritic king, or on his role in the cult. It would be surprising if he were not the central figure, as in Mesopotamia, as the earthly representative of the dying and reviving king-god, but although his sacral status might be a not unreasonable inference from the mythology of the texts,[53] the fact remains that the Ugaritic documents are silent about his position either in the community or in the cultus.

Even in the Keret legend, first published by M. Virolleaud in 1936, that Keret was the Primeval Man who sacrificed to Baal as a king of Ugarit is by no means clear, though the connexion between the Primordial King and the actual ruler has always been very close, as in the Old Testament reference to the king of Tyre as the incarnation of the primeval guardian of Eden.[54] And as Albright says, 'the epics of Keret and Danel are much less purely mythological in character than the Baal epic, and they may have a nucleus of legendary history, heavily embroidered with myth and folk-tale.'[55] Gods intervene in the affairs of men in the usual manner in this type of literature, but the events are located in Tyre and Sidon with a *milieu*, as Ginsberg points out, which was closely connected by cultural ties with what was later known as southern Phoenicia, and also not too far removed from it in space. Indeed, the 'action which it relates actually took place in this region'.[56] But if it be granted, as Pedersen has contended, that Keret was the founder of a dynasty which was still reigning as his descendants when the epic was copied in the reign of a certain Ugaritic king named Niqmadd in the second quarter of the fourteenth century BC, it does not follow that it ruled over Ugarit.

The purpose of the legend was to show how King Keret's line was re-established after it had been wiped out apart from himself. To this end he besought El to give him posterity, and under instructions from the Supreme God he launched a military expedition against Udum with a view to demanding the grand-daughter of the king as the price of peace. These terms were granted and Keret married the maiden Hurriya and begot a numerous progeny. When the children were grown up Keret became seriously ill, and during his convalescence one of his sons, Yassib, tried to make him abdicate in his favour, thereby bringing upon himself the curse of his father, and the succession of the youngest daughter to the throne. Here perhaps may be detected the supersession of the eldest by the youngest son, and the establishment of the royal line in a new dynasty descended through Keret's youngest daughter,[57] which was a very unusual procedure. If a new dynasty was inaugurated in this way, the epic could be explained as a justification of its claims to the throne. In any case, Keret would seem to be a traditional dynasty-founder rather than a vegetation king-god, and in this connexion it is significant that it was El and not Baal who took the initiative in securing the continuance of the royal line. But it can hardly be determined how much of the story can be regarded as sober history and how much was fiction, in the present state of knowledge.[58]

All that can be said is that there was a clear recognition of the vital importance of the maintenance of the dynasty for the well-being of the community, together with the descent of the kingship from El through Keret, and its priestly functions in the desacralization of the new crops for consummation and dispensing the fertility of the earth.[59] The king's illness was said to have brought a drought on the land and upon his recovery Baal bestowed the first rains.[60] It is, therefore, by no means improbable that in the Late Bronze Age the myth had a cultic significance, as Dr Gray has suggested, perhaps in relation to the wedding of the king, which may have coincided with the New Year Festival as the most auspicious occasion for the event, this being the season of the early rains.[61]

Sacral Kingship in Israel

Although similar climatic conditions obtained over the rest of Palestine when the Hebrew tribes settled in the land at the end of the second millennium BC, as they were not typical nomads they readily accommodated themselves to an agricultural *milieu*, but their god Yahweh was not in origin a vegetation god. His traditional background was that of the desert, as we have seen, and when the Israelites established themselves in Canaan an inevitable conflict arose between Yahwism and Baalism. Before the establishment of the monarchy under Saul and his successors early in the tenth century (*c.* 1020 BC), Gideon had succeeded to a kind of hereditary kingship at Ophrah in Manasseh, in the hill-country in the centre. There he placed a gold-plated statue of Yahweh in the sanctuary and made it a popular cult-centre in Israel,[62] having first destroyed an altar of Baal and Asherah which his father had set up, in spite of the fact that he bore a Yahwistic name, Joash.[63] The success of this royal shrine shows that in the eleventh century Yahwism was making considerable progress in Canaan among the Israelite confederation, though the conflict between the two rival cults was strenuously maintained. Baal and the vegetation myth and ritual were too firmly rooted, as the Ugaritic data show, to be ousted by what must have appeared as an alien intrusion from the desert, and it was by no means unattractive to the masses among the Hebrew tribes. Yahweh as the Lord of Sinai might be extolled and his victorious omnipotence stressed in the Song of Deborah,[64] but since both he and Baal were Storm-gods, the givers of rain and fertility, and sky-beings, their assimilation was inevitable, even though in origin Yahweh was not a typical vegetation deity. Therefore, when he became the national god exercising much the same functions as the Canaanite gods and their cults in the control of the weather, as is illustrated by the Carmel conflict, the stage was set for a syncretistic movement which persisted long after the establishment of the monarchy. The nature and attributes of the Canaanite Baals were transferred to Yahweh, and in the sanctuaries devoted to him the cults were indistinguishable from those of their occupants, as is shown by their symbolism and the repeated prophetic denunciations of the syncretism that still prevailed in the eighth century and continued until the Exile, in spite of all attempts at reformation. The bull cult at Bethel and Dan,[65] for example, was not an innovation by Jeroboam, as the later writers contended, viewing the situation in the light of the reform of Josiah in 621 BC. All that Jeroboam did was to restore the earlier cultus with its symbolism and hierarchy in the northern Kingdom, while in the south the temple was constructed on Phoenician models and equipped in the customary manner with the Ark of the Covenant as the principal cult object—the earthly embodiment of the divine presence.[66]

Officially, however, Palestine was 'the land of Yahweh', and the bond between him and the nation of his adoption was dependent upon the observance of the covenant (i.e. the *bĕrith* or cultus) established with the House of David. David, in fact, was represented as the anointed servant and son of Yahweh,[67] and this status made him and his successors sacred persons and cult leaders exercising sacrificial functions like the sacral kings in the neighbouring countries. Thus, David wore an ephod and danced ecstatically before the Ark when it was taken to Mount Zion, after the Jebusite fortress had been made the capital.[68] There he took over the priesthood of the god Zedek and placed himself at the head of the hierarchy with Zadok and Nathan as his *kohen* and *nabi* respectively, while prophets and priests were assigned their ritual duties. When his son Solomon had built the temple he offered burnt offerings and peace offerings three times a year on the altar he had erected to Yahweh.[69]

The covenant, however, with the House of David had a wider significance than the monarchy and was independent of the throne, since behind it lay the covenant of Yahweh with the nation as a whole, thereby differentiating the Hebrew kingship from that in the Nile valley, Mesopotamia and Syria. The Hebrew monarch ruled only by divine permission and the will of the people. Indeed, the monarchy came to be regarded with the gravest suspicion in the prophetic movement before the Exile, largely because of its approximation to the traditional kingship cult.[70] For this reason it was described as an affront to Yahweh.[71] It therefore lacked stability, as the unifying and consolidating force was the covenant, of which kings were merely the instruments. It was not until later that the Davidic king acquired a Messianic significance as the firstborn of many brethren walking in meekness and righteousness.[72] Then the traditional Abrahamic covenant ratified at Sinai and renewed in relation to the House of David, was first interpreted in terms of a 'Messiah' (*mashiakh*) applied to kings, priests and rulers like Cyrus the Persian, Zerubbabel, Jeshua the son of Jozadech and Simon Maccabaeus, who acted as prince, priest and governor,[73] without claiming descent from David, Aaron or Zadok, until at length the office was given an eschatological connotation under a new name—that of Melchizedek, suggesting righteousness (*sedek*) and prosperity[74]—and enthroned in triumph eternally on Mount Zion as Yahweh's vicegerent, 'having neither beginning nor end of life'.[75]

This question of the Davidic covenant with the Son, the Servant and the Messiah of Yahweh, and with the Canaanite royal priesthood of Melchizedek, shows how very deeply laid was the ancient kingship theme in pre-exilic Israel and its conception of the Davidic Dynasty. There is no reason to suppose that any Hebrew king ever assumed the role of the incarnate god like the Pharaoh in Egypt, or of the deified servant of the Goddess and the local god in Mesopotamia, but it is clear, as Dr Snaith says, 'that the well-being of the nation was regarded as being intimately bound up with the well-being of the king.'[76] This found expression in a myth and ritual, which while conforming to the Hebrew *milieu* and interpreted in relation to the conception of the covenant with Yahweh, had their antecedents in the sacral kingship so firmly established in the religion of the Near East.[77]

Even after the fall of the monarchy the kingship tradition survived, when Zerubbabel on becoming governor of Jerusalem in 520 BC as a descendant of David was hailed as the deputy of Yahweh, and occupied a position in the cultus comparable to that assigned to 'the Prince' by Ezekiel and his contemporaries.[78] He ruled, however, in conjunction with the high-priest who was the guardian of the temple and its worship.[79] When his mission came to an end the high-priest alone remained as the consolidating centre of the nation and around him as the alleged descendant of Eleazer, the oldest son of Aaron, the hierarchic organization and the cultus developed. When the temple was rebuilt and the sacrificial system restored, then, reverting to type, the civic and ecclesiastical functions of the ruler were combined in one and the same sacred office as the focal point of the theocratic nation, until its final disruption in AD 70.

The Hittite kingship

In Anatolia the pre-Hittite princes had established a stable civilization in the Middle Bronze Age, in which they became the chief priests of the gods whom they represented in a sacerdotal capacity. Recent excavations at Kültepe, the ancient Kanash near Kayseri, have brought to light a number of tablets on which references occur to local princes and their palaces, among whom one named Pitkhana, king of Kussara, is mentioned, and his son Anittas who appears to have controlled the greater part of the Cappadocian plateau. Such was the fame of Anittas that he became a legendary figure in the second millennium BC. From this 'great prince', as he was described, the royal Hittite line may have descended, though, in fact, it was from King Labarnas that Telipinus began his chronicle and the later Hittite kings traced their lineage.[80] By about 1380 BC the kingdom had been established by Suppiluliumas, king of Hatti, who conquered the Mesopotamian kingdoms of Mitanni and the Hussi lands and incorporated them into his empire, and sent armies into Syria and Palestine, making Lebanon his frontier (c. 1370 BC).

The Hittite states, therefore, were welded as a group under the rule of the 'Great King' and his successors, who in addition to being the heads of the army and the supreme judges were also the chief-priests of the gods in the national cult, and were 'held by the hand' of the Goddess. Although they were never regarded as divine in their lifetime, they were thought to be endowed with supernatural powers at their accession. Thus, Mursilis II in the fourteenth century BC besought the gods in his priestly capacity, at a time of a great plague, to drive forth the scourge from the Land of Hatti and to give it prosperity and happiness to its royal family. Daily the king addressed the vegetation god Telipinu with 'sweet and soothing cedar essence' and 'sacrificed loaves and libations' to secure his favour and clemency, to grant health, strength and enduring years for himself and the queen and his subjects, and 'everlasting fertility to the crops, cattle, sheep, goats, pigs, mules and asses, together with the beasts of the field, and to their people. Let them flourish! Let the rains come! Let the winds of prosperity pass over! Let all thrive and prosper in the Land of Hatti'.[81] Similarly, when Hattusilis II acceded to the throne of Hakpis in 1275 BC, he became priest of the Storm-god of Nerik, the son of the Sun-goddess of Arinna,[82] and adopted the Hurrian Ishtar as his patron goddess. He himself being styled *taberna*, the 'Great King', he told of her divine power as the 'hero, beloved of the goddess' and the incarnation of Labarnas, the founder of the royal line. But it was not until the death of the Hittite kings that they themselves were actually deified, like the

Roman emperors. Nevertheless, they were so essentially sacred personages that they were hedged round with tabus in a manner that hardly differentiated them from the Egyptian Pharaohs in practice.

The queen also had her own place and status in the monarchy (Fig. 45). At the death of her predecessor, the queen-mother, she became the *Tawannannas*, the priestess of the Mother-goddess, and in this capacity she could act as regent during her husband's absence. It seems, in fact, that it was through her that the sovereign was brought into relation with the goddess by means of a sacred marriage, though the evidence for this is obscure, and based solely upon the iconography, mainly at Yazilikaya.[83] The title Tawannannas was derived from the name of her ancestor, the wife of Labarnas, and once she acquired it she might and frequently did take a very prominent and independent part in state affairs, as, for instance, in the case of Puduhepa, wife of Hattusilis III and daughter of the priest of Ishtar of Lawazantiyas. So great was the power wielded by the queen of Mursilis II that he had to expel her and then connived at her murder. Since Puduhepa is depicted at Ferahettin (Fraktin) sacrificing to the goddess, it would appear that like the king the queen exercised priestly functions. Her name, in fact, was compounded with that of Hebat (i.e. Hepit) the consort of the Hurrian Weather-god Teshub who was later identified with the Sun-goddess of Arinna, whose priestess she was. Indeed, in the Egyptian version of the treaty between Hattusilis and Egypt she is represented on the royal seal in the embrace of the Sun-goddess of Arinna, doubtless as the Hittite counterpart of the Hurrian Hebat.

The royal cult

It would seem from the royal archives that the king must have been fully occupied with his priestly and other religious duties. At the round of seasonal festivals, as will be considered later,* he was the chief officiant at the sacrifices and libations offered to a great variety of gods. Sometimes the feasts occupied several days and involved elaborate ritual and the observance of strict tabus, which often included other members of the royal family. Sometimes they required a journey from shrine to shrine, where audiences were assembled together with a staff bearer and other officials (Figs. 46, 47). Generally he was accompanied by the queen, and so vital was his presence at the Spring Festival of the Earth, known as *Purulli*, that Mursilis II, having already performed his functions in honour of the Weather-god of Hatti and the Weather-god of Zippalanda, felt it incumbent upon him to interrupt a military campaign to officiate at the 'Great Festival' of *Purulli*.[84] Indeed,

*cf. Chap. V, p. 157.

its purpose may well have been to renew the life of the king and queen and all that this involved for the health and prosperity of the community. If this were so, the sovereign and his spouse would naturally be very prominent figures in the festival, and we know from other sources that rites were celebrated by or for the king for these ends at the vernal equinox or thereabouts.[85] Just as the return of Telipinu gave the king enduring life, so the fight with the Dragon Illuyankas enacted at the Spring Festival annually at Nerik doubtless had a similar effect, since, as will be considered later, it was so closely associated with the enactment of the Babylonian *Enuma elish* and its combat theme attached to a fertility drama, which is represented on the walls of the sanctuary of Yazilikaya. So vital, in fact, was his presence that when he could not perform his functions in person the festival lapsed.[86]

In the autumnal celebration the king and queen and the heir to the throne visited shrine after shrine for sixteen days on their journey to Nerik. At Arinna, while the king offered sacrifices and libations the queen performed her rites in honour of the Sun-goddess, washing her hands before offering seven lambs to the Goddess under various designations (e.g. 'the Sun-goddess of Arinna of Walanni', Nikalmati, of Henti, of Tawannannas) which appear to refer to deceased queens who had been identified with the Sun-goddess of Arinna.[87] Ultimately, however, the king was himself responsible for the cultus, and any calamity that befell the people or the country might be attributed to some defect or neglect on his part in the performance of his sacerdotal functions. Thus, when Suppiluliumas and his son Arnuwandas II both died during a prolonged pestilence in the middle of the fourteenth century BC, a search was made of the records for possible royal offences that might have been committed to account for the disaster, so that due expiation could be made for them.[88]

The role of the king and queen

Since prosperity was dependent upon the king being 'pleasing to the gods' and he occupied the throne and exercised his rule by virtue of his divine succession and appointment,[89] misfortunes were the inevitable result of any lapse on his part in the fulfilment of his sacred office. The tabus imposed upon him were designed to safeguard his sacrosanct personality and all that entailed and involved. So all-embracing were his functions and his sanctity that they were extended to and shared by his spouse in her royal capacity as the reigning queen. Within his own sphere his authority and judgment were absolute, and the subject-matter of the sacerdotal oracles was for the most part concerned with his cult duties and their correct performance.[90] But in the Old Kingdom the assembly of Elders exercised jurisdiction over royal conduct and that of the courtiers, though this was considerably modified when subsequently the state was organized on a feudal basis enforcing loyalty to the king as the supreme deity. This, however, was a civic rather than a religious obligation, though the oaths taken by royal princes and their vassals were taken in the presence of the gods, who were regarded as the ultimate authority in the exercise of judgment through their human protégé and high-priest the king. But Hittite kings were never represented as divinely born like the Pharaohs or some of the Mesopotamian rulers, even though they might on occasions be described as 'Sun-gods of the gods', a phrase that did not carry a solar connotation in respect of descent. Unless it had some reference to the king's coronation, or sacring, or investiture, the fusion with the divine nature of the Sun-god would appear to have been superimposed on the kingship rather than an essential element in it, and was perhaps in connexion with the administration of justice.[91] But it was not until the statue of a deceased king was placed in the temple that it was accorded divine honours.

The Minoan priest-kings

In the Aegean and the adjacent islands the sacral kingship was no less firmly established than in western Asia. Thus, in Crete the palace of the priest-king was a sacred edifice in which the worship of the gods, and especially of the Mother-goddess, was practised. At Knossos, for example, Sir Arthur Evans has revealed a 'Room of the Throne' in the palace, in which the priest-king as 'the adopted son on earth of the Great Mother of its island mysteries' sat on an elaborately carved throne with frescoes of griffins behind it and guarding the entrance to the inner shrine. Like the Anatolian Hall of Initiation in the sanctuary of Men Askaënos and the Mother-goddess, near the Pisidian Antioch, it was devised for the installation and enthronement of its royal occupant, whose likeness may perhaps be recognized in the relief of a human figure wearing a plumed lily crown and leading a sacral griffin (Fig. 61). The tank opposite the throne may have been used for lustrations, while an overturned oil-jar to the left very likely contained the oil for the anointing in the sacring rite.[92] In any case, the equipment of the palace with its shrines, sacred objects and furnishings leaves no room for doubt that it was a sanctuary, in which the cultus associated with the kingship throughout the Ancient Near East and the eastern Mediterranean was duly performed by Minoan rulers and their deputies, in the customary manner with the Mother-goddess as the central figure.

Whether or not the royal line of priest-kings in Crete was founded by the traditional ruler Minos it is impossible to determine. A cycle of heroic legends has collected around this name, associating him with the origins and administration of Cretan civilization and its position in the Aegean as a maritime power. How much of this is fact and how much romance will probably never be known, though more light may be thrown on the problem when the inscribed clay tablets have been fully deciphered and read. According to the Greek versions of the story he was a divine king, the son of Zeus by Europa, the daughter of the king of Tyre, Agenor, who in the form of a bull carried her away to Crete. There she gave birth to Minos who ascended the throne in the island and married Pasiphae, daughter of Helios, the Sun-god.[93] Thus, both Minos and his consort had a divine status by virtue of their parentage, and from them a sacral dynasty of priest-kings was derived, which was a characteristic feature of the Cretan civilization, now commonly called 'Minoan' after its legendary founder, and having affinities with its contemporary Anatolian, western Asiatic and Egyptian counterparts.

Destined by nature to be a meeting place of streams of culture from the valley of the Nile, Asia Minor and the eastern Mediterranean, Crete became the home of a composite culture in which were combined Nilotic, Anatolian and oriental elements most conspicuous in the Palace régime at Knossos and Phaestos. By the Middle Minoan period (c. 1850 BC) the power of the sacred dynasts had increased enormously in Central Crete by a skilful combination of divine authority, political acumen, and economic enterprise. Trade with Egypt and the Aegean prospered, and these commercial contacts were not without influence on religious practice. They were utilized in the interests of the stabilization of the social structure centred in the sacral kingship and the creation of an independent culture with fresh techniques and refinements peculiar to the island, which persisted in spite of catastrophes attributed to earthquakes, necessitating the reconstruction of the palaces with all their sacred significance, until the final destruction of Knossos in 1400 BC.

The Mycenaean kings
On the mainland a similar royal cult was established in the Mycenaean palaces almost identical with that in Crete. The temples of Hera and Athena were built on the ruins of the royal palaces at Mycenae (Fig. 63), Athens (Fig.76), and probably at Tiryns. Thus, the name of Athena occurs on a bronze plate found in 1939 in the excavation of the temple on the summit of the citadel at Mycenae, where a residence for the kings had been erected; the mortal remains of two of them had been

buried in a shaft-grave, and others interred with their families in the same manner in the Late Bronze Age (1600–1500 BC).[94] Those who were buried in the great beehive tholoi at Mycenae (e.g. the Treasury of Atreus and the Tomb of Clytemnestra) (Fig. 64) doubtless had an appropriate royal residence in the citadel, and the wealth of funerary furniture in both the shaft-graves and the chamber-tombs shows that their mortuary cultus was comparable to that of the Minoan priest-kings at Knossos.[95]

As Mycenae was the meeting-point of the western Asiatic and the eastern Mediterranean cultures in the Bronze Age, two contemporary dynasties coexisted there, the one burying their rulers in shaft-graves, the other in tholoi. From about 1600 BC the rulers interred in the shaft-graves had Cretan affinities though, unlike the Minoan priest-kings, they were not clean-shaven, as their death-masks reveal. Both they and those who eventually occupied the chamber-tombs were the Helladic lords of the indigenous population settled in Greece and the Aegean before the Minoan civilization penetrated the Peloponnese in the middle of the second millennium BC (c. 1600). Their strategic position on the trade-route leading from Corinth to the north and west gave them an essential European (Helladic) status and influence in the Late Bronze Age quite independent of Crete with its Egyptian and Asiatic contacts. Among them no doubt were Minoan colonists under Cretan rulers so long as the Knossian priest-kings were predominant in the region. But the Helladic lords of Mycenae held sway in the Aegean and pursued their own course, culturally, politically and commercially, as is shown by their distinctive sepulture (e.g. tholoi and chamber-tombs) and its magnificent mortuary equipment as well as by their palaces,[96] in spite of the completely Minoan outlook prominent among the ruling classes. Again, while the Minoan priest-kings were relatively pacific, the Mycenaean rulers were warriors and builders of massive fortified cities, engaging in extensive military enterprises which extended their control over an increasing territory and gaining for them no small amount of booty, even though the successors of Minos continued to rule the waves. It is not surprising, therefore, that at their death they were provided with an 'everlasting habitation' in keeping with the splendour of their royal residences and their achievements and their status as sacral kings.

The Archon in the Greek city-states
Although the palaces have not revealed a cultic equipment analogous to that at Knossos, on the north side of the North Corridor in the palace site on the Acropolis at Mycenae the pavement of a room opening off it has been excavated in a Late Helladic deposit which appears to have

been in a shrine containing the remains of two movable stucco altars, hearths, or tables of offering of the same type as the Shrine of the Double Axe at Knossos, partly covered by the terrace of the temple.[97] If a carving in ivory of two squatting women with a youth standing before them, found at the base of the terrace wall on which the foundations of the temple rest at the north end, came from the shrine at the palace, it may represent the divinities to whom the temple was dedicated. If the patron were not Athena, as the inscription already mentioned belonging to the sixth century BC appears to suggest, then it may have been the Eleusinian trio, Demeter, Persephone, and Iacchos, the Young god. The Mysteries at Eleusis were undoubtedly of Mycenaean origin,[98] and they were under the care of the Archon of Athens, who had the title of king, βασιλένς, and were served by ancient priestly Eleusinian families, the Eumolpidae and the Kerykes, probably of royal descent.[99] Sanctuaries of Demeter existed in Argos and Argolis, and another between Argos and Mycenae.[100] On the other hand, as Nilsson has pointed out, Iacchos was not introduced into the Eleusinian cultus until it (Eleusis) had been annexed by Athens.[101]

Nevertheless, whether or not the ivory group represented the Eleusinian trio, behind the Minoan-Mycenaean sacral kingship lay the worship of the Goddess and the Young god so prominent in Crete and the Aegean in the second millennium BC. When in due course the palaces were replaced by the temples in the Greek city-states, and after the monarchy had come to an end, the Archon not only retained the title of king but also the religious functions that formerly had been exercised by the priest-kings. At Athens he was required to marry a carefully selected Athenian virgin who annually on the twelfth day of the month Anthesterion (February) had to contract a sacred marriage with Dionysus in a building on the Acropolis called the Bukolion, or Ox-stall, which formerly was a royal residence.[102] Possibly it was on this occasion that her marriage with the king was celebrated, and its object seems to have been to renew and ensure the processes of fertility over which Dionysus had control, as in the other sacred marriages of the king and queen in the seasonal ritual. Thus, the union of Zeus and Hera, his principal consort, was enacted in many places for this purpose, and in the *Iliad* all manner of flowers and thick soft grass is said to have sprung up to make a marriage-bed for Zeus and Hera on Mount Ida[103] (XIV. 346f.). It would seem, therefore, that the widespread and very deeply rooted fundamental theme of the sacral kingship persisted in Greece in myth and ritual long after the monarchy had ceased to function as a political institution in the city-states.

CHAPTER FIVE

THE SEASONAL FESTIVALS

Egypt, festival of Khoiak, harvest feast of Min of Koptos—New Year festival in Mesopotamia, Akitu in Babylon, Bit Akitu rites, determination of Destiny—Baal cult drama in Syria, Yahwistic cultus in Israel, Passover, Feast of Tabernacles, Day of Atonement—Purulli-Festival in Anatolia—rural rites and festivals in Greece, Thesmophoria, Thalysia, Anthesteria, Eleusinian festivals, Dionysian festivals

THE RECURRENCE of a common cultus, throughout the Ancient Near East and the Aegean, with marked similarities and dissimilarities, centred in the vegetation cycle in which the king and queen impersonated the Young god and the Mother-goddess, has been conditioned very largely by the particular environment in which it has occurred. Seasonal festivals, however, whatever may have been their common or independent features, must of necessity have been related in the first instance to the calendrical course of events. They have always been primarily concerned with the food supply. Under Palaeolithic conditions they tended to centre in the times of breeding among the animals hunted in the chase, or of the appearance of the wild fruits, roots and berries. Similarly, when husbandry and herding became the chief means of subsistence, the festivals were related to these operations which in their turn were governed by the cycle of nature; spring and autumn, summer and winter.

Egypt

Thus, in the agricultural communities that developed in the great river valleys like those of the Nile and the Tigris and Euphrates, sowing and harvest were the principal events in the year, corresponding to the breeding seasons in hunting and pastoral society. But the behaviour of the rivers in Egypt and Mesopotamia, as we have seen, was by no means identical, and these peculiarities were reflected in their respective calendrical observances, notwithstanding the fact that the Egyptian civil calendar bore little or no relation to the seasons. Nevertheless, in theory the beginning of the year on the nineteenth of July coincided with the rise of the Nile at 'The Season of Inundation' (Thoth) in the peasants' calendar. Four months later 'The Season of Coming Forth' (Tybi) was celebrated when the waters were at their height, and in

February or March 'The Season of Deficiency' marked their decline, after the grain sown in November had disappeared and the summer was approaching, from March until June.

The festival of Khoiak

It is significant that the oldest Egyptian festival, the *Sed*, held to rejuvenate the Pharaoh and renew his reign, generally about thirty years after his accession,* was observed in conjunction with the great autumnal feast known as the Khoiak on the first day of the first month of winter. The observance was appropriate at this season as it occurred at a time when the Nile, personifying Osiris, had reached its height and when annually the obsequies of Osiris were enacted. Thus, as they are described in the Ptolemaic inscription on the walls of the Osirian temple at Denderah in Upper Egypt, north of Thebes, they occupied the last eighteen days of the month Khoiak, opening with a ploughing and sowing ceremony on the twelfth day. From then to the twenty-first the effigy of the dead Osiris, moulded in gold in the form of a mummy, was filled with a mixture of barley and sand, wrapped in rushes, laid in a shallow basin, and watered daily. On the ninth day (22nd) it was exposed to the sun just before sunset and sent on a mysterious voyage with other similar images illuminated by lights until the twenty-fourth.

Fig. 7. Osiris rising from a bier

*Chap. IV, p. 112.

135

Then it was buried in a coffin of mulberry wood and laid in a grave, the effigy of the previous year having been removed and placed in a sycamore tree. On the thirtieth day, when the inundation was due to subside and the sowing of the grain to begin, the interment of Osiris was enacted at a subterranean chamber where the effigy in its coffin was placed on a bed of sand.[1]

Osiris is frequently represented in the act of rising from his bier (fig. 7), and on the bas-reliefs which accompany the inscription at Denderah the culmination of the festival is shown to have occurred on the last day (30th) when the ithyphallic dead god, swathed as a mummy, is represented gradually raising himself up from the bier assisted by Nephthys, Isis and Horus, and being presented with the *crux ansata*, the sign of life. Above is the soul of Osiris in the form of a hawk with outstretched wings.[2]

On the tomb of Kheryaf at Thebes the *Djed*-column, resembling a telegraph pole in appearance, is shown in process of being raised up with ropes by the Pharaoh with the help of the high-priest of Memphis in the presence of the queen and her daughters and members of the court (fig. 8). A sham fight is also depicted in progress between the inhabitants of Buto, the Predynastic capital of Lower Egypt, and

Fig. 8. The raising of the Djed column at Memphis, and a battle in progress between two opposed groups. From a relief in the tomb of Kheraf at Thebes

finally the king and his subjects are represented in procession round the walls of Memphis.[3] At Abydos, the reputed home of the body of Osiris, where a similar combat took place, Seti I and Isis are represented in the Hall of the Osirian Mysteries setting up the pillar between them, the *Djed* being swathed in a cloth.[4] In the Denderah inscriptions it is definitely stated to have been raised in Busiris on 'the day of the interment of Osiris'.[5]

Therefore, while the *Djed*-column unquestionably was a very ancient symbol of Osiris before it was identified with Ptah at Memphis, it may originally have been a tree with the branches lopped off,[6] and its ceremonial raising up may have indicated his restoration from the grave as the culmination of the autumnal festival. In Egypt Osiris was always the dead king, the role of the reinvigorated god being reserved for Horus. Nevertheless, if Sethe is correct in thinking that the Memphite Festival of Sokaris commemorated the accession of Menes, the traditional founder of Memphis and of the unified 'Two Lands', the Feast of Khoiak was considered to be the right and proper occasion for the Pharaoh to ascend the throne. For the king and queen to be associated

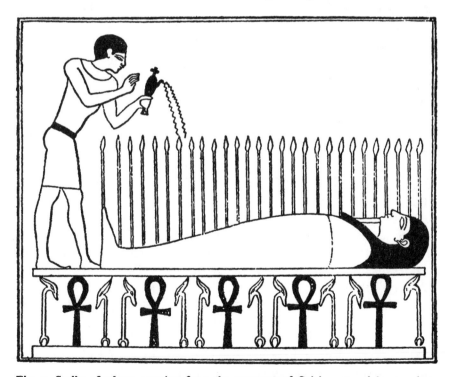

Fig. 9. Stalks of wheat growing from the mummy of Osiris watered by a priest. From the temple of Isis at Philae

with the symbolic erection of the embodiment of Osiris on the first day of the year would therefore be appropriate, the rite being performed to secure his release from the tomb at 'The Season of Coming Forth' when the fertilizing waters of the Nile were beginning the fructification of the land.[7] Even though he was the dead king, his mummy, portrayed in the Ptolemaic temple of Isis at Philae, shows stalks of wheat watered by a priest from a pitcher, to symbolize the sprouting grain in the fields (fig. 9), just as Osirian figures of earth containing germinating seeds were watered for a week and placed in tombs in the Eighteenth Dynasty, to give life to the dead.[8]

These connexions of Osiris with the sprouting grain, taken in conjunction with the autumnal rites, show how very intimately the annual renewal in nature was related to his resurrection interpreted in terms of the rise and fall of the Nile with which the festival and its symbolism coincided. Though he was not strictly a vegetation deity like his opposite numbers in western Asia, Osiris, however, was immanent in the annual germination of vegetation in the soil. In the Memphite Mystery Play performed at the accession of Senusert I in the Twelfth Dynasty (c. 1900 BC), the text of which contains very much earlier material prior to the Middle Kingdom,[9] he is identified with the barley and the emmer that nourished the gods in heaven and man on earth. This deeply laid belief survived in the Ptolemaic period in the temple at Denderah where he was said to have made the corn from the liquid that was in him.[10] Indeed, all the gods connected with vegetation and fertilization were identified with him and he with them, as were all those associated with the dead, while his *Djed*-column became increasingly sacred until at length at Memphis it was deified and transferred to Ptah, the head of the Memphite pantheon. Inherent in the Osirian cultus, be it in the form of mortuary, vegetation or mystery rites and festivals, was the death, burial, resurrection and triumph of the culture hero. This was most apparent in those performed in the month of Khoiak, in which his interment and raising from the tomb were dramatically enacted and inscribed on the walls of the temple of Denderah. But so numerous were the Osirian festivals that they were celebrated throughout the seasons of the agricultural year at a great many places, notably at Abydos and Busiris, his two principal centres.

The Harvest feast of Min of Koptos

In the official calendar, however, it was to Min, the local god of Koptos, that the harvest festival was dedicated. From the dawn of Egyptian civilization he had personified the generative force in nature as the bestower of procreative power, represented in the form of an ithyphallic bearded man with the thunderbolt as his emblem, since he was also a Storm-god and Weather-god. His connexions with Horus, the Falcon-god, began in prehistoric times and were prominent in the Middle Kingdom, while his intimate relation with Amon, the Egyptian Zeus, may have brought him into association with meteorites.[11] In any case he was both a fertility-god and a Sky-god who was chiefly concerned with hoeing the earth, and, therefore, his principal festival was celebrated at the beginning of the harvest, an observance that went back to the Gerzean Predynastic period.[12]

In its Dynastic form as depicted on the sculptures of the temple of Medinet Habu, the ithyphallic statue of the god was carried on poles on the shoulders of the priests who were concealed under the hangings decorated with the names of the reigning Pharaoh (Ramesses III), and preceded by a white bull sacred to Min. Behind the bull bundles of lettuces were carried, this being the plant of Min, and in front of the statue walked the king.[13] The god having been installed on a throne under a canopy and offerings made to him, the Pharaoh then cut a sheaf of spelt which he may have offered to the bull to strengthen his virility and avert sterility.[14] But as Min was regarded as a form of Horus, it would seem more likely that when it was said that the sheaf of barley was reaped by the king 'for his father' he was acting in the capacity of the son of Osiris, and, therefore, that he was impersonating Horus.[15] If this were so, the reigning sovereign as the living Horus was equated with Min, who personified the fertility of the newly-sown fields, and performed his ritual function at the Harvest Festival to secure a plentiful supply of the crop through the liberation of generative power to stimulate the growth of the grain by Min-Horus, 'the bull of his mother' (Ka-mutef), the marital substitute of Osiris.

As a priest proclaimed at a crucial moment at the end of the Festival, 'Hail to thee Min, who impregnates his mother! How mysterious is that which thou hast done to her in darkness', it is not improbable that a sacred marriage was enacted by the king and queen at this point in the rite, Min being so very intimately connected with the manner in which the royal line was supposed to have been maintained in Egypt. Moreover, that the Min Festival had affinities with the Coronation ceremony is suggested by the dispatch of four birds to carry to the four cardinal points of the earth the proclamation: 'Horus son of Min and Osiris has assumed the Great Crown of Upper and Lower Egypt'. This can hardly be other than the counterpart of the release of birds to herald the announcement of the accession of a new Pharaoh after his enthronement,[16] though at the Min feast it was the union of the god with the king that was acclaimed, not the sovereign's actual accession. The state celebrated the reaping of the crops in conjunction with the worship of a god who symbolized the harmonious interlocking of nature and society in a divine source of fertility independent of the chances and changes of the seasonal sequence, and infinitely more dynamic than Osiris.

The New Year festival in Mesopotamia

In Mesopotamia the rise and fall of the rivers was too precarious to be a reliable index for the determination of the calendrical festivals. Recourse had to be made, therefore, to the periodicity of nature and the recurrent decline in and renewal of life as these were observed in the rhythm of the natural course of events. Even so, they were not regarded as natural processes, since they were thought to be under supernatural control and all that this involved in the ritual order. Consequently, the calendrical round of fast and festival, of mourning and rejoicing, represented the collective effort of the community to effect a safe passage from one phase to another, beset as the critical junctures were with so many and such great dangers and hazards. Although the king never occupied the dynamic position of the Pharaoh in Egypt, he began his reign on New Year's Day, and, as we have seen, particularly in Assyria, it was he who approached the gods in prayers and incantations by virtue of his supernatural endowment at his birth and his sacred status with its ritual obligations. Therefore, he played a significant part in the Annual Festival.

The Akitu in Babylon

This became most apparent in the spring and autumn celebrations when the new crops were beginning to germinate in the month of Nisan after the rains, and when their products had been safely gathered in at the end of the summer (i.e. Tishri). On both these occasions festivals were held at Ur and Erech, and in other Babylonian cities. It was, however, at Babylon, when Marduk had become the head of the pantheon in the second millennium BC, that the most elaborate and significant rites were performed, the origins of which go back to early Sumerian times. For two thousand years, in fact, the first eleven days of the month of Nisan in the spring were devoted to the enactment of a seasonal drama which became in due course the pattern of the general observance of the Annual Festival in Mesopotamia, until the establishment of Persian rule in the country. Indeed, after the Persian conquest in 539 BC, Cyrus sent his son Cambyses to take part in the celebrations, and during the rule of the Seleucids after the death of Alexander the Great, Antiochus I Soter (281–261 BC) rebuilt the temple called Esagila in which the festival had been held, presumably for the purposes of restoring its rites.

From the ritual Seleucid texts which are now available [17] and which appear to be copies of earlier documents, it seems that the proceedings opened with elaborate purification ceremonies on the second day of the month (Nisan) two hours before dawn. A priest known as *urigallu* rose and washed himself with water from the river before vesting in a linen garment. He then addressed Bel (i.e. Marduk) calling upon him as 'Lord of Kings, light of mankind, and fixer of destinies', to have mercy upon this city, Babylon, and to 'turn his face to the temple Esagila', the secrets of which were known alone to its *urigallu*—priest of the temple of E-kua. When this prayer had been duly recited he opened the doors of the sanctuary and the priests and singers entered to perform the prescribed rites in the presence of Marduk and his consort Zarpanit.

After a break in this very fragmentary part of the text, on the third day three hours after sunrise a metal-worker and a wood-worker were to be summoned and given precious stones and gold from the treasury of Marduk to make two images for the ceremonies on the sixth day, the one constructed of cedar and the other of tamarisk, and ornamented with the stones set in gold. A snake of cedar was held in the left hand of one, and in that of the other a scorpion raising its hand to the son of Marduk. They were clad in red garments and placed in the temple of Daian, the Judge, and given food from the god's table. The next day the *urigallu*, after having recited prayers for the blessing of Marduk on Babylon as before, and adding a petition to Zarpanit to bless the people of the city which honoured her, blessed the courtyard and the Esagila three times. After the priests had carried out their customary rituals, in the late afternoon he recited the *Enuma Elish* (i.e. the Epic of Creation) to Marduk. While this was being done the crown of Anu and the throne of Enlil were covered.

On the fifth day, two hours after sunrise, the customary ablutions and recitations having been performed, the temple was cleansed and sprinkled with water from the Tigris and Euphrates, and the sacred drum was beaten inside, the exorcist remaining in the courtyard. The chapel of Nabu was similarly purified, the doors were smeared with cedar resin, and the sanctuary was censed. An executioner cut off the head of a sheep and the exorcist wiped the sanctuary with the carcase, whilst reciting spells. He then carried the body of the sheep to the river and threw it in the water facing west, while the executioner did likewise with the head of the animal. This accomplished, as both of them were in a tabu condition, they were required to retire to the country until Nabu left the city on the twelfth day of Nisan, and the *urigallu* was forbidden to see the purification of the temple. 'Three and one-third hours after sunrise' he called upon the artisans to bring out the 'Golden Heaven', or baldachino, from the treasury of Marduk, and to cover the chapel of Nabu, Ezuda reciting a cathartic invocation. When this was done the *urigallu* prepared the table of offerings and its contents, and poured out wine in praise of Marduk, exalted among the gods. The craftsmen carried it to the banks of the canal to await the arrival of Nabu in his ship and to escort the king to Esagila. There he entered the shrine of Marduk and allowed the high-priest to remove his crown, ring, sceptre and *harpé*. He then sat upon a chair before the statue of the god and his regalia was placed on a seat in an inner sanctuary from which the *urigallu* emerged, struck him on the cheek and forced him to his knees before the statue. In this posture the king had to make a negative confession:

I have not sinned, O Lord of the land.
I have not been negligent regarding thy divinity;
I have not destroyed Babylon; I have not caused its overthrow;
I have not neglected the temple Esagila; I have not forgotten its ritual;
I have not rained blows on the cheek of a subordinate;
I have not humiliated them;
I cared for Babylon; I have not broken down its walls.

To this, after a break in the text of about five lines, the high-priest replied by a kind of absolution and blessing from Marduk:

Have no fear, . . .
The god Bel [will listen to] your prayer
He will magnify your lordship . . .
He will exalt your kingship.
On the day of the essesu (new moon) . . . festival do . . .
In the festival of the Opening of the Gate purify your hands;
Day and night
[The god Bel] whose city is Babylon, whose temple is Esagila;
Whose dependants are the people of Babylon.
The god Bel will bless you . . . for ever.
He will destroy your enemy, fell your adversary.

The *urigallu* then restored the sceptre, ring, crown and *harpé*, and struck him on the cheek with the intention of making tears flow, this being a sign that Marduk was friendly and ready to destroy his enemies. At sunset he (the *urigallu*) tied together forty straight reeds of three cubits in length bound together with a palm-branch, dug a hole in the court-yard and planted them therein with honey, cream and oil of the best quality. A white bull was placed before the trench, and the king kindled a fire in the middle of it. They both recited a prayer, the contents of which are lost apart from the opening lines addressed to the bull of Aru as the shivering light illuminating the darkness.

While all this was taking place in the Esagila the city was in a state of increasing commotion because Marduk was alleged to have been imprisoned in the 'mountain' of the underworld, with its reciprocal effects in the desolation of the country evidenced in the annual drought. Mock battles were fought for the purpose of securing his release and the renewal of vegetation. This was accomplished on the sixth or seventh day by his son Nabu assuming the role of the Goddess Inanna-Ishtar in the Tammuz cult when she found the god in the 'mountain' and by her intervention was miraculously restored and emerged from the nether regions. Thereupon vegetation revived with the first winter rains. The warring groups depicted on the seals of the third millennium BC[18] no doubt portray conflicts similar to those re-enacted in Babylon during the Akitu Festival, to free Marduk from his mountain-grave and recall him from death by means of life-giving water, while the state of mourning reflected the lamentations in the Sumerian liturgies during the wanderings of the desolate Mother in the barren fields and sheep-folds, and her wailing for her lost son and lover in her temple.[19] It may be presumed, therefore, that this cult drama was of considerable antiquity in Mesopotamia, continuing the Sumerian tradition of the death and restoration of the Young god of vegetation.

The Bit Akitu rites
This is confirmed by the subsequent course of the Akkadian Akitu, as the events can be determined from the scattered references in the other texts.[20] After the reinstatement of the king by the *urigallu* and the liberation of Marduk in his Tammuz role, on the eighth day of Nisan the statues of the gods were assembled in the Chamber of Destinies in order of precedence, for the purpose of conferring their combined strength upon the restored god for the conquest of the hostile forces, and to give him the right to determine 'the destinies'; that is to say, to renew fruitfulness and life during the forthcoming year. The king,

holding his sceptre in his hand, proceeded to the great hall to receive a fresh outpouring of divine power. 'Grasping the hand of the great lord Marduk', he went in procession from the Esagila with the other gods along the sacred way to the Festival House (*Bit Akitu*) in the outskirts of the city, like the victorious armies of the gods in conflict with Tiamat, depicted by Sennacherib on the copper doors of the *Bit Akitu*.[21] As Sennacherib caused his own figure to be inserted in the chariot of Ashur (i.e. the Assyrian form of Marduk), probably he regarded himself as the personification of the 'victorious prince' who had conquered the forces of evil (i.e. Tiamat), the primeval battle being enacted ritually in the Festival House. Thus, at the conclusion of these rites a banquet was held to celebrate the triumph of Marduk, and all that this involved for the well-being of the country.[22]

On the tenth day of Nisan Marduk and those who had taken part in the procession went into residence in the *Bit Akitu*, and the next day a special festival was held in the Hall. It may have been then that the conflict was given dramatic representation, concluding with the afore-mentioned banquet, before a return was made to the Esagila where, as we have seen, there is reason to think that the king and queen engaged in a sacred marriage in a chamber decorated with greenery (the *gigunu*) on one of the stages of the ziqqurat. If this were so, the rites must have been directed to the maintenance of the fertility of the fields, the flocks and mankind, since fecundity in nature depended upon the union of the Goddess and the Young virile god, enacted on earth by that of the queen and her consort.

The determination of Destiny
There is every indication that the Akitu festival was originally an agricultural cult drama celebrated in all the principal Mesopotamian cities in almost the same form, to ensure abundance and prosperity for the ensuing year. Under urban conditions, however, it tended to acquire a rather different significance, the emphasis being on the 'determination of the destinies'. Thus, on the twelfth of Nisan the gods reassembled in the Chamber of Destinies to ratify the divine decree concerning the fate of society. Moreover, this aspect of the festival was duplicated on the eighth and twelfth days, as in the creation story where the gods were said to have assembled both after Marduk was elected their leader, and again after his victory over Tiamat and her forces, when it was decided to create the human race to supply their physical needs through the offering of sacrifices to provide them with nourishment. It was upon the fulfilment of their obligations as the servants of the gods and the

Goddess that the fates were determined. Being fundamentally pessimistic in their attitude to the course of events in the natural order, the
Babylonians at the beginning of the year engaged in a *rite de passage*
calculated to counteract the hazards of an unpredictable situation at
the moment when rejuvenation in nature was in the balance, and,
indeed, in jeopardy. Unlike the Egyptians, they were more concerned
about the present fate of society than about their own personal destinies
in the hereafter. Therefore they concentrated their attention at the
New Year Festival upon the establishment of the cosmic order in its
various forms and phases against the background of the epic of creation
and all that this implied for mankind, good and evil alike, together
with that which had been accomplished by the due performance of the
Akitu rites culminating in the sacred marriage.

The Festival concluded with the final Fixing of the Destinies before
the gods returned to their cities and men to the cultivation of the
revitalized soil in sure and certain hope that now all would be well
during the forthcoming seasons. So important was this annual observance for the country as a whole that it was celebrated in most of the
cities—at Ur and Nippur in the third millennium BC, and subsequently
at Ashur, Harran, Dilbat, Erech, Nineveh and Arbela, as well as at
Babylon[23]—though it is about the Akitu in the capital that we are best
informed. Since, however, neither the kings, the administration nor the
community at large had an assured and completely secure position
rooted and grounded in a transcendental unifying and stabilizing
divine world standing over the mutable order on earth, gods rose to
pre-eminence by the transference of political jurisdiction from one city
to another—e.g. from Nippur to Babylon. The gods and their status,
therefore, were at the mercy of the ever-changing fortunes of their cult-
centres. The New Year Festival gave a sense of stability in such a
nebulous situation, inasmuch as it was celebrated annually in many
places with the same rites and theme enacted for the same purposes,
whether the divinity were Tammuz, Marduk, Ashur, or any other
vegetation god. This continuity in the myth and its ritual established a
harmony with nature in perpetuity, when the renewal of life was the
most urgent need of the moment.

The Baal cult drama in Syria
That the Ugaritic mythological texts had a similar significance in the
temples at Ras Shamra, in connexion with cult-rituals, is very probable.
Though this has been disputed the fact remains, as we have seen,* that

*Chap. IV, p. 122.

the death and resurrection theme is a recurrent feature in the Baal-Anat cycle, couched in terms of a struggle between two opposed forces in which the antagonists represent personifications of the figures who played the leading roles in the seasonal drama elsewhere in western Asia. Thus, it was in the heat of summer that Aleyan, the Storm-god and Weather-god, was killed by his adversary Mot, the lord of the underworld and the sinister power of death, drought and sterility, and while Aleyan-Baal was in the nether regions vegetation withered and the ground became parched and arid. On his eventual restoration to the kingship and the overthrow of the throne of Mot, the drought ended and fecundity was re-established on the earth.*[24] But although this suggests the recurrence of the decline and restoration of growth in the Syrian agricultural year, interpreted in terms of the struggle between life and death in the customary setting of the cult drama, as the climatic conditions in Palestine were not identical with those in Mesopotamia, the Canaanite rites assumed a character of their own.

It would seem that the Tammuz theme was behind them, even though they may have been celebrated periodically, perhaps septennially as Gordon suggests[25] (though this is by no means certain), rather than annually. The conflict between Baal and Prince Sea may have been enacted at the autumnal festival when the rains were due to begin, Baal playing a role not unlike that of Marduk in his victory over Tiamat in the Babylonian *Enuma elish*. The recurrence of widespread continual drought and famine was an ever-present fear in Palestine, being always in the offing as the Elijah stories and others in the Old Testament indicate.[26] This danger was calculated to produce a state of tension when the seasonal rains were pending, however much its absence may have been taken for granted as normal at other times. Therefore, since Baal represented the wet and more fertile part of the year, his death was equated with the dry months and the languishing of the crops, notwithstanding the ripening of the summer fruits (e.g. figs and grapes) under these conditions. It is the grain that matters most, and wheat and barley require the maintenance of the climatic rhythm in nature without any interruption or abnormality, be it in the dry or the wet season. Moreover, the fact that bad years were exceptional and serious drought when it did occur was prolonged (often apparently of seven years' duration or thereabouts) and devastating, made the emotional reaction so intense that no risks were likely to be taken to avoid such a catastrophe. It was this which found expression in the Danel myth, when the hero cursed the ground where his son had been

*Chap. IV, p. 122.

murdered with seven years of drought, by withholding the life-giving waters which Baal controlled and personified.[27] But the Sabbatical cycle does not rule out the probability of an annual autumnal festival in which the dominant motif and theme were those of the cult drama in its vegetation aspects, directed against the recurrent danger of sterility resulting from unseasonable drought, and also from plagues and pestilences, such as locusts and blight and other similar calamities.[28] Thus, in the Ugaritic texts, although Baal was said to have conquered and destroyed Mot, yet he was not finally and completely defeated since he was represented as returning to the fray in due course like the periodic droughts and famines.[29]

Notwithstanding these divergencies, the Baal-Anat cycle in the Ugaritic mythology conforms in broad outline to the general pattern of fertility rituals centred in the vegetation theme associated with various phases in the agricultural sequence in Syria. Unfortunately we know little about the actual ceremonies performed in these rites. Two lambs were offered at the time of the new moon, and at the dedication of Baal's temple the seventy sons of Anat feasted upon 'oxen, sheep, fatlings, yearling calves and goats' at a heavenly banquet[30] which may have had its counterpart on earth in an annual sacrificial offering to the gods when the episode was recited. But conjectures of this kind throw little light on the nature and purpose of the Canaanite calendrical ritual. The autumnal festival would seem to have followed the normal course, beginning with a period of purification and purgation before the renewal ceremonies were performed to secure the rainfall required to revitalize the ground and its crops, which reached their climax in a sacred marriage of the king and queen in their customary roles, having been enthroned. But while a common purpose and pattern can be discerned in the mythology and its ritual in the form of a cult drama, care has to be taken to avoid generalizations based on similarities, without giving full weight to very real differences in the times and modes of presentation which all these may imply in the underlying function and significance of the actions performed.

The Yahwistic cultus in Israel

This is very apparent in the Hebrew festivals and their cultus. That they owed much to their Canaanite background was the inevitable consequence of the conquest of Palestine by the invading Israelites, however much the traditions may have been reinterpreted in the Deuteronomic literature of the seventh century BC and onwards. During the long process of settlement in the land of their adoption, the Hebrew tribes took over the Bronze Age shrines with their firmly established ritual observances and adapted them to their own requirements. Although the origins of Yahweh are obscure, he was certainly not a vegetation deity, even though possibly he may have been known in Canaan as a minor divinity under the names of *Yau* or *Yo* before the Israelite occupation. Thus, on a cuneiform tablet at Taanach, dated between 2000 and 3000 BC, the name *Ahi-yahu* occurs, and the abbreviation *Yo* appears on the handles of jars at a later date in Palestine, as well as in the form *yw* at Ugarit, if Virolleaud is correct.[31] If Yahweh was in fact a minor deity among the Phoenicians, it is not difficult to understand why Jezebel, herself a Phoenician princess, should have resented the substitution of an insignificant Tyrian god for her great Aleyan-Baal in northern Israel. But however this may have been, primarily Yahweh has every appearance of having been a desert deity who was possibly worshipped among the Kenites before he was encountered by Moses,[32] and as the Phoenicians like the Israelites probably came from the deserts south of Palestine, if the two peoples had a common home in that locality this would explain the similarity between their ritual practices and the recurrence of a divine name among both of them having much the same root but a different status. In any case, it is hardly likely that there was originally a great deal of difference between the attitude of the Hebrews to their national god and that of the surrounding tribes to their respective deities, Baal, Chemosh, or Milcom, however exalted a particular god might be in his own territory. Therefore, the cultus and its calendrical observances would be very similar if not identical.

Nevertheless, the tribes that were with Moses in the desert and had inherited the Sinai-Horeb tradition* doubtless brought with them their own modes of worship of Yahweh with a long history behind them going back to the pre-Mosaic period, if the J document of the Pentateuch is substantially correct in ascribing the beginnings of Yahwism to a very remote age, assigned to the threshold of the human race doubtless because their origins were lost in obscurity beyond memory. But when Yahwism was adopted by a section of the Hebrew tribes, it can hardly be supposed that it did not undergo a very considerable process of adaptation to bring it into line with the memorable experience of the deliverance from Egypt and all that this involved and implied.

The Passover

It was this significant event that was commemorated at the Spring Festival, which became known as the Passover, celebrated at the full

*cf. Chap, I, p. 37.

moon nearest to the vernal equinox when the firstlings of the lambing season were offered, no doubt originally to the fertility-god of the flocks in a lunar context. Although the origins of the festival and its original purpose are obscure, 'the one thing that looms clear through the haze of this weird tradition,' as Frazer says, 'is the memory of a great massacre of firstborn,'[33] for its outstanding feature is the annual commemoration of the historic night on which the angel of Yahweh was alleged to have set forth on his bloody campaign against the Egyptians.[34] But the various accounts of the festival have been so overlaid with later ideas brought into relation with the Exodus tradition, that it is by no means easy to separate the several strands in the complex pattern that has emerged. That it was connected primarily with the sacrifice of the firstlings is highly probable, as is indicated by the injunction to slay a male lamb, kid or goat without blemish on the 14th of Nisan at the opening of the rainy season in the spring. Whether or not in the remote background lay an offering of the firstborn of man, as Frazer suggests, later 'softened into the vicarious sacrifice of a lamb and the payment of a ransom for each child,' transferred in the narrative to the killing of the firstborn children of the Egyptians, the *Pesach*, or pastoral rite, is represented as an offering of firstlings. In the later composite observance when it was combined with the agricultural *Massoth*, or Feast of Unleavened Bread,[35] the Paschal lamb was ordered to be eaten in haste with bitter herbs and unleavened bread, so that it should all be consumed and every vestige burnt up before sunrise. Furthermore, the prohibition that the flesh of the victim was not to be eaten raw would seem to indicate, as Robertson Smith contended, that originally the 'living flesh' with the warm blood was consumed sacramentally.[36]

The sprinkling of the blood on the lintel and door-posts of the houses where the fugitive Israelites were supposed to have concealed themselves was also a later addition, derived from the practice of smearing houses with blood as a protective device to repel demons.[37] This rite clearly has nothing to do with the Paschal festival as such and the explanations given for it are inconsistent, the 'destroyer' and Yahweh being confused.[38] Furthermore, it is not clear whether it was to be a sign to the Israelites or to the 'angel'.[39] As Buchanan Gray has pointed out, 'either the story is intended to correct a popular conception of Yahweh, or to counteract a popular recognition of other divine powers than Yahweh.'[40] In any case, the apotropaic function of the Paschal blood ritual is hardly in doubt.

The *Massoth*, or Feast of Unleavened Bread, on the other hand, belonged essentially to the agricultural tradition, as an offering of the first-fruits, and in all probability it was taken over from the Canaanites and tacked on to the pastoral *Pesach*. That the two ordinances were originally distinct is indicated in the story of the supplementary Passover service in the second month, recorded in the book of Numbers (ix. 1–14), for those prevented by ceremonial uncleanness or absence from their homes from taking part in the festival on the 14th of Nisan. Here no mention is made of the Feast of Unleavened Bread, the first-born rite being regarded as the earlier institution before the two had coalesced. But although at first they were distinct they were both celebrated at the time of barley harvest,[41] when in Babylonia the Annual Festival in honour of Shamash, the Sun-god, was held in Sippar on the 7th of Nisan. Therefore, if it was under Mesopotamian influence that the *Massoth* was observed among the Canaanites, it may have been originally a solar festival, whereas the *Pesach* had a lunar significance, to ensure the fertility of the flocks and herds, the Moon-god being a fertility deity.[42]

Against the precedence given to the pastoral *Pesach* in the desert tradition, with its close association with the redemption of the firstborn of man and beast and the Exodus story, whatever may have been its actual origins, in the J document and in Deuteronomy the predominant observance was the Feast of Unleavened Bread, when at the beginning of the barley harvest a sheaf of the new crop (*'omer*) was waved before Yahweh on the second day, to promote the fertility of the crops in the forthcoming season.[43] Seven days later, at the end of the barley harvest and the beginning of the wheat harvest, the 'wave-loaves' made of fine flour and baked with leaven were offered at the Feast of Weeks (*Shabu'oth*).[44]

These agricultural festivals, which all are agreed were introduced in the Hebrew calendar from Canaanite sources at their arrival in Palestine, were unquestionably first-fruit vegetation rituals and were combined with the pastoral celebrations to form a composite Spring Festival. Since they had both been observed at the same time of year (i.e. in the month of Nisan), they readily became a seasonal sacrificial and sacramental rite for a common purpose in which a number of allied, though formerly distinct, primitive practices associated with the annual Spring Festival were united and reinterpreted as a commemoration of the great deliverance from Egypt.[45] These various strands were brought together and under Deuteronomic influence the J and E stories were revised and combined in a composite narrative, to which the Priestly sections were added after the Exile. That such an amalgam contains many discrepancies and contradictory interpretations that originally belonged to very different traditions is not surprising. The oblation and eating of the Paschal lamb, sheep or goat remained, however, the principal feature until its place was taken by a roast shank-bone when animal sacrifice was abrogated in Judaism, thereby perpetuating the primacy of the blood rite. Moreover, it continued to be essentially a domestic observance, and even when in post-exilic times it was celebrated in Jerusalem and the victims were slain in the Temple and the blood offered at the altar, small groups of ten or twenty of the pilgrims assembled for the sacred communal meal. After the house in which they had foregathered had been carefully swept to remove any trace of leaven (i.e. sour dough left over from the previous day's baking which was associated with corruption), the unleavened cakes known as *Mazuoth* were eaten with bitter herbs, the story of the deliverance from Egypt was recited, and the Hallel (i.e. Psalms cxiii–cxvii) was sung.

After the destruction of the Temple in AD 70 the sacrificial and sacerdotal aspects of the Passover necessarily ceased, and the observance assumed a domestic character. The head of each family, surrounded by his children and guests, gave the prescribed explanation of the rite in answer to the question 'why is this night different from other nights?'[46] to emphasize the deeper spiritual significance of the commemoration of the deliverance of the ancestral Hebrews from oppression in Egypt. An element of festivity, in hopeful anticipation of the restoration of Israel, was and has been maintained in the later annual observance of the Paschal Feast in its domestic guise, shorn of the grimmer side of the original rite and its subsequent priestly slaying of the victims and the oblation of the blood at the altar, with all its lunar, apotropaic and vegetation calendrical associations in the Mesopotamian and Canaanite background of the Spring Festival. When the celebration was revived and centralized before the Exile in the reign of Josiah,[47] the rites as practised after the settlement in Palestine in the time of the Judges underwent a good deal of transformation to bring them into line with the tradition of the Exodus that they then commemorated. This was further developed in the Priestly additions and reinterpretations after the Exile,[48] as well as in the Temple ritual, until after AD 70 it became a domestic observance, thereby losing to a considerable extent its sacrificial significance.

The Feast of Tabernacles

In the earliest references to the Passover in those sections of the book of Exodus known as 'The Book of the Covenant' (chapters xx. 22–xxiii. 19(E), and xxxiv. 18–26(J)), the Feast of *Massoth*, or Unleavened

Bread, is described as having been held in the month of Abib, the Babylonian Nisan, at the beginning of the spring. But the Hebrew agricultural year commenced in the autumn when the Feast of Tabernacles, or *Sukkôth*, was held[49] in the month of Ethanim, described after the Exile as 'the seventh month' (Tishri), when the vintage had been completed. The connexion with the ingathering of the grape-harvest shows that it was borrowed from the Canaanite rather than from the desert tradition, and that it coincided with the autumnal equinox, when the harvest moon was full and the agricultural work of the season had come to an end. In the pre-exilic community it was this observance that was really the New Year Festival, and when the Babylonian autumnal rites at 'the going out of the year' continued to be observed, although Nisan or Abib now became 'the beginning of months' when the Passover was held.[50] Therefore, like the Babylonians, Israel virtually kept a dual observance of the New Year, the one at 'the going out of the year' (*Rosh hashshanah*) in the autumn in Tishri when the ingathering of harvest was celebrated;[51] the other in the spring at the beginning of the barley harvest.[52]

The autumnal festival marked the end of the agricultural year, when the rains were due to begin to revivify the earth and cause it to bring forth abundantly in the months ahead. Therefore, its rites were directed to the accomplishment of this end, upon which the well-being of the community depended, and in the post-exilic book of Zechariah it is affirmed that 'whoso of all the families of the earth goeth not up to Jerusalem to worship the King, the Lord of Hosts, upon them the rain shall not come'.[53] This forward look of the Feast of Tabernacles in connexion with 'the former rains' is suggested in the lists of agricultural operations set forth in the so-called Gezer Calendar, assigned to the tenth or ninth century BC, beginning with that of the Ingathering at the commencement of the rainy season.[54]

In short, the autumnal festival in Israel, later called the Feast of Tabernacles or Booths, was held at the turn of the year for much the same purposes as the corresponding festival in the agricultural ritual among the Canaanites and elsewhere in western Asia. Behind it lay the drama of the dying and reviving Year-god, however much the theme may have been modified under Yahwistic influence and made to conform to the status of the god of Israel standing over and above creation and its processes as a transcendent rather than as a vegetation deity. But the belief in Yahweh's lordship in the natural order carried with it his control both of the nation's vicissitudes and of such natural events as the rainfall.[55] This is particularly apparent in the psalms in which the enthronement of Yahweh is celebrated.[56] Whether or not they were an integral part of the New Year liturgy is still a matter of dispute.[57]

Thus, Mowinckel maintained that they were composed for use at the Feast of Tabernacles, at the autumnal New Year Festival marking the annual commemoration and re-enactment of the victory of Yahweh over the forces of primeval chaos, reflected in his domination over the kings and nations of the earth. This was symbolized by the carrying of the Ark in solemn procession to the Temple where he was acclaimed as the universal triumphant sovereign Lord of the universe,[58] and his blessing was sought on the fortunes of the forthcoming year. This was secured by the renewal of the covenant (*bĕrith*, i.e. cultus) with the House of David. It is true, as we have seen,* that the king in the Hebrew monarchy was never the dynamic centre in the nation that Pharaoh was in Egypt, but the relationship between David and his successors with Yahweh was unquestionably an important factor in the stabilization of the cultus and the social structure, and in maintaining right relations between Yahweh and his people and the natural order (i.e. rain and fertility).[59]

It is unfortunate, however, that most of the evidence based on the 'enthronement psalms' comes from sources which hitherto have been regarded as post-exilic, though there is good reason to think that Psalm lxxxi, which is parallel to Psalm xcv, was composed for use at the Feast of Ingathering at the full moon of Tishri,[60] whatever may be said about some of the rest of the collection. If they did in fact originally belong to the New Year liturgy, as is by no means improbable, they must have lost a good deal of their significance when they became Sabbath Psalms in the later post-exilic worship, the New Year Festival having then become associated with the Kingdom of God.

Although many of the psalms listed by Mowinckel may be subsequent to the Exile, some at least are prior to this event, going back to the days of the monarchy (e.g. xlvii, xciii, xcv–c), and they may have influenced the thought of the Deutero-Isaiah at the end of the Exile. The theme is that of the domination of Yahweh over the physical universe manifest in the seasonal rains and over the prosperity of the nation, along the lines so familiar in the cult drama in the Mesopotamian and Ugaritic texts. The appropriate occasion for their recital would be the celebration of the triumph of Yahweh as the universal King at the Annual Festival, when his victory over the forces of death and destruction was enacted in a triumphal procession, as described in several of the psalms (xxiv,

*cf. Chap. IV, p. 125.

xlvii, lxviii), reminiscent of the progress of the Ark from the house of Obed Edom to its abode on Mount Zion, but shorn of its ecstatic dance in which David engaged.[61]

Of the details of the pre-exilic Feast of *'Asiph*, or Ingathering, no information is available, but in its later form as the Feast of Booths or Tabernacles, recorded in the Rabbinic literature, a dance was held with blazing torches on the second night in the Court of the Women in the Temple, together with a procession round the altar each day of the festival in which branches of palm were carried and waved and a fruit like a lemon (*ethrog*) was held as a fertility charm.[62] These may be assumed to have been survivals of the earlier harvest observance at the end of the agricultural season when the moon was at its fullness, having a solar as well as a lunar background. Thus, a procession of priests proceeded to the eastern gate at sunrise and turned westwards facing the Temple, as a protest against the former custom of facing the rising sun when Yahweh took up his abode in his tabernacle on Mount Zion as the King of glory.[63]

The booths made of greenery have been compared with the *gigunu* in the Babylonian Akitu festival connected with the royal sacred marriage as the consummation of the rites, and it is possible that a similar fertility observance was an integral element in the earlier Hebrew ritual.[64] Thus, as we have seen, Yahweh was associated with Anat in the Elephantine Papyri, presumably as his consort, and the worship of the Queen of Heaven was firmly established in Israel before the Exile.[65] Again, libations of water drawn from the pool of Siloam were poured out from a golden vessel by a priest at the altar each day of the festival, originally doubtless as a rain-making ceremony since in the Talmud it is affirmed that the waters were offered to Yahweh on the Feast of Sukkoth 'that the rains of the year may be blessed to you'.[66]

Although the dominant note in the festival was that of joy and victory, there was an underlying minor key of sorrow and weeping.[67] It was at this season, in Ezekiel's vision, women were seen weeping for Tammuz in the Temple,[68] and in Israel there was, it would seem, a corresponding ritual of mourning, as is suggested in the 'lamentation psalms', the counterpart of the Tammuz liturgies.[69] In the first instance these rites were expressions of sorrow for the Young god, so fundamental in the vegetation cult drama and its weather motif, in relation to the fertilization of the earth by the seasonal rains.

The Day of Atonement

Moreover, closely associated with the Feast of Booths were the very primitive expiation rites for the nation and all its members on the first day of the seventh month. According to Ezekiel the sanctuary was ritually cleansed twice a year, on the first day of the first month as well as on the first day of the seventh month.[70] This, however, is the only reference to a twofold purification. In the post-exilic account of the event the ancient symbolism of the blood as the life was the most prominent feature,[71] interpreted in terms of an act of reconciliation between Israel and its god which reached its climax in the rites performed on the tenth day of Tishri. In the Levitical narrative in its present form, three stages in the development of the rite can be detected. The first belongs to the middle of the fourth century BC, recorded in chapter xvi, 3, 5–10, describing the simple act of atonement. The priest was to sacrifice a bullock for a sin-offering for himself and the rest of the priesthood and a ram for a burnt-offering. Then he was to 'set before Yahweh' two he-goats. Lots were cast upon them to determine which of the two was to be assigned to Yahweh as a sin-offering, and which was to be presented to a goat demon, Azazel, as the sin-receiver. Yahweh's victim was then slain, and Azazel's live goat was dispatched to the desert carrying with it the uncleanness of the sanctuary and its servants.

This expiation in the next stage (verses 11–28) was transformed into an elaborate cathartic ritual with detailed regulations concerning censings, the manipulation of the blood of the bullock on the mercy-seat in the Holy of Holies, and on the altar, 'to make atonement for the holy place, and because of the uncleanness of the children of Israel'. No mention is made of the casting of lots over the two goats, but the transference of the iniquities of the people to the one to be driven forth was effected by the priest laying his hands upon its head and confessing all their sins over it to bear them away to a solitary land. The carcases of the bullock and of the goat slain as a sin-offering were to be taken without the camp (i.e. the city)* and destroyed by fire. The man allotted this task became tabu, having contracted ritual uncleanness by his contact with the sacred victims, and so he was required to make a thorough ablution of himself and his clothes before he returned to the community, lest he should be a source of contagion. Finally (verses 29–34a) a note was added explaining that the Day of Atonement was to be regarded as a 'high sabbath', set apart as a fast for the people 'to afflict their souls', and 'to do no manner of work'.

*The scene is laid in the desert because the observance is referred back to the time of Moses and Aaron to give a divine origin and sanction to the rites as they were to be performed in the Temple.

Although the rite is only described in the book of Leviticus—the *rituale* of post-exilic Judaism—and its significance is interpreted in spiritual concepts in the Rabbinical literature, the ceremonial was obviously based on the primitive conception of evil as a substantive pollution, or miasma, removable by the sprinkling of blood, censing and lustration, and transferable to a sin-carrier in the form of an animal described as a 'scapegoat'. The blood made atonement by reason of the *nephesh*, or soul-substance, contained in it[72] as a life-renewing agent, and applied to cover up or wipe away the defilement, and confer non-moral holiness by its sanctifying power and atoning efficacy. The smoke of the incense and the holy water were endowed with the same numinous potency, while the 'scapegoat', like the bird in the purification of the leper,[73] was a vehicle for the removal of the pollution transferred to it.

The ceremonial of the Day of Atonement, therefore, and its underlying beliefs must go back to a very remote period when sin and its removal were regarded in this way. In post-exilic Israel it was Yahweh alone who could forgive sin and pardon iniquity, and he demanded a clean heart and a broken spirit.[74] Without these essential requirements the blood of bulls and the ashes of a heifer could not avail, and so in the later literature just as the daily sacrifice was held to expiate unintentional breaches of the Law (the Torah), the Day of Atonement piacula removed *ex opere operato* sins committed with a 'high hand', but always on the condition that the offering was accompanied by repentance.

A violation of the divine law was an affront to the holiness of Yahweh, and, therefore, genuine penitence and ceremonial amendment were required to effect expiation when there had been any brⁿach of the prescribed rules of conduct and worship, whether in the sphere of ethics, theology or ritual, intentionally or accidentally. Animals and inanimate objects like the sanctuary and its vessels were always liable to the pollution, as well as human beings, and so they required the same purification as the priests who ministered at the altar. The 'scapegoat' was laden with *all* the sins of the nation, ethical and ceremonial, human and non-human alike, to remove these harmful influences wherever they might occur. This was done at the 'turn of the year' in conjunction with the New Year Festival in the autumn, because it was the most appropriate occasion for the putting away of defilement contracted during the year that had come to an end, in order that a fresh start might be made annually with a completely clean slate. To this end the Day of Atonement was set apart as a 'Sabbath of great sanctity' on which work of every description was absolutely forbidden and a fast ordered to be strictly observed.[75] For the benefit of those who were prevented from taking part in the Temple rites, provision was made in the synagogue liturgy for special confessions of sin and prayers for forgiveness corresponding to the penitential aspects of the ritual of the high-priest in the Holy of Holies in the Temple. When the ceremonial expiation automatically ceased with the destruction of the Temple in AD 70, this symbolic synagogue service alone remained to perpetuate the annual expiation and piaculum on the tenth day of the seventh month.

The Purulli-*festival in Anatolia*

In Anatolia what appears to have been the New Year Festival, known as *Purulliyas*, probably a Hattian derivation, *purulli* meaning 'of the earth', was celebrated in the spring, and since at it the myth of the slaying of the dragon Illuyankas by the Weather-god of Hatti was enacted, it would appear to have centred in a ritual combat. So important was this annual event that, as we have seen,* Mursilis II felt compelled to return to Hattusas to celebrate it there, even though he had already performed its rites elsewhere in honour of the Weather-god of Hatti and his counterpart of Zippalanda;[76] there was no single cult-centre like Jerusalem in Judah after the Josiah Reformation and in the post-exilic community. Although the details of the ceremonial and its significance have not yet been determined from the mutilated thirty-two tablets recording the ritual, they contain the cult-legend in two versions.[77] The first relates the struggle of the god with his adversary, the dragon, ending, after a temporary defeat, in the slaying of the monster with the help of the gods and the goddess Inaras, who employed as her agent one Hupasiya. Here the main story finishes, but the text goes on to narrate how Inaras built Hupasiya a house on a cliff in the land of Tarukka as a reward, but instructed him not to open the window on any account lest he should see his wife and children. After twenty days he disobeyed the command and presumably paid the penalty either of death or expulsion, but the text is broken at this point and so the conclusion of the story can only be conjectured.

The second version is more elaborate. Illuyankas vanquished the Weather-god and took away his heart and eyes at the first fight. To recover them and avenge his defeat, he took a mortal woman and begat a son whom eventually he married to the daughter of the dragon. The son was instructed to demand as a bride price his father's eyes and heart. Having secured them, he restored them to his divine father,

*Chap. IV, p. 128f.

157

thereby giving the Weather-god renewed strength and so enabling him to slay Illuyankas. Then, at his own request, the son was killed because he had betrayed the laws of kindred and hospitality by becoming a member of the dragon's family by his marriage.[78]

These two dragon stories with their points of contact with the Babylonian epic of creation and the Egyptian Osiris, Isis, Horus myths, were recited at the *Purulli*-Festival at the beginning of the dry season when the winter rains had ceased and drought was imminent. Dr Gaster, in fact, regards the myth as the libretto of an ancient Hittite ritual drama, comparable to that celebrating the victory of Marduk over Tiamat or of Horus over Seth, and the Rogationtide rites and Mumming play in Europe.[79] In all these the dominant theme was a sacred combat between the forces of good and evil, personified in the victory of the beneficent Weather-god responsible for the rainfall over the dragon of drought or flood. Hupasiyas is supposed to have had sexual relations with the Goddess Inaras to enable the Weather-god to acquire strength for the fight, while his incarceration in the house was to conserve his supernatural power. The request of the son of the god to be slain in the second version is explained as the betrayal of the sacred laws of hospitality, because he allowed his father-in-law to be killed while he was in his house. The concluding fragment is interpreted as a ritual epilogue describing the procession of the gods and goddesses and the installation of the Weather-god in the temple at Nerik, the cult-centre of another Storm-deity, as in the Babylonian Akitu.

Whether or not the myth was the libretto of a cult drama, it unquestionably represents the legend of the festival as the text affirms, and it conforms to the Babylonian-Egyptian theme, and that of the Greek Typhon myth where Zeus, after losing his sinews, regained his strength and slew his enemy with the help of the dragon's daughter. The king was the celebrant and the royal ritual recorded on the festival tablets follows the usual procedure. The king and queen are described as escorted from the palace to the temple by a bodyguard and servants, with statue-bearers and heralds. There they kneel before the sacred spear, and the king is given the cloth covering it. A banquet is then prepared and the dishes are brought in ceremonially, the cloth covering them being removed by the king. The ritual meal then doubtless proceeded in the usual manner, though at this point the texts are silent; however, sacrifices are said to have been offered at the end of the observance.[80]

In the autumn (i.e. the eighth month in the Hittite calendar), at a city called Gursamassa, in the presence of the cult-image of the god

Yarris, there was feasting, singing and a mock battle in which 'the men of Hatti', carrying bronze weapons, engaged in combat with 'the men of Masa' bearing weapons of reed. When the 'men of Hatti' prevailed, they were said to seize a victim and dedicate him to the god; they then carried his image to the temple and poured out libations before the altar.[81] It was, however, at the beginning of the year at the vernal equinox that the principal festival was held in honour of the Storm-god and Weather-god, enacting the heavenly gathering at which all the gods assembled to engage in a ritual banquet and 'pronounce the life of the king and queen, and the life of heaven and earth',[82] as in its Babylonian counterpart. As has been considered,* it is by no means improbable that it was celebrated at the great rock-shelter at Yasilikaya near Boghazköy adorned with the bas-reliefs of the procession of gods and goddesses and also because of its associations with the Weather-god and his consort, the Young god Sharma and the daughter and grand-daughter of the Sun-goddess of Arinna and the vegetation deity Telipinu.

The so-called 'Festival of the Year', however, about which very little is known, does not appear to have been the Spring Festival, as it was celebrated by the king in the winter months, though on the Anatolian plateau wintry conditions continued much longer than in the more temperate regions. Its title suggests that it was in fact a New Year Festival normally celebrated by the king, but until the very large collection of Hittite tablets dealing with the festival rituals have been read and studied, so far as this is likely to be possible in their fragmentary condition, their precise purpose and significance cannot be ascertained. That their celebration was a principal preoccupation of the kings is apparent from the repeated references to their journeyings from shrine to shrine for these purposes.[83] As they frequently bear the names of the seasons or the months of the year they must have been calendrical rituals, and they all seem to have conformed to much the same procedure, which included preliminary ablutions and the investiture of the king and queen in a special building used as a 'sacristy', before proceeding to pour libations at the table of offerings, the hearth, the throne, the window and the bolt of the door in the temple. The ceremonial meal in the presence of the gods followed, and since at it the king is said to 'drink the god', it probably had some kind of sacramental significance, especially as the wine and beer were partaken of by the officiants and those who were assembled as a sort of 'audience' or 'congregation'.[84]

*Chap. III, pp. 93, 94.

Rural rites and festivals in Greece

Passing from Anatolia to the Aegean, we are much better informed. As regards the Greek evidence, the greater part of the agricultural community engaged in cult dramas at the times of ploughing, sowing and reaping, to control the processes of vegetation at these important and often critical junctures in the seasonal sequence. Nearly all the early Greek festivals were, in fact, agrarian, as ancient Greece was essentially a country of peasants and herdsmen. As such, long before the urban developments and commercial enterprises arose, the foundations of the cultus were laid. The Greeks, subsisting as they did on the fruits of the earth, depended upon the weather for their food supply; corn, wheat or barley, with figs, olives and a little wine, were the staples of their diet. It was mainly on festal occasions, like seed-time and harvest, when the people assembled at sanctuaries to perform the rustic rites appropriate to the season, that communal feasts known as *panegyreis* were held. Then animals were slain for sacrificial purposes and eaten to the accompaniment of music, dancing, merrymaking and games, originally religious in their character and setting (Fig. 67). Thus, Aristotle says that in early times sacrifices and assemblies took place chiefly after the ingathering of harvest, when there was more leisure to engage in these festivities.[85]

It was from this seasonal routine of agricultural rites that the Greek calendar emerged and was eventually placed under the aegis of Apollo (Fig. 78) and the Delphic Oracle, as the urban administration gained more and more control over the religious and social life of the city-states. But in the rural provinces (e.g. Boeotia, Thessaly, Phocis, Messenia and Arcadia) the rustic observances remained predominant, surviving little changed throughout the ages as an integral element in folk life and its cultus. It is true that when they became public cult dramas in the city-states in classical times they rapidly acquired a new splendour and elaboration, but in their essential nature and function they were little changed. In the sixth century BC tragedy began to appear and gave expression in literary form to death and decay in nature and in human experience, with comedy as the revel-song designed in the rural ritual to make the crops grow, and held in an atmosphere of general license amid merry-making and the relaxation of all restraints.

The Thesmophoria

The ancient Corn-goddess and/or Earth-Mother, Demeter, with her daughter Kore, the Corn-maiden, embodied the new harvest and was very closely associated with these agricultural operations (Figs. 65 and

66). At Eleusis she was the giver of the corn on the Rarian plain, and while this was always her principal function, her Mysteries had a wider and deeper significance which extended far beyond the cornfields into the realms of the hereafter. But in the beginning Demeter and her worship centred in her control of the processes of vegetation, causing the corn to germinate and the fruits of the earth to spring forth. At the autumnal sowing of the crops in October or November (11th to 13th of the month Pyanopsion) the festival of the Thesmophoria was held in her honour, celebrated solely by women who erected bowers with couches and sat upon the ground to promote the fertility of the corn that had just been sown, and to secure their own fecundity—hence the presence of sexual symbols. The casting of pigs sacred to Demeter into subterranean chasms (μέγαρα) during the course of the rites, probably represented the descent of Kore into the nether regions of Pluto, and the bringing up of the putrefied remains of those thrown in the previous year, placing them on an altar and mixing them with seed-corn to secure a good crop, was said to commemorate the swallowing up of the swineherd Eubuleus by the earth when Kore was abducted, and the engulfing of his herd in the chasm. The festival, therefore, was regarded as an annual commemoration of the Corn-maiden's descent into the underworld.[86]

Now it was at this season that ploughing began in Attica, and when the seed was sown the fields became green again after the summer drought, for the crops sprouted in the mild winter months. It is not improbable, as Nilsson has suggested, that the Demeter cult and its legend arose out of a very ancient agricultural festival celebrating the bringing up of the corn from the silos in which they had been stored away after threshing in June until it was ready to be sown in October.[87] During the four months when it was concealed in the silos the fields were barren until the autumnal rains began, and, if Nilsson is correct, it was then, in this arid season, that the Corn-maiden was in the realm of Plouton, the god of wealth, who later became Pluto, the god of the nether regions. When the silos were opened in October and the seed-corn was brought up and sown in the newly ploughed fields, her release was celebrated at the Greater Eleusinian Mysteries which coincided with the Thesmophoria, both of which appear, therefore, to have been in origin agrarian rites to promote the fertility of the corn.

In Greece the year was divided rather arbitrarily into twelve months, and as the seasons varied in different parts of the country they could not be correlated exactly everywhere with the agricultural sequence of ploughing, sowing and reaping. The peasants held their rustic rites at the appropriate times irrespective of the official calendar with its urban subtleties and precise calculations, chronological and lunar, beginning approximately at midsummer with the month of Hekatombaion, which derived its name from the 'great sacrifice' at which a hundred head of cattle were offered in honour of Apollo. All the months in the Athenian calendar, in fact, were called after the festivals, many of which are very obscure and often bore little or no relation to the events commemorated in the earlier vegetation cycle. In Attica these followed a regular pattern, opening with the autumnal ploughing and sowing so that the barren fields immediately became green again, as the crops sprouted in the winter. After a lull in January the flowers appeared in February and March, and by May the grain was ready to be reaped and then threshed at the beginning of the dry season in June.

The Thalysia

At the ingathering of the harvest in the month of Hekatombaion (i.e. June or July) a festival known as the Thalysia was held, when sacrifices were offered on the threshing floor at the altar of Demeter in recognition of her bounty, as a sort of 'harvest home' domestic observance, rather than a state festival as at the autumnal sowing. These first-fruit rites had no fixed date; they were held whenever the threshing was concluded and the first loaf was baked from the new corn, called the *thalysion arton*, with which Demeter was associated as 'the goddess of the great loaves'. Eventually the Thalysia in Attica was brought under Apollan influence, and a criminal known as the 'pharmakos' was fated and flogged at it as a kind of scapegoat in an expiation rite to expel the evil accumulated during the year and to allay the supernatural dangers attendant upon the annual slaying of the corn-spirit at the harvest, lest the new crop and the community should be contaminated by evil influences. It would seem, therefore, that behind these ingathering rites lay the normal complex of primitive customs connected with the cereal harvest, just as in the late autumn in the month of Pyanopsion a similar observance, the Pyanopsia, was held to celebrate the gathering of the fruit.

The Anthesteria

In the spring when the crops were ripening, the vines were pruned, the wine was ready for drinking and the flowers were in bloom, the Anthesteria—the 'Festival of Flowers'—was observed from the 11th to the 13th of the month named Anthesterion. The wine jars were opened amid general rejoicing, and in Athens their contents were taken to the sanctuary of Dionysus in the marshes and distributed among the citizens (including children above the age of four years) in small jugs. The god (Dionysus) was then taken to the city on a ship set on wheels and a sacred marriage with the wife of the Archon of Athens was contracted to promote fertility. In the evening vegetables and pots containing cooked food were taken to the dead, and libations were poured out to them; the Anthesteria being also the Athenian Feast of All Souls. At its end, as in the Lemuria in ancient Rome in May, the ghosts were summarily dismissed with the formula, 'Be gone spirits, the Anthesteria are over'. Thus, like many spring festivals, it combined a joyous and a more sombre character, represented respectively by the Dionysian and the funerary rites; the one was Bacchic and hilarious, the other chthonian and in a measure sinister.

The Eleusinian festivals

This association of the seasonal cycle in the growth of the grain and of the vine, and of vegetation in general, with death and the afterlife, was very prominent in the Greek mind. It was in the spring when this connexion was most apparent, and the Lesser Eleusinian Mysteries were held at Agrae, a suburb of Athens; this ceremony eventually became an essential preliminary to initiation at Eleusis in the autumn, at what originally was a festival of the sowing of the new crops (Fig. 75). That these primitive agrarian rites were very ancient is shown by the Mycenaean foundations of the sanctuary, as well as by the character of the ritual and its affinities to the Thesmophoria. These festivals appear, as in Crete, to have been held at first in the open air for the benefit of the newly sown seed-corn, and the *telesterion*, where the initiates assembled on the night of the 22nd of the month of Boedromion (which coincided with the autumnal sowing) was a rectangular hall resembling a Mycenaean *megaron* or a Minoan 'theatre' rather than a Greek temple. It would seem, in fact, that it was in Crete that the rites were originally performed. There, solemn processions of sacral kings on portable thrones, followed by their worshippers, made their way along the *Via sacra* to the enclosed paved 'theatrical area' in the palace sanctuaries, designed for small performances of sacred dances and similar rites depicted on the frescoes.[88] The excavation of these sites at Knossos, Phaestos and Gournia have shown that they were not intended for large gatherings, and may have been confined to a very carefully selected audience who sat or stood on the stone steps to behold the sacred scenes portrayed on the 'orchestra', in which no doubt the Minoan Goddess played an essential role. Indeed, Hesiod says that the birth of Pluto, the god of wealth, was the result of the union of Demeter with Iasion 'in the rich land of Crete'.[89]

Little is known of what was done in the *telesterion* at Eleusis, when the neophytes (*mystae*), having undergone a course of secret instruction in what was to be revealed to them after the purifications and asceticisms of various kinds, were led forth in procession along the Sacred Way from Athens to the sanctuary of Demeter at Eleusis. On their arrival they bathed in the sea and roamed about the shore with lighted torches enacting the search of the Goddess for her abducted daughter. Then came the nocturnal vigil in the hall of initiation where, veiled in darkness and in complete silence, they sat on their stools covered with sheepskins to behold sacred sights which might never be revealed. The secret has been well kept, for apart from a few scattered allusions to the cult by Christian writers, such as Hippolytus and Clement of Alexandria, of very uncertain veracity, what was displayed and represented during the solemn hours in the *telesterion* when the initiation rites reached their climax, can only be conjectured.

The tabu extended to visible portrayals of what was done, and so the iconography throws little light on the problem. According to the cult legend in the so-called *Homeric Hymn* assigned to the seventh century BC, the story with which the agrarian festival became so intimately associated, centred in the Corn-maiden being carried off to the nether regions in the golden chariot of Pluto while she was gathering flowers in the rich Rarian meadows. The sorrowing mother, Demeter, wandered far and wide in search of her, carrying a torch to light up the deep recesses where she might have been concealed. Such was her grief that she withheld her fructifying gifts from the earth, until universal famine was threatened. Disguising herself as an old woman, she came eventually to Eleusis. There, sitting on a seat covered with a ram's skin by a wayside well, she met the daughters of the ruler, Keleos; she told them a fictitious story about her escape from pirates and was taken to their home, where she became nurse to their baby brother Domophoon, the infant son of the queen. Demeter thereupon began the process of making him immortal by anointing him secretly with ambrosia, the food of the gods, by day, and at night placing him in the fire to consume his mortality. Disturbed in these operations by his mother, who screamed with terror at the sight of her son in the fire, Demeter revealed her identity. Thereupon she abandoned her intentions to make Domophoon immortal, but before she left the royal household she commanded the people of Eleusis to build her a sanctuary on the hill above the 'fountain of maidenhood' where she first met the daughters of Keleos. There the rites she would teach her votaries should be performed to bestow immortality on all who were initiated into her Mysteries.[90] For another year, however, the drought and famine continued, until Zeus intervened and persuaded Demeter to accept an arrangement whereby her daughter would spend a third of the year in the underworld with Pluto and the remaining two-thirds in the upper world with her. Then the new life began to appear again and the fructifying rains to fall, until with the return of Kore to the nether regions in the autumn sterility prevailed, pending her ascent in the spring.

In this complex legend a number of myths and traditions have been amalgamated, but behind it there is clearly the motif of the agrarian festival centred in the Goddess of fertility who was also the giver of immortality. Before the rites acquired a more personal application in the bestowal of eternal life upon the initiates in their individual capacity, it would seem that it was the renewal of vitality in the regenerative process as a whole that was their primary purpose. Although Hippolytus seems to have confused the Phrygian Attis rites with those of Demeter,[91] if, as he maintained, an ear of corn was reaped in a blaze of light before the wondering eyes of the *mystae* in the *telesterion*, and the birth of a divine child Brimos (i.e. Iacchos, a variant of Bacchus) was announced,[92] it may have had reference to a sacred marriage between Zeus and Demeter, or Plouton and Persephone, symbolized by the union of the hierophant and the chief priestess in their respective roles. Such a rite would be in accordance with the agrarian origins and vegetation setting of the festival and its mystery at this season of the year. The germinating wheat would be at once the symbol of the harvest of the grain and of the immortality of the human soul, falling into the ground and dying in order to bring forth much fruit either here or hereafter, like the corn which the Athenians sowed on their graves.[93] A corn-token symbolism would be in keeping with the idea of rebirth alike in nature and in man.

The fact that these two concepts were fundamental in the Eleusinian Mysteries throughout their long and chequered history is shown by the myth and ritual from their earliest rustic beginnings to their latest manifestations. The Neoplatonist writer, Proclus, in the fifth century AD, in a passage emended by Lobeck, records that the worshippers were said to have gazed up to the sky and cried aloud at the appropriate season, 'Rain (O Sky) Conceive (O Earth), Be fruitful'.[94] This formula, as Farnell has pointed out, 'savours of a very primitive liturgy that closely resembles the famous Dodenaean invocation to Zeus, the Sky-god, and Mother-earth; and it belongs to that part of the Eleusinian

ritual "*quod ad frumentum attinet*".' Late though it be, it has every indication of being, as he says, 'the genuine ore of an old religious stratum
sparkling all the more for being found in a waste deposit of Neoplatonic
metaphysic.'[95] It is, therefore, highly probable that the seasonal cult
drama and its theme to promote the fertility of the soil, and especially
of the corn, occurred at Eleusis, and was vested as a hereditary possession in the ancient priestly families of the Eumolpidae and the Kerykes
(heralds) as the successors of the king, having been originally a family
cult before it was transformed into a death and resurrection esoteric
mystery to bestow a blessed hereafter on its initiates. Then it became
open to all who could speak Greek, and who lived in a circumspect
manner worthy of the brotherhood to which they sought admission.
But its principal celebration continued to be held at the autumn sowing,
thereby preserving, as in its ritual, its deeply laid agrarian foundations
in the seasonal cult drama.

Dionysian festivals
Unlike the Thraco-Phrygian Dionysiac, however, it never adopted the
orgiastic and ecstatic rites of the vintage festivals, though Dionysian
elements were incorporated in the Eleusinian Mysteries at an early
period (i.e. in the fifth and fourth centuries BC). This is apparent in the
prominence given to the figure of Iacchos in the procession, represented
in the likeness of Dionysus-Bacchus, and in his appearance on late vase
designs and in statuettes among the Eleusinian goddesses and heroes.
But though its wild revels continued to be held on Mount Parnassus,
the Dionysiac became more sober in Greece when it gained a place in
the Olympian tradition and in the Orphic *teletae*, or initiation rites, and
under the restraining influence of Delphi. The cult then acquired a
mystical significance, and its myth and ritual, originally so closely
associated with the death and resurrection cult drama and the festival
of viticulture, were transformed into an allegorized eschatology and
hope of immortality, in terms of the Orphic doctrine of reincarnation
leading at last to the Elysian Fields. Then the maenads turned their
nocturnal flight to the mountains in spring and autumn to more serious
account in the Orphic quest of release from the Titanic element in
human nature through a series of rebirths, when at length the Dionysian
divine soul, incarcerated in a mortal body, attained deification and
eternal bliss.[96]

Nevertheless, as the son of the Phrygian Earth-goddess Zemele, who
in the Greek Olympian theology became Semele the spouse of Zeus,
he stood in the vegetation tradition, and in the Orphic literature

Demeter was identified with **Rhea** as the mother of Zeus, by whom she conceived Kore, who in her turn bore Dionysus to Zeus, so that the Cretan Rhea displaced the Thraco-Phrygian goddess, Zemele. Behind this mythological confusion stood the union of heaven and earth symbolized by the sacred marriage of the Sky-Father and the Earth-Mother, and it was this aspect of the cult drama that persisted, first in one form and then in another, in the *teletae* associated with the names of Dionysus and Orpheus, and the mysterious Demeter with whom they coalesced. Moreover, the Maenad tradition was never wholly repressed, and at stations such as Panopeus on the road from Athens to Parnassus, its Thyad tumultuous dancing survived at Dionysian festivals[97] after it had been brought into relation with the Eleusinian Mysteries. Indeed, when eventually it reached Rome, the wild Bacchanalia had to be suppressed by the Senate in 185 BC.[98]

CHAPTER SIX

THE CULT OF THE DEAD

Egyptian funerary cult, conception of the soul, afterlife, judgment, Ushabti figures, Fields of the Blessed—Sumerian mortuary cultus, Babylonian afterlife, Gilgamesh epic, myth of Adapa—Baal and Anat epic in Syria, burial of Aqht, Canaanite and Hebrew obsequies, mortuary equipment, Hebrew modes of burial, necromancy and Sheol, Hebrew conception of immortality, Jewish apocalyptic eschatology—Helladic and Mycenaean burial customs, Homeric conception of the soul and Hades, Mystery afterlife

THE CLOSE association of the seasonal drama with death and resurrection to a newness of life beyond the grave shows how very intimately the quest of life in this world and the next has been related the one to the other. The extension of the process of rebirth and regeneration to human beings when their allotted span has come to an end under temporal conditions is apparently almost as old as mankind, since in the archaeological record, as has been considered, indications occur of mortuary practices suggesting a cult of the dead going back to the beginning of the Old Stone Age.

Taking the evidence collectively, it seems that the mystery of death called forth a combination of very deeply seated emotions of fear, respect and veneration rendering not only the corpse in a tabu condition but everyone who was intimately connected with it. But because the dissolution was not the final end of existence, attempts had to be made to promote and facilitate the renewal of life, wherever and however it might be lived in the hereafter. All this no doubt was very vaguely conceived prior to the rise of civilization in the Fertile Crescent and throughout the Ancient Near East, where mortuary ritual became such a very prominent feature from the Neolithic and Chalcolithic onwards. This was most apparent in Ancient Egypt as has been shown in the increasing elaboration of tomb construction and equipment, and in the preservation of the physical body by a highly technical process of mummification, and by the provision of carefully designed plastered heads, death masks and portrait statues as permanent simulacra of the deceased.*

The Egyptian funerary cult
In conjunction with these mortuary devices a funerary cult developed,

*cf. Chap. II, p. 58ff.

to secure for the dead the requirements of the living, such as a worthy and enduring habitation, sustenance, apparel, rest and recreation. At first for kings and the nobility, and later for commoners, the major consideration was an assured status in the afterlife when they joined their *kas* and were destined to become an Osiris. Hence arose the care bestowed upon the tomb as 'the castle of the *ka*', with its separate compartments, lavish offerings of food and drink, and sacerdotal 'servants of the *ka*' to minister to the daily needs, both spiritual and material, of the occupant. Since grain was buried in the Predynastic graves at Merimde-Benisalame, Naqada and el-Amra, the widespread practice of including objects with life-giving qualities in the funerary furniture was established in the Nile valley long before the Dynastic royal cultus concentrated immortality on the cosmic figure of the Pharaoh in the Pyramid Age, as the texts reveal. It was from the Fourth Dynasty and onward, under the influence of the Heliopolitan Sun cult, when all the available resources were employed in the construction of the colossal royal tombs, and the ingenuity of the embalmers was centred in the mummification of the deceased occupant of the throne, that every other aspect of the cult of the dead was obscured. So vital to the well-being of the nation and of the cosmic processes was the complex personality of the Pharaoh, that his rebirth in the realms of his heavenly father, the Sun-god, and all that this involved, was the primary preoccupation. To prevent any interruption in the natural order and its forces, his immortality had to be made secure at all costs, whatever happened to the rest of mankind.

With the diffusion of the Osiris cultus from Busiris in the Delta to Upper and Lower Egypt by the end of the Fifth Dynasty, the mortuary situation assumed a different character. Osiris being himself at once the Lord of the underworld and the son of the Earth-god Geb and the Sky-goddess Nut, who was slain by his brother Seth and restored to life by his wife and sister Isis with the aid of his posthumous son Horus, he became the earnest of the resurrection of all mankind. So powerful was the influence of this Osirian faith centred in the belief in his resurrection and all that this involved, that the Heliopolitan theologians were compelled to incorporate it in their solar creed, and ascribe to Osiris the status, some of the attributes, and the prerogatives of Re, the Sun-god, and to give him a place in the celestial realms. This Osirianization of the Heliopolitan solar-worship carried with it after the end of the Old Kingdom (*c.* 2250 BC) the extension of the hope of immortality to ordinary mortals who had no claim to divinity like the Pharaoh. They too could undergo the same process of restoration to life beyond the grave as that by which Osiris was resuscitated by Anubis with the help of Isis and Nephthys. This included the technique and rites of mummification performed on the corpse of the Pharaoh.

As attempts had been made to preserve the body after death from the very beginning of the Dynastic period,[1] this was not wholly an innovation. Once the Osirian interpretation of the afterlife was established, the ceremony of mummification became an elaborate imitation of what had been done to Osiris himself after his dismembered mortal remains had been collected, restored and revived, the embalmers assuming the roles of Thoth and Horus and wearing their masks. The water used for the lustration of the portrait statue of the deceased in the *serdab*, or cult-chamber, having come from the Nile, which was identified with Osiris, it was interpreted as the purifying and regenerating fluid that issued from him,[2] bestowing on the corpse below the reciprocal effects of the libations. All deceased persons, therefore, could be treated in much the same way as was the Pharaoh, if their resources permitted, when the funerary cultus was democratized at the beginning of the Middle Kingdom (*c.* 2000 BC). As we have seen, the 'Opening of the Mouth' ceremony in connexion with statues was a very ancient rite,* and in both the solar and Osiris mortuary ritual it was a fundamental element, first on behalf of the dead in general, celebrated either in the mortuary temple for kings, or in the tombs or graves for commoners.

The mortuary liturgy regularly followed the pattern of the daily ceremonial in the House of the Morning,† consisting of the preliminary ablutions in connexion with the 'Opening of the Mouth' as a preparation for its anointing, censing, and feeding. The actual burial rite was preceded by a procession from the house of the deceased to the tomb after the embalmment of the corpse had been completed in the 'mortuary workshop', known as 'The House of Gold'.§ The cortège moved off amid the wailing of the mourning women beating their heads and rending their garments in the prescribed manner (Fig. 73). As shown in the scene in the mastaba of the vizier Mereruka at Sakkara in the Sixth Dynasty, the mortal remains were carried to the river in a cradle with long poles followed by the celebrants impersonating Isis and Nephthys, and individuals described as 'the seal-bearer of the god' and the 'embalmer', preceded by the 'lector Priest' holding a scroll[3] (fig. 10). The objects to be buried with the body came next and shrines with the canopic jars. On reaching the river the coffin is represented as being

*Chap. II, p. 61.
†Chap. IV, p. 113.
§Chap. II, p. 61.

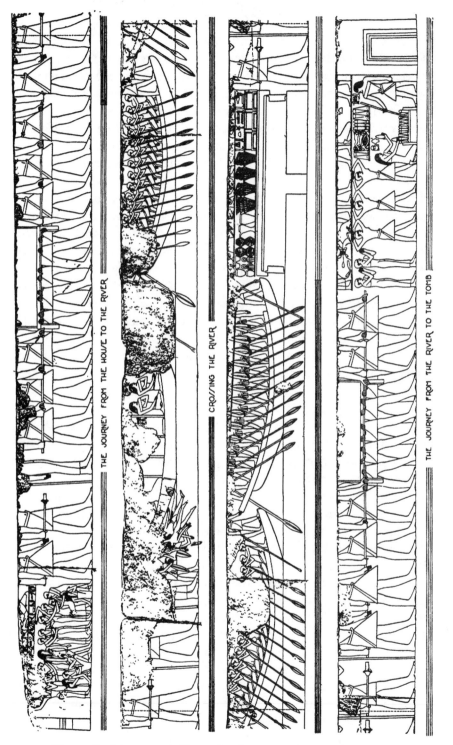

THE JOURNEY FROM THE HOUSE TO THE RIVER

CROSSING THE RIVER

THE JOURNEY FROM THE RIVER TO THE TOMB

Fig. 10. Burial scene at Sakkara, showing the cortège crossing the river

conveyed to the funeral barge, shown to be launched with difficulty. From other similar scenes of funeral processions in the Old Kingdom, it seems that the deceased, or his statue, was placed in a shrine facing the west in the boat with the lector before him reciting the sacred texts from his scroll, the passage of the river symbolizing the 'crossing of the firmament going down into his house of eternity in very good peace, when he has reached a good age in the presence of Osiris'.[4]

On arrival at the western bank the contents of the barge were disembarked and the procession moved on to the necropolis where sacrifices appear to have been offered, beatifications uttered by the lector, and services rendered by the embalmer in the presence of Anubis. A meal was then prepared to give sustenance to the reanimated spirit before a ceremonial entrance into the tomb was made. What followed within the necropolis is not depicted in the scene, but judging from a reference in a Sixth Dynasty text to eighty men entering the necropolis, who included all the principal officiants, the rites must have been of an elaborate nature completing the process of dispatching the deceased to his *ka* and making him an effectively blessed spirit. In the later cult this constituted identification with Osiris and all the prerogatives hitherto reserved for the Pharaoh.

The conception of the soul
That the cult of the dead was at first centred in the tomb where the soul had its home under ground, or in some subterranean world, with needs similar to those it had in this life, is apparent from the increasing care bestowed upon interment and the construction and furnishing of the grave with everything necessary for the comfort and well-being of the occupants. So firmly rooted was this practice that after the conception had arisen of the soul leaving the body and flying up to the sky to meet its *ka* in the celestial realms, the two ideas of the afterlife persisted side by side. Like the gods, first the Pharaoh and then the dead in general were thought to be in heaven and on or under the earth at the same time, equipped as they were with an immortal *ba*, or ghost, and an imperishable body or portrait statue, in addition to the *ka* as the protective genius guiding their fortunes in this world and the next. At death the *ba* left the body, normally in the form of a bird, or whatever external manifestation it might assume, and went to its future abode, whether above or below ground, or in the tomb, while the *ka*, being equated with the 'personality' (*akh*), or entire ego, exercised its functions both here and hereafter as a quasi-divine entity closely associated with the body but independent of it and separable from it.

The complications and contradictions in the Egyptian conception of the psycho-physical constitution of the human organism and the destiny of man in the afterlife were due partly to a general confusion of thought and speculation about the nature and attributes of the Pharaohs as divine beings and their application to mankind as a whole, and partly to the Osirianization of the solar theories. Thus, in the Pyramid Texts the basic theme is the procurement of eternal life for the occupant of the throne in the celestial realms of Re, coupled with that of the identification of the king with Osiris in terms of the Isis-Horus myth, transferred from the nether regions and the western desert of the Delta to the sky-world whither the deceased ruler ascended on a ladder, or on the tail of the heavenly cow, or in the smoke of incense, unless he flew up as a human-headed bird. There he might become one of the stars visible at night adorning the body of Nut the Sky-goddess, symbolized in the tomb by the stars painted on the ceiling of the burial chamber, and by the figure of the goddess on the underside of the lid of the coffin. But as Osiris he had to be revivified by the 'Opening of the Mouth' ceremonies and the offerings in memory of the bestowal of the eye of Horus on the dead Osiris, inscribed on the walls of the tomb. Then the *ba* could leave the body in the grave and rejoin its *ka* for ever in heaven. Precisely what was the relation of the spiritual double to the mortal remains in the grave is by no means clear, and probably it was never determined, as logical thought and neat and tidy concrete determinations of abstract concepts were outside the sphere of mythopoeic speculation and its cultus.

The afterlife
Moreover, when these conceptions and the magical use of the Pyramid Texts were extended from the Pharaoh to all his subjects, the earlier Osirian afterlife was reinterpreted in terms of the Heliopolitan solar hereafter, originally prescribed for the royal physical son of Re, so that the king became at once Re and Osiris, reigning in the capacity of Horus. From the Middle Kingdom (*c.* 2000–1780 BC), when everyone at death hoped to be Osiris, and might even sometimes become a star on the horizon of Nut, and take part in the nightly journey of the sun through the underworld (*Duat*) to rise in the newness of life in the morning, the spells hitherto employed in the royal obsequies were taken over for use among the masses to enable their *bas* to leave the tomb and enjoy the delights of the next life, depicted on the walls of the necropolis and on the sides of the coffins. These consisted of spells in the Pyramid Texts, The Book of the Dead, and the Coffin Texts. The Pyramid Texts,

however, were essentially solar in their eschatology, portraying the afterlife as a heavenly kingdom of the Sun-god. At first it was restricted to the Pharaoh, who was ferried across the river and guided by Nut; or who flew to the sky as a falcon, or was transported to the realms of Re by mounting the celestial ladder.[5] On his arrival the double doors of the sky were opened and his advent was announced by heralds. Having been greeted by the gods he sailed with Re in his boat, ate divine food and was suckled by a goddess.[6] As the son of his heavenly father, with whom he became completely identified, and even sometimes was represented as his superior,[7] he enjoyed all the delights of eternal blessedness.

The judgment

When the afterlife was Osirianized and democratized, these privileges became a common possession of all who fulfilled the conditions and could pass muster at the judgment after death, when they stood before Osiris as their judge and his forty-two assessors in the Hall of the Double Truth. It no longer sufficed to depend upon the possession and knowledge of the spells in the Pyramid Texts, as in the case of the king who was himself divine, though the magical agencies of The Book of the Dead still played an important part in the determination of the final destiny of the deceased. It is true that the conception of judgment included a detailed scrutiny of all transgressions in which moral qualities were a factor,[8] but when the heart was weighed against Truth, symbolized by either a feather or an image of the goddess Maat, the personification of justice as the divine order of the cosmos and of society and the moral law, it was not to vindicate his righteousness in the ethical sense as this was understood in prophetic and post-exilic Judaism. All that had to be established was that the individual was in harmony with the divine order as registered by the equilibrium of the balance manipulated by Thoth (Fig. 69).

To be 'true of heart and voice' like Osiris, was a calculation of Maat, in the determination of which there would appear to have been some assessment of good actions against bad actions. At any rate, the presence of the 'devourer' as a hybrid monster in the form of a crocodile, hippopotamus and lion at the foot of the scales suggests that the result was not an inevitable foregone conclusion in favour of the soul in the balance. Indeed, in the Middle Kingdom, although Osiris was the god of the democratized afterlife, reference was still made to 'that balance of Re in which he weighs justice'[9] as the moral arbiter before whom all might receive justice if their deeds merited this reward. As Osiris had been tried and found innocent in the Judgment Hall at Heliopolis, so mortals who appeared before the Osirianized solar bar of justice might hope to be vindicated at the great assize. Nevertheless, the issue was too serious for any risks to be taken. Resort, therefore, was made to the old magical devices calculated to make an effective 'declaration of innocence' when their good deeds and negative confessions were duly inscribed on the papyrus or scarab inserted among their grave furniture. Then they could be certain that their faults would be expelled and their guilt wiped out by 'the weighing of the scales on the day of reckoning characters', and that they would be permitted to 'join with those who were in the sun's barque'.[10] This accomplished, the case would not be contested at the tribunal, it was felt, by any god or goddess, and the balance would record an excess of good against evil.

It was this combination of spells and a weighing of justice that constituted the Egyptian conception of the judgment of character in the Osirianized afterlife in the Middle Kingdom. But even the denial of having committed a long list of offences in the form of a 'negative confession', and the extreme care taken to insure against an adverse verdict, implies some realization of a condition of righteousness as a crucial factor in the attainment of eternal bliss over and above the funerary ritual. This involved a test that had a latent moral content even though justice and truth were largely cosmic concepts, and, particularly in the New Kingdom, the efficacy of magic played an increasingly significant part in preparation for the Judgment. Then, under the new Theban priestly influence, the spells and amulets attained such prominence that the ethical requirements of sinlessness were rendered completely null and void, the state in the hereafter being made more and more dependent upon magical incantation of The Book of the Dead and the use of the appropriate charms. This was in line with the reconstitution of the faculties in the 'Opening of the Mouth' ceremonies, since it was carried to a further stage in the reanimation process by magical agencies, extending it to the status in the next life. Thus, a scarab was placed over the heart to prevent it witnessing against the *ba* when it was weighed in the balance, The Declarations of Innocence were sold by the scribes to be filled in, in the name of the deceased, declaring that he was a righteous man, and had been acquitted of all evil by the Sun-god, and sometimes threatening the deity with drastic penalties if he did not secure the justification at the Judgment.

Moreover, these mortuary texts from The Book of the Dead were claimed to be efficacious in securing not only the vindication of the dead irrespective of their moral character, but also all the delights of the afterlife. Thus, in 'The Book of Ani the Scribe' it is asserted that if it be written on the coffin the occupant 'shall come forth by day in any form he desires and he shall go into his place without being prevented. There shall be given to him bread and beer and meat upon the altar of Osiris. He shall enter in peace to the field of Earu, according to this decree of the one who is in the city of Dedu. There shall be given to him wheat and barley there. He shall flourish as he did upon earth. He shall do his desires like these nine gods who are in the underworld, as found two million of times. He is the Osiris: the Scribe of Ani.'[11]

Ushabti Figures

In addition to all these spells, charms and magical tomb texts to expel evil, justify the soul, guard it against encounters by malignant foes, and enable it to attain the joys of the next life, the ancient practice of depositing in the tomb small wooden figures of servants was developed. From the end of the Old Kingdom these Ushabti statuettes (i.e. 'answerers') of workmen carrying agricultural implements were supplied as servants to take the place of the deceased whenever he was called to work in the Elysian fields. Sometimes the names of individuals were scratched on pictures of servants carrying sacks of grain and engaged in other menial tasks inscribed on the walls of the tomb, suggesting that those who had been in the service of the occupants would continue their customary occupations and status after death. So they too were believed to have immortal life beyond the grave, and in their turn apparently to have resorted to Ushabtis, since on some of the statuettes a spell was inscribed, 'O Ushabti if N [name of the deceased] is called upon to perform any kind of work that is done in the underworld as a man to carry out his duties, to cause the fields to flourish, to irrigate the banks, to convey the sand from the east to the west, thou shalt say, here am I.'[12]

In the New Kingdom these Ushabtis, represented in the form of a mummy (Fig. 70) impersonated the dead as well as acting as their servants with specified labours. Their numbers rapidly increased until eventually one was provided for each day of the year. Hence the numerous examples of them now displayed in museums everywhere. That they were for the most part assigned agricultural duties shows that the idea survived of a terrestrial paradise in which work of this nature was required in the Elysian fields, where conditions were identical with those on earth, except that they were idealized. Freed from manual labour and menial tasks, the rulers, officials, artisans and soldiers sailed on the canals of the heavenly Nile, played draughts (Fig. 71), told tales

2 Man in Sumerian or Semitic clothes with two dogs beneath him, in Mesopotamian fashion. Reverse of knife handle from Gebel el-Arak. (*See p.* 30)

1 Asiatic influences in Predynastic Egypt shown in the panel depicted on an ivory knife handle from Gebel el-Arak. (*See p.* 30)

3   Pharaoh (King Scorpion) inaugurating
an irrigation canal with two fan-bearers
behind him. Mace-head from Hierakonpolis. *c.* 4000 BC. (*See pp.* 107 and 115)

5   Reverse of the Nar-Mer palette, showing the king with his standard-bearers and fabulous monsters.

4   King Nar-Mer smiting a prisoner kneeling before him. Palette of King Nar-Mer from Hierakonpolis, Egypt. *c.* 3500 BC. (*See p.* 30)

6   Terra-cotta female figurine from Tepe
Gawra, near Nineveh. Halafian period of the
Chalcolithic culture, *c.* 3800 BC. (*See p.* 48)

7 & 8 Nude female figurines, from Palestine. *c.* 2000 BC. (*See p.* 47)

9 Figures of the Eye-goddess, excavated at the Eye Temple, Tell Brak, Mesopotamia. *c.* 3000 BC. (*See p.* 48)

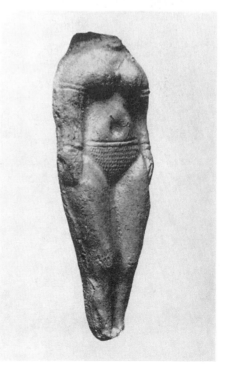

10, 11 & 12 Female clay figurines from Warka, the ancient Uruk. *c.* 2500 BC. (*See p.* 48)

13 Female figurine in lead from Alishar
Hüyük, Anatolia. *c.* 2000 BC. (*See p.* 49)

14　Faience figure of the Minoan Snake-
goddess from Knossos. *c.* 3000 BC. (*See p.* 54)

15 Life mask from Egypt. It was found in a sculptor's workshop where apprentices tried to gain experience in portraiture. *c.* 1370 BC, reign of Akhnaton. (*See p.* 58)

16 Neolithic plastered skull found at Jericho. The lower part of the face was modelled in plaster, and the eyes were sometimes marked with cowrie shells in an attempt to give an accurate informal portrait of the head. *c.* 5000 BC. (*See p.* 56)

17 Limestone relief of a substitute head from the wall of a tomb, Egypt. *c.* 4000 BC. (*See p.* 58)

18 Gilded cartonnage mask of a royal
princess, placed over the head of the deceased, inside the mummy wrappers. *c.*
1700 BC. (*See p.* 58)

19 Step pyramid at Sakkarah, built as a tomb for King Zoser, Egyptian 3rd Dynasty. (*See p.* 60)

20 Opening of the Mouth ceremony. Egyptian papyrus sheet. *c.* 1550–1090 BC. (*See p.* 61)

21 Gold Jewellery of Queen Shub-ad, from the Royal tombs at Ur, Mesopotamia. *c.* 2250 BC. (*See p.* 65)

22 Goat in a thicket, part of the grave goods in Royal tombs at Ur. Gold and lapis. *c.* 2250 BC. (*See p.* 64)

23 The falcon God Horus, with a human body, the form in which he usually appears. Bronze. Egyptian, late Dynastic to Ptolemaic period, 663–30 BC. (*See p. 70f.*)

24 Statuette of the God Horus in the form of a hawk, wearing the crown of Upper and Lower Egypt. Bronze. Twenty-sixth Dynasty to Ptolemaic period. Approximately 663–30 BC. (*See p. 70f.*)

25 Pharaoh offering to the God Horus,
relief from the tomb of King Seti at Abydos,
Egypt. 1318–1301 BC. (*See p.* 108)

26 Ea (Enki), Sumerian and Akkadian God of
Wisdom and Water. Black serpentine cylinder
from Sumeria. *c.* 2360–2180 BC. (*See p.* 74)

27 The Goddess Ishtar standing on a lion, stela from Til-Barsilo, Mesopotamia. About 4 ft. 8th century BC. (*See p.* 78)

28 God of vegetation in the role of Tammuz. Alabaster relief from Mesopotamia. First half of second millennium BC. (*See p.* 78)

29 Marble head of the Goddess Ningal, from Ur. 2300–2200 BC. (*See p.* 80)

30 Gudea and the God Ningizzida (*right*), basalt Chaldean stela from Susa of the Hammurabi epoch. About 1½ ft. (*See p.* 73)

31 The Assyrian God Ashur. Marble bas-relief, *c.* 1000 BC. (*See p.* 213)

32 A winged deity standing at each side of a stylized tree. Relief of Ashurbanipal II from Nimrud. *c.* 1000 BC. (*See p.* 100)

33 The God Osiris holding the sceptre and flail. Bronze figurine. *c.* 16th Dynasty. (*See p.* 108)

34 The Goddess Neith crowned with red crown of Lower Egypt. Bronze figurine of the Ptolemaic period. (332–330 BC.) (*See p.* 84)

35 The Sky-goddess Nut, supported by the Air-god Shu. Papyrus from Deir el-Bahri. 10th century BC. (*See p.* 85)

36 Shamash-resh-usur, governor of Suhi
and Mari, standing before the deities Adad
and Ishtar. Limestone relief from Babylon.
About 4 ft. 8th century BC. (*See p.* 74)

37 The Goddess Astarte at a window.
Ivory inlay from Khorsabad, Syria. 8th–
7th century BC. (*See p.* 86)

38 The Syrian Goddess. Copper figurine
from Ras Shamra, Syria. *c.* 19th–17th
century BC. (*See p.* 87)

39   The Goddess of wild beasts. Ivory from
Minet el-Beida. *c.* 14th century BC. (*See p.* 104)

40 The Storm and Weather-god Baal. Limestone relief from the sanctuary to the west of the great temple at Ras Shamra, Syria, c. 1900–1750 BC. (See p. 87)

41 El, the Ugaritic Supreme God. Stela from Ras Shamra, c. 13th century BC. (See p. 88)

42 Hittite rock sanctuary entrance, Yazilikaya, Anatolia. Mid-13th century BC. (*See p.* 93)

43 Yazilikaya: procession of the goddesses, part of the frieze in the sanctuary. (*See p.* 93)

44 Anatolian Weather-god and King Tudhaliyas, rock sculpture, Yazilikaya. (*See p.* 94)

45 The Hittite king and queen worshipping a bull. Rock carving from Alaja Hüyük. *c.* 1500–1200 BC. (*See p.* 128)

46 The processional entry of offering-bearers at Carchemish. Basalt relief. 9th–8th century BC. (*See p.* 128)

47 The processional entry of offering-bearers carrying animals at Carchemish. Basalt relief. (*See p.* 128)

48 The naked Hittite Goddess, from the Long Wall of Sculpture, Carchemish. Rock relief. *c.* 920 BC. (*See p.* 93)

49 Cult scene on a sarcophagus at Hagia
Triada, Crete. *c.* 14th century BC. (*See p.* 100)

50 Minoan Snake-goddess. Ivory and gold statuette. 16th century BC. (*See p.* 105)

51 The boy-god. Wooden Minoan statuette. 16th century BC. (*See p.* 105)

52   Athene. A Greek statue of the fifth century BC. (*See p.* 106)

53   The Themis of Chairestratos. Statue in marble. Early 3rd century BC. (*See p.* 133)

54 Jupiter. Roman statue of the Greek Supreme God Zeus. (*See p.* 75)

55 The birth of Venus. From the marble back of the Ludovisi Throne. Sicilian or South Italian. *c.* 470 BC. (*See p.* 106)

57 The Goddess Isis with King Seti I, relief carving from the tomb of Seti at Abydos, Egypt. *c.* 1318–1301 BC. (*See p.* 108)

53 [2472C]
ISIS & HORUS.

56 The Goddess Isis with Horus on her lap. Egyptian statuette. Saïte-Ptolemaic period (500–200 BC.) (*See p.* 82)

 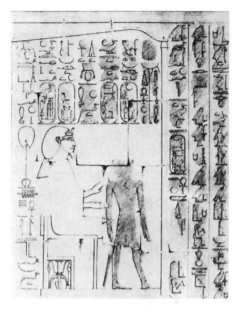

58 Ptah enthroned, with Pharaoh kneeling before him. Relief from chapel of Ptah at Abydos, *c.* 1318–1301 BC. (*See p.* 108)

59 Hathor presenting Queen Hatshepsut to Amon. Drawing of relief from temple of Deir el-Bahri. *c.* 1486–1469 BC. (*See p.* 110)

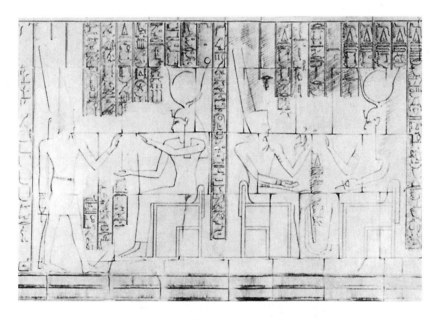

60 Queen Hatshepsut crowned by her father in the presence of the high officers of the kingdom. Drawing of a relief from the temple of Deir el-Bahri. (*See p.* 111)

61 The throne room at the Palace at Knossos, Crete. *c.* 1800–1709 BC. (*See p.* 130)

62 Vapheio Golden Cup, from the Mycenaean Vapheio tomb. *c.* 1500 BC. (*See p.* 193)

63   General view of the tombs at Mycenae. (*See p.* 131)

64   Treasury of Atreus at Mycenae. One of the great
Tholoi of the middle of the 2nd century BC. (*See p.* 132)

65   The Demeter of Cnidus. Statue in marble. *c.* 4th century BC. (*See p.* 160)

66 Demeter and Persephone consecrating Triptolemus. Votive relief from Athens. 5th century BC. (*See p.* 160)

67 Sacrifice to Dionysus. Scene on a Greek red-figure vase. 5th century BC. (*See p.* 160)

68 King Seti I offering before
the sacred boat of Amen Re,
relief from Abydos. *c.* 1318–
1301 BC. (*See p.* 109)

69 Weighing the heart, in the Egyptian
judgment scene. From the Papyrus of Ani.
c. 1500 BC. (*See p.* 174)

70 Ushabti figure of the Lady Tahured. Limestone statuette. *c.* 1550 BC. (*See p.* 176)

71 The Elysian Fields. From the Papyrus of Ani. *c.* 1500 BC. (*See p.* 176)

72 Bull men fighting with bulls, from a Babylonian cylinder seal. *c.* 2000 BC.

73 Lamentation scene on a limestone relief from Memphis. Height about 0.52m. 19th Dynasty. (1350–1200 BC.) (*See p.* 170)

74 The temple at Eleusis, Greece, the foundations of which appear to go back to Mycenaean times. *c.* 1500 BC. (*See p.* 163)

75 The Theatre at Epidaurus. Built probably about the middle of the 4th century
BC. (*See p.* 240)

76 Temple of Athene at Efestos, built *c.* 420 BC. (*See p.* 131)

77   Temple of Apollo at Delphi, rebuilt 370 to 330 BC on site of earlier temple. (*See p.* 242)

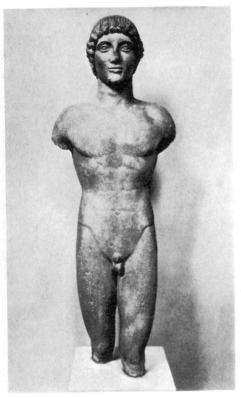

78 The 'Strangford' Apollo. Lifesize marble statue, *c.* 480 BC. (*See p.* 160)

79 Maat as the Goddess of Truth. Bronz statuette, Saïte-Ptolemaic period (500–20 BC.) (*See p.* 261)

80 The Ziggurat at Ur, the original of the
'Tower of Babel', built *c*. 3000 BC. (*See p*. 234)

81 Karnak; the Hypostyle Hall, from above. *c.* 1250 BC. (*See p.* 71)

82 Luxor, general view of the great temple. *c.* 1400 BC. (*See p.* 71)

83   Temple of Ishtar-Kitium, at Ishoali,
built *c.* 1763 BC. (Reconstruction by
Harold D. Hill.) (*See p.* 86)

84 The bull Apis, wearing a disc between his horns and an uraeus. Bronze statuette, Saïte period. (*See p*. 86)

85 Mithras and the Bull. Roman statue of 2nd century AD. (*See p*. 317)

and sang love-songs, in addition to enjoying celestial repasts and the offerings of food and drink made to them at their tombs by their survivors on earth, thus remaining in touch with this world.[13]

The Fields of the Blessed

The setting of this conception of the afterlife shows how very prominent was the belief in the continuation of earthly existence under perfect conditions affording the maximum of pleasure, at any rate for the more fortunate and privileged section of the community. But this was by no means the only interpretation of immortality. The earlier idea of the underworld persisted in the Osirian tradition and found expression in these Fields of the Blessed. It may have been overlaid and reinterpreted, however, by that of the heavenly solar kingdom ruled over by Re in his various manifestations, as set forth in the Pyramid Texts; it was confined originally to the King and was then extended to all who fulfilled the preliminary requirements and passed the test at the Judgment. Or, again, a third possibility was to ascend to the sky to dwell there as stars in celestial glory remote from terrestrial conditions and contacts. But the prevailing conception was that of a combination of the nether regions, the sky world and the Western paradise, in which, with the help of magical devices and sacrificial offerings, the status and occupations of the dead were maintained; the underworld had thus lost its sombre character and been transformed into a delectable paradise with rivers, lakes, and islands, and fertile land ploughed by heavenly oxen and bringing forth its fruits in ever-increasing abundance and perfection.

From the time of the Middle Kingdom this realm of Osiris, known as the Duat, was divided like Egypt itself into Upper and Lower divisions with a river running through it corresponding to the Nile, along which the Sun-god, accompanied by several gods, such as Geb and Thoth, made his nightly journey from west to east to give light, air and sustenance to its denizens. In the morning he emerged between two mountains to start his passage across the sky in his boat. This was an anomaly, in so far as strictly the Sun-god had no rightful place in the domain of Osiris, any more than had Osiris in the solar realm. But the Egyptian eschatology was never consistent, and the account of the nocturnal journey of Re in the 'Book of Gates' and the 'Book of Am Duat' (i.e. 'Of him who is in the underworld') originally had little or nothing to do with either Osiris or the hereafter, until in due course the solar theology was Osirianized. It was then that in The Book of the Dead the Judgment Hall of Osiris was placed between the fifth and sixth divisions in the Duat, and the Osirian eschatology was incorporated in the solar symbolism, together with an emphasis on the Western paradise. The emergence of the Sun-god from the Duat was equated with the resurrection of Osiris, as the Osirian doctrine of the afterlife became more and more dominant, in spite of recurrent attempts by the Theban priesthood to resuscitate the solar tradition.

The Sumerian mortuary cultus

In Mesopotamia the sustained preoccupation with the afterlife which remained such a prominent feature in the civilization of Ancient Egypt was conspicuously absent. The climatic and geographical conditions in the valley of the Nile and that of the Tigris and Euphrates, as we have seen, appear to have played some part in this differentiation in mortuary belief and practice.* But in spite of the absence of monumental sepulchres (apart from the royal tombs at Ur) and elaborate methods of mummification, the Sumerians made provision for the sustenance and well-being of their dead by placing in their earth and brick graves an adequate supply of food and drink, which sometimes seems to have been renewed by monthly offerings, together with personal belongings.[14] By comparison with Egypt, however, the equipment was very meagre, and, with the outstanding exception of the Ur royal burials, there are no indications of a developed funerary ritual. Indeed, while the grave goods suggest a belief in human survival, individual immortality may not have acquired a cultic significance. This is supported by the absence of documentary data bearing upon a mortuary cultus at all comparable to the Egyptian textual evidence, as well as by the very simple modes of disposal of the body, usually under the floor of the court or of a room in the house of the deceased rather than in cemeteries.

Even in prehistoric times the early Egyptian farmers expended more care on the tombs and their furniture than any contemporary western Asiatic community. Thus, the Badarian graves in the cemeteries in Middle Egypt with their female figurines, imported malachite and turquoise, and oxen, sheep and dogs, were considerably in advance of the Sumerian interments, or of those of the surrounding region in Mesopotamia. This was conspicuous at Hassuna near Mosul in Assyria, where although mortal remains have been found at all levels of the mound, there seems to have been no uniformity in burial practice in this period.† Indeed, the skeletons in a grain bin and in a rubbish pit suggest that often no attempt was made to give the dead decent burial at all, in striking contrast to the care bestowed upon them in the Nile valley.

*Chap. II, p. 62f.
†cf. Chap. II, p. 63.

Only a breath-like double survived the dissolution, earlier associated with certain organs of the body. This doubtless explains the vital connexion between the fate of the physical integument and the liberated phantasmal breath-soul, so that what happened to the one had a reciprocal effect on the other. Therefore, to remain unburied, or to be disturbed in the grave, was the worst fate that could befall a man after death.

The Babylonian afterlife

In Babylonia the inevitability of death was accepted as an indisputable fact, and the importance attached to proper disposal of the body and tendance on the part of the survivors suggests some conception of conscious existence in the hereafter. But what lay beyond the grave was so obscure and became so unattractive that it afforded little or no opportunity for reflection or speculation. As far back as our written records go the dead were assumed to continue a shadowy existence in Irkalla, a sombre land of 'no return' beneath the earth ruled by the goddess Ereshkigal and her husband Nergal. To this House of Dust and Darkness, surrounded with huge walls and having strongly guarded gates secured with bolts and bars, all descended irrespective of status, class, age or ethical behaviour, when the span of life on earth ended. Sometimes it was represented as a hollow mountain difficult to approach, into which the Apsu, or watery deep, flowed; or the entrance might lie in the west across the sea reached by a ferry. None might leave it, this dreary abode, once having entered it. There, huddled together amid dust and dismal shadows in a semi-conscious condition, they were destined to wither away like the vegetation in the devastating heat of a Mesopotamian summer.

This mood of despair found expression in the lamentations for Tammuz or Marduk imprisoned in the subterranean mountain which symbolized the nether regions. Though his liberation was celebrated with rejoicings at the New Year Festival, when death appeared to have been vanquished in nature at the return of the rains,* it was only life on earth that was renewed. For man the gods had decreed that death should be the portion, having reserved immortality solely for themselves.[15] It was a perilous undertaking for them even to visit the dread abode on ceremonial occasions or, like Gilgamesh or Ishtar, for specific reasons, and its permanent denizens were never allowed to leave it.[16] Gods and heroes alone could be revived and live for ever on the Island of the Blest, Dilmun, at the confluence of the Tigris and Euphrates, as in the case of Utnapishtim (Ziusudra), the Babylonian Noah, and his

*Chap. V, p. 144f.

wife and daughter, on whom 'life like a god' was bestowed after the Flood to enable them to live for ever in the mountain of Dilmun, where the sun rises.[17] But even great kings, such as Dungi or Sargon, suffered the same fate as the rest of mankind, as did Enkidu.

The Gilgamesh Epic

When Gilgamesh, the semi-divine founder of the city of Erech, went in search of immortality, and passed through the waters of death and encountered Utnapishtim in Irkalla, he was led

'To the house which none may leave who have entered it,
On the road from which there is no way back,
To the house wherein the dwellers are bereft of light,
Where dust is their fare and clay their food.
They are clothed like birds, with wings for garments.
And see no light residing in darkness.'[18]

Since Enlil, the father of the gods, had not destined him for eternal life, the attempt of Gilgamesh to obtain this boon proved to be fruitless. On his way back to earth he was cheated by a serpent of the magic rejuvenating plant he had secured to renew his youth,[19] and so all that he could hope for was the kingship, prominence and heroism in battle in this life until at length, like all mortals, he passed to the sinister Land of No Return.

The famous legend in its final Akkadian form on twelve tablets as a national Epic was the product of a long and complicated literary process incorporating elements from a number of different sources at different times unified in and around its hero. Combining the Tammuz theme, the Deluge myth, and the adventures of Utnapishtim, and the quest of immortality, in what seems to be a *rite de passage* through the waters of death, with nature myths, necromancy, and the cult of the dead, a heroic tale has been produced of profound human interest, to give purpose and meaning to decent burial and its cultus.[20] But throughout the story the frustration which characterizes Mesopotamian mortuary myth and ritual is apparent, ending in the disillusionment of its hero, who in spite of his relentless endeavour to discover the secret of immortality in the sombre country beyond the waters of death, failed to secure the priceless boon.

The Myth of Adapa

This verdict is confirmed in the myth of Adapa, in which mankind is represented as having lost eternal life by a trick of the gods. Here, again, a semi-divine being was the hero, in the figure of Adapa, who was the son of Ea (Enki), the god of the waters, begotten by him to be a leader among men and endowed by his father with divine wisdom but not with immortality. He was also a fisherman, and one day when he was fishing on the Persian Gulf his boat was overturned by a sudden south wind and he was thrown into the water. Infuriated, he cursed the wind and broke one of its wings, so that it was prevented from blowing for a week. When Anu, 'the Father and King of the gods', was informed of the cause he summoned Adapa to appear before him in his heavenly abode. Acting on the advice of his father, Adapa put on a mourning garment to excite the pity and win the favour of Tammuz and Gizzeda, who guarded the gate of heaven, by explaining that he was mourning their having disappeared from the earth. Touched by this expression of grief at their demise, it was hoped that they would intercede for him with Anu. Having gained entrance by this ruse, Ea warned him against eating and drinking the beer and water of death that he would be offered by the gods, telling him to accept only a garment and the oil which would be presented to him. Following these instructions, he was acquitted by Anu and the food of life was brought to him. This he refused, acting on the injunction of his father, and so lost the gift of immortality. As a result he was sent back to earth to die like other men, thereby suffering the fate of Gilgamesh.[21]

The conclusion of the story cannot be determined as only a few lines have survived on the last of the four fragmentary tablets from the library of Ashurbanipal at Nineveh. These refer to the clothing of Adapa with the garment, his anointing with oil, and the passing of the verdict on him. Heidel maintains that had he accepted the water of life he would have lived for ever, but by refusing the offer of Anu he not only missed immortality himself but brought illness, disease and death upon the human race as a whole.[22] In the text, however, all that is stated is that 'what ill he has brought upon man, and the disease that he brought upon the bodies of men, these Ninkarrak (the goddess of healing) will allay.'[23] But, whatever its effects, the breaking of the wing of the south wind certainly was not the first sin committed by human beings. So far from transgressing a divine command, Adapa is represented as having lost eternal life through acting in strict obedience to the injunctions of his wily divine father, Ea. No moral issue, therefore, was involved in the episode.

As in the Gilgamesh Epic, everlasting life was sought, but it proved to be a hopeless quest because the gods had decreed when they created man that death would be his portion. Adapa and Gilgamesh were given a chance to secure immortality presumably because they were divine heroes, but even for them the odds were weighted too heavily against them. They had to accept, therefore, the inevitable, in spite of their privileged status, having been outwitted in the quest on which they embarked. Where they failed, less exalted mortals could not hope to succeed. So in Babylonia life was regarded as ending in a cul-de-sac, a land of no return, in which even Inanna-Ishtar, the queen of heaven, was deprived of her regalia and robes until on reaching the temple of her elder sister, Ereshkigal, she was reduced to a naked corpse.* She, it is true, was able to make her escape, being the embodiment of the creative process in nature. But, nevertheless, it required a special divine intervention to restore her vitality and secure her release from the land of the dead. Throughout Babylonian mortuary myth and ritual there is this fundamental strain of frustration. But although the quest of immortality is continually defeated by the wiles of the gods and their agents in accordance with their original decree, in the background lies a more positive attitude to the afterlife, which found expression in an adequate if not very elaborate equipment of grave goods and offerings in the relatively simple interments in or near the home of the deceased. But the Babylonian cult of the dead never developed a conception of immortality at all comparable to that in Ancient Egypt, the Graeco-oriental mystery religions, or in post-exilic Judaism, Christianity and Islam.

The Baal and Anat epic in Syria

In Syria, as throughout the Near East and the Aegean, the cult of the dead was bound up with the seasonal fertility ritual in which the revival of life in the spring was connected with regeneration beyond the grave, until eventually in Babylonia and Assyria and among the Hebrews in Palestine, the conception of immortality underwent considerable restriction. In the Ugaritic texts from the Ras Shamra library, the descent of Baal to the underworld, as we have seen, was the occasion of the familiar search for the dead god by his sister-spouse Anat, the goddess, and the reciprocal effect on the life of vegetation. After the mourning rites had been duly performed, resembling the weeping for Tammuz in Mesopotamia and Jerusalem, when she had recovered his body with the help of the Sun-goddess and buried it with considerable ceremony, a funeral feast was held. Then she avenged the murder of Baal by killing Mot, the god of sterility, and as a result 'the heavens rained with fat', we are told, 'and the wadis flowed with honey'.[24]

*Chap. III, p. 79.

Here, again, the decline and revival in nature in the seasonal sequence were interpreted in terms of the fortunes of the two divine personifications of the vegetative processes in a death and resurrection myth and ritual enacted in all probability at the appropriate times in the year. But the cultus was confined in intention to life on earth and to the growth of the crops during the ensuing year, under the precarious conditions of time and space. There are no indications in the texts of a reciprocal effect on the destinies of mankind beyond the grave in a blessed immortality, as in the Egyptian cult of the dead. Mot was the sinister power of drought and sterility whose home was in the underworld, symbolizing the land of the dead. Baal was equated with the regenerating rains and the life awakened and restored on earth, the land of the living.

The burial of Aqht

Thus, in the Aqht text in which the interment of the dead is described and its significance is stressed, the hero Danel, when his son Aqht was killed through the machinations of Anat, placed a ban of seven years upon the rain-clouds of winter and the heavy dews in summer,[25] being, like Baal, the dispenser of fertility. Following the example of Isis in Egypt, he endeavoured to recover the fragments of his son's body, which he discovered in the gizzards of vultures, and give them decent burial.[26] The shedding of the blood of the youth, at the time of the harvest, had, however, polluted the land, made the fields infertile and produced the prolonged drought. It was not until Anat had repented of her instigation of the murder and mourned the demise of Aqht, and her sister Paghat had avenged the crime by slaying the soldier, Yatpan, who slew the lad, that the curse was removed. The sequel of the episode is missing in the texts, but doubtless it followed the Tammuz-Adonis theme and described how Aqht was restored to life and fertility returned to the arid country.

In both the Baal and Aqht myths the emphasis, however, appears to have been on proper burial and the due performance of the mourning rites. The prolonged search for the body recalls that of Ishtar for Tammuz and of Demeter for Kore, or of Aphrodite for Adonis, and it concludes with a detailed account of the way in which the lamentations were conducted. On the death of Baal El sat on the ground, loosened his turban and the knot of his girdle, covered his head with dust and wallowed in it, tore his face with his nails, and made the mountain re-echo with his lamentations, crying 'Baal is dead.'[27] Anat seems to have joined in this grievous mourning,[28] like the women weeping for

Tammuz and mourning for Hadad-Rimmon in the valley of Megiddo,[29] or the Israelite maidens who lamented their virginity in an ancient funerary rite in the mountains of Gilead.[30]

Canaanite and Hebrew obsequies
The mortuary ritual recorded in the Ugaritic texts is, in fact, in accord with that to which reference is made in the Hebrew scriptures. In both communities in Palestine the proper burial of the dead was regarded as a matter of supreme importance for the safety and well-being of the body politic, as well as for the welfare of the departed. Although in this region what lay beyond the grave was obscure, the mystery surrounding death and the awesomeness of a dead body rendered the condition, and everyone and everything intimately connected with it, sacred and tabu. Therefore, they had to be approached with great caution, respect and ritual devices as protective measures. These included segregation on the part of the mourners, and ablutions at the end of the period of contagion before returning to normal life in society, the obsequies being in the nature of a *rite de passage* from a holy to a profane state, from the sacred to the secular. Thus, after the death of the infant son born to Bathsheba, we are told that David, when he had performed the lamentation ritual, 'arose from the earth, and washed and anointed himself and changed his apparel, and came into the house of the Lord and worshipped.[31] Then he returned to his own house.

In this incident as it has been recorded, the customary order was reversed, ostensibly on the ground that the mourning rites were performed before rather than after the child's death, to avert his demise, in the hope that Yahweh would be gracious and merciful and grant the boy recovery.[32] Whatever may have actually happened on this occasion, as the story has been handed down in Holy Writ it constitutes a break in the established mortuary practice in Palestine and the rest of western Asia, by interpreting the ceremonial abstentions and lamentations in terms of personal grief and the rescuing of the child from death rather than his initiation into the afterlife. Nor did David refrain from returning immediately to normal intercourse in the community as soon as he had performed the traditional desacralization rites. In this form the narrative indicates an ethical approach to a personal situation transcending a ritual social observance of readjustment after a disturbing critical event. The enactment of the prescribed customs does not appear to have been regarded as having any particular effect on the status of the infant in the next life; the purpose was to appease Yahweh in the hope of saving the life of the infant in this world. Here, no doubt, can be detected later prophetic influence, in which the cult of the dead and the afterlife were looked upon with the gravest suspicion as being in conflict with Yahwistic ethical monotheism and its ideals of humiliation and self-abasement in the approach to the Holy One of Israel.

Mortuary equipment

It was generally admitted both by the Canaanites and the Hebrews that death was not the final end of existence, though more is known about the methods of burial practised by them than about their beliefs about immortality. That it was a life like that lived in this world is suggested by the mortuary equipment in the graves in the hillsides where these obtained. Thus, it apparently required food and raiment and personal belongings, including tools, weapons, cups, dishes, jars, lamps and amulets; these were whole and entire, or not infrequently 'killed' by breaking or piercing the objects, possibly to place them at the disposal of the dead by liberating the sacredness inherent in them. In the massive sarcophagus of Ahiram king of Byblus about 1200 BC and the father of Ithobaal, the sovereign was seated on a throne flanked by winged sphinxes and holding a lotus in his hand. In front of him stood a table of offerings and attendants were portrayed bringing food, while dancing and weeping women were depicted with hands on their heads, like Tamar in her distress.[33] On the coffins of Ahiram curses were engraved against any rebel who robbed or disturbed the tomb.[34] But, as in the case of the royal tombs at Ur, sumptuous burials of this kind were confined to the privileged few, and in Palestine itself they are conspicuously absent. Food and drink offerings to the dead survived, at any rate sporadically, in the second century BC, as is revealed in the Tobit legend,[35] while figurines, scarabs and Horus eyes, and numerous other amulets, vessels, rattles, toys, ornaments and the remains of animals abounded in Palestinian tombs at Gezer, Ain Shemesh, Beth-Shemesh and elsewhere,[36] in spite of rifling by grave-robbers in the first instance seeking gold, and more recently by tourists in search of souvenirs. At Jericho, infants, often buried in jars, were prevalent, besides the plastered skulls,* as they were also at Gezer and elsewhere, deposited below the floors of houses. But offerings in the Bronze Age graves were for the most part meagre and sometimes confined to a single dagger in the graves of men, and a few beads and pins in those of women, successively pushed on one side to make room for later burials. The equipment sometimes included portions of wooden furniture as well as scarabs, pottery, pins and beads.[37]

*Chap. II, p. 56.

Hebrew modes of burial

Until the time of the Hebrew monarchy the dead were normally buried in caves, but in the relatively few shaft-graves the goods were placed in the chamber at the bottom of the shaft sunk in the rock. As Dr Mackenzie has pointed out, these chamber tombs were modelled on the general plan of the abodes of the living, and the figures put in them were the same as the images of domestic divinities in the early Canaanite cult, placed there to protect the dead by warding off evil influences.[38] After the Israelite occupation of the land the bodies were laid on benches cut in the walls of the small chambers, though kings would seem to have been deposited in a more elaborate hypogaeum with several chambers containing the mortal remains of their predecessors. The so-called 'Egyptian' tomb at Silwan near Jerusalem was quarried out of the rock and later remodelled after the manner of a mastaba. In its original form, however, it must have been a simpler construction with a much smaller door leading into the chamber. Those of the Ptolemaic and Maccabaean periods were entered by a square shaft-opening in the roof, with a block of stone raised on the floor to act as a step. Stone slabs, on or beneath which the offerings were laid, covered the graves.

Sometimes horizontal shafts were cut into the walls at right angles large enough to receive a single corpse endways, though in some of these *kokim* it was possible to thrust in two bodies side by side. Occasionally they served the purpose of a passage leading to a subterranean secret chamber as a protection against rifling. In the sepulchre of Apollophanes of Marissa constructed along these lines, entrance was through a sort of vestibule to transverse chambers with *kokim* opening out of each wall, and through a door to a long hall similarly arranged with horizontal shafts, decorated above with a frieze depicting animals having Greek names intermingled with the figures of men, which have been obliterated.

Generally, family graves were located as near the home as possible. Samuel was buried in his house in his native town of Rama,[39] a practice, as we have seen, that was prevalent in Mesopotamia and Syria. Similarly, when Joab was killed by Benaiah, the son of Jehoiada, he too was buried in his own house in the desert,[40] just as Asahel, one of David's servants, after he had been slain by Abner, was taken to Bethlehem to be interred in his father's sepulchre there.[41] When Ahitopel found to his chagrin that the advice of Hushai was taken rather than his own counsel in the strategy to be employed in the campaign against David, he saddled his ass and went to his house in his native city. Having put his affairs in order there, he hanged himself and was buried in the tomb of his father.[42] David, on the other hand, although a native of Bethlehem, had his grave in the capital he had founded,[43] and from henceforth the kings of Judah were buried with their fathers in Jerusalem.[44]

With the exception of Hezekiah who was buried in 'the ascent to the graves of the sons of David' on crown land outside the city,[45] and his descendants who appear to have been interred in the garden of the house of Uzza[46] below the oldest royal tombs, all the successors of David were gathered into the family necropolis at death. In the former capital, Hebron, was the ancestral burial cave of Machpelah containing, as it was believed, the mortal remains of Abraham and Sarah, Isaac and Rebekah, and Jacob and Leah,[47] within the sanctuary of Mamre. The reputed grave of Rachel near Ephrath (Bethlehem) in Benjamin was marked by a sacred pillar said to have been erected by Jacob,[48] and that of the nurse of Rebekah was marked by an oak to which resort was made for divination,[49] while the sepulchre of Joseph at Shechem was similarly equipped.[50] Indeed, throughout the whole land sacred sites were regarded as the place of burial of the ancestors of Israel, where libations and offerings were made suggestive of a cultus centred in the veneration of the illustrious tribal heroes in the Patriarchal tradition. Hence arose the importance attached to their graves and to the mummified remains of Joseph, which are said to have been carried away with the escaping Israelites at the time of the Exodus to be reinterred on ancestral soil in Canaan.[51] But, except under Egyptian influence, no indications have been found of embalming or mummification in Palestine.

Necromancy and Sheol

These customs and cult practices suggest that the pre-prophetic beliefs of the Hebrews about the dead and their requirements in and beyond the grave were much the same as those that had always prevailed in Palestine and the rest of western Asia. The importance attached to lamentation, laceration and other mourning rites, and to the disposal of the body and its provision with offerings of food and drink, platters, jars, bowls and lamps—women with beads and other ornaments and men with their weapons—attest to the belief that the afterlife was conceived in relation to an earthly pattern in which these gifts were essential requirements. It was, in fact, because the cult of the dead, like that of fertility, was so firmly established in Hebrew tradition that the Deuteronomic legislation before the Exile prohibited and denounced the time-honoured beliefs and customs. These included not only the mortuary ritual but also such practices as necromancy. So intimate was the relation between the living and the dead that, not content with venerating the patriarchal heroes at their reputed graves, intercourse was held with the departed through the medium of oracles, divination and spiritualist séances.

In the early days of the monarchy after the death of Samuel, Saul is said to have taken measures 'to put away those that had familiar spirits, and the wizards, out of the land', [52] because this illicit recourse to necromantic practices conflicted with the absolute claims of Yahwism over the living and the dead. This was the pre-exilic Deuteronomic interpretation of the situation, but in fact eschatology in Israel was in a state of confusion in the time of Saul. The popular belief still held sway that the individual not only survived after death but had supernatural power as *elohim* possessing superior divine knowledge. Moreover, the idea prevailed of a ghost or double as a shadowy replica of the self (the *nephesh*) with animistic powers and properties. Therefore, despite his efforts to prevent traffic with the deceased by necromantic methods, when Saul himself was at the end of his tether in his campaign against the Philistines, the oracle of Yahweh having been as silent as that of Apollo at Delphi in AD 362 when Julian the Apostate had recourse to it, on the night before the fatal battle on Mount Gilboa he stole away to a medium at Endor to gain occult knowledge of his fate. When she called up Samuel the seer appeared as a ghostly figure wrapped in his familiar cloak as during his lifetime. From the depths of his subterranean abode he was called back to earth and confirmed the sentence passed upon the terror-stricken king. Because Saul had not obeyed the voice of Yahweh, the kingdom, he was told, had been rent out of his hand and on the morrow he and his sons would be in the nether regions, and Israel would be delivered into the hand of the Philistines. [53]

In this graphic account of that tragic night, some light is thrown on the situation in Israel at the beginning of the monarchy respecting the state of the dead and their provenance, making allowance for the narrative having assumed its present form when the reactionary doctrine of Sheol had become more clearly defined. In the days of Saul it was believed that the dead could be invoked and materialized by women who had 'a familiar spirit' (i.e. by mediums), and that they were the ghostly counterparts of themselves as they had lived and appeared in this life. Thus, Samuel was at once recognized both by the woman and Saul, and he was sufficiently conscious of past, present and future events in this world to remember what had happened in the relations of Yahweh to the king, and to know what was about to transpire in the forthcoming battle with the Philistines. Furthermore, he was able to engage in conversation with Saul and to communicate the sentence of death to him through the medium in intelligible terms of language. In fact, the method of consulting departed spirits seems to have been much the same as that employed in respect of the oracle of Yahweh,[54] and because it was a rival mode of divination it was prohibited and condemned.[55]

No doubt it was very largely to stop the traffic with the dead, and the practice of necromancy in general, that Sheol was represented in the pre-exilic period as a subterranean 'land of no return' on Babylonian lines in which the shades of all men, without respect of persons or ethical considerations, lived in a state of silence and forgetfulness as *rephaim*, or 'powerless ones', rather than as *elohim*, or 'divine beings'.[56] So far from having supernatural knowledge which they could impart to those who inquired of them on earth, they did not even know their own sons.[57] Furthermore, it was maintained that since Yahweh was 'the god of the living', whose concern was with his people and their fortunes in the land on earth he had given them for a possession, Sheol was outside his jurisdiction, and its denizens were remembered no more and cut off from his hand.[58]

The Hebrew conception of immortality

Exactly when this interpretation of the afterlife arose in Israel, and to what extent, if at all, it was borrowed directly from the Babylonian notion of the land of no return, are questions of dispute. It may well be that the idea of Sheol developed out of that of the tomb as the chthonian abode of the dead, going back to the nomadic period,[59] where they lived on and continued to experience the same needs as the living— food, drink, clothing, light and implements—but by no means as shadowy replicas of their former selves. On the contrary, since the *rephaim* were called *elohim*, and the term (*rephaim*) was applied to an ancient race of giants[60] as well as to the shades of the dead, they were hardly regarded as 'weak ones', or as devoid of knowledge and consciousness. Indeed, it has been suggested that originally they were 'sons of god' like the *nephilim* in the very ancient piece of folklore incorporated in the Genesis pre-Flood narrative.[61]

Certainly the ancient Hebrews appear to have ascribed considerable power to the dead, and to have venerated their heroic ancestors. With the rise of Yahwism their status was no doubt reduced to the level of only semi-divine beings in the cultus, and with the development of the conception of the *nephesh*, or breath-soul, withdrawn at death, the indwelling life (*ruach*) breathed into Adam at the creation, and repeated at every subsequent birth,[62] left only a shadowy ghost-soul as the replica of the living organism. Thus, in the relatively late post-exilic book of Ecclesiastes, the process of creation is represented as being reversed at death, when the physical elements of the body return to the dust of the earth and the spirit (*ruach*)—the impersonal divine energy—returns to God who gave it,[63] while the soul (*nephesh*) as only a function of the material body merely survives in Sheol in the form of a phantasmal ghost or shade. The general trend of Hebrew thought, therefore, was in the direction of a nebulous afterlife in which conscious personal immortality had no real purpose and dynamic function, quite apart from extraneous Mesopotamian influences.

A man might hope to live in his descendants as his ancestors lived on in himself, the son being responsible for the due performance of the mortuary rites of his father—hence perhaps the levirate which required a man to marry his dead brother's widow to raise up seed to the deceased for this purpose.[64] But it became increasingly a group-survival. As an individual he was destined to survive as a shade of the double that in former times had been thought to inhabit the grave as a duly venerated vital being and repository of superhuman knowledge and wisdom. From the ninth century BC, at any rate, this prophetic doctrine prevailed in pre-exilic Israel, and it survived the Exile among the Sadducees and the more conservative element in the restored nation. Thus, Ben-Sirach, for example, writing just before the Maccabaean revolt, regarded the graves as the common home of all men, whence by divine decree there was no return,[65] though he dimly perceived that the bones of the Judges of old might yet flourish again out of their place.[66]

Despite, however, this Yahwist attempt to reduce Sheol to the inert state of the Babylonian Aralu, which can hardly have failed to influence the Hebrew conception of the nether regions, the earlier belief in a conscious afterlife never completely disappeared in Israel and Judaism. Warriors continued to be buried with their swords and shields,[67] corpses to be gorgeously arrayed, and enemies were mutilated,[68] while Rachel wept for her children at the time of the Chaldaean invasion.[69] It was not, however, until the universal sovereignty of Yahweh was at length extended to include the land of the dead, that a new attitude to the doctrine of immortality was adopted.[70] So long as the dead in Sheol were cut off from their god and were thought to pass out of his presence and power, there could be no promise of eternal life. But once he was recognized to be the god of Abraham, Isaac and Jacob as individuals, and not merely as ancestors of Israel as a nation, then their final destiny could not lie beyond his power.

Jewish apocalyptic eschatology

Job had expressed the conviction that in the end God would vindicate him of his innocence in Sheol, where he would see Him after worms had destroyed his body,[71] though this personal venture of faith does not bear the interpretation of the resurrection of the flesh given to it in the texts translated under Christian influence. Only in one place in the Hebrew canonical scriptures, in fact, is the belief in eternal life and retribution in the afterlife affirmed,[72] and then the reference is to a return of the soul to the earth in a restored body in which it would receive its deserts. Job had cried in despair, 'Oh that a man might die and live again',[73] but with no hope that the wish would be fulfilled. Eventually, however, in the apocalyptic literature in the centuries immediately preceding and succeeding the rise of the new era (180 BC– c. AD 100), when Iranian eschatology made its way into Judaism and Yahweh's jurisdiction over the dead was established, Sheol was transformed into an intermediate state of the faithful Israelite, although it remained the final abode for the rest of mankind.[74]

By about 170 BC it had been sub-divided into departments for particular cross-sections of the community with appropriate rewards and punishments respectively for the righteous and the wicked,[75] and located in the far west, as in the Babylonian, Egyptian and Greek eschatologies, though the Hebrew conception of the underworld also still survived elsewhere in the book of Enoch. With the rise of the belief in retribution in the next life, in addition to a penal Sheol, heaven became the dwelling-place of God and the angels above the celestial spaces,[76] resting on pillars and having gates and portals whence the stars appeared.[77] In the seven heavens into which the celestial realms were divided[78] the various angelic hosts had their several abodes, together with the righteous in their duly allotted resting-places.[79]

Paradise is represented as the heavenly estate of the righteous, situated according to the Book of Adam and Eve in the third heaven. Thither the soul of Adam was taken at his death,[80] and it was to this abode that St Paul said he had been caught up.[81] In the first century AD, however, the final habitation of the righteous was placed in the seventh heaven,[82] this privilege having hitherto been reserved for Elijah and Enoch.[83] Paradise is not mentioned as the abode of the dead in the Hebrew canonical scriptures, the term almost certainly being of Iranian origin. Since originally it designated a 'park' or 'garden', it was readily adopted in the apocalyptic literature to denote the heavenly counter-part of the Garden of Eden.[84] Then, in the first century BC, it became an intermediate state for all the righteous rather than a special preserve for Enoch and Elijah at their translation.

Conversely, the wicked, from being assigned a special penal section of Sheol, were destined to be consumed in a place of torment which derived its name from the valley of Hinnom to the south-west of Jerusalem, long associated with child sacrifices to Molech and similar abominations.[85] Therefore, it readily became a symbol for the final state of apostate Jews and those who oppressed the elect people of God.[86] At the beginning of the Christian era, however, these eternal torments of the damned were thought to be meted out in various localities, such as the third heaven, the nether regions, and an 'inaccessible part of the earth',[87] associated with Azazel in the desert, or the 'murky Tartarus and the black recesses of hell'.[88]

At the general resurrection at the Final Judgment 'the pit of torment shall appear and over against it the place of refreshment. The furnace of Gehenna shall be made manifest, and over against it the Paradise of delight' with its sweet-flowering trees and delicious fruits, and the tree of life in the midst,[89] the Jewish equivalent of the Egyptian Elysian Fields. There, guarded by angels, the righteous were thought to dwell for ever in joy, peace and infinite happiness,[90] in striking contrast to their predecessors in Sheol. Equipped with a heavenly body, those who had been accounted worthy to attain to this final state of eternal bliss were clothed in 'the garments of God's glory' immediately on leaving the intermediate abode, while the wicked passed to the place of torment on the northern side of the third heaven, or, to the lowest hell where 'the prisoners are in pain, expecting limitless judgment'.[91] At the resurrection their souls would waste away, and they would depart to the place of torment and have their dwelling in the fires of Gehenna.[92]

No attempt has been made to systematize this apocalyptic eschatology either in its Jewish or Christian aspects. Gehenna, for example, has many shades of meaning ranging from the valley of perpetual fires of the Hinnom or Topheth imagery, to the penal divisions of Sheol as the final and eternal abode of torment, or the temporary sphere of those awaiting either resurrection to the life everlasting or the destruction of the damned. The New Testament is no more precise. In the Synoptic Gospels the word 'Gehenna' occurs about a dozen times in connexion with the doom and judgment of sinners destined to perish in 'un-quenchable fire' in 'the place of weeping and gnashing of teeth'.[93] In some of the passages the punishment is represented as being of endless duration, while in others it would seem to be remedial and variable, except in the case of the sin specifically described as unforgivable.[94] In the Fourth Gospel, on the other hand, the emphasis is on eternal life which Christ as the Logos possesses in himself and dispenses to his followers who believe in him and participate in his life sacramentally.[95] At the Parousia his elect, it is said, will be gathered to himself and be 'raised up at the last day' to share in the general resurrection.[96] Only once is it asserted in this Gospel that the wicked will have any part in this consummation,[97] though it is affirmed that 'he who believeth not the Son shall not see life but the wrath of God abideth on him'.[98] It was with these modifications that the apocalyptic eschatology found a place in Christian tradition.

Helladic and Mycenaean burial customs
In Greece the conception of immortality developed along lines parallel to those in Israel, the Homeric shades being the counterpart of the Hebrew *rephaim* in their respective nether regions. Moreover, in the Mycenaean background of the Homeric poems there was a more defined cult of the dead comparable to that which seems to have occurred among the early Hebrews. Thus, a great wealth of funerary equipment has been recovered from the shaft-graves of the Helladic kings and the Mycenaean tholoi, bearing eloquent testimony to the deep regard in which the memory of the great princes was held in the Aegean (Fig. 62). In Mycenaean Greece the head of the state (*wanax*) was accorded virtually divine honours, perhaps under Egyptian influence, and in the beehive tombs in which the kings were buried in the second half of the second millennium BC they lived on as deified heroes, probably with a cultus closely associated with that of the gods.[99]

Since many of the tholoi (e.g. at Kapokli, Dimini, Menidi, Vapheio, Messenian Pylos, Chalcis) have yielded pottery of Late Minoan style, and others are Late Mycenaean, they belong unquestionably to a period succeeding that of the shaft-graves. The excavations at Mycenae since the Second World War have brought to light a number of Middle Helladic shaft-graves in the Grave Circle west of the so-called 'Tomb of Clytemnestra' near the Lions' Gate, which contain the skeletons of children and adults with a number of vases, bronze swords and daggers, gold ornaments, an ivory plaque, and a silver jug. In some of them rich furnishings were found *in situ* beside the skeletons, in others a succession of members of the family had been interred, the graves having been opened three or four times for this purpose. Collectively they show that in the closing years of the Middle Helladic period (*c.* 1650–1500 BC) rich gifts were placed in carefully constructed graves, presupposing a developed cult of the dead, at any rate so far as the more important sections of the community were concerned,[100] preparing the way for the great tholoi monuments in the next half of the second millennium BC.

This elaborate tendance, which at Drachmani and Dendra near Midea included sacrificial pits filled with ashes and the charred remains of burnt offerings,[101] supports Nilsson's contention that a developed conception of the afterlife and a hero cult was a distinctive feature of the Mycenaean phase of Aegean religion, in contrast to the absence of a similar mortuary equipment in Minoan burials in Crete.[102] At first these sumptuous rites in shaft-graves and stately beehives may have been reserved for the rulers, but if so they were soon adopted by their subjects, judging from the contents of their tombs. In Crete it was mainly under Mycenaean influence that these distinctive Aegean features were introduced, as is shown, for instance, on the sarcophagus from Hagia Triada* where Egyptian and Mycenaean traits can be discerned in the scenes depicted, and in the number of Egyptian vases, and other objects, including death-masks, ostrich eggs and an isolated example of embalming in Helladic shaft-graves, as well as in the construction of the chamber tombs and their gold.[103]

The Cretan communal ossuaries can now no longer be regarded as the prototypes of the Mycenaean tholoi, as Evans supposed,[104] since the antecedents of the chamber tombs in Greece are to be sought in Egypt rather than in Crete. But the great beehives were specially constructed, in all probability for the Mycenaean rulers, on the plan of the Grave Circles covered with a corbel vault and a mound, when burial in rock chambers was adopted by the populace and a hero cult was becoming established at Mycenae. This was centred in the king in the Egyptian manner, in all probability, and very different from the simple Helladic belief in human survival among the indigenous inhabitants of Greece indicated by the grave goods of the more important section of the community. The bodies of the commoners, however, were disposed of with little or no ceremony or provision for their needs in any afterlife which they may or may not have expected.

Even more marked is the contrast between the Mycenaean burial customs and those recorded in the Homeric literature. Thus, inhumation gave place to cremation, and such funerary goods as are mentioned are said to have been burned with the corpse on the pyre while the shaft-graves, chamber tombs and monumental tholoi were reduced to a mound surmounted by a menhir covering the urn in which the ashes

*cf. Chap. III, p. 100.

of the dead had been deposited.[105] There is nothing to suggest a cult of heroes in these mortuary practices, however much the exploits of Agamemnon, the leader of the Greek expedition against Troy, and his confederates were eulogized. A warrior killed in battle, or under any other similar circumstances, was incinerated as a matter of course because this innovation was regarded as the normal mode of disposing of the body of the dead in the Heroic Age as described by Homer, although, of course, it was only one method adopted in classical Greece.

In the Homeric account of the funeral of Patroclus there are indications of the survival of the earlier Mycenaean customs. The immolation of four horses, nine dogs and twelve prisoners, together with sheep and oxen on the funerary pyre,[106] may have been just a piece of ostentatious barbarism on the part of Achilles and condemned by the poet as an 'evil deed'. But, as Nilsson suggests, it is more likely to have been a carry-over from the rites performed at the tomb of the prince of Midea near Dendra in pre-Homeric times, which included both human and animal sacrifice, and other objects burnt at a fire over two pits.[107] The funeral of Patroclus would seem to have been conducted according to long-established custom in which the earlier procedure was retained. Thus Achilles, as the chief mourner, fasted and remained unwashed throughout the entire ceremony;[108] the corpse was lamented over by wailing women;[109] and carried in procession by warriors with shorn hair to the funerary pyre where the immolations were duly made and the ashes placed under the mound in an urn.[110]

The Homeric conception of the soul and Hades
The earlier belief in a conscious existence after death was retained in the description of the psyche of Patroclus as 'marvellously like himself' standing over Achilles all the night. This was a conception of the state of the dead very different from the normal view of the Homeric poems. At the dissolution the psyche, or breath of life, escaped from the body with the last gasp (represented on vase paintings as a miniature of the deceased), and as a powerless shadow and insubstantial phantom (εἴδωλα)[111] took up its abode in the gloomy realm of Hades in the far west, or beneath the earth. Instead of continuing its customary life in association with the body in an elaborately constructed tomb supplied with adequate sustenance, furnishings, goods and creature comforts, the mortal remains were destroyed by fire as soon as possible, lest they should hinder the departure of the soul. But since that which is felt (θυμός) and perceived (νοῦς) had its seat in the heart and diaphragm, or midriff (φρένες), and, therefore, belonged to the physical organism,

the liberated psyche was devoid of consciousness. When the corporeal life came to an end emotions and perceptions ceased, so that all that survived was a shadowy ghost (σκιά) or image (εἴδωλον) without substance.

Making due allowance for the literary nature of the poems, which set forth in noble language the adventures of the gods and men without much regard for the current theological speculations about the afterlife, it is quite clear that a fundamental change had occurred in the cult of the dead and its associated beliefs in the Homeric tradition. The earlier customs and ideas in some measure doubtless survived, but for ordinary mortals, at any rate, death now meant passing virtually into oblivion in the nether regions from which, as in Babylonia, there was no escape, and in which there was no conscious existence. The witless and feeble shades are represented as flocking together like bats incapable of either joy or sorrow. The mother of Odysseus gazed vacantly at her son, and only when they drank the dark blood as a vitalizing agent did consciousness return to the phantoms.[112] An exception was made in the case of Teiresias, the blind Theban seer to whom Persephone had granted reason (νοῦς) as a special favour, but the other souls flitted about as shadows.[113] Though Orion pursued the wild beasts over the cheerless plains of Asphodel and Minos held his golden staff and sat in judgment over the dead, yet all were insubstantial and devoid of conscious life and activity. Only a few favoured heroes like Kadmos, Harmonia, Herakles and Menelaus, the younger brother of Agamemnon, and the husband of Helen, as the son-in-law of Zeus, were promised Elysium without dying in the Islands of the Blest, where the sky was always clear and the refreshing westerly breezes blew.[114] But these retained their bodies, and as gods escaped imprisonment as disembodied shades and fluttering shadows. Only a few notorious immortal sinners, such as Tantalus, Titysus and Sisyphus, were destined to endure the sufferings of Tartarus, but so grim and uninspiring was existence in Hades that Achilles, like Enkidu in the Babylonian Land of No Return, opined, 'speak no comfortable words to me, glorious Odysseus, concerning death. I had rather be another man's serf of the tilth, a portionless man whose livelihood was but small, rather than be lord over all the dead that have perished.'[115]

As in Israel, this, however, could not be the final verdict on the ultimate end of struggling humanity. In the Homeric Age interest may have been centred in this life, and the story of the descent of Odysseus to the underworld was primarily a literary narrative in noble language, telling the adventures of the Trojan hero and his relations with his former companions. It was not the intention of the poet to give a detailed description of the land as such, as in the case of Dante, still less to formulate a doctrine of immortality. A theory of the soul was often assumed, which ill consorted with the current practices in relation to the dead handed down from former ages when very different ideas about the afterlife prevailed. This was very apparent in the funeral rites of Patroclus which, as has been considered, presupposed a developed cult of the dead, with an elaborate tendance quite out of accord with the Homeric conception of powerless phantom souls. Blood and wine were poured out and sacrifices offered to give life and nourishment to the psyche, just as Circe made Odysseus promise to the gibbering shades that he would offer a barren heifer on their behalf on his return from Ithaca.[116]

Here the revivification of the dead by life-giving blood as a vital essence is implied, and it cannot be reconciled with the Homeric conception of survival in terms of chthonic witless shades as 'the floating images of those who have toiled on earth' beyond reach either by man or to man. Nevertheless, taken collectively 'the Homeric picture of the shadow-life of the disembodied soul,' as Rhode has said, 'was the work of resignation, not of hope. Hope would never have beguiled itself with the anticipation of a state of things which neither afforded men the chance of further activity after death, nor, on the other hand, gave them rest from the toil of life; one which promised them only a restless, purposeless fluttering to and fro, an existence, indeed, but without any of the content that might have made it worthy of the name of life.'[117] The songs of the brave days of old when gods and heroes freely intermingled, sung in the courts of the princes of Ionia, dealt with the glories of the past; but the nobles for whom they were composed and rendered derived no more inspiration from them concerning their destiny in the afterlife than did the rest of the community.

Unlike the Hebrew prophets and psalmists, however, they were not antagonistic to the cult of the dead for theological reasons, and they had no wish to exclude the gods from the land of the dead. On the contrary, in the *Odyssey* Erebus was represented as being under the control of Hades and Persephone, and the Olympian gods themselves were anthropomorphic figures with human qualities and attributes, though they did not concern themselves with human destinies beyond the grave. Only gods were immortal but, nevertheless, heroes were endowed in varying degrees with divine ancestry and superhuman powers. In short, the Homeric tradition, while it contributed a permanent element to Greek religious thought and practice, failed to provide for the deeper spiritual needs of mankind. Side by side with the gloomy abode of Hades was the blissful corporeal existence in a land of Cockaigne, or terrestrial Elysium at the borders of the earth, with its Minoan background, enjoyed by the privileged few. It was only a matter of time before the latent earlier hope of the fuller and better life beyond the grave found its realization for all who were anxious and willing to embrace it, when new religious movements swept through Greece in the sixth century BC, introducing the mystery conception of a blessed afterlife secured through a process of initiation into esoteric cults.

The Mystery afterlife

As we have seen,* although the rites assumed very different forms and could be interpreted in a variety of ways, the main purpose of these secret cults was to obtain a happier lot beyond the grave. In the words of Plutarch, 'death and initiation clearly closely correspond, word for word, and thing for thing. At first there are wanderings and laborious circuits, and journeyings through the dark, full of misgivings where there is no consummation; then, before the very end, come terrors of every kind, shivers and trembling, and sweat and amazement. After this, a wonderful light meets the wanderer; he is admitted into pure meadow lands, where are voices and dances, and the majesty of holy sounds and sacred visions. Here the newly initiated, all rites completed, is at large.'[118]

At Eleusis this was attained by the aid of sacred symbols and sights revealed in the *Telesterion*, whereas in the Thraco-Phrygian cults of Dionysus and Sabazius the Maenads engaged in wild revels to become Bacchoi, and in that status they were made one with the god and so immortal. Sobered under Hellenic influences, in its Orphic guise the Dionysiac acquired a dualistic interpretation in terms of the myth of Zeus and Kronos and the wicked Titans, brought into relation with the doctrine of metempsychosis. The divine origin of the soul having been affirmed, eternal blessedness could be achieved by the adoption of the Orphic way of life with its purifications, asceticisms and sacraments through cycles of rebirth, until at length, when the Titanic nature had been eliminated, the soul was liberated from its imprisonment in the body and so reached its final Elysium. Since this involved rewards and punishments after death, an ethical element was introduced into the conception of the afterlife[119] far removed from the non-moral Hades in the Homeric tradition.

As conceived by Pindar (*c.* 476 BC) games, music and pleasant

*Chap. V, p. 165.

odours were among the rewards of the righteous in the Isles of the Blest, but, nevertheless, this eschatology of Judgment, based on ethical considerations, constituted a definite advance in the moralization of the doctrine of immortality in Greece, even though Homeric ideas were by no means wholly eradicated.[120] It remained for Plato, by a combination of Orphic and animistic imagery, to bring into the full light of philosophical thought the origin and destiny of the soul as the real self of which the body was the instrument. A conception of the soul's moral responsibility involving judgment after death with rewards and punishments, and cycles of lives in this world or in some other sphere in the afterlife, was inherent in the Platonic myths.[121]

Behind all these later speculations lay the primitive conception of human survival in a condition not very different from that of this world but in which the body tended to play a secondary though not always an unimportant role. The Eleusinian Mysteries being in origin Mycenaean with a Minoan background, the optimistic notion of an idealized continuation of terrestrial existence was retained against that of the more pessimistic Homeric subterranean realm of witless shades whither Persephone was represented as being abducted with disastrous consequences in the upper world. Combined with Orphic assurances of an eventual blessedness for the initiated when the shackles of the corporeal life were finally removed, the Pindaric Elysium remained a eulogized Land of the Blest either below ground or at the extremities of the earth. For Plato the pre-existent immortal soul of simple structure akin to the immutable Idea, when it divested itself of its fleshly integument and earthly interests for good and all, was destined to regain its place in the eternal world in accordance with its true nature. This, however, might involve rebirth for anything up to ten thousand years for the majority of mankind, unversed in philosophy or reason before the state of pure intellectual knowledge and understanding could be attained in the Isles of the Blest.[122] It is hardly surprising, therefore, that in the Graeco-Roman world many turned to the hellenized Mysteries of Isis and Attis, which offered to their votaries a more immediate assurance of a blessed afterlife through a ritual process of initiation.

CHAPTER SEVEN

COSMOLOGY

*Egyptian cosmogony, Memphite theology, Heliopolitan Ennead, cosmology of the Two Lands,
Ogdoad of Hermopolis, Amon-Re at Thebes, fashioning god Khnum, cosmological order—
Akkadian creation epic, Sumerian cosmogonic myths, Mesopotamian cosmology—Anatolia—
Ugaritic Baal epic, Israelite cosmogony, Hebrew creation stories—Olympian cosmogony in
Greece, Hesiodic and Orphic theogonies, the One and the Many*

TURNING NOW from the human to the cosmic order, it was by analogy
with the prevailing conditions of mankind that the creation of the
universe, or of that part of it which was the centre of interest and
knowledge, was conceived in the Ancient Near East as a process of
birth from the gods and goddesses primarily concerned with its
generation. In the Fertile Crescent, therefore, western Asia and in the
Aegean, generally it was from either a primal pair or from a single
progenitor, male or female, that all things were thought to have come
into being, though very seldom *ex nihilo*.

The Egyptian cosmogony

Thus, in Egypt the Creators themselves emerged from a watery chaos
and then proceeded to call into existence other divinities who were
personifications of the cosmos in its various parts and aspects. From
Nun, the primordial abyss, came all life, and ever since the sun has
continued to be reborn from these subterranean waters every morning,
just as from them issued the annual inundation of the life-giving Nile,
equated with Osiris, upon which vegetation depended for its growth
and renewal when the waters subsided and the fertile soil appeared.
It is not surprising that they should have been personified as divinities,
since, taken in conjunction with the sun which was thought to arise
from them on its daily course across the horizon, they were the source
of all vitality. Indeed, any god might be said to have 'come forth from
Nun'. For in the last analysis the primordial abyss was regarded as the
father of the gods who gave rise spontaneously to the Creator of the
world known under his several names at his respective cult-centres, as
Atum-Re at Heliopolis, Ptah at Memphis, Thoth at Hermopolis and
Khnum at Elephantine, though each might be subordinate to the other
elsewhere. It was, therefore, from Nun that both the divine and cosmic
orders were established, and it is not improbable that behind the

multiplicity of deities concerned with creation there was originally one Supreme Being as the transcendent source of universal creative activity summing up in himself the various attributes and aspects of the cosmos, and responsible for the control of the cosmic processes.

In this way the same linguistic root connects the heavens, the clouds and the rain, with their principal personifications in the Creator and his manifestations in nature, such as the storm and the thunder. Zeus or Dyaus Pitar among the Indo-Europeans, or Teshub in Anatolia, was primarily the god of the sky, the storm and the weather, known under a number of names before he assumed the functions of the various gods whom he assimilated, and in Egypt the Falcon-god Horus, the 'Lofty One', was regarded as a celestial deity with a creative capacity before he acquired a solar significance and eventually an Osirian role. In view of the place occupied by the sun in the Nile valley as a life-giving and as a destructive force, it was not surprising that it became the dominant creative symbol, even though the self-created Memphite Ptah retained his position as the sole Creator of the universe and of the gods who were objectified conceptions of his mind.[1]

The Memphite Theology
Ptah, however, was originally represented in the Memphite Theology as anterior to the Sun-god Atum, because the eight gods who brought forth the sun from the primeval waters were his creation, as were the eight primeval elements in chaos with which he was identified as Ptah-Ta-Tjenen, 'Ptah of the Risen Land', the Primordial Hill which he created out of Nun to become the centre of the earth. Therefore, all that exists came from him and functioned through him as the ground of all creation. By thinking as the 'heart' and commanding as the 'tongue', Ptah fashioned an egg on his potter's wheel from which the earth was hatched, or as was sometimes supposed, he carved it as a statue.[2] In this more abstract conception of creation in the Memphite Theology, Ptah became the 'mighty great Creator' from whom the cosmic order emanated virtually *ex nihilo*. It was 'in his heart and on his tongue' that something in the form of Atum came into being, and by this creative process of thought the rest of the Ennead of gods were created and placed in their temples. This accomplished, 'men, animals, all creeping things and whatever lives' were similarly created by the thought and word of Ptah. So it became understood that his power was greater than that of other gods, and, like Yahweh in the Hebrew Priestly story, as will be considered, he then rested from his labours well content with everything that he had made.

When Memphis suddenly rose to pre-eminence in the First Dynasty, its theologians realized that its god Ptah had to be greater than all other deities, including even the Heliopolitan Atum, who was represented as having resorted to masturbation to create Shu and Tefnut, the atmosphere and moisture, by receiving his own semen in his mouth. Ptah, however, conceived all things in his 'heart' (i.e. mind) and brought them forth by words of his mouth ('tongue'). To this end the available resources were utilized—that of the Sun-god rising from chaos; the creation of the eight heavenly and earthly gods of the abyss; an Ogdoad transformed into an Ennead by the addition of Atum. It then only required the substitution of Ptah for Atum as the head of the pantheon, and to make him the ultimate source of the process of creation, to establish him as 'the Creator upon the great throne', and identify him with the original gods of the Ogdoad—

> Ptah-Nun, the father who begot Atum;
> Ptah-Naunet, the mother who bore Atum;
> Ptah the Great, that is, heart and tongue of the Ennead;
> Ptah . . . who gave birth to the gods.[3]

These he created out of nothing, prior even to chaos as well as to Atum, the head of the Ennead, with whom the work of creation began when the gods and the divine cosmic forces were brought into conjunction with the physical universe.

Whereas other gods created by physical methods, Ptah exercised his functions spiritually in the realm of ideas by thought and speech, thereby taking precedence over the rest of the pantheon as the 'Great One', the 'Lord of the Two Lands'. All the rest of the gods did homage to him, and were content because they were associated with him. And, as Breasted has pointed out, there would seem to be in these early speculations an anticipation of the Logos doctrine of Philo and the Fourth Gospel within the context of Egyptian cosmology.[4] It was, however, a cosmos in which gods and men were interrelated and shared a common nature and modes of behaviour with the Supreme Creator still rather far removed from the monotheistic transcendent living God of Hebrew and Christian faith and practice, or from the Hellenic First Cause of the universe as a principle of divine intelligence and cosmic order. The primary purpose of the Memphite Theology was to stabilize Memphis as the new centre of a theocratic state, and to unify Upper and Lower Egypt as a single duality ruled over by a Pharaoh who was himself the epitome of all that was divine in the Nile valley. Although the act of creation was described in spiritual terms in relation to the utterances of the thought of the Source of everything that exists, human and divine, Ptah was in the first instance the power in the earth, though he was transcendent rather than immanent in nature. But he made the local gods and their cities, and ordered their estates in a polytheistic pantheon.

Moreover, the Memphite Theology never gained universal recognition in Egypt. It was too abstract to be generally acceptable, and it was to Atum and Amon-Re, immanent in the sun and the wind, and incarnate in the reigning king on earth, that the nation as a whole turned as the dynamic centre of the cosmic and political order. In the solar mythology the all-enveloping sun was represented flying across the horizon like a falcon, or as the self-created scarab beetle rolling the ball of the sun across the sky in the morning, and in the afternoon as an ageing man who in the evening tottered down to the west. The earth was depicted encircled by mountains on which the sky rested, personified as the goddess Nut. Below was the great abyss from which the Sun-god was born every morning as at the beginning of creation, when he arose from it as the first-born of the primeval sea, Nun. Until Shu, the Air-god, the father of Nut, stood on the earth and lifted her up and supported her with his arms, the sky and the earth were not separated. Alternatively, the vault of heaven was depicted as an immense cow upheld by the gods, which had a star-spangled belly; under this was the Milky Way which was traversed daily by the morning boat of the sun manned sometimes by the personified stars.

The Heliopolitan Ennead

In the celestial realms Atum became supreme and exercised his creative functions whilst his worship and its cosmic symbolism became predominant in the Old Kingdom under the powerful influence of Heliopolis. In the Fifth Dynasty (c. 2380 BC), when the city became the capital and the centre of the solar cult, he was the head of the Ennead, and the Pharaoh assumed the title 'Son of Re'.* There the 'House of the Obelisk' in the temple was alleged to stand on the Primeval Sandhill on which Atum first appeared. Consequently, it was regarded as the centre of the creative forces which he combined within himself when he became the progenitor of the Great Ennead—Shu (air) and Tefnut (moisture), Geb (earth) and Nut (sky), Osiris and Isis, and Seth and Nephthys, the offspring of Geb and Nut. As Atum-Re a complex mythology developed around him in the Pyramid Age in which as the Supreme God he

*Chap. II, p. 71.

became the self-created Creator, the source of life and generation as well as the father of the gods and the personification of the sun in its manifold forms and capacities.[5] He was the ruler of the world in all four directions of the horizon, and at the same time he exercised protective control in a special sense over Egypt, as the Pharaoh was his son and incarnate embodiment on earth.

The cosmology of the Two Lands

The cosmological symbol, however, in the Nile valley was that of the 'Two Lands', not the four cardinal points of the world. According to Frankfort this very ancient conception of the Kingdom of the Two Lands recurring analogically in a dualistic symbolism long after the unification of Upper and Lower Egypt attributed to Menes was an accomplished fact, satisfied the Egyptian mode of thought, which was always prone to understand the world in dualistic terms as a series of pairs and contrasts balanced in an unchanging equilibrium—heaven and earth, north and south, Geb and Nut, Shu and Tefnut.[6] Wilson, on the other hand, has come to the conclusion that it was the duality of the Two Lands that produced the dualism.[7] This is by no means improbable since Egypt has always been primarily 'the gift of the Nile', and, in conjunction with the sun, the Nile was the source and symbol of the vitality of the country and its inhabitants.

The upper and lower reaches of the river were the outstanding divisions, perennially in conflict until they were unified as a dualistic whole, and subsequently brought into relation with the solar cultus and its four-dimensional cosmic conceptions. The world of the horizon and the world of the Two Lands were not infrequently in a state of tension and conflict at that time, expressed in terms of Horus and Seth with the Pharaoh mediating the divine forces of the cosmic order on behalf of the well-being of the unified nation.[8] He was the dynamic stabilizing centre of the country, uniting it with the divine sources and controlling agencies of the universe in a sacramental process of mediation, himself being a cosmic figure and the embodiment of its forces.[9] He was, in fact, the god by whose dealings all things lived and moved and had their being in the Nile valley, consubstantial with his heavenly father Atum-Re.[10]

As he was the fount of all life and order, so he was the champion of justice because he 'lived by Maat', dispelling the darkness of disorder and radiating the brightness of Maat in its cosmic, social and ethical sense of the rhythm of the universe, of good government, harmonious human relations, law, justice and truth. The universe, in fact, was regarded as a monarchy, the king of the world being the first Egyptian Pharaoh, and his successors, by virtue of their descent from Atum-Re, had consolidated the Two Lands into a single nation balanced in unchanging equilibrium, like the always dependable seasonal rhythm in the Nile valley pursuing its annual course with phenomenal regularity.

The Ogdoad of Hermopolis

In addition to the Memphite and Heliopolitan cosmogonies, Hermopolis had a Primordial Hill which was alleged to have appeared at the beginning of time as an island of flames in the midst of the primeval waters,[11] and an Ogdoad of gods and goddesses personifying the formless chaos before the creation. The first pair of these eight gods was Nun, the primordial waters, and his consort Nunet, the celestial expanse above the abyss. The next two were Huh and Huker, the boundless imperceptible expanse of chaotic formlessness, followed by Kuk and Kuket, darkness and obscurity. Finally, Amon and Amonet, the intangible and secret aspects of chaos, emerged, blowing where it listeth like the wind, without revealing whence it comes and whither it goes.

At the head was placed Thoth, probably an ancient Delta god who was already a member of the Little Ennead of Heliopolis, and he, with Horus, was the heart and tongue of Atum and of Ptah. Although he was never actually one of the Ogdoad, the eight primeval gods were thought to be the souls of Thoth. As an ibis he laid an egg on the waters of Nun out of which the Sun-god appeared, though he was also said to have come into being in a lotus-flower. In his Hermopolitan guise Thoth himself was self-begotten, the personification of divine intelligence, omniscience and omnipotence, exercising his creative powers by divine utterance—'the word of his voice'.[12] But the Hermopolitan mythology is hopelessly confused, and it is impossible to be sure whether it was the Ogdoad who created Atum or Atum who produced the eight gods, while the precise relation of Thoth to them, and his cosmological functions, cannot be determined with any degree of certainty. Thus, in the New Kingdom Amon became the leader of the pantheon and head of the Theban Ennead, having been brought into conjunction with the Heliopolitan Re and his cultus at the new capital (Thebes) where the cosmology and theology of Amon-Re of Heliopolis and Thoth of Hermopolis were merged with Amon-Re as the supreme solar deity. Thoth ceased to exercise creative functions and became the god of wisdom and eventually the virtual judge of the dead, since he pronounced the verdict when the souls were weighed before Osiris. His earlier connexions with the moon may have been responsible for his being regarded as a reckoner of time and of numbers, as calculations were made by the moon.

Amon-Re at Thebes

In the New Kingdom Thebes rose to pre-eminence as the principal sacred city, 'the Eye of Re', having absorbed the Memphite, Heliopolitan and Hermopolitan cosmogonies and their respective systems of gods, by making Amon the body of Ptah and the face of Re, who controlled and pervaded the entire universe together with the heavens and the underworld. There was no single god worshipped as alone supreme anywhere in Egypt, except during the Ikhnaton interlude when the Aton, the monotheistic Power manifested in the disk of the sun, was temporarily exalted as the one and only god. This was foreign to the Egyptian conception of Deity, and after the death of Ikhnaton (c. 1366 BC) the normal polytheistic combination of gods in pantheons unified in a primary creative power was restored with the Theban Amon-Re as the ultimate source of existence.

The Pharaohs were his embodiment and representative, but they were also equated with a series of gods concerned with the cosmic processes and comprehended as a divine unity in the several forms of the Ogdoad manifesting the qualities, attributes and activities of Amon in the universe and on earth in Egypt. Having brought all things into being, he continued to rule the seasons and the days, to sail over the heavens and in the underworld in his boat, to control the winds and the clouds, to speak in the thunder, and to give life to man and beast and vegetation. Thus, Tutankhamen restored the Amon succession at Thebes after the death of Ikhnaton, and re-established it as the capital of the empire; he was then said to have 'driven out disorder from the Two Lands so that order (Maat) was again established in its place as at the first time (i.e. the creation).'[13] As society was an integral part of the universal divine order of the universe, which included truth and justice, its laws were identical with those of nature and its processes, and all alike were originated by and under the control of the Creator and his incarnation on earth. Therefore, any disturbance in the one, such as the Ikhnaton heresy, had a corresponding effect in the other sphere of cosmic operations. Consequently, to maintain the flourishing condition of the country as in primeval times, Maat has to be put in the place of disorder and falsehood.[14] This was accomplished by the Pharaoh and his priesthood who transmitted the Maat of the cosmos from the gods, to give stability and good government on earth.

The fashioning god Khnum

But no single god had an absolute monopoly of all the powers and forces involved in this complex cosmological conception in the Nile valley. While at Heliopolis, Hermopolis and Thebes it was the Sun-god who was its primary source, at Memphis the Earth-god Ptah reigned supreme. At Elephantine and Philae Khnum, an ancient god of the First Cataract, was 'the maker of heaven and earth and the underworld, and of water and of the mountains', who produced mankind out of clay, fashioning them on a potter's wheel.[15] He raised up the heavens on its four pillars, and made the Nile. So all-embracing were his powers as a 'fashioner' not only of gods and men but also of cosmic phenomena, that he occupied an important position among the great Creator-gods not very different from that of Ptah. His symbol the ram became 'the living soul of Re', and he was represented with the head of a falcon to identify him with Horus the Sky-god.[16] So close was his relationship with Re, in fact, that he often was known as Khnum-Re, and in this capacity he was a manifestation of the power of the Sun-god in his various aspects, particularly in respect of procreative force. Therefore, the king as the vital centre in Egypt was equated with Khnum as the fashioning god, 'the begetter who brings people into being'.

The cosmological order

Such was the situation in Egyptian cosmology. The physical universe, of which the Nile valley was the focal point, was conceived as having emerged from the primeval ocean, Nun, which remained below the earth and surrounded it as the Okeanos, the 'Great Circuit'. Whether the earth and the sky were supported by a cow, a goddess, a mountain chain, or posts at the four cardinal points, or the sun was the son of the Sky-goddess, the calf of Hathor, or the self-created Atum-Re-Khepri, depended upon the principal cosmogonic myth that was adopted, and the centre with which it was associated—Heliopolis, Memphis, Hermopolis, Thebes or Elephantine. The creation stories in which their several gods were represented as the primary and contemporary source of all existence—Atum-Re, Ptah, Thoth, Amon-Re or Khnum—all had behind them, notwithstanding the inconsistencies, the conception of divine creative activity manifest in the sun, the wind, the earth and the heavens, making and fashioning all things according to predetermined designs and purposes. This was achieved either by sexual processes of procreation on the part of the Creator-god, or by the projection of thought given expression in divine utterance.

In this cosmological symbolism, the Nile, the sun, the sky, the bull,

and the cow predominate, personified as divine creative powers manifest in cosmic phenomena. The waters of the inundation, sharply
divided into south and north, upper and lower Egypt, constituted the
earliest and most fundamental imagery in their recreative aspects, while
the sun, especially in the south, did not become the dominating feature
until later. From Heliopolis the solar theology spread over the whole
country, so that practically every local god became identified with the
Sun-god in some way, and the temple cultus was everywhere based on
the Heliopolitan liturgy, while its Great Ennead and Primordial Hill
set the pattern of the cosmic mythology.

Next to the solar cosmology, that of the primeval ocean with its many
ramifications on, around and below the earth was of widespread
occurrence. This was extended ultimately to the celestial realms, when
the home of the dead became the Duat in the Elysian Fields in the
northern part of the sky, where the circumpolar stars were located.
The underworld of Osiris was situated in the west, until he became
Orion—'He of the horizon from which Re goes forth'—rising and
setting daily, and Isis followed after him as the dog-star Sothis.[17] The
waxing and waning moon was also equated with Osiris, typifying his
death and resurrection, the waning moon being the Eye of Horus lost
in the fight with Seth.[18] Originally the moon may have been a form of
Horus, the twin of the sun, personified as Khonsu, who at Thebes
became the son of Amon and Mut. In the New Kingdom he was
identified with Thoth, who, however, was primarily the god of Wisdom.
As Horus he was represented as a handsome young prince with a lunar
disk and crescent on his head, holding in his hands the whip and
shepherd's crook.[19]

The Akkadian creation epic

In Mesopotamia the cosmological order was constituted in relation to
the divine powers in and behind the various phenomena of nature, who
determined the course of the universe and the political organization,
which was based on the cosmic order of the gods. At their head stood
Anu, the god of the sky, who was the most potent power in heaven and
on earth, though it was not until the time of Gudea of Lagash in the
middle of the third millennium BC (c. 2060–2042 BC) that he attained
supremacy, having risen from obscurity in the Sumerian period.
According to the Babylonian creation story (i.e. the *Enuma elish*), in the
beginning the primal male Apsu, personifying the 'sweet waters' of the
abyss, mingled with his consort Tiamat, the salt-water of the ocean, to
produce a son Mummu, representing the mist and clouds arising from

the watery chaos. From these primeval divine relationships all life emerged in much the same way as the luxuriant growth in the marshes in southern Mesopotamia seemed to have proceeded spontaneously from the conjunction of the waters of the Tigris and Euphrates with those of the sea. So in the primeval cosmogony the first two gods appeared in this watery chaos, Lahmu and Lahamu, as the offspring of Apsu and Tiamat, and from them the next divine pair, Anshar and Kishar, issued as two aspects of the horizon composed of the silt circumscribing the sky and the earth. It was this second couple who gave birth to Anu. He took up his abode in the third heaven and begot Nudimmut, or Ea (Enki), the god of the sweet waters and of wisdom, and as Enki he was 'the lord of the earth'.

The boisterous behaviour of these youthful deities, however, became so disturbing to their progenitors that, acting on the advice of Mummu, they determined to destroy them, that peace might again reign. Tiamat refused to acquiesce in this drastic course of action, and when the news of the proposal reached the younger gods it caused great consternation among them, until Ea/Enki surrounded Apsu and his allies with a magic circle and rendered them helpless by an overpowering spell which he cast on the water. He then slew Apsu and imprisoned Mummu, the vizier, passing a string through his nose to hold him fast. As Tiamat had not been party to the proposed massacre, she was left unmolested by Ea, who now assumed the leadership and produced a son, Marduk, destined to become the wisest of the gods, omnipotent in magical power.[20]

By the time that Marduk had grown to manhood, further disturbances had arisen among the gods until at length Tiamat was aroused to action by her new husband Kingu, whom she placed at the head of her forces, giving him supreme power over the universe by entrusting to him the 'Tablets of Destinies'. After both Ea and Anu had failed to mollify Tiamat, Anshar proposed that Marduk should be sent to vanquish her. The young warrior god assented to this on the condition that he be made head of the pantheon and be given 'kingship and power over all things'. The gods thereupon assembled at a feast, and after Marduk had proved his magical powers by causing a garment to disappear and reappear, he was invested with 'irresistible weapons' for the fight. Clad in a terrifying coat of mail, he was equipped with every possible aid to victory, including arrows of lightning, a rainbow and a net held by four winds

Thus arrayed, he set forth to meet Kingu and his forces, who at the very sight of him fell into disorder. Tiamat alone remained unperturbed, and calling down vengeance upon him engaged him in single combat.

Thereupon he entangled her in his net as she opened her mouth to devour him and drove in an evil wind to keep her jaws extended while he shot an arrow through them to her heart. Like David triumphing over Goliath, he stood upon her dead body while her followers were caught in his net while attempting to flee. Kingu was then bound and the Tablets of Destinies were taken from him. He returned to Tiamat, split her skull and divided her body into two parts like a mussel. With one half he formed the sky as a roof, fixing a crossbar and posting guards to prevent the waters of Tiamat from escaping. He installed the three great gods—Anu, Ea and Enlil—in this upper firmament in their respective residences, and set the constellations in their stations, ordering the phases of the moon to determine the months and days in the calendar and the sequence of night and day.[21]

The universe having been established and the lunar fluctuations arranged, Ea's creation of man from the blood of Kingu, to relieve the gods of all menial tasks is described, after a break in the text in Tablet V. Marduk then divided the gods into two groups (Anunnaki), the one celestial and the other those of the lower regions, and stationed three hundred of them to protect the earth, assigning to them their appointed portions. In gratitude for having been relieved of compulsory service they erected the Esagila in honour of Marduk in the temple at Babylon, and built themselves shrines. When the sanctuary was completed a great banquet was held, attended by the fifty great gods, at the end of which Anu conferred upon Marduk the fifty names and his status and functions in the universe indicated by each of the designations.[22]

In this great Akkadian epic, assigned to the early part of the second millennium BC, the creative activities of the ancient Sumerian gods, Ea, Anu and Enlil, were centred in Marduk and his city Babylon. In the background may lie the perennial struggle against the recurrent floods in Mesopotamia, interpreted mythologically in terms of the primeval conflict between Tiamat and the waters of chaos, and Marduk, the son of Ea, as the young virile Storm-god and Weather-god.[23] Since it was this cosmic struggle that was repeated annually at the New Year Festival in order to maintain the right ordering of the universe and its processes, and to secure the renewal of life at its source, it is not surprising that the enactment of the creation story occupied a dominant position in the *Akitu* celebration in the Esagila at Babylon.

The Sumerian cosmogonic myths
In the cosmological myths current in Sumer in the later half of the third millennium BC, although the creation of the universe is not des-

cribed, there are references to the goddess Nammu, the primeval ocean, giving birth to heaven and earth which were united as a vast cosmic mountain until they were separated by Enlil, the Air-god. Then Anu carried off the heaven and Enlil the earth, later identified with the goddess Nunmah or Ninhursaga.[24] In the sky world the Moon-god Nanna, a son of Enlil, 'caused the good day to come forth', and in conjunction with Ea, the Water-god, produced vegetable and animal life on earth. They also sent the Cattle-god Lahar and the Grain-god Ashnan to make cattle and grain abundant, so that the gods (Anunnaki) might be supplied with food and clothing.[25]

As in the later Babylonian creation story, human beings were made by the joint efforts of Nammu, her son Enki, and Ninmah 'for the sake of the welfare of the sheepfolds and good things of the gods', to free them from labouring for their sustenance. Six types of men were fashioned by Nunmah from the clay of the Apsu, two of whom were sexless. Enki then tried his hand at creating clay men, with little success since his manikins could neither speak, eat nor stand.[26] Although the texts fail us at this important point in the story, eventually the joint efforts of the gods appear to have been successful, as man is represented as having been created for their benefit after heaven and earth had been engendered by the primeval sea and separated by the air, from which also the moon was made and became the matrix of the sun. Plant, animal and human life then appeared on the earth by the union of air, earth and water, conceived in terms of gods and goddesses, the Sumerian prototypes of their Babylonian and Akkadian counterparts.

Mesopotamian cosmology

These deities, however, were essentially an integral part of the cosmic order and its creative processes, just as the social and political structure on earth was represented as an event in the cosmic order of the gods. Both the cosmic and social organizations were thought to have emerged out of a constant state of ferment, the one being dependent upon the other. Thus the kingship was said to have come down from heaven and to have resided in the rulers in the great ancient Sumerian cities as the earthly analogues of the cosmic order.

With the rise of Babylon and its god Marduk to pre-eminence, it (Babylon) became the *omphalos*, 'the navel of the world', occupying much the same position as the sacred cities of Egypt that claimed to possess a Primordial Hill (e.g. Heliopolis, Hermopolis, Memphis, Thebes and Philae), equated with their temples alleged to stand upon it, or with the stone at Delphi in Greece which marked the centre of the universe. In the Code of Hammurabi it is said that when Anu and Enlil determined the destinies of the land Babylon was 'made supreme in the world established by him (Marduk) in the midst of an enduring kingship whose foundations are fit as heaven and earth.' It was then that Hammurabi was called by them 'to cause justice to prevail in the land, to destroy the wicked and the evil that the strong might not oppress the weak'. Thus he rose 'like the sun over the blackheaded people, to light up the land'.[27] Nippur occupied a similar position in Mesopotamian cosmology prior to the rise of Babylon, and as early as the middle of the third millennium BC the Sumerian ruler of Umma, Lugal-zaggisi, 'the shepherd' of his people, assumed the title 'King of the Land' at the end of the Early Dynastic period, on the authority of Enlil.[28] This gave him not only dominion over Sumer but a unique status in the world, by divine decree coextensive with the cosmic rule of Enlil.

Although in fact the rulers of Ur, Kish and Lagash had exercised similar jurisdiction on the same grounds, Lugal-zaggisi went further than his predecessors by claiming universal sovereignty over all countries from the Persian Gulf to the Mediterranean. Therefore, when he was defeated by Sargon of Akkad, his son Naram-Sin adopted the title 'King of the Four Quarters (of the world)' which was the designation of the Great Gods, Anu, Enlil and Shamash.[29] At the centre stood the principal temple of the god and the king, which acquired a cosmic significance, though in Mesopotamia, as we have seen, the kingship was never a really cohesive force in the country as a whole until the time of Hammurabi. The title, however, did carry the implication of universal rule comparable to that of the divine heavenly counterparts of the king, and Hammurabi was not slow to maintain these implications and to be styled the sun of Babylon and of all peoples. Celestial emblems were included in the regalia, and the imperial robe was ornamented with the zodiacal constellations, just as celestial revolutions and fertility cycles were interpreted in relation to aeonic and astrological phenomena. It was an accepted principle that events on earth were controlled by those that occurred in the celestial sphere, and this was in line with the cosmic counterparts of the established social and political régime. All existence, in fact, was part of a unified cosmological order as a coherent cosmogonic whole, as set forth in the creation stories which can be traced back from the Assyrian and Babylonian epics to the Sumerian myths of origins.

Because the Mesopotamian gods were regarded virtually as the universe in its several aspects, they were not exactly creators in the theistic sense of the term. As in Egypt, they were themselves products of a creative process in which primeval parents gave rise to theogonies; in these contending factions of older and younger gods struggled for the mastery and a cosmogony developed out of this conflict. In the first half of the second millennium BC this became the great Akkadian epic known by its opening words *Enuma elish*, 'When Above', with Marduk as its central figure and Babylon as its cult-centre and hub of the universe. In the first millennium, when Assyria attained predominance in Mesopotamia, Marduk was replaced by Ashur (Fig. 31), but apart from minor adjustments, the cosmic drama remained essentially unchanged.

Anatolia

Although in Syria and Anatolia a corpus of myths occurred which had parallels to the Mesopotamian cycle, in which the divine cosmic order was regarded as being intermingled with events on earth, cosmogonic texts comparable to those in Egypt and Mesopotamia have not been found in the Hurrian, Hittite and Ugaritic tablets. As we have seen, the Tammuz motif seems to be inherent in the Hittite cultic myth of the god who disappeared in a rage and thereby caused a drought to devastate the land, connected with the figures of Telipinu, the Weather-god, and the Sun-god.[30] Nothing is said in it, however, about the origin of the universe, any more than in the story of the combat between the Weather-god of Hatti and the dragon Illuyankas. In the Kumarbi theogony the triad of gods, Anu, Alalu and Kumarbi, appear to correspond to the Sumerian Anu, Alalu and Enlil, but again they do not occur in a creation context. No doubt behind these myths lay the ancient conflict between the older and younger gods, as in Mesopotamia, and the recurrent vegetation theme, but in neither the Hurrian nor the Hittite versions has the cosmological content survived.

The Ugaritic Baal epic

In the Ras Shamra texts El is represented as a remote shadowy Supreme Being living in a cosmic paradise, 'a thousand fields, ten thousand fields at the sources of the two rivers, in the midst of the fountains of the two deeps', as 'the father of years' and of man, the progenitor of the gods. His localization was the 'Mount of the North', the Ugarit Olympus, identified with Mons Cassius, the modern el-Akra to the north of Ras Shamra, and other Syrian cosmic paradises, such as Sheizar in the Orontes valley, south-east of Ras Shamra, Sapon, the seat of the victorious Baal after his conflicts with Mot, and the Tyrian 'garden of god'.[31]

These sacred heights were commonly regarded as 'the navel of the earth' and acquired a cosmic significance not very different from that of the Egyptian 'Primeval Hills'. As Mons Cassius was the highest mountain in Syria, it may have been thought to mark the place where the waters of the upper and lower firmaments met.[32] It was where 'two streams converge' that El was said to have met Asherah, very much as in the Gilgamesh Epic the abode of the gods was situated at the mouth of the cosmic streams, and the Hebrew terrestrial paradise was watered by two rivers, Pihon and Gihon, which became four heads.[33] In any case it was in these inaccessible lofty regions that El dwelt and exercised his cosmic functions, like his counterparts elsewhere in western Asia, until at length his supremacy was usurped by Aleyan-Baal, full of strength and vigour like Marduk in Babylonia when he replaced Enlil.

Baal, the equivalent of the ancient Semitic Storm-god and Weather-god, Hadad (i.e. the Akkadian Adad), also had his habitation on a lofty mountain in the northern heavens as 'the exalted Lord of the Earth'. There in his celestial palace he caused a lattice to be inserted to allow the fructifying rain to fall on the world beneath, so that he became known as 'the lord over the furrows of the field' controlling the processes of fertility,[34] having conquered his enemies and installed himself on the throne of El. His main task, however, as King of Sapan appears to have been the rejuvenation of vegetation and the maintenance of the seasonal sequence, rather than the creation of the universe and the establishment of the cosmic order. This involved defeating his opponent Mot, just as Marduk had to dispose of Tiamat and Ea to remove the threat of the monster Illikummi. But although he acquired the leadership of the gods and became the central figure in the Ugaritic cult, he was honoured as the god who guaranteed rain and fertility, but there is no suggestion that he was regarded as the creator of all things and the author and giver of life. On the contrary, he had replaced El as the most potent figure in the pantheon, and whatever creative functions were exercised, they were originally in all probability performed by El as the ancient Supreme Being, who passed into obscurity with the rise of the dynamic Young god Aleyan-Baal.

It is possible, in fact, that Baal was identified with the Hurrian Storm-god and Weather-god Teshub and the Semitic Hadad before he was introduced into the Canaanite pantheon in northern Syria.[35] Certainly he was not the only god on whom fertility was thought to depend; Mot, for example, was treated as a Grain-god, and had rival claims to the kingship. Moreover, the name ba'lu was a generic term for 'lord', and, therefore, readily applicable to a number of gods. Hence arose the identification of Baal with other local gods of western Asia—Hadad, Yahweh, Aleyan and El—as a composite deity combining a number of creative activities. In this guise he was a recurrent figure in widely dispersed theogonies in which a creation story was inherent rather than defined. Nevertheless, the Baal epic in the Ugaritic texts lacks a cosmogony comparable to that in the Egyptian, Mesopotamian and Hebrew literature, as there is no account of the origins of the Canaanite pantheon or of the emergence of the universe from a primeval chaos and its organization as a cosmic order.

The Israelite cosmogony

In Israel, on the other hand, when Yahweh became the consolidating centre of the Hebrew tribes and was represented as the god under a new name whom their fathers had worshipped from the beginning, although it was not denied that the neighbouring nations had their own deities, he occupied a unique position in the cosmogony. If he assumed the functions of the indigenous vegetation gods in Palestine, he stood apart from them in Israel, jealous of his position as the sole legitimate object of worship among his chosen people. Occasionally, as at Elephantine, he may have been assigned consorts from other pantheons, but for the most part he was kept free from compromising relationships with rival local divinities, until eventually he became the one and only Supreme Deity by whose act and word order was brought out of chaos, and all things visible and invisible were created.

When he engaged in battle with other gods it was for the purpose of deposing them and asserting his absolute sovereignty as a result of his victory, seizing their power and occupying the throne in unchallenged might.[36] In fighting against dragons and demons, like Baal and Marduk, he did so as the supreme Creator[37] conquering chaos and creating an orderly cosmos, endowing it with light and life and setting the sun, moon and constellations in their respective courses.[38] There are, however, also references to a creation story in which Yahweh was in conflict with mythical primeval monsters, such as Leviathan and Rahab, indistinguishable from those which recur elsewhere in the Near Eastern cosmology.[39]

Even as late as the end of the Exile in the sixth century BC, the Deutero-Isaiah called upon him to awake and put on the strength of his arm 'as in the ancient days' when he clave Rahab in pieces and pierced the crocodile (*tannin*), and dried up the abyss, as when he delivered his people from Egypt he dried up the Red Sea and made a similar way for the ransomed to pass over to the safety of the desert.[40] Here the reference is to the creation of the universe from the body of Rahab, when Yahweh had fought and destroyed the monster of the deep just as Marduk employed the body of Kingu for the same purpose, and also to the piercing and driving away of the flying serpent, a dragon associated with eclipses and the sky.[41] Rahab, in fact, seems to have been synonymous with the serpent, the crocodile and sea monsters in general,[42] while Leviathan was another name for Lotan, the Ugaritic Prince of the Sea, said to have been punished by Yahweh with his great sword when he slew the crocodile that was in the sea.[43] In the book of Job he is depicted as a cosmic dragon breathing out fire and smoke, impervious to attack by sword, spear or arrow.[44] Clubs and sling stones were treated by him as stubble, he laughed at the lance; iron was a chaff and brass was as rotting timber. He left a gleam behind him in the sea and on earth none was like him, feared as he was alike by gods and all the creatures over which he ruled as lord of the beasts, while by swallowing the sun or the moon he produced eclipses.[45]

He was a many-headed demonic being, like Lotan, connected with the primeval abyss with whom Yahweh was in conflict, and the victory was later interpreted as a foreshadowing of the deliverance of Israel from bondage in Egypt. In the earlier mythology, however, of which only a few traces remain, the theme undoubtedly was that of the conquest of the dragon under a variety of designations—Leviathan, Rahab, Tehôm, Tannin, and the Serpent (*Nakhash*)—and identified with the primordial waters of the abyss. When it was broken in pieces and its hosts scattered, chaos became an ordered cosmos. Then the Creator divided the sea and caused the mighty rivers to dry up. The destructive waters were transformed into life-giving rains, wells and springs, as the dry land appeared, ready for vegetation to spring forth and the seasons to be established.[46]

Thus the ancient cosmic struggle with the hostile forces was personified as Leviathan and Rahab, while the surrounding waters were regarded as a destructive and sinister element that had to be conquered and tamed before the earth could be made habitable. This was in accord with the Mesopotamian mythopoeic thought but not with that of Palestine; where water was regarded as beneficent. The victory of Yahweh was extolled by the Psalmists in transcendental terms in which he is represented as standing over and against creation, weighing the wind and measuring out the waters, making a decree for the rain and a way for the lightning and the thunder, upholding the earth on its pillars and the heavens with their stars; this was in Semitic cosmological fashion but he had complete dominion over all foreign gods and the entire order of nature.[47] Heaven was his throne and the earth his footstool, for he transcended the whole creation. He had stretched out the sky as a curtain, spreading it as a tent, and like Aleyan-Baal he made the clouds his chariot and the winds his messengers who laid the foundations of the earth.[48] Yahweh was conceived as enthroned in transcendental might and splendour on the dome-shaped upper firmament (i.e. the sky) which rested on the circle of the earth with its pillars and the bases of the mountains on which it rested, deeply laid in the abyss (Tehôm) (fig. 11). From this exalted position he had only to

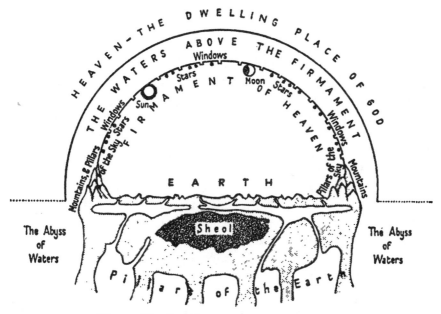

Fig. 11. The Semitic conception of the Universe

touch the mountains to make them break into volcanic eruption, to look at the earth and it trembled in seismic disturbance, and to walk upon the wings of his ministers for the wind to come and flaming fire to burst forth.[49]

In this monotheistic interpretation of the primeval victory over the hostile forces of chaos resulting in the complete and final sovereign rule of Yahweh in the cosmos he had established, he alone was supreme. Unlike Marduk, instead of being made king and head of the pantheon by decree of the rest of the gods, he exercised universal dominion by divine right as this was conceived by the Hebrew prophets. 'I am Yahweh, that is my name, and my glory I give not to another.'[50] His unique glory and absolute sovereignty were derived from his status as the Creator of heaven and earth whose works proclaimed his divine power and excellence.[51] By him all things were upheld and acted in accordance with his decrees as the controlling force in creation.[52] Thus, the entire universe came to be regarded as subordinate to him, and such was his power over nature that little or no room was left for other divine beings in the ordering and control of the cosmos.

The Hebrew creation stories

Hence, when the creation story in the opening chapter of the book of Genesis was compiled after the Exile by the Priestly school of redactors in the middle of the fifth century BC, although the Babylonian *Enuma elish* was made the basis of the narrative to a considerable extent, with the ancient primeval conflict between life and death, chaos and order, in the background, the Yahwistic monotheistic approach was maintained. It is apparent that the old myths and the conception of the universe lay behind it, because of the sequence of creative activities beginning with a primordial ocean, the Hebrew Tehôm or 'deep'—a corruption of the Babylonian Tiamat—out of which the heavens and the earth were fashioned. But instead of the firmament, the spirit of God was said to have hovered over the waters of chaos dividing the light from the darkness and the upper from the lower waters, out of which the land emerged. No mention was made of the battle of the gods, or of the fight between Yahweh and Rahab and Leviathan; these episodes were doubtless regarded by the Jewish priests as unworthy of their theme. From the charismatic victory over chaos, rain descended upon the earth from the heavenly ocean while springs and rivers emerged from the abyss beneath, making the newly formed soil fertile. Then vegetation appeared, followed by birds, beasts, fishes and reptiles; the succession of events reached their climax in the creation of man in the image and likeness of the Creator himself, given dominion over all the earth and its animal life.[53] No reference occurs, however, to the purpose of his creation, that it was for the benefit of the gods as in the Babylonian Bilingual texts, and the *Enuma elish*.

Nevertheless, virtually the same order was preserved in the Hebrew and Mesopotamian stories, beginning with a desolate waste with darkness covering the abyss, before it was dispelled by light prior to the creation of the luminaries, and ending with the human species as the culmination of the momentous week, occupying six days of creative activity and followed by the sabbatical rest of the Creator on the seventh day in the Hebrew version; probably one of the purposes of the story in this form was to afford a divine sanction for the observance of the Sabbath. This took the place of the fixing of the destinies and the conferment of his titles upon Marduk in the Babylonian epic. The, Tehôm, unlike the *Apsu*, was not personified in the Genesis narrative but it was connected with the traditional monsters, Rahab, Leviathan, the serpent and the dragon in the background of the cosmology. Though at first the earth was without form and void, when the abyss was still wrapped in darkness, and may have been thought to have existed before the divine spirit hovered over the waters of chaos, the transcendent Creator alone was responsible for calling all things into being; if it were not *ex nihilo* like Ptah, at least it was by a succession of creative acts, which included plant and animal life only incidentally mentioned in the Mesopotamian stories.[54]

Taking the similarities and the differences together, the Priestly narrative appears to have been drawn up under Babylonian influences by redactors who assembled and interpreted their source material in accordance with their monotheistic theology and to meet the ritual requirements, if, as is very probable, the creation story was recited in the Temple at Jerusalem to extol the work of Yahweh as the victorious Creator at the annual enthronement celebrations.[55] The didactic character of the myth with its repeated refrain is indicative of a liturgy, while the closely associated dragon mythology in the 'enthronement psalms' accords with the victory of Marduk over Tiamat, and at a higher level with the vindication of the creative work of Yahweh.[56]

In an orderly sequence of mighty acts, he had called all things into being by his word, from the cosmic order derived from the disordered chaos of waters to the creation of man from the dust of the earth. Moreover, this was represented as a prelude to the subsequent course of events, following the initial creation and the human catastrophe in Eden with its resultant recession culminating in the Flood tradition and the covenant with Abraham. The next successive phase in the unfolding of the order in human history, interpreted in terms of the Abrahamic covenant, moves through the Exodus and the wandering in the desert to the conquest of Canaan, as recorded in Psalm cxxxvi in which the drama of creation is set forth in three acts—first, the creation of the world; second, the deliverance from Egypt; and third, the conquest of Palestine, concluding with an invocation and thanksgiving to 'the god of the heavens', appropriate in a liturgical enactment of the historical panorama. Similarly, Psalm civ, with its liturgical background, reiterates the Priestly creation story in the same manner, doubtless for the same purpose. Thus, at every stage in the unfolding drama of Hebrew theocratic history the significant events from the Creation, the Covenant and the Exodus, through the conquest of and settlement in Canaan and the monarchy to the Exile and the re-establishment of the nation in a new covenant with Yahweh, were given liturgical expression in the myth, ritual and hymns, in order to secure a fresh outpouring of re-creative power, primarily in the spring and in the autumn at the New Year Festival.

The pre-exilic Paradise story in Genesis ii and iii is less liturgical in its form and more Palestinian in its cosmology, though it too has a Mesopotamian background. The narrative as it now appears in the Hebrew scriptures is the combination of two myths, one from the Yahwist collection of documents in the southern kingdom of Judah (J), and the other from those of the Elohist in the northern kingdom of Israel (E), distinguished by their respective use of the Hebrew names for God, Yahweh and Elohim. The accounts of the course of events of these two compilers were by no means identical, and in combining them into a composite continuous narrative the original stories have undergone a good deal of revision by the pre-exilic editors in the process of amalgamation and in adapting them to current monotheistic doctrines.

In its present form, instead of emerging in the primordial watery abyss, the earth is represented as being originally a barren waste before Yahweh-Elohim planted a delectable garden 'to the east in Eden' watered by four rivers which apparently include the Tigris and Euphrates (Hiddekel), and rendered fertile by a mist descending upon the ground, or perhaps springing up as a fountain from beneath. Then man was made out of the dust of the soil (*adamah*) and the Creator breathed the breath of life into his nostrils, so that he became a living soul. In the early forms of the story this Primal Man was probably a divine or semi-divine being, just as the serpent he was to encounter may have been a demon.[57]

In its Yahwistic guise, Adam, though he bore the divine likeness, was represented as human but not apparently mortal. Two magical trees were retained in this paradise, but it was a faint shadow of the Garden of God on the holy mountain, where the king of Tyre dwelt in a quasi-divine status and environment.[58] Nevertheless, the tabu placed on the tree described as that of the knowledge of good and evil was to prevent the first parents of the human race becoming *elohim*, or divine beings endowed with superhuman powers and qualities akin in their nature to divinities. In the Phoenician Garden of God the Primordial Man appears to have been the gardener and guardian of the paradise, like the angelic custodian of the tree of life in Eden.

Having made man, Yahweh-Elohim then produced the animals out of the soil of the ground and birds to be his companions in the garden, but as they failed to meet his requirements, a 'helpmate' of human status was created by extracting a rib from Adam, to relieve his loneliness and to be his wife. It is by no means clear whether the breaking of the tabu by eating the forbidden fruit at the instigation of the wily serpent, and the expulsion from the garden, was part of the original story or not.

In the sources of the Yahwistic myth the Paradise story was distinct from that of the fertilizing of the barren world. Whereas the Eden episode had Mesopotamian and Phoenician affinities, the background of the opening verses of the narrative (Gen. ii. 2–7) were Palestinian in their setting. The Yahwist incorporated these in his account of the fertile garden and its Mesopotamian characteristics (Gen. ii. 10–14), and interpreted the composite narrative in terms of pre-exilic ethical monotheism. Many of the naïve anthropomorphisms and magical elements in the ancient myths were retained, as for instance the fashioning of the human species from clay and the bone of a rib. Or, again, Yahweh-Elohim is represented as walking in the pleasant garden and talking with Adam and Eve in the cool of the evening as though it were his own abode and he was on intimate terms with the man and woman he had placed in it. There, too, the woman held converse with the serpent, to her undoing and also that of her husband and their offspring when their disobedience to the divine injunctions had been discovered. So they were driven forth from their paradise: the man and his descendants to labour in the sweat of their brow, the woman to be in subjection to her husband and to bear children in sorrow and travail. The serpent, as the instigator of the fall from a state of primeval innocence, was condemned to go on his belly for all time and eat the dust, and eventually his head would be bruised by the seed of the woman.[59]

This series of events leading up to the expulsion and its aftermath was not without its Mesopotamian parallels in the Adapa and Gilgamesh stories. Thus, it will be recalled,* both these heroes were semi-divine beings endowed with wisdom, who were cheated of immortality by a ruse which in the case of Gilgamesh was effected by the serpent, who stole from him the magical regenerating herb. But although the underlying theme is the same, or very similar, in the Hebrew and Babylonian myths, both turning on supernatural knowledge and the loss of eternal life, the details and purpose are very different. Adapa was the first man, but so far from error lying in an act of disobedience to divine commands, the fall was the result of following the advice of his father, Ea, the god of wisdom. Moreover, there is no suggestion of the Fall of mankind as a whole in these versions; the conflicts on earth are the counterparts of the battles among the gods in their own domain rather

*cf. Chap. VI, p. 181.

than the outcome of the 'original sin' of the first parents of the human race, when they usurped divine prerogatives,[60] like Prometheus when he stole the fire of the gods.

In the cosmic setting of the Yahwistic narratives, however, the initial sin left an entail for all the descendants of the Eden defaulters, because the universe was responsive to the dictates of the living God who was its sole creator, and the process of history was inextricably interwoven with that of creation, in a pattern of emergence and recession. Thus, the expulsion from the garden began the long trail of misery and woe that filled the earth with so much violence and corruption that the Creator is represented as regretting having made man at all. Only Noah, the Hebrew Ut-Napishtim, found favour in his eyes, and, therefore, it was resolved to bring the existing order to an end with its Nephilim strain, and re-create a new state of affairs interpreted in relation to the Mesopotamian Deluge stories, with Yahweh made solely responsible for the cataclysm, and the depravity of man taking the place of the noisy behaviour of the gods as the root cause. A fresh start having been made, a new world-order was established with the rainbow as the sign of the covenant between Yahweh and Noah, the prototype of that subsequently made with Abraham as the founder of the Hebrew theocracy, and the connecting link with the civilizations on the other side of 'the flood' (i.e. the Tigris and Euphrates). Therefore, the ancestors of the chosen people are said to have moved westwards from 'the land of Shinar' in the east and to have scattered throughout the earth.[61]

In spite of the Palestinian colouring of some of the sources of the Yahwistic narrative, the creation and deluge stories are fundamentally Mesopotamian in their origin and setting. It was, therefore, in the Sumerian and Babylonian cosmology that the Hebrew conception of creation and the cosmic order was rooted and grounded, though in coming to fruition in Palestine as the higher religion of Israel, the ancient stories were expurgated, arranged and adapted by the Yahwist and Priestly editors to serve the purposes of its fundamental doctrine of ethical monotheism.

The Olympian cosmogony in Greece
In Greece on the other hand the Olympian gods, unlike Yahweh in Israel, never transcended the universe and mankind. On the contrary, they shared human weaknesses, passions, and intrigues, behaving as conquering chieftains rather than as creators or cosmic deities. True, Zeus as the Indo-European Sky-god and Weather-god combined the functions of a nature god with those of the head of the anthropomorphic

pantheon centred on Mount Olympus towering above the plain of Thessaly. From his exalted abode the divine 'cloud-gatherer' poured the refreshing fertilizing rain on the earth, but he also blasted gods and men alike with his terrorizing thunderbolts when they thwarted his irascible will or frustrated his plans and purposes. Every hill-top and every town, in fact, had its localized Zeus who gathered the clouds and produced the rain and the tempest. But he never lost his earlier connexions with the sky, when before his arrival in Greece at the beginning of the second millennium BC in his Vedic aspect as Varuna 'the broad heaven was his portion in brightness and in cloud alike'.[62] He continued to be portrayed in these celestial realms from the time of Homer onwards, and was sometimes equated with the sky itself, as in the case of many of his counterparts elsewhere.

The Greek gods, however, fell into three main divisions: the Olympians whose abode was in the heavens and on the sacred mountain and the Chthonians who dwelt in the earth; those who made their bed in the sea and exercised their functions in great waters occupied an intermediate position between the upper and the lower divinities. In the background of this tripartite pantheon was the ancient but not very clearly defined figure of Kronos, who originally may have been a harvest deity transformed into the lord of the universe and married to Rhea his sister, the Cretan Earth-Mother. Three sons were born from this union, Zeus, Poseidon and Hades, who cast lots for the possession of the universe when their father ceased to rule over it. As a result Zeus obtained dominion in heaven, Poseidon obtained the sea, and Hades the nether regions. The earth was their common property and they lived there together on Mount Olympus.[63]

This seems to have been a Greek variant of the Anatolian Kumarbi myth in the Hurrian texts,[64] so that in the theogony of Hesiod, Ouranus, the heavens and the first of the gods, the begetter of Kronos and the Titans by Ge (Gaia), the Earth-goddess, became the father of Zeus. Therefore, he was the counterpart of Anu, Kumarbi and Teshub. Emasculation is a common feature in all the myths, as is the impregnation of the Goddess by the castrated organ or its phallic symbol in the form of a stone. The Hurrian myth, as has been considered, goes back to Mesopotamia,[65] and it is not improbable that it passed to Greece through Phoenicia and Cyprus in the middle of the second millennium BC where eventually it was developing into a theogony by Hesiod, who made his way into Boeotia from north-west Asia Minor. As the Aryan, Anatolian and Aegean elements were fused into composite stories the tradition found a common centre in the syncretistic Zeus as the Sky and Weather Olympian leader, the cloud-gatherer, thunderer, rain-giver, and despotic ruler, 'the father of gods and men', who gradually assumed a cosmic significance. Without essentially changing his charac-ter and functions he became at length the Creator and prototype of mankind, the one Primary Being and Life Force, from whom all existence emanated and to whom it was destined to return. Finally, by the middle of the first millennium BC he became the Eternal God, the ground of creation, in whom all things lived and moved and had their being. The Pindaric poets conceived him pantheistically, but in the Hymn of Cleanthes in the third century BC his monotheistic attributes were scarcely distinguishable from those of Yahweh in post-exilic Judaism.[66]

So long as the Greeks were confined in their circumscribed environ-ment in the Aegean and Asia Minor, their theogonies and the associated cosmological mythology were conditioned by these topographical con-ditions. The earth appeared as a vast plain encircled by streams (Okeanus) resembling the waters of Nun in Egypt, from which the gods and mankind sprang.[67] Above was the sky as a great dome wherein the upper gods dwelt, unless they were in residence on Mount Olympus, though they were not in lonely seclusion and remoteness like many Supreme Beings in primitive society. They were essentially human by nature and in their relationships, sharing the weaknesses of mankind and other characteristic features. The heavens were, in fact, so accessible that, as in the Hebrew, Babel and Bethel traditions, the possibility of scaling them by some kind of ladder was contemplated.[68] Similarly, the sky and the earth were thought to meet at some point on the extremities of the horizon in Greek as well as in Egyptian cosmology, the entrance to the underworld being situated in the west where the sun descended into the nether regions, and the stars arose on the other side. It was possible, however, to reach Hades through rifts in the rocks at certain places on the earth's surface.[69]

The struggle between Zeus and the Titans, representing the conflict between heaven and earth, may be a reflection of the defeat of the chthonian indigenous cult of the soil by the Olympian Sky-religion. When we encounter the Olympian theology in the Homeric literature, the gods are organized on the human model in a class of fighting chieftains behaving, as Gilbert Murray has said, as conquering royal buccaneers. Though they were manifest in nature they made no claim to have created the world or to have disposed of creation by divine right as its sovereign lords. They were content to fight against each other and apportion the spoils like the invading Nordic princes on whom they were modelled. That Zeus and his confederates defeated Kronos, the pre-Olympian ruler of the universe, is not surprising since they became the dominant power in Hellas under their overlord Zeus, who distributed the kingdom among his brothers and numerous offspring— Hades, Poseidon and the rest—'living on the revenues and blasting with thunderbolts the people who did not pay'. They fought and feasted, drank deep, played, made music and thwarted one another.[70] In short, they were typical Indo-European chieftains in the guise of mountain-gods.

The Hesiodic and Orphic theogonies

How this state of affairs came to prevail is explained by Hesiod in accordance with the current cosmology, for clearly the Olympians were firmly established when the Homeric literature was compiled about 750 BC. Starting with chaos as the ultimate source of the universe in the manner of most Near Eastern cosmogonies—the equivalent of the Babylonian Apsu, the Egyptian Nun and the Hebrew Tehôm—the Earth (Gaia) is represented as emerging as Tartarus, 'a dark place in the depths of the ground', together with Eros (love) and Erebos (darkness), leading up to Night. It is not explained how and by what agencies that was accomplished, but there is no suggestion of a creation *ex nihilo*, chaos being said merely to have come into being (γένετο). From the union of Night and Erebos Aither, the 'upper air' or sky, was born, while the Earth produced of its own accord as a cosmic principle the Heavens (Ouranus), the mountains and the sea.[71] Although this theogony conforms to the normal procreative method in its generation, and follows the Egyptian Geb and Nut sequence in its general genealogical scheme, there is underlying it an impersonal conception of a cosmic order couched in familiar mythological forms and nomenclature that were still surviving in the Boeotian peasant lore and tradition, in which Eros is made the dynamic force in the creative process.

This is more apparent in the closely allied Orphic cosmology, although it is known almost exclusively from post-Aristotelian and Neoplatonic sources, when a new type of Greek thought had emerged. Nevertheless, a few fragments of Orphic texts reveal that they contained a cosmogony that was dependent upon Hesiod. Thus the same sequence is maintained with Kronos at the head as the Time that never grows old. From him were begotten Aither, Chaos and Erebos, and in Aither, the upper air, he fashioned an egg from which sprang Phanes, the Creator. As the source of all life he was also called Protogonus, the first-born, Eros or Metis, in his several aspects of generation and light. In the late Rhapsodic version of the poem he was light *par excellence*, existing before the sun which was created by him. He was the light of reason, the light of life, and the light of love, the author of wisdom responsible for bringing the gods and the world into being.

In the process of cosmic procreation he was assisted by his daughter Night who bore to him Ouranus and Gaia, and by an ingenious fusion of the Orphic, Hesiodic and Olympian theogonies, which was brought into relation with the pre-Hellenic Thraco-Phrygian cult of Zagreus and its mythology, and that of the Cretan Rhea, Zeus was said to have swallowed Phanes and his whole creation in order that, as in the Hebrew Flood myth, a fresh start could be made by the establishment of a new creation. He then contracted an alliance, first with Demeter who gave birth to Persephone (Kore), and then with Persephone who bore Zagreus-Dionysus, whom Zeus purposed to make the ruler of the universe. This aroused the jealousy of Hera, the official wife of Zeus, who conspired with the Titans to kill and devour the child. They gave him toys to distract him and then they slew and ate him. Thereupon Zeus in his anger hurled a thunderbolt upon them and burned them up, making mankind from their ashes. Athena secured the heart of Zagreus and gave it to Zeus who swallowed it and so was able to beget him again by contracting an alliance with Semele, the Phrygian Earth-goddess. It was this second Zagreus who became Dionysus, and as the Titans had eaten the original Zagreus before they were annihilated, the human race that sprang from their ashes was partly divine and partly evil, combining in its nature both a Dionysian and a Titanic element.[72]

Although the story is relatively late in its developed form, there can be little doubt that it was based on a Phrygian or Thracian myth, which was incorporated in the Orphic cosmology to account for the Dionysiac *omophagia*, when the raw flesh of bulls and calves was devoured by the maenads to become sacramentally united with Zagreus-Dionysus, and also to establish the twofold nature of mankind, good and evil. As this duality was fundamental in the Orphic doctrine of metempsychosis and salvation* it had to be given a cosmogonic basis, which the crude tale supplied with its affinities with the Hesiodic theogony and its Olympian background. Under Orphic influence, however, it acquired a philosophic and mystical context which Pindar and Plato were not slow to recognize and develop. As Dr Guthrie says, 'the Orphic showed a genius for transforming the significance of his mythological or ritual material, and sometimes saw an opportunity of preaching his religion through the medium of symbols which were in their origin of the crudest and most primitive.'[73]

*Chap. VI, p. 199.

While the Hesiodic and Homeric tradition was maintained in which the gods played their customary roles in the cosmic drama with Zeus taking the lead, new features were introduced. The ancient pre-Olympian Kronos was transformed into Chronos and made the personification of 'Time which never grows old', as the abstract principle in which all things take their origin and to which they are destined teleologically to come to their appointed ends. Then came the world-egg in the Orphic cosmogony, according to the Neoplatonic interpreters, from which proceeded the first god Phanes, the Creator of the earth. By swallowing Phanes Zeus succeeded in acquiring this status as the beginning, middle and end of creation by incorporating Phanes in himself, while Time remained as the first principle. The problem of the One and the Many latent in the growing curiosity about the origins of the universe and the relations of the parts to the whole, and the union of the human and the divine, eventually found expression in words attributed to a pupil of Orpheus Musaios, 'everything comes to be out of the One and is resolved into One.'[74] Thus, in the Orphic cosmology it was out of a confused mass that creation emerged, the process being one of separation and division, bringing order out of chaos, until eventually at the end of the era there will be a return to the primitive chaotic condition.[75]

The One and the Many

Speculation about the One and the Many became the central theme of philosophical reflection among the Milesian thinkers when in the sixth century BC they broke away from the polytheistic tradition in an intellectual search for the first cause and sustaining cosmic principle (ἀρχή) in the universe and its processes, without reference to the gods and their theogonies. With the problem of ultimate origins they were not concerned, being content to seek the universal ground of existence in relation to some material entity—for Thales (*c.* 625–547 BC) it was water, and for Anaximenes it was air, the 'Boundless' or Infinite, while for Heraclitus fire was the fundamental principle. Xenophanes (*c.* 570–480 BC), the founder of the Eleatic school, categorically dismissed the Homeric gods as 'thieves, adulterers and deceivers', and put in their place a changeless, imperishable, timeless Being conceived as a unity endowed with intelligence, ruling all things by the power of mind alone.[76]

Similarly, Heraclitus of Ephesus, who flourished about 500 BC, affirmed that 'this world which is the same for all, none of the gods or men has made, but it was ever, is now, and ever shall be an ever-living fire, with measures of it kindling and measures going out.' It is always in a state of flux between the tensional opposites, never continuing in one stay, all things emerging and being absorbed. But the divine law that controlled the cosmic process, reconciling all opposites, acted rationally. Deity, in fact, was the principle underlying all harmony in tension and the rhythm of opposing forces, day and night, summer and winter, peace and war, plenty and hunger. It was, in short, the unity of opposites and movement, or incessant change, that was the lord of the universe.[77]

That a pantheistic strain, however, ran through the Ionian and Eleatic cosmology was inevitable, since all things were reduced to a single substance immanent in the natural order and in its relation to change and generation. The quest of the One that remains was in great measure lost in the confusion and complexity of the Many. When the cosmos was regarded as eternal, sentient and intelligent it was difficult to set it over against a Creator in a theistic sense. Thus, for Parmenides (c. 475 BC) the concept of Being was that of the eternal One as an Absolute. This ruled out altogether the sensible world of motion, change and becoming, as an illusory process as in Indian cosmic mysticism. Everything proceeded from the primal ground and to it returned, True-being having no place in Not-being.[78] The force of law alone was unchangeable and held the existent order together in the world of appearances, but absolute Being was never identified with Deity in any intelligible theistic sense of the term, however much it might be interpreted as rational, timeless and indestructible. Therefore, it was virtually a static form of pantheism.

Anaxagoras (c. 500–428 BC) in tracing the world to a non-material agency and trying to find a place for Mind (*Nous*) in the ordering of its processes, introduced a teleological interpretation of the cosmos. But although it was Mind that controlled everything having a soul, and ruled over the entire natural order of living species of which it was independent, it was nowhere represented as divine, though divinity was attributed to its epithets.[79] Diogenes equated Mind with air, and sharply distinguished it from everything else in the physical order, standing both behind and within the universe[80] as a single conscious Creator to account for the rational purposefulness underlying creation. But the dualistic distinction between mind and matter was retained, and it was latent in the Platonic differentiation of the phenomenal visible order from the invisible, permanent, real world of Ideas (i.e. of perfect and timeless absolute form or pattern) resting on a single ground, the Good.[81]

Nevertheless, though the Olympian pantheon was not entirely excluded,[82] the polytheistic tradition was as foreign to the Platonic cosmology as it was to the Aristotelian conception of motion, which was based on a Prime Mover himself unmoved as the first and final cause of all things. By this original divine essence of pure actuality, 'Prime matter' (πρώτη ὕλη) was endowed with the potentiality of becoming a substance when it received a 'form' (εἶδος) which made it what it was (i.e. an individual concrete object) as an indissoluble union of matter and form related to each other as potency and act.[83] All nature was represented as potentially divine being, the realization of the thought of God who is Himself Supreme Mind. This eternal Thinker can be but One, but so completely distinct from the Many, so wholly transcendent, that He is not even aware of the existence of the universe, and, therefore, mundane affairs are not His concern.[84]

Throughout this attempt to emancipate the cosmology of the ancient Near East and the Aegean from its cosmogonic mythology, the Ionians and their successors maintained that the universe was an intelligible cosmos capable of elucidation in the light of reason, without recourse to mythopoeic divine personifications, creative generation, and genealogical ancestry and relationships which hitherto had constituted the recurrent basic conception everywhere. The influence of these earlier notions can be discerned in much of the reflective speculation of the early Greek thinkers, so that, for example, Thales and Anaximenes believed that 'all things are full of gods', and the cosmological inquiry in general was pursued on the assumption of a material primal principle or first cause of things,[85] not very different in method or aim from the former approach shorn of its personifications.

Now, however, attention was concentrated on speculations about causation, the permanent element and sustaining principle in real existence, and their nature and constitution. But because the universe was knowable by the processes of thought and rational reflection, mythopoeic cosmogonies could be dismissed, and in their place cosmic order was determined reducible to a single principle irrespective of the gods. Nevertheless, the cosmological problems of which this rational solution was sought by natural causes and primal substances were not very different from those inherited from the earlier tradition. The quest of 'the One that remains' was lost in great measure in the confusion and complexity of the Many, but the substitution of fixed laws for the transcendental control of natural phenomena marked a genuinely new cosmological approach in the ancient world.

CHAPTER EIGHT

DIVINATION, ASTROLOGY AND PROPHECY

The Mantic tradition, divination in Babylonia and Assyria, Barû and hepatoscopy, Astral science and astrology, exorcism and expiation, therapeutic divination in Egypt, incubation and the cult of Asklepios—Delphic oracle, Exegetai of Athens, vicissitudes of Delphi, Sibylline oracles, Theophanies and oracles in ancient Israel, divinatory prophecy in Israel, literary Hebrew prophets

THE DIVINE CONTROL of the cosmic order and of natural processes, which was so conspicuous a feature in Near Eastern and Aegean religion, found expression in a highly developed divinatory technique, especially in Greece and Mesopotamia, for the purpose of gaining superhuman knowledge, foresight and guidance in the conduct of everyday affairs. So important was this aspect of the cultus, that highly trained professional experts were set apart as diviners, astrologers, seers and exorcists to interpret signs and omens, dreams and movements of the heavenly bodies, to proclaim oracles and make known revelations, in the belief that the gods employed inspired men to communicate their will and power to mankind. Thus the mantic tradition developed into a pseudo-science under the direction of diviners and seers who often by genuine psychic and occult powers stimulated by technical training, disclosed hidden wisdom and determined the course of events by ecstatic visionary experiences, portents, augury, auspices, hepatoscopy and astrological prognostications.

The Mantic tradition

Their principal work was in relation to omens, dreams and oracles, but it also included in some instances priestly duties in temples, shrines and sanctuaries, incubation, trance and the wilder forms of ecstasy and sacred utterance. Thus the office of the seer was very closely connected with that of the diviner, as the spoken word has been regarded as a means of establishing a 'phatic communion' with a deity by a sacramental exchange of words between the human speaker and the divine hearer.[1] But the revelation received directly through visionary or ecstatic experience, or whatever form the prophetic manifestation may have taken, was made known as a divine oracular pronouncement having an absolute validity, being nothing less than the expression of the will and purpose of the god with whom the seer had been *en rapport*. The divine voice spoke through its human instrument in words intended to convey either a message, a warning or a declaration; when devoid of symbolic meaning or intelligible thought and utterance, it gave expression to an intense, deep-seated state of emotion. The agent then felt himself filled with the divine inspiration and compelled to give vent to prophetic oracles like Balaam, the Syrian mantis, who could only speak the words put into his mouth as an inspired utterance of his divine control.[2]

It might suffice merely to utter a sacred formula or exclamation in relation to a rite or gesture, such as the reiteration of the syllable OM (Om man padmi Om) by the Vedic *hotr* reciting priests in India, or the singing of the Rigveda as Words of Power filled with Brahman, the sacred power or energy by which a constraining influence was exercised over the gods and their votaries, at once coercive, persuasive and pro-pitiative.[3] The good will of the gods was thus secured and they could then be induced to bestow their benefits on their worshippers in response to the service rendered in the cultus. The Words of Power uttered and the sacred actions performed established a condition of rapport in rela-tion to the objective environment and its mysterious characteristics, portents and hidden potencies independent of any intelligible meaning the words may have conveyed. Their utterance had a sacramental numinous and consolidating effect upon those who heard and repeated them, very much as has the recitation of the Qur'an in the mosques in non-Arabic speaking Islamic countries, the saying of Mass in Latin or the reading of the Pauline epistles in the presence of an uneducated congregation unfamiliar with the language employed.

When the purpose of mantic devices was to establish union with the sacred order, to convey supernatural power and to influence the course of events, gaining access to superhuman knowledge was of secondary importance. But however efficacious ecstatically and phatically Words of Power and glossolaly (i.e. speaking in an unintelligible manner) may have been, it did not fulfil the practical purposes of the mantic art directed to the interpretation of omens and prognosis. Thus, although it has been a recurrent phenomenon, as, for example, in Christianity where it was prominent in Apostolic times as 'speaking with tongues' or 'prophesyings',[4] and reappeared in revivalist movements notably among the Quakers, Ranters, Methodists, the Irvingites and other Adventist sects,[5] it has only been a temporary occurrence at any time.[6] The main function of the seer and diviner always has been to supply information about current or future events, whether trivial or important, thought to be known only to the gods with whom they were *en rapport* or in some way in communication. Agis inquired of Zeus Naos and Dione whether his coverlets and pillows had been lost or stolen, just as Saul repaired to Samuel the seer to discover the whereabouts of his father's asses, and incidentally found a kingdom. Before engaging in battle with the Syrians at Ramoth Gilead Ahab consulted his prophets, and at Delphi the framing of laws, the founding of colonies, the launching of wars, the fortunes of dynasties, the healing of disease and the legal suits of individuals, were referred to the judgment of the Pythian Apollo from the seventh century BC, and probably the famous shrine had been an oracular centre long before this time.

Divination in Babylonia and Assyria
It was, in fact, in the Hellenic world and in Mesopotamia that divination and mantics in general were most widely practised as a firmly established tradition in the official cult as well as unofficially by an array of private augurs whose services could be secured by payment of a small fee. In Babylonia most great temples acquired in due course a full complement of diviners, soothsayers, exorcists and astrologers, many of whose offices went back to Sumerian times. Thus the most ancient manual of Mesopotamian astrology belonged to this period, and omen texts and inscriptions, such as the *Enuma Anu-enlil* series (i.e. 'When Anu and Enlil', etc.), are believed to go back to the third millennium BC in view of the references to the fourfold division of the world into the lands of Akkad, Elam, Subartu and Amurru, and to early kings like Rimush and Ibin-sin. Similarly, in the Sumerian version of the Flood story Ziusudra, or Ut-Napishtim, the Babylonian Noah, is represented as resorting to divinatory practices, and one of the kings of this age, Enmeduranki of Sippur, was alleged to have obtained from the gods the arts and insignia of divination.[7] Divination by the behaviour of oil in water was in use in the reign of Urukagina of Lagash (*c.* 2800 BC), and an omen obtained from liver is mentioned in the time of a pre-diluvian ruler, Enmeluanna.[8]

The Barû and hepatoscopy
Indeed, the designation of the special class of Akkadian seers known as *barû*, who were set apart to communicate knowledge of the will of the gods by oracles, dreams, visions and omens, had its Sumerian equivalent applied to diviners who consulted the gods by the inspection of the liver and entrails as the seat of the soul-substance. But the natural

meaning of the term 'to see', is that of beholding in the mantic sense, of ascertaining the will of the gods by oracles, visions and dreams. As the practice developed, therefore, in addition to divination by noting the behaviour of the liver of a sheep employed as a sacrificial victim, (*hepatoscopy*), or of water (*hydromancy*), or oil (*lecanomancy*), the observation of celestial phenomena, physiognominal omens, the flight of birds, and similar devices, the *barû* also resorted to more direct methods, such as night visions, to obtain their portents.[9]

It was, in fact, through these *barû*-diviners that inquiry was made of the gods by all the various methods employed on the diverse occasions on which they were consulted, some depending upon observation, others on special communications, or particular omens or casting lots, while their office was intimately connected with that of the obscure officials called *šabrû*, who appears to have been the recipient of dream-visions and the incubation oracle, associated with healing.[10] But it does not seem to have included that of *asipu*, or incantation-priest, and exorcist, whose functions were directed more specifically to determining the course of events by magical coercion, the expulsion of evil and de-sacralization.

The principal method adopted by the *barû* was that of *hepatoscopy*, the elaborate practice of divining by the inspection of the lower lobes and upper lobe of the liver of a sacrificial victim, together with its two appendices, the gall-bladder, the cystic duct, the hepatic duct, vein and the *porta hepatis* (the 'liver-gate'). The markings on the right side were regarded as auspicious, those on the left as sinister, while a swollen bladder indicated increase of power, and a depression of the *porta hepatis* portended a decrease in power.[11] Models of livers have been found in terracotta in Babylon with oracular divisions marked to specify particular areas connected with the predictions, and in the cuneiform texts constant reference is made to hepatoscopy. In the omen-texts and oracle-tablets appeals are made to the gods in the form of prayers related to divination and the oracles are addressed on the issues at stake. Sometimes they take the form of questions, and the answers are sought in the portents revealed by the liver. On occasions of grave national concern and before important events kings like Esarhaddon and Ashurbanipal consulted the oracle to ascertain the will of the Sun-god Shamash, or that of Ishtar; the answers were recorded on the tablets, presumably after a successful issue had been achieved.

It was apparently from Babylonia and Assyria that hepatoscopy made its way among the highly trained Etruscan diviners known as *haruspices* and thence into the Graeco-Roman world. Clay models of livers with

Hittite cuneiform inscriptions found at Boghazköy may be a connecting
link between the Babylonian and Etruscan cults, while occasional
references in the Old Testament to the liver of a sacrificial victim having
divinatory powers by its convulsive movements suggest that hepatoscopy
was practised in Israel.[12] In the book of Tobit the liver of a fish is
connected with exorcisms,[13] and it caused no surprise to the Hebrew
writer that Nebuchadnezzar should have 'looked in the liver' to divine
the road he should take when he stood 'at the parting of the ways'.[14]
In the passage of the cult from its Mesopotamian cradleland to Palestine, Anatolia and the Graeco-Roman world, the Hittites doubtless
played an important part. That the spread was in this direction is
shown by the model of a sheep's liver in bronze found at Piacenza in
Italy in 1877 displaying the Babylonian method of hepatoscopy by
divisions of the sky inscribed with the names of the gods associated
with the several sections.[15]

Astral science and astrology
Omens were also obtained from the position, appearance and colour of
entrails, and the condition of the heart, kidneys, gall-bladder and other
internal organs, and the flight of birds, strange portents like eclipses,
unusual atmospheric conditions, violent storms, manifesting either the
good will or malevolence of the gods concerning some known or unknown event in the offing. Signs in the heavens encouraged increasingly
careful observations of the sky for celestial phenomena and their
variations. The moon seems to have been the first of the heavenly bodies
to have become the subject of careful observation in the ziggurats and
bittamarti, or 'houses of observation' at Babylonian temples (Fig. 80). As
it was the nearest to the earth, and its changes were both regular and
spectacular, its importance for divination was recognized very early.
Since its phases could not be determined with mathematical precision,
its appearance and disappearance had to be observed with great care,
and the variations given an ominous and astrological interpretation.
The concurrence of the sun and the moon in the sky could also be seen
between the 12th and 20th days of the month, and this phenomenon
was noted and interpreted in relation to the fall of the dynasty and other
unpropitious events. On and after the 14th day it betokened prosperity.
The periodic repetition in the movements of the heavenly bodies was
calculated and tabulated for future reference, so that each observer
had at his disposal collections of these observations which he could
consult in arriving at his prognostications.

As a result of these calculations the year was divided into months in which the occult character of each day was noted, and observations were made in the clear Mesopotamian air which were quite remarkable for their accuracy, taking into account the absence of instruments. Thus the greater part of the twelve constellations in our modern zodiac are identical with those distinguished by the Chaldaean astrologers, and the zodiacal system as a whole is a product of their attempts to map out that part of the sky in which the movements of the heavenly bodies were thought to occur as a circle or 'girdle of signs' influencing events on the earth. The course of the moon and of the planets was determined with reference to the sun's ecliptic and the five planets, now called after the Roman deities, Venus, Mercury, Mars, Jupiter and Saturn, were identified with the corresponding Babylonian gods—Ishtar, Nabu, Nergal, Marduk and Ninib—whose movements were believed to be related to the fortunes of mankind. Groups of stars or asterisms were formed into a well-defined system of stellar names, and the chief constellations known to the Greeks seem to have had their origin in Mesopotamia.

A complicated astral science was developed there by a highly organized body of augurs, seers and astrologers with an extensive omen literature comprising long series of tablets dealing with every aspect of augural phenomena. If many of these belonged to a relatively late period, about 668–626 BC in the time of Ashurbanipal at the close of the Assyrian period, they refer to a firmly established tradition and represent the product of much earlier editing and redaction. Thus, as has been pointed out, the omen-texts and astrological inscriptions go back to a much earlier period, probably to the middle of the third millennium BC, though it was not until very much later that an astrological system was devised which was based on the movements of the heavenly bodies and the identification of the planets and fixed stars with certain gods. Then professional astrologers were employed in casting horoscopes and predicting the fortunes of individuals and of the community at large. When calendars of favourable days had been drawn up, the royal astrologers were continually on the look-out for events that might portend public and political disasters, but eclipses and similar occurrences were too occasional to serve their general purposes. Therefore, while great importance was attached to them, it was the more ordinary and recurrent phenomena that were usually studied by astrologers, particularly the changes in the clouds and in the position of the planets and the stars.

Every celestial phenomenon, in fact, was held to have its counterpart in human events, and every individual was at length brought under the influence of a planet or a fixed star which determined his fate from the cradle to the grave. For example, if an eclipse of the moon took place in the month of Nisan in the first watch there would be destruction, and brother would slay brother. If it happened in Iyyar, the king would die and his son would not succeed him. If it occurred in Tammuz, agriculture would prosper and prices would rise. If it took place in Ab, Adad would send a flood upon the land. But when Adad caused his voice to be heard in the thunder in Nisan the rule of the enemy would cease, and when he did so in Tammuz agriculture would prosper.[16] Similarly, solar eclipses generally were regarded as ominous, varying in degrees according to the month and moment when they appeared. The stars acquired a more personal significance, and together with the sun, moon and the planets, they determined human destinies with an elaborate astrological lore which reached the eastern Mediterranean and the Aegean in the wake of the conquests of Alexander the Great in the fourth century BC.

Behind the determination of the course of events by the position and behaviour of the heavenly bodies lay the recognition of laws governing their movements amenable to calculation. The gods might be thought to behave in an arbitrary manner, but at least their ways and purposes were sufficiently intelligible to be ascertainable by natural occurrences, so that they could be calculated by the time of the appearance of the new moon and the periodical appearance of lunar and solar eclipses. This was made possible by the knowledge gained by observation and the association of ideas by the astrologers, who in Babylonia in particular made such remarkable strides towards the scientific study of astronomical phenomena.

It was not only, however, upon the heavenly bodies that inquiry was pursued. In the conviction that all things in the universe proceeded along parallel lines by fixed laws, controlled by the celestial stellar world as the province of the gods, hepatoscopy, oracular dreams and omens and almost every aspect of divination were brought, in the course of time, within the embrace of astrology in some manner and related to the horoscope and the planetary deities. But astrological diagnosis was a later development of therapeutic divination, and when it was established various substitutes for it were adopted, as it was by no means always easy to obtain the requisite facts concerning the planets. The interpretation of horoscopes was a very complicated procedure, and in the considerable number of medical texts examined, collated and translated by Campbell Thompson from the royal library of King Ashurbanipal incantations and the accompanying rites to be performed when the spell was recited were the main features of the prescriptions.[17] While the Assyrians had an extensive knowledge of medicines, including animal and vegetable drugs, magic unquestionably played a conspicuous part in the treatment of disease.

Exorcism and expiation

Behind the various methods adopted in the healing art in Babylonia and Assyria lay the elaborate system of demonology with its jinn, ghouls, vampires and vast hordes of hostile spirits roaming about the streets of cities, sliding through doors and the walls of houses, as well as lurking in cemeteries and solitary places, on marches and mountains, and in dens of the earth. Wherever they occurred they brought in their train sickness, death, and misfortune of every kind.[18] It was this widespread belief that found expression in the practice of exorcism and incantation in the healing of disease, and the expulsion of evil wherever it occurred. The cuneiform texts from the middle of the third millennium BC bear witness to its prevalence and prominence as a bulwark against the assaults of these hostile supernatural forces which were unfriendly to man and ever on the alert to bring upon him the ills to which flesh is heir.

While Anu and Enlil were never well-disposed towards the human species, Ea, the third god of the Great Triad, the personification of divine healing power, and his son Marduk, were the protectors against these malign assaults. Standing as they did nearest to mankind, these two deities were invoked by the aid of the healing waters under the control of Ea and his mediator, Marduk, in such 'Words of Power' as 'Marduk hath seen him (the sick person) and hath entered the house of his father Ea, and hath said, "Father, headache, from the underworld hath gone forth".' Then follows the prescription for the patient, ending usually with the incantation, 'By Heaven be ye exorcized, By earth be ye exorcized!'; the formula was addressed to the appropriate god concerned with the particular disease. In addition to pronouncing the name of the divinity in which the magic virtue resides, the exorcist had to mention that of the demon to be driven forth. This involved the recitation of long lists of devils and ghosts (*edimmu*) in order to include the one that might be the cause of the malady.[19] The patient was then sprinkled with water, censed, surrounded with flour or some other magically protective substance such as black and white yam fastened to his couch, while the exorcist held in his hand a branch of the sacred tamarisk, 'the powerful weapon of Anu', during the incantation.[20]

The 'curse of Eridu' (*Siptu*, i.e. the curse of expiation) derived its efficacy from the potency ascribed to water as the incantation *par excellence* in overcoming the ban of demons, and in the consecration of sacred objects. The words of the formula have not been recorded, but doubtless they contained the name of Ea, since its mystic power was ascribed to the Water-god, though originally it was the life-giving water itself that drove forth the malevolent influences and by absorbing them into itself freed those beset by them from evil contagions. The expulsion sometimes involved the offering of a kid or sucking-pig to drive the demon into the body of the victim, which was then destroyed.[21] In a Sumerian ritual-text Ea is said to command Marduk to take to the king a scapegoat in the form of a horned wild goat bound by a curse and place its head against that of the king so that 'his poisonous tabu into his mouth may be cast'.

'May the king be pure, may he be clean,
He who knows not the curse by which he is cured,
From his body may he chase it away.
May the demon of his device stand aside.'[22]

Similarly, seven loaves of pure dough were carried into the desert in order to remove the pollution after the exorcist had transferred to them the evil incurred by the breaking of a tabu.[23] The Assyrians modelled the dough into an effigy of the sick man and censed and sprinkled it with water, but whether or not it was then treated as a 'sin-carrier', or scapegoat, is not recorded.[24] But a specially woven white and black woollen cord bound upon the hand, head and foot of a man under a curse was sent forth to the desert as an expiation rite.[25]

Surrounded on every side with such an array of ill-disposed forces personified in a variety of forms and guises, the exorcist occupied a position of supreme importance. Not only was he in demand in his capacity of physician, but he was called upon to assist at the consecration of temples, at funerals, and at seasonal ceremonies; in short, on all occasions when hostile powers might be lying in wait, or already in possession of places, objects or persons. He was, indeed, one of the principal functionaries in Babylonia and Assyria, and without his aid and intervention at critical junctures evil was almost certain to befall the nation and its people. He was, therefore, held in high esteem, as was Eridu, the seat of the worship of Ea and the original centre of the rites of exorcism. But the office was not without its dangers for its practitioners, since, like those who engaged in other aspects of the healing art, failure to effect a cure might render the exorcist liable to a fine, or even bodily injury, on the principle of the *jus talionis*.

Therapeutic divination in Egypt

Similarly in ancient Egypt, disease or injury was attributed for the most part to demonic or some kind of malign spiritual agencies. On certain days and at particular hours, especially at specific seasons, these influences were thought to be most active. Even the gods themselves were not exempt, as they, too, were always liable to be stricken with diseases, and in the medical books and papyrus documents, written in hieratic script, prescriptions occur used to restore ailing deities to health.[26] These deities were, however, more favourably placed than human beings to discover the secrets of the healing art and its magic, and it was those men who were able to obtain this information from the gods who laid the foundations of Egyptian medicine and the therapeutic techniques employed.

First the name of the demon had to be discovered and that of the god who could be adjured to expel it by his divine power. When the secret knowledge had been gained, the exorcist either summoned the god or disguised himself as the god and imitated his actions. Alternatively, he might be content simply to rely on the divine magical devices which had proved to be efficacious on previous encounters in heaven and on earth. The hostile force was not always personified, though it usually was addressed in personal terms and bidden to depart. 'Flow out thou poison, come forth upon the ground. Horus conjured thee, he cuts thee off, he *spits thee out*, and thou risest not up but fallest down. Thou art weak and not strong, a coward and dost not fight, blind and dost not see. Thou liftest not thy face. Thou art turned back and findest not thy way. Thou mournest and dost not rejoice. Thou creepest away and dost not appear. So speaketh Horus, efficacious of magic!' When these words were recited over a hawk made of ivy-wood with two feathers on its head, and bread, beer and incense offered to it, the poison was slain by the magic of Horus, as soon as the object was placed on the face of a sufferer from snake-bite.[27]

Sometimes the exorcising magician spoke in his own name, but when he gave vent to threatening utterances to the malignant power, demon, spirit, ghoul or vampire, he usually attributed the spell to a god. 'It is Isis who says it', or 'I am Re in this his mysterious name'.[28] In addition to the knowledge of secret names and mystical numbers as potent means of expelling and gaining control over evil influences, statues animated by the spirit of the god whose help was sought were employed, together with images and amulets charged with magical power derived from the statue in which the divine essence dwelt in its plenitude.[29] Care had to be taken to make sure that the incantation was performed at the right time on the lucky day of the appropriate season in the temple calendar, so that the role of the god or spirit invoked might be reproduced by the sorcerer under the most advantageous circumstances in relation to the calendrical conditions.[30]

The *Sunu*, or 'priest-physician', exercised his functions as the controlling agent of the supernatural powers, particularly the gods of healing on the one hand and the demons of disease on the other. He was believed to have secret sources of information and to have been the repository of magico-religious knowledge and potency which empowered him to work cures.[31] But although he might have been specially trained, he was not necessarily a member of a priestly order, and incantations could be uttered at any time by any one, as, for example, when mothers put their children to bed at night they invariably invoked divine aid against malign influences which they believed were on the alert to perform their nefarious deeds.[32] Nevertheless, the offices of magician, priest and physician were frequently combined in ancient Egypt.

Incubation and the cult of Asklepios

In the Nile valley, however, the mantic tradition never reached the heights it attained in Mesopotamia, and in the astrological texts of the Ptolemaic period Babylonian, Assyrian and Iranian influences were very apparent. Among the numerous priests and priestesses and their lay assistants attached to the great temples there was no specific office of exorcist, though divination by incubation was widely practised. In the sanctuary of Ptah at Memphis therapeutic oracles were given and various remedies were revealed through dreams to those who slept in the temples with this end in view. But it was in Greece in the fifth century BC, when the cult of Asklepios was established in Argolis, and elsewhere, and brought into conjunction with that of Apollo at Delphi, that incubation became widely recognized to be an essential element in the healing magical art.

The sick resorted to his shrine near Epidaurus (Fig. 75) in very considerable numbers to sleep in the temple of Asklepios; they saw a vision in the night watches and awoke cured of their ailment. The procedure as it has been recorded by Aristophanes in his comedy *Plutos* (c. 388 BC), consisted in the patient who was suffering from blindness being put to sleep in the precinct of the temple in order to be visited by the god,

who touched his head and wiped his eyes. Two large snakes then darted
out of the temple and licked his eyelids. This completely restored his
sight. On one of the Epidaurian inscriptions a man whose fingers were
paralysed saw a vision during his sleep in the temple, in which he
thought he was playing dice, and just when he was about to make a
throw the god suddenly appeared, jumped on his hand and stretched
out his fingers and straightened them one by one. As the day dawned
he left the temple cured, although at first he had doubted the accounts
of the cures he read on the tablets in the precincts of the sanctuary.[33]
Sometimes in their hypnotic sleep the sick appear to have dreamed that
they underwent ecstatic experiences not very different from those of
medicine-men or shamans in primitive society at the time of their
initiation. These experiences included having their abdomens cut open
by the attendants of the gods and then stitched up again, like the
Australian medicine-men who received a new set of internal organs,
together with magical stones, when they repaired to the depths of a cave
to be so equipped during their initiation rites.[34]

The crowds who flocked to Epidaurus from far and near to seek from
Asklepios either immediate relief or advice that would lead to a cure,
and the long list of successes recorded on the inscriptions at the
sanctuary, leave little room for doubt that from the end of the fifth
century BC Epidaurus occupied a position in Greece comparable to that
of Lourdes in Western Christendom today. From Argolis the cult spread
to Athens and thence to Memphis in Egypt, where the god reappeared
under the guise of the sage Imhotep, until in 293 BC in response to a
Sibylline oracle during a pestilence when the aid of Asklepios was
sought, it found a home on an island, the Insula Tiberina, on the Tiber.
Here a shrine was erected in honour of the son of Apollo, latinized as
Aesculapius, and his partner Salus, the Roman counterpart of Hygieia
(Health) in the Hellenic cult, and served by priests who were probably
Greeks skilled in the healing art.[35] The island was eventually shaped like
a ship in commemoration of the legendary arrival of the god under his
form as a sacred serpent, when he escaped in this guise from the boat
which was taking him from Epidaurus and landed there.

In the Roman Aesculapium the inscriptions suggest that the remedies
were not wholly magical, but the practice of incubation was retained.
The dream oracles of Fannius in Virgil[36] may be merely poetic fancies,
but within the Epidaurian cult in hellenized Rome incubation survived
as an integral p: .t of the healing art of Aesculapius.[37] It was, however,
foreign to the R man tradition, in which neither mantic possession nor
exorcism was firmly established. In Italy divination was centred in an

elaborate system of augury as the official means of ascertaining the will of the gods in all matters of moment, by signs as the flight or cries of birds, lightning, dreams and the prognostications of the authorized augurs. Not until inspired seers, sorcerers and healers were introduced from Greece, Asia Minor and Mesopotamia, largely as a result of Etruscan contacts with Hellenistic civilization, did the dream-oracles of Epidaurus and the ecstasies of Delphi reach the Roman Empire. Nevertheless, the cult of Asklepios was widely practised among all sorts and conditions of men and women, rich and poor, bond and free, in Greece and Rome, until the healing art was taken over by the Church at the beginning of the Christian era and the functions and offices of the Epidaurian patron of physicians were carried on by SS. Cosmas and Damian.

The Delphic oracle

Similarly, for a thousand years of recorded history Greeks and Romans consulted the Pythia, the prophetess of Apollo, seated on her tripod at Delphi, on all matters great and small, for such was the reputation of the famous oracular shrine. Its foundation is wrapped in obscurity as it was the most ancient sanctuary in Greece, going back to the Mycenaean period (Fig. 77). It was regarded as the centre of the earth with its *omphalos*, or navel-stone, in the adytum of Apollo's temple where the Pythia gave her oracles. The Greeks recognized that Apollo was a newcomer, and he was said to have been preceded by the Earthmother, Ge-Themis, and probably by Poseidon.[38] In the Homeric period it had become an Apolline centre, and the legend of the killing of a chthonian monster[39] may indicate that it was originally connected with the underworld cult.

It was also associated with the ecstatic worship of Dionysus, but whether or not it was ever its home before it was occupied by Apollo has yet to be determined. In any case, from the fifth century BC references to Dionysus became increasingly frequent at Delphi, and by the third century BC the monument in the inner sanctuary was regarded as his grave. By the time of Plutarch two centuries later he was believed to take the place of Apollo at the shrine during the three winter months when Apollo retired to the north,[40] a tradition that may go back to a much earlier period, since the winter absences were established by the sixth century BC. Who then presided at the sanctuary is not recorded. But the partnership of Dionysus and Apollo at Delphi had a moderating influence on the Thracian Zagreus orgies, and though it introduced an ecstatic element into the procedure of the Pythia at Delphi, inspiration took a different form from that manifested in the Thraco-Phrygian frenzies, in spite of the fact that its prophet and *katharsis* had much in common with the Dionysian cultus.

Thus the Pythia exercised her office in a state of frenzy induced by means which remain conjectural. While the information available on the entire procedure is extremely vague, it seems that when an oracle was demanded of her she arrayed herself in long robes, a golden head-dress and a wreath of laurel-leaves, before drinking of the sacred spring Kassolis. To make sure that the day and the omens were auspicious a goat was sprinkled with cold water to see if it would tremble throughout its limbs, this being the favourable indication. When the sign had been given the Pythia took her seat on the tripod over a vaporous cleft in a chasm or cave below, though sometimes she was said to have entered the cavern to encounter the vapour. The accounts, however, are derived mainly from relatively late sources.[41] No allusion to the cave or chasm occurs before the fourth century BC and only very sporadically in the later literature until the first century. Clefts of this nature had been found in the limestone mountains in the neighbourhood of Delphi[42] but excavations at the site of the shrine have not produced any conclusive results, except to show that no subterranean cleft existed in the rock beneath the sanctuary.[43] Therefore, although the vapour theory is by no means improbable it lacks confirmation.

Whatever may have been the cause of the phenomenon, the words uttered by the Pythia, though doubtless unintelligible, were interpreted by the 'prophet', or chief priest, and often written down in hexameters as the oracles of Zeus given through Apollo, with whom the prophetess (Pythia) was thought to be *en rapport*. Like the Cumaean sibyl, she was an inspired figure, and in giving utterance to divine revelations she made known the will of Zeus through his son Apollo. So sacred was the office that she was forbidden to live with her husband and was subject to a number of tabus, but anyone with the essential occult powers might be selected to become the Pythia, irrespective of lineage, social status, or training. At the height of its prosperity three women served the tripod, but normally it was confined to a single occupant with an understudy who was her potential successor.[44] Doubtless there were various attendants occupied with the duties of the shrine, such as tending the sacred fire, and offering the sacrifice and sacred cake required before inquirers entered the temple. It was not until the beginning of the Christian era (*c.* 300 AD) that this service was associated with priestly families.

If, as is very probable, the original home of the oracle was in Anatolia,[45] it had an ecstatic background, however much this may have been modified under Apolline influence at Delphi. Indeed, as Dr Guthrie has pointed out, it is significant that the Hyperboreans, with whom Apollo is traditionally associated, geographically and etymologically have northern Asiatic affinities,[46] in which the shamanistic tradition was firmly rooted. Therefore, long before it was mellowed and modified in Anatolia and subsequently combined with the cultus of the Pythia, its ecstatic antecedents were probably firmly established. While opinion is divided about the priority of Apollo and Dionysus at Delphi, when they were brought into relation with each other on 'rocky Pytho', as the two cults coalesced, so the prophetess and her ecstatic oracular utterances gave expression to a common tradition.

In addition to Dionysus and Apollo, Orpheus, the prophet and hero of the Dionysian cult and priest of Apollo, found a place in this complex oracle at Delphi, and as a result many Apolline modifications were introduced into the Thracian orgiastic tradition. Under Orphic influence the Delphians cultivated hero-worship[47] and ritual tendance of the dead,[48] and the gulf was bridged between mortals and immortals first by crude ecstatic frenzy, and then by metempsychosis and *teletae*, as a means of getting into touch with the chthonian powers and purging the soul of its Titanic defilements. The Pythian Apollo, therefore, was responsible to no small extent for directing the wilder forms of ecstatic revelation into new and more refined channels, at once oracular and animistic, which ultimately acquired a philosophic content in the Platonic *soma-sema* doctrine of the soul and of its pre-existence and reincarnation.[49]

So great became the fame and influence of Apollo that all Greece resorted to his instrument and mouthpiece at Delphi for information on cult procedure, politics, law and personal conduct in everyday affairs, from monarchs and tyrants to ordinary individuals, in spite of the fact that the responses were for the most part vague, evasive and ambiguous,[50] especially on critical questions. When empire building made increasingly heavy demands on the oracle, local *exegetai* had to be appointed to give advice to the administration and to deal with the direction of the citizens of Athens, Sparta and other cities. To enable them to act in this capacity of legal advisers in private and local affairs they had to be equipped with some powers of divination,[51] but the Pythia remained the final voice of the god and Delphi the centre of spiritual authority. Thus, when a new colony was to be founded, the oracle was consulted in advance by any Greek community, to make sure that the venture had the approval of Apollo.[52] Even Socrates did not disdain to turn to it for guidance, although the Pythia had declared him to be the wisest of men, and he in return regarded himself as in the service of Apollo and under his protection.[53] Thus, the oracle retained the allegiance of the entire nation from rulers, statesmen and sages to citizens and athletes, who assembled periodically at Delphi to take part in the sacred games held in his honour. Therefore, its influence was very considerable as a consolidating force.

The Exegetai of Athens

In addition to the Delphic oracle Apollo had officials known as *Exegetai Pythochrestoi* who were either named by the oracle or selected by the Pythia from among a short list of nine Athenians submitted to her; they were nominated by the citizens but, like the Eumolpidae at Eleusis, they were usually equipped with hereditary qualifications.[54] Their function was to give advice on cultic matters such as sacrifices, festivals and purificatory rites, as well as to act as interpreters of the sacred law, omens and oracles, and to deal with questions affecting the relations of Athens with Delphi in an official capacity as officers of the state. When they were elected by popular vote, as recommended by Plato in his conception of the ideal Republic,[55] the people as a whole had a voice in their nomination, even though the final choice of three lay with the oracle; and Plato allowed that the Pythian Apollo was the external authority to whom all must submit in spiritual matters.

If no attempt was made to unify the cults of the Greek states in a single deity together with his worship, Delphi and its *exegetai* and ministers occupied a unique position, situated as they were at the centre of oracular inquiry both public and private. The rest of the pantheon played their several roles in their duly appointed and localized spheres, but Apollo said the last word on how their worship and the cult of the dead were to be conducted, and in respect of matters of legal and statutory procedure, the elucidation of ancestral custom, international colonization, vendetta, homicide and in times of crisis. His oracular decrees bestowed upon colonists a title of possession in the territory they occupied, just as they were largely responsible for the abandonment of the blood-feud and the substitution of ritual purification for homicide.

In short, by 600 BC Apollo became the chief standardizing agency in the religious organization and in the social structure in Greece, with Delphi as the *omphalos*, the navel of the earth. Thus Solon, when he reformed the state in 594 BC instituted the provision of three *Exegetai Pythochrestoi*, thereby showing his dependence upon the Pythian Apollo and his Delphic seat. This is clear from the fact that the *exegetai*, although they were state officials residing in Athens, were appointed by the oracle and acted as its interpreters. Moreover, they were not confined to the capital, as the institution had been extended to other cities to maintain the supremacy of the Pythia as widely as possible against the various other rival forms of divination and prognostication. Thus, Delphi did not possess a mantic monopoly and its 'priesthood' lacked any ultimate authority other than the pronouncements of the Pythia as the voice of Apollo. In the absence of a stable hierarchy independent of the oracular tradition, if the inspired utterance failed to be justified in practice, its prestige was liable to be diminished and recourse made to other seats of oracular inquiry.

The vicissitudes of Delphi

In the sixth century BC, for example, after the Persian wars, it proved unequal to the exacting demands made upon it, and so for a time Delphi lost the confidence of the nation by its partial and inaccurate judgments. In the Second Sacred War (357–346 BC) it was despoiled of its treasures by the Phocian generals, and when they were defeated by Philip of Macedon, it ceased to occupy its focal position as the Panhellenic sanctuary, though the oracle supported the conqueror and his successor, Alexander the Great.[56] In the Hellenistic period after the death of Alexander in 323 BC it was reduced to little more than a local court of appeal on doubtful questions touching the gods and moral conduct, giving advice on matters of conscience. In the ethical sphere generally its standard was high, but faith in its oracular pronouncements had so declined in the prevailing atmosphere of decadence and scepticism that no attempt was made to rebuild the temple after its destruction, probably by an earthquake, in 371 BC. In spite of the legends to the contrary, the Hellenistic kings ignored the Pythia, and on one occasion one of them is said to have seduced her without incurring any penalties for his sacrilege.[57] In short, they paid lip-service to Apollo without honouring his prophetess or consulting his oracle.

It was not until 279 BC when Celtic hordes invaded Macedonia and sacked the temples, that consolidated effort was made to save Delphi from their hands, on an assurance from the god that he would protect his shrine—'I and the white maidens shall take care of these matters.'[58] National sentiment rallied to the cause, and convinced that Apollo had intervened by an earthquake and thunderbolts, and appeared as a youth of superhuman size and surpassing beauty, the prophetesses and the priests rushed into the fray clad in their sacred vestments to complete the discomfort of the enemy, who withdrew to the north and was then driven back into Macedonia.[59] Though the attack was beaten off with sufficient success to stimulate the growth of the legend, nevertheless, the shrine appears to have been plundered by the Celts.[60] However, a festival called Soteria was instituted to commemorate the saving of Greece by this alleged intervention, in honour of Zeus Soteria and the Pythian Apollo.[61]

The episode is very obscure and controversial, but whatever may have happened in the second century BC the vitality of Delphi was renewed. Roman envoys consulted the oracle in 207 BC at the end of the Hannibalic war before approaching Attalus of Pergamos (who himself had founded his Dynasty on the word of Apollo)[62] with a request for the transportation to Rome of the meteoric stone that symbolized the Magna Mater[63] and on the strength of its verdict successfully fulfilled their mission in Pessinus, thereby introducing the cult of Kybele in Rome. Before founding a temple of Aphrodite Stratonicis in Smyrna in honour of his wife, Seleucis II (245–226 BC) sought the sanction of the Pythia,[64] and Ptolemy VI (173–146 BC) is said to have obtained the blessing of the Pythian Apollo in the transference of the image of Serapis from Sinope to Alexandria.[65] While this doubtless was only the popular version of the arrival of Serapis in Alexandria, elaborated by Plutarch to enhance the reputation of Delphi in the second century BC, at least it suggests that the authority of the oracle was still recognized, though in the early years of the Roman Empire it appears to have been completely ignored in matters of state. Later it was revived after the temple had been restored and repaired by Domitian in 84 AD, and the Pythian games reinstated.[66]

In the reigns of Trajan and Hadrian it again became a sacred city, but after a few sporadic utterances in the time of the Antonines and Severus, the oracle became silent;[67] this was explained by Christian apologists as the direct result of the incarnational revelation of Christ, regardless of its post-Christian pronouncements.[68] The attempt of Julian, however, to resuscitate it failed and his emissary Oribasius, on his return from the shrine, could only bring back the message, 'Tell the King, the fairwrought hall has fallen to the ground. No longer hath Phoebus a shelter, nor a prophetic laurel, nor a spring that speaks. The water of speech is quenched.'[69] How this information was obtained is not explained, but the fact remains that the temple was closed in AD 390 by Theodosius and demolished by his successor, Arcadius. So came to an end one of the most remarkable oracular influences in the history of the mantic movement, and a factor of no small importance in Greek civilization; Delphi was at once the geographical and spiritual centre of the Hellenic world, like Jerusalem in the medieval maps of Christendom.

It never, however, occupied the position of Rome as a focal point of a centralized hierarchical and ecclesiastical organization. The most it could claim was to declare the will and purposes of Zeus as revealed by Apollo and his instrument the Pythia, often in the face of the rival seats of mantic prophecy and of other modes of prognostication. Adopting the policy of being all things to all men its carefully devised ambiguities could not conceal its failure to give positive direction. Therefore, it was always in a precarious position, and once the mantic tradition of the Graeco-Roman world in which it had arisen and functioned ceased to operate, the role of the oracle lost its *raison d'être* and inevitably it was reduced to silence for ever.

The Sibylline oracles

Christianity, however, did not deny that behind the oracle were spiritual powers; it considered them demoniacal and, therefore, in line with other manifestations of possession by evil spirits.[70] The Sibyls, on the other hand, although like the Pythia they were thought to have derived their frenzied inspiration from Apollo, were supposed by some of the early Fathers and other Christian writers to have borne witness to Christ by their prophecies.[71] But, in fact, these prophetic priestesses had spread in Greece from Asia Minor in the sixth century BC and became closely allied with the Orphic movement before they passed to Italy, where one of the leaders established a seat, probably among the Greek settlers at Cumae near Naples. There a temple is said to have been dedicated to her in 493 BC in response to directions found in the Sibylline Books, which a strange old woman had succeeded in selling at an exorbitant price to Tarquinius Superbus, the last of the Tarquin kings, after she had burned the earlier collections of prophecies that he had refused to purchase. Behind the story lies the fact that Sibylline oracles from Greek sources reached Cumae in the sixth century, and gained a footing in Rome at the beginning of the Republic, bringing with them the Hellenic gods and their cultus.[72] In the disturbances and famine that occurred in the next century during the Etruscan struggle for the restoration of its dynasty, the Sibylline books were consulted and called for the foundation of the worship of Demeter, Dionysus and Kore, these deities being latinized as Ceres, Liber and Libera. Thereupon a temple was erected in their honour on the side of the Aventine Hill in Rome towards the Circus Maximus, and dedicated to them.[73] Nearly three hundred years later, after a violent storm of pebble-rain in

205 BC towards the end of the Hannibalic war, as has been mentioned above, recourse was made to the oracular books; this resulted in the Phrygian Magna Mater being installed in the temple of Victoria, until in 191 BC her own temple was erected on the Palatine.

If, as is very probable, the tradition arose in Asia Minor, where the head of 'the Sibyl of Erythrae' appears on Erythraean coins in the seventh century BC, it was in Greece that the floating oracular dicta on many themes flourished before it reached Etruria and became established at Cumae. Very soon a collection of the prophecies was kept in the Capitol at Rome under the care of the *duoviri sacris faciundis* as their guardians became, who consulted them as occasion arose, upon the application of the Senate for oracular direction in the maintenance of the *pax deorum*. This included the introduction of new gods and new rites, sometimes of a barbarous character, involving the burying alive or beating to death of those to whom were attributed widespread disasters.[74] As a result of these Sibylline pronouncements the entire character of the official State cult was changed by the introduction of an ever-increasing number of Greek deities with their western Asiatic and Etruscan ecstatic affinities, which were foreign to the indigenous Roman religion of the field and the farm and the hearth.

When eventually the books containing the collection of prophetic verses were destroyed in the burning of the Capitol in 83 BC during the civil wars, men were sent to Erythrae and elsewhere by Augustus in search of Sibylline records. The thousands that were brought back were inspected by the *duoviri*, and having been considerably reduced by the Emperor, they were re-copied and carefully preserved for future consultation in the base of the statue of Apollo in the new temple on the Palatine. Thus, by the beginning of the Christian era the Sibylline movement had acquired a new official status in the Empire with Apollo as a rival to Jupiter, the Roman Zeus, on the Capitol. As in due course it gained a measure of recognition from the Church, in the second and third centuries AD, a new class of oracles came into being from Christian sources, closely related not only to the pagan prophecies but also to those that had grown up at Alexandria in Hellenistic Jewish circles during the second century BC. These adaptations of the Sibylline books consisted of hexameter verses written in the same manner as those of the Graeco-Roman originals, and attributed to Sibyls who were inspired, it was said, to propagate the faith and teaching of Israel among the heathen. Old Testament incidents were combined with legends borrowed from the Sibylline writings, so that the destruction of the tower of Babel, for instance, was represented as the work of mighty winds before the reign of Cronos, Titan and Iapetus and the birth of Zeus, and foretold by the prophetic seer.[75]

The success of this method of propaganda as a proselytizing force led Christian writers in the second and third centuries to carry on the tradition. Some of the oracles were revised and worked over by the Christian Sibyllists,[76] while others were composed entirely afresh.[77] Most of them, however, are composite documents, and the last four books (XI–XIV) deal mainly with historical persons and events, with varying degrees of accuracy and written in Sibylline language by Jews and Christians from the third century onwards.[78] Notwithstanding the widespread acceptance by the Early Fathers of the inspiration of the Sibyls as spontaneous witnesses to Christ, the real nature of the fabrications was recognized by such discerning minds as those of Lucian and Celsus, who used all their skill and wit to discredit this method of Christian propaganda.[79] Nothing daunted, the Latins continued the tradition, and at the Council of Nicaea Constantine appealed to the oracles[80] while St Augustine placed the Sibyl in the City of God.[81]

Theophanies and oracles in ancient Israel
It is hardly surprising that in an uncritical age ecstatic inspiration readily survived, considering how very deeply laid it was both in the Graeco-oriental and in the Judaeo-Christian tradition. In the State religion of Rome it offered a way of escape from the formalism and remoteness of the official cultus, while in Christendom the discredited occult and esoteric mysteries and mysticisms were transformed by the new spiritual dynamic, interpreted in terms of divine charismatic forces such as had been manifest from time immemorial in the theophanies and revelational experiences in ancient Israel prior to the later developments of prophecy in the pre-exilic period from the eighth century BC onwards. Thus, the traditional founder of the 'chosen people' was represented as having been called out of Mesopotamia to what was to become the 'promised land' by a theophany which was succeeded by a series of divine disclosures at an oracle-bearing terebinth at Shechem, where the nature of his mission was made known to him.[82] At Bethel the foundation of the sanctuary was interpreted in relation to an incubational experience there by Jacob (later represented as having been accidental), and the disclosure of the divine occupant of the sacred place in a dream-oracle.[83] Other important shrines in the Patriarchal tradition—e.g. Beersheba, Hebron, Mamre and Ophrah—are represented as places at which the god of Israel disclosed himself to the

ancestors of the nation in special theophanies, either in person or through a supernatural being.

Often these manifestations are presented as spontaneous in some tangible form or visionary experience, as in the case of Jacob who is said to have declared, 'surely Yahweh is in this place, and I knew it not.'[84] Similarly, later in Midian, Moses is alleged to have encountered the same deity under the form of fire in the midst of a bush which was not consumed, when he turned aside in the mountain of God to see this mysterious phenomenon and to receive instructions from the god who 'dwelt in the bush'.[85] On the holy mountain known as Sinai or Horeb both Moses and Elijah are said to have met Yahweh 'face to face' in direct and immediate intercourse,[86] like Adam and Eve, though in a more dramatic setting and devoid of any mantic mediation through dream, vision or spirit-possession, sacramental channel, 'riddles' or 'dark speeches'.[87] In the wilderness Yahweh is held to have walked in the midst of the camp, and to have descended to 'the tent of meeting' in the outward and visible sign of a pillar of cloud, and to have stood at its door.[88] From the mountain top and out of the fire and in the tabernacle he spoke to his servant Moses 'mouth to mouth' continually, in contrast to the transient prophesying of the seventy elders, which was confined to a single occasion.[89]

These naïve anthropomorphisms are very different from the ambiguous and enigmatic pronouncements of the Pythia at Delphi, the obscure oracular utterances of the ecstatic prophets, or the prognostications of the diviners elsewhere in the Near East and the Aegean, including Palestine. In Hebrew tradition Moses occupied a unique position, combining the offices and functions of prophet, law-giver, cult-leader and ruler endowed with supernatural powers.[90] In these several capacities he was enabled to have intercourse with Yahweh in a more intimate manner than was possible in the case of those who depended upon less direct means of communication. Nevertheless, notwithstanding his privileged status, it was only at particular times and places that a theophany occurred, so that even Moses was virtually a cult-prophet, in the sense that he exercised his functions in relation to a prescribed ritual order and on the authority of his vocation and its spiritual endowments.

It is not always easy to determine to what extent the practices in vogue in Palestine and the surrounding region at the time of the Israelite occupation were transferred to the pre-exilic cultus and referred back to the desert and the tent of meeting by the later compilers of the narratives. But there can be little doubt that the mountains, caves, oracle-trees, wells and stones already sacred to the Canaanites were taken over with the beliefs and rites firmly attached to them from time immemorial and little changed in content or purpose. In the desert the Hebrew tribes carried on the tradition which was subsequently interpreted in relation to the ancestral history of Israel and its personnel, as the Yahwistic faith and its cultus took shape. Many of the customs, in fact, have persisted among the Arab peasants and Bedouins little changed to the present day. It would, indeed, be remarkable if they had not survived in Palestine after the settlement of the invading tribes. That they did persist is made clear by the equipment of the local sanctuaries with a sacred tree, a spring, alignment, mazzebah or 'gilgal' (i.e. stone circle), and adytum, as late as the time of the Josiah reformation in 621 BC. This brought them into line with the shrines of all the other Semitic peoples, Aramaeans, Canaanites, Akkadians or the Phoenicians, in spite of the Deuteronomic claim of an injunction to destroy the 'high places' and the groves and megalithic sanctuaries with their graven images at the time of conquest.[91] If any serious attempt was made to eliminate the Canaanite cultus at that time, or subsequently, it was abortive until all worship was centralized at the temple in Jerusalem as a temporary expedient during the Josiah reform.

In this way oracular divination persisted in Israel in association with the local shrines throughout the period of the monarchy. For example, the oak of Meonenim, 'the soothsayers' terebinth'[92] at Shechem in the days of Abimelech,[93] was doubtless the same 'oak which giveth oracles' (Moreh) to which reference is made in the Patriarchal narrative,[94] and at the time of the conquest of Palestine[95] diviners derived omens from this tree by the rustling of the leaves.[96] The principal function of the seers attached to these sacred places was to consult the god rather than to engage in sacrificial or cultic worship. They had, therefore, to be in possession of the technical knowledge required to give oracular direction, including augury, incubation, the drawing of lots and inspection, and divinatory prophecy.

Divinatory prophecy in Israel

It is indicated that cultic prophecy was practised in Israel little changed after the settlement in Canaan by the Hebrew designations for those who occupied these offices—*kohen*, *lewi*, *nabi* and *roeh*. Thus, the *kohen* was the equivalent of the Arabic *kahin*, diviner, who was mainly concerned with obtaining oracles by the aid of the Urim and Thummim, the method of securing a 'yes' or 'no' answer to specific questions, or by some similar mode of oracular inspiration and knowledge.[97] But the Hebrew seers differed from other Semitic and Mesopotamian diviners in that they were primarily professional ecstatics rather than mantic soothsayers, sorcerers and inspectors of entrails. Like the *Kohnim* and the hereditary Levites, these *Nebi'im*, as they were called in Israel, or 'sons of the prophets', were associated with particular sacred places and exercised their functions as cult officials. Thus, as confraternities, they were attached to sanctuaries such as Bethel, Gibeah, Rama, Jericho and Carmel,[98] in the service of the god who disclosed his will and purposes to them in a state of possession. It can hardly be questioned that they were pre-Israelite in origin, in view of the widespread range of this type of psychic phenomena and shamanistic behaviour, which was characteristic of Semitic prophecy in general. It was, in fact, identical in its essential characteristics with that exhibited by the Mesopotamian *makku*, or visionaries, believed to have been animated by a divine oracular 'breath' and to have derived their powers direct from the god with whom they were *en rapport* and to whose words they gave utterance.[99]

But while it is possible that priest (*kohen*) and prophet (*nabi*) may have had a common origin,[100] in Israel the *nebi'im* very soon became differentiated from the *kohens* of the sanctuaries, in so far as they assumed an independent role with little or no official status in the community, roaming about in the northern kingdom in ecstatic bands, like those encountered by Saul on his arrival on Mount Gibeah after his consecration by Samuel. Such was their contagious 'enthusiasm' that he was himself immediately infected by it, and the spirit (*ruach*) of Yahweh came mightily upon him and turned him into 'another man'.[101] Henceforth he displayed ecstatic symptoms from time to time, even though the divine afflatus is said to have left him and descended upon his successor after the anointing of David.[102] The position of Saul, however, is obscure, as he is represented as having been intimately associated with the sacrificial cultus in his royal capacity, and this brought him into conflict with Samuel.[103]

It is not improbable, in fact, that some of the incidents attributed to Samuel may have been told of Saul originally and subsequently transferred to Samuel by the anti-monarchical Deuteronomic school. Apart from the word-play in the story of the birth of Samuel being more relevant to the name of Saul,[104] as 'because I have asked him of the Lord' is nearer to *sha'ül* (Saul) than to *Shmü'el* (Samuel), the divine wrath the king is alleged to have incurred in offering sacrifice at Gilgal in the customary manner to consecrate the battle against the Philistines[105] is inconsistent with his having built an altar to Yahweh at the beginning of his reign and offered upon it the blood of the victims without any question of sacrilege;[106] to say nothing of his successors performing these functions as a matter of course, as, for example, in the case of Solomon in the temple at Jerusalem.[107]

Samuel, as depicted in the present narratives, was not a typical *nabi*, though he was subject to night-visions, mystical auditions hearing supernatural voices, and predicting future events,[108] knowing about the discovery of Saul's lost asses and ascertaining the divine will as a seer as and when occasion required, even beyond the grave.[109] His communications were in the nature of typical prophetic oracles, and although he was not of the tribe of Levi and was never described as a *kohen*, he is represented as having been consecrated to the service of the sanctuary at Shiloh from his birth, and to have been girded with the sacerdotal ephod.[110] Before the word of Yahweh had been revealed to him he experienced an audition which Eli realized was an oracular voice calling him,[111] but there is no suggestion of it having been an ecstatic possession. In short, Samuel appears to have been a priestly diviner or a seer alert to whatever was made known to him by a process of interior spiritual seeing and hearing, and so having occult knowledge beyond the range of normal perception. It is doubtful, therefore, whether he can be regarded as the originator of *Nab'ism* in Israel, as has been suggested.[112]

Elisha, on the other hand, was essentially an ecstatic engaged in shamanistic feats, including signs and wonders such as making iron swim, producing healing waters, restoring the dead to life by contact with his bones, foreseeing future events and exercising abnormal psychic powers, as in the account of his encounter with Hazael, or of his parting the waters with the aid of his staff, having been filled with the double portion of the spirit (*ruach*) of his predecessor.[113] Elijah, however, was a rain-maker rather than a charismatic *nabi*, fulfilling the role of the Al-Khidr, or 'Green Man' of folk tradition, with whom he was equated in his legendary guise. Thus, the Al-Khidr of Near Eastern popular lore suddenly sprang into being with no ancestry or genealogy like the Tishbite. After performing many remarkable deeds both of them disappeared mysteriously, and their respective legends have been intermingled.[114]

Elijah occasionally behaved ecstatically, as for instance when he was suddenly 'seized by the hand of Yahweh' and ran before the chariot of Ahab, outstripping the approaching storm-cloud.[115] But he chiefly exercised his supernatural power by controlling the weather. He was accredited with having brought a three years' drought upon Palestine, during which he was miraculously fed by ravens and the widow of Zarephath was sustained by a barrel of meal that wasted not and a cruse of oil that did not fail.[116] Then followed the contest on Mount Carmel with the frenzied priest-prophets of the Phoenician Baal in which Elijah, without becoming 'god-possessed' like his rivals, succeeded in vindicating Yahweh by commanding lightning to consume his sacrifice and causing the rain to descend on the arid land.[117] This is the outstanding event in the tradition, though he is represented as being carried from place to place by the spirit of Yahweh, continually appearing on the scene with dramatic suddenness and confronting Ahab with messages from 'the god before whom he stands' in prophetic guise. He discerned the divine presence in the rustling of a gentle breeze on the holy mountain, and went forth from Horeb to do the bidding of Yahweh, anointing Hazael to the kingship of Syria, Jehu to that of Israel, and Elisha to be his own successor in the prophetic sphere.

In these popular traditions, which are at variance with the events as they are recorded in the other documents preserved in the book of Kings,[118] Elijah stands out as a heroic figure, the stalwart defender of Yahweh, in violent opposition to the Canaanite cultus and all its ways and works. He is therefore represented as exercising his prophetic functions in accordance with the Yahwistic rather than the indigenous mantic tradition current in the northern Kingdom in the reign of Ahab. That the Hebrew cult-prophets were connected with local sanctuaries is shown by Elijah erecting an altar on Mount Carmel and lamenting the wholesale destruction of the Yahwistic altars elsewhere.[119] The rain-making ritual and its results conformed to the normal procedure[120] directed to Yahweh, who, he maintained, was the only one among the gods who could break the drought he had produced. In carrying on the Yahwistic campaign Elisha appears to have employed more shamanistic abnormal psychic methods, if the legends reflect his manticism, for each prophetic confraternity had its own traditions, rules and experience, were they ecstatic or thaumaturgic and magico-religious.

Little, however, has been recorded in the Old Testament about what was actually done by the prophets in these Israelite societies, and it is only by the few hints given here and there in the narratives that some idea can be gained of their behaviour. In the northern Kingdom *nebi'ism* seems to have been more ecstatic than in Judah in the south where Nathan and Zadok occupied a predominant position in the Davidic hierarchy and the temple ritual, as the official court priest-prophets. Moreover, it was in the north that the prophetic movement became most prominent in times of crisis. Ahab certainly could not ignore Elijah, and he and Jehoshaphat consulted the four hundred ecstatic opponents of Micaiah before the fatal battle at Ramoth-Gilead,[121] in the hope of ensuring victory over the Aramaeans. Elisha was behind the Yahwistic *coup d'état* of Jehu, and it was at Bethel that Amos, the earliest of the canonical prophets, himself a southerner, proclaimed 'the Word of Yahweh' as he had perceived the disclosure he had received in his visionary experience in Tekoa in the middle of the eighth century BC.

The literary Hebrew prophets
These new prophets displayed the phenomena of inspiration by means of their own peculiar endowment of spiritual vision which they claimed to have come direct from Yahweh. They were not mystics, nor were they *nabi* in the strict sense of the term, though they were in a very intimate relationship with the god whose message they believed themselves to have been called to deliver. Thus, Amos the herdsman of Tekoa declared that he had seen the words he was about to utter concerning Israel in a vision in the days of Uzziah king of Judah and Jeroboam II king of Israel,[122] while he was tending his flocks and dressing his sycamore trees in his Judaean homeland. But he did not belong to one of the guilds of the prophets, and for this reason he was expelled from the royal shrine at Bethel by Amaziah. He could not, however, be silenced, because he had shown himself to have been the recipient of a visionary message from Yahweh. For no matter how irregular a prophet might be and unpopular and unwelcome his prophesyings, his status as an instrument of Yahweh, albeit that of 'free-lance', made him a sacrosanct person immune from physical attack, by reason of his sacredness and its tabus. Therefore, the so-called literary or canonical prophets in Israel in and after the eighth century BC continued to denounce the depravities of the backsliding nation and to pronounce its approaching doom, and none prevented them by violence or death.

If they did not work themselves up into a state of ecstasy by occult methods and in companies, their prophetic experience was not fundamentally different from that of the *nabi*, inasmuch as it was based upon inspiration derived, as it was claimed, from Yahweh himself. They, too, felt themselves to be filled with divine afflatus (*ruach*) and moved to speak words which they regarded as divine oracles in the form of revelations received in visions. Therefore, they proclaimed that they were moved by a transcendent power which invaded them, being none other than that of the god of Israel. Consequently, they often prefaced their pronouncements, spoken in the first person, with the refrain, 'Thus saith Yahweh', and concluded them with the words 'Oracle of Yahweh',[123] the divine Word having objective reality. Conscious of being his 'messenger' sent by him, and, indeed, almost indistinguishable from the Deity,[124] they held converse with him and received their orders from him, which they proceeded promptly to carry into effect. By sharing in the divine nature (*ruach*) they partook of the Spirit of God as an extension of himself,[125] and so were brought within his 'corporate Personality' as a living part of his divine being.

This was a natural conclusion from the Hebrew conception of man as an aggregate of elements of the conscious life, physical and psychical, animated by a breath-soul or *nephesh*, and standing in a peculiar relationship to God by virtue of having been created in the divine image and likeness and brought into a covenant relationship with him as a member of the holy nation. Whether or not the initial inbreathing of the breath of life was equated with the divine energy, called *ruach* after the Exile, this charismatic endowment cannot be confined to the breath-soul (*nephesh*) of man. It had a wider significance denoting the spirit of Yahweh in its various and manifold operations, and filling the prophets with ecstatic power and visionary experiences.[126] As the god of Israel was conceived as a person, the personality of the Israelite was directly related to his fellowship with the ultimate source of his life. In the case of the prophet, however, this relationship was so intimate that it became a projection of the divine Personality, which rendered him, when he was in the service of Yahweh, virtually a divine being like the *malach*, or 'divine messenger'. In this status he perceived some aspects of the being and nature of God and had a transcendent insight into his will and purpose for his 'chosen people' and for mankind at large, be it a message of hope or of judgment, whether they would hear or whether they would forbear. For the literary prophets the 'messenger' had ceased to be a supernatural *malach* and become a human being in a particular relation with God, delivering the special message Yahweh had consigned to him.

Precisely how the 'true' and the 'false' prophets were to be distinguished, when both of them spoke with oracles attributed to the same divine source was no easy matter. Jeremiah, for instance, condemned the contemporary prophets in no uncertain terms because they relied on 'the visions of their own hearts' and on 'the dreams they had dreamed' rather than on the revelation of Yahweh spoken directly to them without any traditional oracular medium.[127] But, in fact, dreams and ecstatic visions were a recognized feature in pre-exilic prophecy in Israel, however much he might repudiate the tradition of Hananiah and his company.[128] Jeremiah did admit that the truth of their respective portents would be decided by the course of events, though subsequently he pronounced a further and conclusive word of doom against Hananiah and the nation.[129] Where the classical prophets were all agreed from Amos to Ezekiel was in their condemnation of the syncretistic cultus, for they saw behind all the phenomena of nature and the vicissitudes of the history of the nation the one omnipotent will of the Holy One of Israel, the righteous ruler of creation and doer of justice, whose law was holy and whose power was infinite.

Unlike the indigenous Canaanite gods and those of the surrounding countries, whose existence was not denied, Yahweh was not sporadically beneficent when in a favourable mood, nor was he dependent upon the fate of competing priesthoods, cities or nations. His tender mercies were over all his works, but he demanded of every member of the holy nation obedience to his commands and conformity to his standards. In the prophetic consciousness it became increasingly apparent that each individual had a personal responsibility in the maintenance of the prescribed religious and social order of the theocracy, as the will and purpose of God were made known through the voice of prophecy as well as by the Torah as a sacred oracle. As they were divine disclosures and precepts, the Law and the Word of Yahweh constituted an absolute standard of belief and conduct binding on the nation as a whole and on each individual in his personal capacity.

Since the great prophets received their message through their own experience of a direct encounter with the god of Israel, they interpreted the social problem in relation to the character of the individual.[130] While they proclaimed a social ethic the corporate personality of the nation could fulfil its vocation only by every member realizing his responsibilities and the demands made upon him by the Holy One of Israel as a righteous God, as will be considered in greater detail in the next chapter. Nothwithstanding the fact, however, that the Hebrew prophets gave a new significance and ethical interpretation to the Word of Yahweh, they exercised their functions along the same lines as their predecessors, and their oracular methods were not very different from theirs, except that they claimed to have received unsolicited revelations which, as they maintained, were of unimpeachable authenticity. Amos denied that he was a mantic professional prophet, but he was absolutely convinced that he had been the recipient of a divine command to 'go, prophesy unto my people Israel', received in a series of oracular visions.[131] Jeremiah declared that he had 'stood in the council of

Yahweh' and 'heard his Word' which he transmitted to the people along familiar lines.[132] Isaiah in a visionary experience saw Yahweh sitting upon a throne, high and lifted up and surrounded with angelic beings. In this ecstatic condition he heard the divine voice saying unto him, 'Whom shall I send and who will go for us?' And in abasement, filled with numinous awe and wonder, he replied, 'Here am I, send me.'[133] Again and again he had similar experiences which compelled him to utter the messages that resounded in his ears from the eternal world,[134] just as Ezekiel was continually subject to prolonged super-normal psychoses indistinguishable from those characteristic of the *nabi*.[135] But the great prophets were not content just to be filled with the prophetic spirit. They saw the truth in the same measure as they were convinced that they had received it from Yahweh. They knew the will and mind of the god in whose service they were enlisted, and that any prophecy that was not strictly in accord with his commands was not in fact derived from him.[136]

CHAPTER NINE

THE GODS AND THE GOOD LIFE

Egyptian conception of good and evil, the 'heart' the seat of conscience, the 'silent man', moral responsibility and personal piety, mortuary morals and magic, divine guardianship of morality—sin and transgression in Babylonia, ritual lamentation texts and penitential psalms, cult of Ea at Eridu, code of Hammurabi—Hebrew legislation, the sacred and secular in Israel, prophetic ethic, ethical monotheism, post-exilic Judaic ethic, dualism and the problem of evil—Zoroastrian ethic, Mazdaean dualism, religion of the good life, Iranian influence on Judaism—Iranian and Ionian dualism, pre-Socratic pluralists, ethics of the Pythagoreans, Orphic life, Orphism and the Homeric and Hesiodic Olympian ethical tradition, Platonic conception of God and the Good

The Egyptian conception of good and evil

AMONG THE PEOPLES of western Asia, the Fertile Crescent and the Eastern Mediterranean, the ancient Egyptians were outstanding in the interest they displayed in the moral aspect of the world. It is true that their sages made no attempt to construct and enunciate a system of ethics, but they recognized that the good and the right had a cosmic significance. Their physical environment gave them confidence in the order of nature and its rhythm and made them fundamentally optimistic in their outlook and also ethically minded. The good was that which was pleasing to the gods, and the evil that which was displeasing to them, though evil was held to have come from them. Moreover, they were themselves subject to the same weaknesses, attacks and influences as were human beings. So far from being omnipotent, omniscient, all-righteous and infallible, the gods sometimes might champion the good and at other times support the malign forces, as in the case of Seth, who was at once the ally of Re-Atum and the adversary of Osiris and Horus. Even Horus, in spite of his vindication of his father Osiris, was alleged to have decapitated his mother Isis when she enraged him, and Hathor had as many sides to her character as she had offices and functions.

Therefore, the Egyptians considered that the good was not that which in our sense is ethically 'right' or the evil that which is morally 'wrong'. These concepts were conditioned by the environment in which they arose, the divine ordering of the cosmic forces and the natural processes on which well-being depended, although it was thought that the gods willed the good, which was conceived as the right ordering of all things in heaven and on earth and personified in the goddess Maat who embodied truth, justice, right and order (Fig. 79). It was she, as the daughter of the Sun-god, who stood beside Thoth in the boat of Re when he arose out of Nun, and accompanied him on his nightly passage through the underworld. She was 'the brightness by which Re lives', and ushered the soul on its arrival into the judgment hall of Osiris and Re to be weighed by Thoth and Anubis.

Maat, however, was essentially a divine attribute of the universe and of the structure of society, having a cosmic, social and ethical connotation. By it Re lived, ruled and dispelled the darkness when he put order in the place of chaos in the beginning and he repeated the process in rising in the east daily at dawn. Consequently, it was the duty of his son, the Pharaoh on the throne, to maintain 'justice' (i.e. Maat) by ruling the nation with 'truth', preventing anarchy, strife and lawlessness, and preserving the rhythm of nature.[1] Therefore, 'living in truth' (Maat) was appended to the official name of the reigning Pharaoh, and during the Ikhnaton monotheistic movement in the Eighteenth Dynasty the new capital Amarna was described in one of the hymns as 'the seat of truth'. Similarly Tutankhamen, when he restored the worship of Amon-Re at Thebes, was said to have 'driven out disorder from the Two Lands so that order (Maat) was again established in its place as at the first time (creation).'[2]

In this complex conception of Maat, the gods, the universe and the sovereign ruler were inseparably combined in a fundamental enduring principle 'the good and the worth of which was to be lasting. It had not been disturbed since the day of creation; whereas he who transgresses its ordinances is punished'.[3] As it was this changeless universal divine right, ordering of all existence, it was of the essence of the good life, and the entire universe was regarded as a divinely constituted monarchy, in which the king in his capacity of the son of the Sun-god and the living Horus, occupied the key position alike in the physical, social and ethical spheres. He was, in short, the personification of the good life because he had 'made bright the truth (Maat) which he (Re) lives'. He knew what he lived by, since he was the likeness of Re, 'one with him'.[4] And right conduct was 'doing what the king, the beloved of Ptah, desired'.

The 'heart' the seat of conscience

As the ka was originally the exclusive possession of the Pharaohs, in the same way Maat in all probability was a royal prerogative, until in process of time the good life became universal among the whole nation, when it was recognized that all men were capable of understanding the nature of the universe and of entering into a harmonious relation with it. Doubtless it was primarily officials and leaders who strove after this knowledge and endeavoured to fashion their lives according to its tenets. But 'it lay as a path in front even of him who knows nothing'.[5] Every man had the faculty associated with the heart (*ab*) as the seat of the mind, reason or conscience, to recognize the right course of action. It was the 'heart' that brought forth every issue as the guiding principle in the life of man and by determining conduct became 'character'. It was, indeed, described as 'the voice of God that is in everybody: happy is he whom it has led to a good course of action'.[6]

In the Old Kingdom this was centred exclusively in the monarchy as the sovereign protector and defender of the right order. Under feudal conditions in the Middle Kingdom (*c.* 2000–1780 BC) when the stress was upon social justice and righteousness, it was declared that 'every man had been made like his fellow', and since the social order was part of the cosmic order, social inequality was contrary to the proper equilibrium of society, and no part of the divine plan. Only evil in the heart of man had upset the balance, and when the ancient divinely ordained Dynasty broke up at the end of the Pyramid Age before the invading Asiatics, Maat was said to have been 'cast out and iniquity to sit in the council chamber. The plans of the gods are destroyed and their ordinances transgressed. The land is in misery, mourning is in every place, towns and villages lament'.[7] This was a state of evil *par excellence*, because it represented the collapse of the established order with the inevitable disorder, strife, falsehood and chaos following in its train. Thus, in a static régime such as prevailed in the Nile valley, so long as the existing order remained undisturbed, its ethic, conceived in terms of Maat, was a powerful cohesive dynamic welding together as a composite whole the divine cosmic and human orders as a single entity governed by a transcendental principle making for 'righteousness' (i.e. justice, harmony and equilibrium), permanence and stability, and all that is involved and implied in the Egyptian conception of the good life.

The monarchy, by virtue of its divine foundation and function, was the unifying centre, and so when the royal power was again able to assert itself as a world power, alike cosmic and political in its range, it became the rallying point. Later the Ikhnaton interlude in the Eighteenth Dynasty failed, because the heretic king was not able to transform the royal divine Maat incarnate in him into an effective social order as a political and administrative force. It collapsed, therefore, at his demise about 1366 BC and a return was made at once to the orthodox solar worship of Amon-Re at Thebes. To be efficacious the Maat of the cosmos had to be transmitted from the gods through the Pharaoh and his priesthood and administrators to society at large, in order that good might be counterbalanced against evil by transforming cosmic divine Maat into the Maat of a firmly established social order with good government maintaining peace, justice and stability.

The 'silent man'

In its personal application the good life was living in attunement with Maat, exemplified in the self-discipline of the 'silent man' who is always patient, calm and self-effacing, master of his impulse, 'striving after every excellence until there is no fault in his nature'.[8] Yet in the Egyptian Wisdom literature of the New Kingdom 'silence' had a more positive connotation than in the Chinese quietistic conception of Tao, the 'path' that lay at the heart of all existence and the order of the universe, with which it was closely associated in idea. Although it was linked with humility, weakness and meekness,[9] it was 'submissive silence which could give you ultimate success related to the designs of the god', to be practised in everyday life rather than in seclusion.[10]

In the restless age after the expulsion of the Hyksos Asiatic invaders with perpetual threats at the extremities of the newly-established Egyptian Empire from the Hittites, the Assyrians, the Libyans and the 'Peoples of the Sea', dependence upon the gods for help and succour gave rise to a deterministic philosophy based on human insufficiency, in contrast to divine ability with the emphasis on the needs of the nation rather than on the individual, who was constrained to cultivate a spirit of submission to the group and reliance upon the divine ordering of events. In quietness and confidence lay his strength alike in relation to the gods and to the community. The source, however, from which the 'quiet' or 'silent' man drew his strength and consolation was a cosmic principle and established divine order manifest in nature, in harmonious society, and in the good life of the individual who strove after its excellence.

Moral responsibility and personal piety

In the Middle Kingdom the sense of individual moral responsibility became paramount, and with it went that of the worthy character and personal right. The virtues extolled and sought after in the moral treatises of the period were honesty, truthfulness, justice, generosity and frankness; the vices condemned were robbery, adultery, and violence.[11]

The maxims of the Egyptian sage Ptahhotep, in fact, provide the earliest formulation of right conduct and the content of life's worth, in spite of the pragmatic pronouncements in which truth and honesty were commended because they represented the best policy, and justice (Maat) was of advantage because its usefulness endured. Nevertheless, these virtues were comprehended as the highest ideal in the conception of Maat which, as we have seen, was primarily and essentially the divine order established at the creation of the universe, the essence of existence. To follow this way of life, therefore, was to live in harmony with the highest good, and not merely to pursue an opportunist course. As Frankfort has pointed out, when it was said that 'Maat has not been disturbed since the day of its creator', this was not the expression of complacent optimism, as Breasted contended,[12] because it represented a deep religious conviction concerning the changelessness of this cosmic order by divine decree.[13] This applied equally to the Misanthrope's exhortation 'speak with truth, do the truth, do that which conforms to truth, because truth is powerful, because truth is great, because it is lasting, and when its paths are found it leads to a blessed state of existence'.

Mortuary morals and magic

With the democratization of the afterlife in the Middle Kingdom, notwithstanding the widespread use of magical charms to protect the dead from the dangers and ordeals which beset them, and to enable them to attain a blessed eternity, there are unmistakable indications of a moral consciousness in the 125th chapter of *The Book of the Dead*. The emphasis given to the enumeration of the good deeds of the deceased and admonitions against the use of false weights, robbing a widow and the poor and stealing in general,[14] shows the importance attached to right conduct. The deplorable traffic with the magical charms to prevent the heart witnessing against the dead man at least represented an attempt to silence the voice of conscience, magic being employed as an agent for moral ends. The declaration of innocence, in fact, was the positive aspect of the confession of guilt, when at a higher ethical level the sinner humbly acknowledged his unworthiness in the presence of an all-righteous God on whose mercy and forgiveness he depended for his salvation in this life and beyond the grave. In ancient Egypt this stage in the development of conscience had not been reached in respect of the hereafter, since an adequate magical equipment was deemed sufficient to secure vindication. But this may be in some measure the result of a deeply laid consciousness of the far-reaching consequences of evil, and the fear that the wrong that had been done in this life would have eternal consequences, unless drastic steps were taken to silence the voice within which was called the 'heart'.

The belief in a judgment after death, however, inevitably carried with it some conception of moral responsibility in relation to the gods and the afterlife, as otherwise such an assize would be unnecessary and meaningless. All that would be required would be the adequate provision of charms and sustenance, and the due performance of the prescribed rites, without any assessment of behaviour in this world. Egypt, in fact, stands out above the surrounding ancient nations by reason of the way in which conduct during this life was expected to affect that on the other side of the grave. Moral requirements in themselves were by no means rare, for righteous behaviour was not without avail in the attainment of immortality, and even Osiris had to be vindicated or 'justified' before he gained his status in the celestial realms as the personification of all that is good and the judge of the dead. And those who hoped to share in his victory over death had to be pronounced 'true of voice', however much charms and amulets played their part in securing the verdict by protesting their innocence and preventing the conscience from witnessing against the deceased.

The divine guardianship of morality
It was the height of wisdom to be just, righteous, godly and humane, and especially in the literature of the last millennium BC, divine consciousness became the determining factor in the Egyptian ethic, coupled with social justice and truth. Seth was opposed against Osiris as the essence of evil, but collectively the gods were regarded as good and the guardians of morality, even if some might have malevolent qualities themselves. They were, in fact, held to have been responsible for the creation of evil as well as of good, but, nevertheless, they loved and upheld the right and the true (i.e. Maat), and hated and destroyed error and disorder. Therefore, they were regarded as righteous judges having knowledge of all that took place and watching the actions of every man, punishing wrongdoing and rewarding virtuous acts. Consequently, the good life was 'to do all the gods loved',[15] be it the virtues personified in Osiris or those concerning the right ordering of the city or nome over which the local deity presided.

All destinies were under divine guidance, and men were safe only when they placed themselves in 'the hand of god', the determiner of fate. From being associated mainly with evil and malevolence, destiny came to be regarded as beneficent when the gods were thought to be essentially the benefactors of mankind who dispensed their good gifts to those who merited their bounty. But so fixed were the fortunes of all men, that by the Middle Kingdom it was felt to be useless to try to alter that which had been predetermined by the gods, or to pry into their intentions and decrees. The lot of everyone had been duly apportioned and predestined, and, therefore, it was foolish to trouble further about what cannot be changed; this was in contrast to the earlier belief that the good life was capable of achievement by human endeavour under the guidance and guardianship of the gods.

Nevertheless, if free will had tended to give place to predestination, by the time of the sage Amenemope, which seems to have been in the Eighteenth Dynasty,[16] the conception of conscience was firmly established, 'the heart of man' being described as 'the nose of god', open to the divine voice.[17] For this ethical teacher the power to distinguish between good and evil was a human endowment, and this carried with it moral responsibility and a duty to God in the abstract, as the term Deity is used in respect of either Atum-Re or the Aton as the ruler of man's mind and destiny and his judge. The plans for each individual had been divinely formulated, and so no attempt must be made to discover or disarrange them, founded as they were upon Maat in its cosmic, spiritual and ethical aspects, embracing law and order, justice, righteousness and truth.[18] To do the will of God was the moral ideal. To attain this *summum bonum* the wise man must 'seat himself on the arms of the God', and in silence, tranquillity, humility and meekness rest upon them in confidence, trust and complete submission to that which has been determined by divine Providence for the eternal good of those who accepted the will of God and its appointed ends and endeavoured to walk in the paths he had set before them. But while the gods were the guardians of morality and determiners of destinies, they were never regarded as the saviours of mankind from the evils of the flesh, or as in any way altering the prescribed course of events.

Sin and transgression in Babylonia
In the less stable and predictable environment of Mesopotamia with its scorching and suffocating winds, torrential rains, devastating floods and uncertain seasons, the cosmic, social and ethical orders could not be interpreted in terms of Maat, as in the Nile valley. Under these conditions the human situation and its destinies were as indeterminate as the processes of nature, involving a continual struggle for existence and survival in a world in which evil was more apparent than good, and

malevolence more than beneficence. For man death was no less the perennial challenge to the will to live than were the floods which every spring threatened the return of the primeval watery chaos, and all bodily ills and misfortunes which were the work of the gods or of demons. Thus a list of possible offences occurs of which the sufferer might have been guilty in the Sumerian and Babylonian incantations and prayers, and since every aspect of life was thought to be under divine or demonic control, morality was essentially a magico-religious discipline.

It is not surprising, therefore, that ritual errors occupy a very prominent position in the lists inasmuch as human transgression was generally regarded in the last analysis as sin against or neglect of a god or goddess, the breaking of a tabu, the failure to perform a prescribed cult observance, or an offence of some kind in which supernatural sanctions and the divine ordering of the universe were involved. As every phase of existence, cosmic, civic, domestic and personal, was brought within the orbit of the gods, ethics and religion were inseparable, and much that appears on the surface to have had little or no moral purpose on further examination is found to have a more ethical significance than was at first apparent. The emphasis was often on offences committed unwittingly, involving at most unconscious guilt, and encouraging resort to charms, divination and other magical devices to rectify them. Similarly, the behaviour of the gods, as has already been made clear, was frequently far from ethical. But, nevertheless, regarded from the standpoint of the ethico-religious conception of the universe that prevailed in Mesopotamia, moral and ceremonial offences against men, the gods, and the super-sensuous forces governing the cosmic order, could not be differentiated. They were all equally harmful, dangerous and brought their consequences and punishment on mankind at large, and they were requited in this world.

Ritual lamentation texts and penitential psalms
In the ritual texts, such as the collection of prayers and spells in the incantation series called *Shurpu*, the various causes of the contraction of evil are set forth in a long list of questions by an exorcist:

> Has he sinned against a god,
> Is his guilt against a goddess,
> Is it a wrongful deed against his master,
> Hatred towards his elder brother,
> Has he despised father or mother,

Insulted his elder sister,
Has he given too little,
Has he withheld too much,
For 'no' said 'yes'
For 'yes' said 'no'?

Has he used false weights,
Has he taken an incorrect amount,
Not taken the correct sum,
Has he fixed a false boundary,
Has he removed a boundary, a limit, or a territory,
Has he possessed himself of his neighbour's wife,
Has he shed the blood of his neighbour,
Robbed his neighbour's dress,
Was he frank in speaking,
But false in heart,
Was it 'yes' with his mouth,
But 'no' in his heart?[19]

The list, which in its totality enumerates more than a hundred possible offences, covers a very wide field, including many ethical as well as ceremonial misdemeanours and transgressions, which Marduk is called upon to remove, even though these may have been inserted by later redactors when higher precepts of right and wrong had emerged. But the intermingling of ethical concepts and ritual holiness is a characteristic feature of Babylonian and Assyrian texts and penitential psalms at all times. Thus, the lofty prayer to Ishtar in which the goddess is besought by the penitent to 'forgive my sin, my iniquity, my shameful deeds, and my offence; overlook my transgression, accept my prayer', concludes with a rubric concerning the ceremonial lustrations with pure water and cleansings by means of aromatic woods and sacrificial offerings.[20] Nothing could sound more sublime than the prayer:

The sin which I have done turn thou into goodness;
The transgression which I have committed, let the wind carry it
    away;
My many misdeeds I strip off like a garment;
O My God, my transgressions are seven times seven: remove my
    transgressions.
O My Goddess, my transgressions are seven times seven: remove
    my transgressions.[21]

Yet the sins bewailed were for the most part ritual errors, often committed unwittingly, and the general outlook was that of the primitive conception of propitiation.

The same is true of the public lamentation rituals which from early times formed part of the official cult on occasions of calamity. Thus, in the Sumerian texts and their Babylonian translations, the land is represented as being in a tabu condition, in consequence of which the gods had forsaken the cities and brought disaster upon mankind. A fast was demanded to restore their beneficence, together with purificatory ceremonies and appropriate magical lamentations.[22] Usually the king is the speaker and by uttering laments in his official capacity he voices the complaint of his people. It was upon these royal public lamentations that the Priestly and private psalms, hymns, dirges, litanies, confessions and incantations were modelled, and having been originally compiled for the use of the king as the chief and all-embracing penitent they could easily be adapted to individual use. But whether public or private, there is little expression of sin and righteousness in the ethical sense. Moral faults are seldom enumerated, and often the suppliant is quite at a loss to know why a calamity has fallen upon him. Thus, he declares, probably quite truly, that he has not neglected any of the ritual prescriptions, failed to observe the appointed feasts, or despised the images of the gods. The daily cry of the penitent was the pathetic protest: 'I know not the sin which I have done; I know not the error which I have committed.' Somehow he had 'missed the mark' and brought upon himself the wrath of tyrannical deities who were ever on the alert for the slightest infringement of the ritual order.[23]

Nevertheless, on the Assyrian bilingual recensions in which the Penitential Psalms occur in the library of Ashurbanipal, going back in origin to a very much earlier period, the king, as the ideal man, is represented as suffering vicariously for his people, in spite of the psalms being an essential part of the magico-religious cultus. Moreover, the more he 'thought only of prayer and supplication', made 'sacrifice his rule', 'the day of divine worship the pleasure of his heart', and 'the procession of the goddess his riches and delight', the more did he suffer. 'He cried to his god' but 'he did not vouchsafe his countenance to him', and 'entreated the goddess but her head was not vouchsafed'. He taught his country to respect the name of god, and to revere the name of the goddess, but 'what seems good to oneself that is evil with god; and what is evil to one's own mind that is good with his god.' Indeed, 'before god false things are acceptable!' Yet this depth of despair was followed by a psalm of thanksgiving for deliverance when he was brought back to life and power by Marduk; 'the rust was wiped off', his 'troubled course became serene', 'the stain of slavery was cleansed away and the chain unbound'.[24]

Although this Babylonian Job raised the problem of the divine moral ordering of human affairs, he arrived at the conclusion that the ways of the gods were past finding out, defying the diviner and the soothsayer as well as the unaided wit of man. The most that could be hoped for was the restoration to health and prosperity in this life, as the gods had denied the boon of immortality to the human race. And even this consolation was abandoned in a pessimistic dialogue between a master and his servant in a later text, in which all moral values were denied and the only good that was left was to break both their necks and throw them into the river.[25] Nothing was worth while and death alone remained the end of man.

The cult of Ea at Eridu

Surrounded on all sides with so many and great dangers, tribulations and malign forces and machinations, an elaborate penitential and propitiatory system of ritual protection, purification and atonement was developed in Babylonia centred notably at Eridu where the cult of Ea, the god of wisdom, was firmly established. Situated at the head of the Persian Gulf, where formerly the Tigris and Euphrates flowed into the sea, this oldest of the Sumerian cities was known as 'the Good' because there stood the temple of Ea, 'the house of the depth of the ocean', or 'the house of wisdom'. As the Delphi of Mesopotamia the wise counsels of Ea were sought at his sacred *Kishkanu*-tree in this hallowed acre (*Engurra*), as had been revealed in the beginning to his son Adapa, the first man and the king-priest of Eridu. From the potency of its waters 'the curse of Eridu', or *siptu*, derived its efficacy as the curse of expiation which was destined to become the all-important spell in exorcisms. Originally it was the life-giving waters that neutralized, expelled or absorbed the malevolent influences and so freed those who had come into contact with evil from its contagion because being the substance out of which the universe was created it was endowed with all its creative potentialities. The location of the ancient city made it the natural cult centre of the god of the waters whose function was that of 'washing away', purging, or in some way removing evil as a miasma. So in the texts Ea is represented as the god who above all delivered men from sin, disease, pollution, and demoniacal assaults, as well as being the source of supernatural knowledge.

The code of Hammurabi

With the rise of Babylon to supremacy when Hammurabi consolidated the city-states in the Empire in the second millennium BC (*c.* 1750 or 1728), the new capital gained precedence over Eridu and its god Ea gave priority of place to Marduk, as Hammurabi claimed to have been called by him and Anu to reign as 'king of righteousness' in order that 'justice might appear in the land'.[26] This he is said to have accomplished in the second year of his reign, but it is not clear when in fact he promulgated his great code in its final form with the divine authority of Marduk. Until he had completed the subjugation of the country he could not have enforced the legislation, even though a good many of the laws had been embodied in the earlier collections of judgments of very considerable antiquity issued by the Sumerian rulers and recorded by their successors (e.g. those of Urukagina, *c.* 2700 BC, and of Gudea, *c.* 2450 BC). He did not succeed in subduing Elam, Sumer and Akkad until the thirtieth or thirty-first year of his reign; nor did he complete the subjugation of the west until five years later.[27] Then he became 'king of the west-land', and about the same time extended his dominion in the north by conquering Nineveh and Ashur, thereby becoming 'the king having the obedience of the four quarters of the earth'.[28] His intention, therefore, to govern the empire with justice and righteousness was not in all probability finally accomplished until the end of his lengthy reign of forty-three years, when the code in its present form was published and became the basis of all subsequent legislation.

Once the centralization of jurisdiction was established at Babylon, 'the gate of the gods', with the divine sanction of Marduk, his 'exalted prince' Hammurabi was able 'to give justice to the people and to grant them good governance, to set forth truth and justice within the land and prosper the people'.[29] In the exercise of his quasi-divine rule, however, he kept in the background as far as possible, and when he bought land as a private individual he tended more and more to employ his stewards to carry out the transactions on his behalf as 'the king of justice'. He constructed canals and controlled dredging and similar operations connected with their use and maintenance. He gave instructions concerning the enforcement of the laws against bribery and money-lending, upheld the just claims of debtors and supervised the regulations of food supplies, transport, public works, and the care of the royal flocks and herds. A breach of contract was decided in a local court consisting of one or more judges together with the elders of the city acting as assessors after the inspection of the deed. The oaths were taken in the temple, or at its gate, and referred to the judgment of the god, but the judges were not necessarily priests. Indeed, the code and the administration of its legislation were essentially secular and made no claim to have been divine pronouncements, in spite of their having been issued with the sanction of Marduk.

Hebrew legislation

In this respect this remarkable legal document, which represents the high-water mark of legislation in the ancient Near East at the time of its promulgation, and which influenced to a very considerable extent the regulation of conduct and behaviour in the adjacent countries, was in marked contrast with the Hebrew laws regarded as divine oracles. A legal decision, however, was generally looked upon as in the nature of an oracle indicative of the will of the god, and both the Babylonian word for 'law', *tertu*, and its Hebrew equivalent, *tôrah*, meant 'omen'. Hence arose the dogma concerning the divine origin of the Pentateuch as the code revealed on the Holy Mount to Moses, who, it was alleged, wrote down and taught it to the congregation of Israel as the decrees of Yahweh, without any clear distinction between ecclesiastical, civil and criminal procedures.

How much, if any, of this heterogeneous legislation actually emanated from Moses cannot be determined, but the distinctive character of many of the laws (e.g. those on slavery, holiness, and the *lex talionis*) suggests that they were the product of independent legislative schools in Israel, like the Priestly Code drawn up by the priests after the Exile in the time of Ezra (*c.* 444 BC) which represented the result of a process of careful collecting and sorting of tradition by a skilled body of sacerdotal canonists and legislators. It is apparent that they borrowed directly and indirectly from Mesopotamian sources, but they also developed their own traditions, behind which it would seem was the shadowy figure of a supreme legislator who was also a lawgiver and stood in a peculiarly intimate relation with the god of Israel and the cultus. Therefore, some of this legislation may go back to Moses, and behind him to the Code of Hammurabi and the Sumerian jurisprudence of the third millennium BC. The Book of the Covenant in Exodus xxi-xxiii. 19 is now recognized to have been a fragment of a much longer Hebrew analogue to the Code of Hammurabi, comparable to similar Hittite and Assyrian legal codes, and belonging to a more or less common corpus of ancient customary laws current probably in Palestine and elsewhere in western Asia at the time of the Israelite settlement in Canaan between 1500 and 1000 BC.[30]

The sacred and the secular in Israel

Living, as it was claimed, under a special dispensation of divine government, the 'chosen nation' was subject to the laws and sovereign rule of Yahweh exercised through his earthly agents and the cultus. The *Torah* (i.e. Law) was its sacred and treasured possession, and its decrees and prescriptions were absolute in their demands for explicit obedience. At first it consisted mainly of cultic and secular formulations in the name of Moses and giving the norm of the covenant relationship between Yahweh and Israel, until under prophetic influence in and after the eighth century BC, it was moralized in accordance with the ethical standards and moral judgments of an all-righteous God. When the bond between the tribes and their local god was that of a covenant-unity comparable to the social nexus that united desert folk on a family basis in a kindred group and blood brotherhood, the good life was centred in the mutual obligations which each owed to the other members of the clan, strengthened by their collective relationship with Yahweh, under whose rule and jurisdiction they professed to live and prosper. Their first duty was to the theocracy and its god-given laws and institutions as administered by its duly appointed agents and made efficacious in the cultus.

So long as the religious and civic observances and the prescribed ethic were interpreted in terms of non-moral sacredness as an irreducible datum *sui generis*, the holy denoted that which was set apart from the secular and consecrated to the service of religion. It was in this sense that Israel was regarded as a sacred congregation, or the Nazarite was 'separated' from the rest of the community,[31] while Yahweh himself was a holy god, because he was the personification of the numinous, the *mysterium tremendum* transcending the natural and commonplace and controlling the universe and its processes.[32] With the fuller moralization of the conception of sacredness, he became the Holy One of Israel, the righteous Ruler of the world, absolute in goodness and truth.[33] Divine righteousness, however, retained a forensic quality, meaning conformity to the proper norm or standard in respect of correct weights, true speech, or right paths.[34] Therefore, as a category of value it characterized the conduct required of every member of the 'holy nation' standing in a covenant relationship with the Holy One of Israel. Right and wrong were defined not by reason, reflection, custom or common consent, but by the revealed will of God made known through the Torah, the cultus, the sacred oracle and the voice of prophecy.

The prophetic ethic

The Hebrew ethic had a legal character, inasmuch as the Torah was

T

regarded as a divine injunction resting on the righteousness of Yahweh disclosed to the Patriarchs and Moses. These regulations took the form of categorical commands, prohibitions, hortatory utterances, legal prescriptions, and in the later literature they included wise sayings, pious aspirations, and prophetic denunciations. Finally, the rabbinic interpretations and applications of the revelations to Moses and the Prophets were recorded in the Mishnah and the Talmuds, and ethical principles and legal sanctions were inextricably fused as several aspects of one divine ordering of all things in accordance with the righteous purposes of God.

Taken collectively these divine disclosures and precepts constituted an absolute standard of conduct binding on the conscience of Israel. The Deuteronomic and Levitical Codes were drawn up for the purpose of maintaining the religious and social structure of the nation free from the contaminations of the Canaanite cultus and that of the surrounding countries. Emphasis was laid on the spirit of love towards God and one's neighbour as the crux of the good life within the sacred congregation of Israel, summed up in keeping the commandments of the Law, observing justice and doing righteousness, and walking in the ways of Yahweh.[35] By these things was the world sustained—by the Law, by worship, by charity—while social stability rested upon justice, truth and peace.[36] From the greatest to the least Yahweh demanded obedience to his righteous will, rewarding those who walked according to his laws, and punishing those who sinned and came short of the prescribed criterion of conduct.

Ethical monotheism

It was not, however, until the Deity was conceived monotheistically as transcendent moral perfection, the one ruler and judge of all the earth with one Law for the universe and for all mankind, that a morally religious ethic was established. This was the notable achievement of the great eighth-century Hebrew prophets, from Amos onwards. It was they who revealed Yahweh as the one God perfect in righteousness, absolute in power, and omniscient in wisdom and knowledge, fulfilling His purpose in accordance with His will, hating iniquity and loving goodness, mercy and truth. Therefore, perceiving that human nature was equipped with the power of discerning between right and wrong, good and evil, they ceased not to declare the degradation into which the nation had sunk by following the abominations of the Canaanite cultic tradition, especially child-sacrifice and sexual licence, harlotry and drunkenness, together with vice and cruelty, manifest on all hands as the result of an obdurate choice of evil rather than good.

In reaction to the indigenous Canaanite practices associated with the local shrines, they looked back with approval to what seemed to Amos to have been the golden age of the nomadic culture. Thus, in the name of Yahweh they opined, 'have ye offered unto me sacrifices and offerings in the wilderness forty years, O house of Israel?'[37] Similarly, Hosea proclaimed, 'I have found Israel like grapes in the wilderness: I saw your fathers as the first ripe in the fig-tree at her season: but they came to Baal-peor, and consecrated themselves unto that shame: and became abominable like that which they loved.'[38] To go to Bethel was to transgress and to visit Gilgal was to multiply transgression,[39] because the syncretistic cultus at these sanctuaries obscured the ethical demands of Yahweh. Reformers are always inclined to be reactionary and iconoclastic in their endeavours to sweep away abuses, and the Hebrew prophets were not an exception to this propensity. But though their movement was short-lived and virtually came to an end during the exile in Babylon, nevertheless, they made a permanent contribution to ethical development by their insistence on a standard of conduct that would satisfy the demands of an ethically righteous God who had showed man what is good, and what is required of him: to do justice and to love mercy and to walk humbly with his God.[40]

The secret of the good life was shown to lie in a changed attitude towards God, with a corresponding disposition towards mankind at large as the corollary. This prophetic interpretation of the Hebrew ethic went far beyond the conception of non-moral holiness and numinous awe in the presence of the *mysterium tremendum*. The transcendent majesty of God inspired awe, loyalty and obedience, which introduced a new standard of the good life. Moreover, it gave a fresh emphasis to the fact that moral goodness was a quality that had to be won in conflict with evil, whether evil be interpreted theologically in terms of sin, biologically as an inheritance from man's forbears, human or animal, or sociologically as a result of the demoralization of society and its institutions, beliefs and customs.

The post-exilic Judaic ethic

After the Exile when the prophetic movement had lost its spontaneity, having accomplished its main function and purpose, attention was concentrated on the establishment of Judaism on a firm theocratic basis in which morality and the divinely ordained institutional faith and practice were combined in an effort to bring back the nation to its god and to re-establish the temple and its worship. The reorganized Aaronic priesthood and the cultus became the unifying dynamic. The compilation and editing of the sacred literature by the sacerdotal schools resulted in the five books attributed to Moses being canonized as the Torah, or 'teaching' (i.e. the Law), and assigned supreme authority as the verbally inspired Word of God. This made prophecy of secondary importance, and with the rise of the synagogues those who sought to know the will of Yahweh betook themselves thither, where scribes as the official teachers gave instruction in the written Law.

While the holiness of God remained the ultimate reason and interpretation of this corpus of sacred tradition and precepts, the legal and the purely ethical were treated as concomitant principles, the one depending on the other. Thus no distinction was made between the pious duty of burying the dead, emphasized in the Testament of Tobias and the prophetic injunction to do justly, to love mercy and to walk humbly with God. As the centre was the Deuteronomic command to love God and man as the first principle of right conduct, only by fashioning one's life in accordance with the statutes and judgments of Yahweh could true blessedness be attained, and these immutable divine dictates were enshrined in the Law and its requirements. Therefore, as the scribes sat in Moses' seat, all that they taught and commanded had to be obeyed,[41] and generally speaking joy and satisfaction were felt in the fulfilment of the Law, which for the most part did not consist of excessive demands. Daily God was praised for having sanctified His people by His commandments and they rejoiced in the words of His teaching, for they were their life and 'the strength of their days'. It laid upon them the primary duty of loving God as their Creator and sustainer, and as a corollary to manifest their love for their neighbour in human intercourse and everyday affairs in a social ethic.

Dualism and the problem of evil

The absolute transcendence of Yahweh interpreted in the ethical terms of the prophetic movement raised a problem in post-exilic Judaism in relation to the origin of evil. So long as the universe was represented as being under the control of beneficent and malevolent divine beings, the struggle between good and evil could be explained as emanating from these two opposed supernatural forces. But once all things were grounded in a single all-righteous omnipotent Creator the origin and persistence of evil in a creation that *ex hypothesi* is and ought to be essentially good became a serious challenge to the conception of ethical monotheism. In Judaism an 'evil imagination' (*yetser-ha-ra*) was thought

276

to have been implanted in the heart of man for the purpose of developing his character as a moral being with the aid of the Law.[42] Indeed, the Deutero-Isaiah did not hesitate to affirm in the name of Yahweh: 'I create evil,'[43] perhaps in the physical rather than in the moral sense, and when he was angry with Israel he was said to have prompted David to a sinful act in taking a census in order to bring disaster upon the people.[44] Later in the book of Chronicles this was modified by Satan being made responsible for the provocation of David.[45]

The Satan, however, was at first represented as one of 'the sons of God' in the court of heaven assigned the task of testing the sincerity and integrity of men, and acting only as the prosecuting counsel.[46] In the role of 'the adversary' he was not fundamentally evil in direct opposition to the beneficent Deity, like the Devil of apocalyptic theology. Nevertheless, since he came to be regarded as the accuser of Israel leading David astray, when once a dualistic conception of good and evil had emerged, he was well on his way to becoming the Prince of Darkness and Leader of the rebel angels, intent on seducing mankind and filling the world with corruption.[47] Once this was conceded he could hardly be other than the arch-enemy of Yahweh, from whom he was supposed to have wrested the control of the earth, which henceforth was his domain, though his reign ultimately would be brought to an end when the all-righteous and beneficent Creator became all in all.

It is difficult to believe that this reversal of divine omnipotence was a natural development of the prophetic and post-exilic conception of ethical monotheism. There was a latent dualism, it is true, in the doctrine of Yahweh's choice of Israel, but so far from 'the world lying in the Evil One', in the Hebrew tradition creation had been pronounced 'very good'.[48] Nevertheless, the course of events made it increasingly hard to reconcile the world as it actually existed with the beneficent rule of a single omnipotent Creator and controller of all things. The sequel to the prophetic movement with its insistence on ethical monotheism was the Exile, and when hope was renewed with the re-establishment of the post-exilic community in and around Jerusalem, it proved to be but an Indian summer. With the rise of a new antagonistic secular authority in the days of Antiochus Epiphanes, it doubtless seemed that demonic supramundane powers were at work frustrating the designs of Yahweh for his chosen people. In the book of Daniel, which was a product of these turbulent times, each of the adjacent nations, Greece, Persia and Israel, was represented as having a 'prince', or guardian angel, as its tutelary protector,[49] very much as Babylonian cities had their own gods. Therefore, the stage was set for a gigantic struggle of contending spiritual hierarchies with Michael, 'one of the chief of the princes', fighting on behalf of Israel as a divine agent.[50] The struggle, however, was between angelic beings, not between rival equally powerful gods, as in the contemporary Mazdaean dualism.[51]

The despondency that descended upon the Jews in their sorry plight during 'the abomination of desolation spoken of by Daniel', and the disillusionment in the Hasmonaean degradation that followed the temporary recovery under Maccabaean rule, gave rise to serious misgivings about the providential care of Yahweh for his people, and gave a new emphasis to the problem of evil in the setting of ethical monotheism. Various attempts were made to explain the corruption of human nature and the triumph of evil in a 'fallen world' as an inheritance from the ancient past, without throwing much light on the conflict as an ever-present reality. At first in this period the initial cause was sought in the unnatural alliance between 'the sons of God' and 'the daughters of men' which resulted in the procreation of an evil progeny of Nephilim and their exploits,[52] but as this stock was supposed to have been wiped out by the Flood it did not help by way of explanation of the existing situation. Recourse was then made to Adam's transgression in Eden[53] at the threshold of the human race, and while this remained the popular interpretation of 'original sin' in the Judaeo-Christian tradition, until it was confronted with the biological and anthropological evidence in the latter part of the last century, it left unsolved the problem of the Devil in the context of ethical monotheism.

Thus, in apocryphal, rabbinical and early Christian literature good and evil spirits stood in contrast with one another as clearly defined as in Iranian dualism, whence it would seem the post-canonical Jewish apocalyptic conception of Satan and the doctrine of the twin spirits were to a considerable extent derived. In the Wisdom literature it was God who was represented as having created two mutually antagonistic powers, the evil within the soul and the Law without, and a man was free to make his choice between them.[54] Ben Sirach maintained that the grain of evil seed was sown in the heart of Eve and brought death in its train,[55] which, as was subsequently contended, was transmitted to all her descendants.[56] Moreover, in the Wisdom of Solomon it was affirmed that this evil seed was sown by the Devil,[57] though the rabbinic theory of 'the evil imagination', or *yetser*, as part of the divine constitution of man, remained the official doctrine in Judaism.[58]

The Zoroastrian ethic

That Iranian influences played a significant part in the development of these dualistic interpretations of good and evil in the post-biblical period is suggested by the form they assumed, especially in the apocalyptic tradition. Nowhere did the problem of evil occupy a more prominent position in the Near East than in the great religious movement initiated by Zarathushtra in the middle of the first millennium BC. Having revealed Ahura Mazda, the All-wise Lord and Fountain-head of the Good Mind, as the sole Creator of the universe and wholly beneficent, he postulated the primeval twin-spirits, Spenta Mainyu (Good Mind) and Angra Mainyu (Evil Spirit), with their respective angelic and demonic followers in eternal conflict since the dawn of creation. They did not exist independently, but each was in relation to the other, according to the Gathas, meeting in the higher unity of Ahura Mazda. From the Good Spirit proceeded pure words and deeds, and it was right speaking and right conduct that constituted the good life.

The Zoroastrian ethic was summed up in the conception of *Asha*, which was regarded as a cosmic principle equated with righteousness and more or less the equivalent of the Egyptian Maat and the Vedic Rta. But while it was the universal principle of the right ordering of the universe it was also essentially the 'path of righteousness' as an ethical law revealing itself in order, symmetry, harmony, truthfulness, discipline, moral purity and spiritual and physical health. Therefore, to uphold *Asha* was to live the good life to which all free moral beings were called by the Wise-Lord, who himself was the originator and embodiment of the right law, or moral order (*Asha*), ruling all things in respect of his absolute perfection.

Mazdaean dualism

In the earlier Gathas of the Avesta, which may go back to the time of Zarathushtra, probably about the seventh century BC, Ahura Mazda is represented as opposed by Angra Mainyu, or the Druj, as this evil spirit was called. Since he seems to have been regarded as evil in his nature, it would appear that a fundamental dualism was latent in Zoroastrianism, though it was only in the later Mazdaean literature that the Lie emerges as Ahriman, coeval with Ahura Mazda. Then it only remained for the Magi to divide the world into two diametrically opposed and balanced creations—the one the work of the beneficent Ormuzd (a combination of Ahura Mazda and Spenta Mainyu), and the other that of Ahriman—to complete the process. If this involved an absolute dualism, it unquestionably became an inspiration in meeting the challenge of evil in creation and in man, not least since good was destined to triumph[59] at the consummation of all things.

In the later Avesta, however, the Wise-Lord was equated with the Good Spirit, and was identified with light as against his rival Ahriman who was darkness, whereas in the Gathas Ahura Mazda was said to have created both light and darkness.[60] Originally Zarathushtra appears to have regarded the One God, holy, righteous and true, as the author of both good and evil, including the destructive twin-spirit Angra Mainyu, the Lie. This left the problem of evil unsolved and opened the way for a dualistic solution. Sooner or later the Wise-Lord and the Evil Spirit were almost bound to be opposed in the manner of Ormuzd and Ahriman as two co-eternal principles of good and evil by their respective natures, personified as God and the Devil, Light and Darkness. Some of the Median Magi tried without much success to mitigate this absolute dualism by making Ormuzd and Ahriman emanations of a primeval principle, Zervan, but this interpretation was declared to be heretical, even though the victory of Ormuzd was represented as being vindicated at the last, when the good was destined to be established and evil finally destroyed.

The religion of the good life

Nevertheless, this dualistic ethic of self-salvation was essentially the religion of the good life in the service of Ahura Mazda, dedicated to the setting up of righteousness on earth. Evil was a force to be met on its own ground and conquered by the might of the Spirit of goodness and beneficence. It was the sacred duty of man to uphold and maintain purity, righteousness and morality, and this constituted the essence of the Zoroastrian ethic (i.e. *Asha*), which aimed at nothing less than the regeneration of the world by the elimination of evil. Apart from the observance of certain prescribed ritual rules and duties, these things were enjoined: personal purity, honesty and straight dealing, charity towards the poor, hospitality towards the stranger, care for cattle, the cultivation of the fields, the destruction of noxious creatures and the veneration of the dead. By these means the powers of evil could be kept at bay.[61] The social ethic was based on the sense of duty and responsibility to the community in such matters as ministering to those in need, tilling the ground, the preservation of trees, the cutting of canals, the construction of roads, bridges and houses, the propagation of the species, and the maintenance of a healthy and harmonious home and family life. In principle the ideal was humanistic, humanitarian and utilitarian. Justice, truthfulness, benevolence, contentedness and thankfulness were extolled, because they were regarded as essential for the well-being alike of the individual and the practical needs of society.

If moral concepts were combined with primitive tabus concerning contact with corpses, menstruation, and flaying, right conduct transcended such survivals and became equivalent to the eternal truth and divine law of Ahura Mazda. Those who followed this Path of Righteousness increased in strength, power and wealth, and laid up a store of merit which not only enabled them to expel the evil spirits but also at death safely to cross the perilous *chinvat* bridge connecting this world with the next world, since only those righteous souls who had lived the good life could successfully negotiate it and enter the heavenly realms confident that at the final judgment their good deeds would be recompensed.

The Iranian influence on Judaism

To assume that the good would ultimately overcome the forces of evil merely by the inherent goodness of human nature doubtless was to take too optimistic a view of the situation. This may account for the resort to Magian magic and superstition to supply the dynamic that was lacking in Zarathushtra's lofty conception of the good life. Nevertheless, the fact remains that Zoroastrianism became the State religion of Persia during the Sassanian Dynasty (224–650 AD); this was perhaps the greatest period in its history, and although it succumbed to the impact of Islam after the conquest of the country by the Arabs in the seventh century AD, its influence on Jewish, Christian and Muslim apocalyptic literature was very considerable. As has been considered, this was most apparent in Judaeo-Christian eschatology and angelology,* and it recurs in relation to dualism and the conception of evil. Thus, the transformation of Satan and the rebel angels into figures not very different from those of Ahriman and his demonic host in the apocalyptic literature has every appearance of having been due to Iranian contacts.

This is further indicated in the *Manual of Discipline* now recovered among the Dea Sea Scrolls, where God is said to have 'created man to have dominion over the world and make for him two spirits, that he might walk with them until the appointed time of his visitation; they are the spirits of truth and of error. In the abode of light are the origins of truth, and from the source of darkness are the origins of error. In the hand of the prince of lights is dominion over all sons of righteousness: in the ways of light they walk. And in the hand of the angel of darkness is all dominion over the sons of error; and in the ways of darkness they walk. And by the angel of darkness is the straying of all the sons of righteousness . . . but the God of Israel and his angel of truth have

*Chap. VI, p. 191.

helped all the sons of light. For he created the spirits of light and darkness, and upon them he founded every good work and upon their ways
every service. One of the spirits God loves for all the ages of eternity;
as for the other, he abhors its company, and all its ways he hates for
ever'.[62]

This identification of truth with light and error with darkness is
definitely Iranian, but as interpreted by the Qumran sect in Judaic
terms, Yahweh is represented as having created the twin-spirits,
contrary to the Gathic doctrine of the evil spirit being evil through his
own will. Again, the underlying predestination in the Jewish document
constitutes a departure from the Zoroastrian free choice, bringing it
more into line with the Iranian Zurvanite myth than with the theology
of the Gathas. There the primeval Being, Zurvan, Unlimited Time,
was identified with Destiny, the father of the twin-spirits who made
light, Ormuzd, to rule the world of spirits above, and dark, Ahriman,
to be prince of this world,[63] just as the Satan became the lord of the
earth, and light and darkness, truth and falsehood, were contrasted.

Nor were the parallels confined to the Qumran literature. They are
characteristic of the Essenes, and they are deeply laid in the Fourth
Gospel and in the First Epistle of St John in the New Testament,[64]
and they recur in the Pauline doctrine of the 'two Adams' and in the
distinction between the 'flesh' and the 'spirit', though the dualism be
but relative and temporary.[65] At the end of the first century AD, however,
the evil world was set against the world of light and life in the Johannine
cosmology in such a manner that under Alexandrian influence they
became two opposed realms with their respective spiritual forces in
perpetual conflict, as in the Gnostic dual control of the world by the
good and evil deities respectively. But it is still in debate to what extent,
if at all, Gnosticism was of Iranian origin.[66]

Iranian and Ionian dualism

The Greeks, unlike the Hebrews and Iranians, developed ethical
concepts subsequent to the efforts of their pioneer thinkers and philosophers to find a single principle capable of explaining all the
phenomena of the material world. Moreover, they were not averse to
acknowledging foreign influences on their religion and civilization, from
western Asia and the Fertile Crescent, or from Crete and the eastern
Mediterranean. As F. M. Cornford says, 'whether we accept or not the
hypothesis of a direct influence of Persia on the Ionians in the sixth
century, no student of Orphic and Pythagorean thought will fail to see
between it and the Persian religion such close resemblances that we can

regard both systems as expressions of one and the same conception of life, and use either of them to interpret the other.'[67]

The pre-Socratic pluralists

Aristotle recognized an affinity between the dualism of the Magi and that of the Platonic distinction between Form and Matter, the Good and its negation, but the problem had long exercised the minds of the pre-Socratic thinkers in Greece. While their approach was primarily materialistic and monistic, since as empiricists they reduced the world to a primary substance—water, fire, air or earth—nevertheless, they distinguished between mind and matter, perception and the thing perceived, the void and the plenum. The Pythagoreans made a similar distinction between the principles of good and evil, corresponding to the contrast of soul and body. For Empedocles these primary elements, or 'roots of things', were held together by two contrary forces, love and hate, producing a state of tension with order and harmony emerging from strife and discord and the reign of chaos. All constructive forces of Reality arose from love, but only as a temporary measure destined to give place to the dominance of discord as the ever-recurrent sinister element in the world.[68]

In this dualistic ethic the gods played no part, for the opposed principles, love and hate, moved the elements impersonally from without as the efficient causes of good and evil. All that happened in the cosmic order was the result of these external changes in the four primary 'roots', love acting as the combining force and hatred as the separating force of dissolution, in a cyclic process. For him (Empedocles) the divine were universal powers active in the cosmic cycle as the primary forms of corporeal existence and the forces of love and hate producing goodness and perfection by their interaction in nature and in the human soul.

Anaxagoras, who was born in Clazomenae in Ionia about 500 BC and carried on the Milesian tradition, posited in place of the four elements innumerable seeds, each composed of eternal homogeneous particles held together by an ethereal vapour until the vapour and ether separated themselves from the primeval mass. Then came mind (νοῦς ἐλθών) as something distinct from the world and its elements, which set all things in order as the moving cause separate from matter, 'existing along and by itself'. It 'controls all things that have a soul' and 'the whole whirling movement and made it possible for it to whirl at all'. It knew 'all the things that were then being mixed, and separated off and parted from one another'. In fact, mind arrayed 'all such things as were to be and which are not, and such as are at present',[69] though as a purely mechanical cause which hardly can be said to have anticipated the Platonic and Aristotelian ethical teleological dualism. *Nous* may have ordered all things from the beginning according to a definite plan, but as Aristotle said, it was only dragged in when no other explanation could be found to account for mental and spiritual phenomena.

Democritus (*c.* 460–370 BC), on the other hand, included within the scope of his interpretation of the origin of the physical universe in relation to quantities of invisible atoms devoid of qualitative differences, the consideration of the problem of human conduct viewed from the side both of the State and the individual. The true end of life was not pleasure as the Cyrenaic school contended, but a state of thought and feeling attained only by a proper control exercised over pleasures and pains, and promoted by philosophical training and cultivated living. 'Peace of soul comes from moderation (μετριότητι) in pleasure and harmony of life', and 'the crown of righteousness is a mind confident and unamazed; but the end of unrighteousness is the fear of impending calamity'.[70] But these moralizings were based on his crudely materialistic physical speculations rather than upon anything in the nature of a systematic ethic or a transcendental theology.

The ethics of the Pythagoreans

The first serious attempt in Greece to establish a rule of life on an ethical basis was that of the Pythagoreans in the fifth century BC. As an organized religious community they were committed to a prescribed routine which involved a careful scrutiny of daily conduct in an 'examination of conscience', fragments of which have survived in all probability in certain hexameter verses which assume that the body as the seat and source of sin was the prison-house of the soul. The mortification of the flesh by abstinence and asceticism, therefore, was essential for the purification of the soul and the development of the higher life through a process of metempsychosis. As the evil contracted during each rebirth was carried over to the next reincarnation, life here in this world became a penance for the sins committed in a former state of existence. Consequently, every man as a moral being was confronted with a choice between a morally good life and a bad one; this was directed especially to self-restraint and the control of the passions, particularly anger and the cultivation of the power of endurance, and the contemplation of the 'wisdom' of the eternal world of the soul and its virtues. The gods were the guardians and guides of the good life, and as men grew in their likeness they became better and nearer to perfection in the protracted ascent to the final goal, when the soul was released from the chastisement of corporeal imprisonment. Those who failed to emancipate themselves from the dominion of sensuality in its various forms and aspects were condemned to transmigration into the bodies of animals, and, if they proved to be incurable, to be consigned ultimately to punishment in Tartarus, the Pythagorean hell which was opposed to the bliss of incorporeal heavenly existence.

It is highly conjectural to what extent, however, the Pythagorean ethic can be attributed to Pythagoras, who was a native of Samos in southern Italy and migrated about 530 BC to Croton, where Orphism was established. There can be no doubt that much that was a product of the later brotherhood was assigned to the founder of the school, and was brought into relation with the Orphic doctrines current in the sixth to the fourth centuries BC. Furthermore, it may well be true that an 'Orphic religion' as an organized and unified system of belief and practice did not actually exist in the Hellenic world, as has been generally supposed.[71] Nevertheless, a number of closely related ideas and customs finding expression in a specific mode of conduct and incorporated in a literature, prevailed around the name of Orpheus during this eventful period and had a permanent influence on Greek religious thought and practice.

Thus, 'the Pythagorean way of life', as Plato described it,[72] bore a general resemblance to the Orphic counterpart in respect of rules of abstinence and asceticisms for the purpose of securing the release of the soul by means of reincarnation. On the other hand, Pythagoreanism was essentially a highly intellectual movement with an ethical dualistic philosophy based on the contrast of good and evil interpreted in terms of a cosmological principle of the Limited and the Unlimited, or of the Odd and the Even. It cannot be regarded as in any sense an offshoot of a hypothetical Orphism, however much the two disciplines may have had common ideas and aims with regard to a conception of the good life directed to release, or 'moral salvation' (λύσις), secured in the case of the Pythagoreans by the pursuit of 'knowledge' or 'wisdom' as well as by asceticism and *teletai* (rites of initiation).

The Orphic life

Plato leaves us in no doubt that the Orphic life was intended to promote ethical uprightness and moral righteousness, however much its rites may have been misused by the unscrupulous and superstitious. The initiates were animated by the desire not only to be released from the wearisome round of rebirths but to emerge at length as a god, like the

Bacchoi who attained complete union with Dionysus-Zagreus in their Thraco-Phrygian ecstatic frenzies. They, too, sought liberation from the Titanic element in their dual nature and the realization of their diversity by the cultivation of the Dionysian side in their inheritance and the purging away of the evil, through the due performance of their *teletai* and the adoption of the Orphic way of life with its rules and injunctions and purifications. These were always liable to degenerate into ritual holiness, upon which Plato poured such scorn in no uncertain measure. But Socrates realized that 'those who established rites and initiation for us were no fools, but that there is a hidden meaning in their teaching when it says that whoever arrives uninitiated in Hades will lie in mud, but purified and initiated when he arrives will dwell with the gods'. The initiated, in fact, are identified with the true philosophers, having become 'the sons of the gods (*theologoi*) who may be expected to know the truth about their own parents'.[73]

The Orphic life, in short, was ambivalent. At one level it might be merely a routine of ritual purity like any other mystery cultus or institutional religion; while at another it reached very considerable heights of spiritual and ethical attainment. In the background lay the Thraco-Phrygian orgies and Iranian dualism, out of which emerged a predominantly Graeco-oriental mystery cult, less Hellenic than that of Eleusis but sobered under the influence of Apollo and brought within the Hesiodic theogony and the Olympian theology by Zeus having destroyed the Titans and caused Dionysus to be reborn. In such a composite and syncretistic tradition the good life of its adherents could hardly be other than many-sided. Its prohibitions were numerous and for the most part they had been inherited from these earlier substrata, often preserving primitive traits like those of the closely allied Pythagoreans. Here the emphasis was on the negative side of behaviour.

There was also, however, a positive aspect in which moral actions were enjoined, though precisely in what they consisted besides expiation, prayer and sacrifice to the gods for the bestowal of divine favour we cannot be sure, in the absence of *teletai* on the subject in the Orphic literature, apart from the descriptions in very general terms mentioned by Plato. We know it involved self-denial and rules of conduct to secure the purification of the soul from sin and to advance its status in the next earthly life through the discipline of asceticism, which was not without some sense of moral consciousness. Those who made progress in the Orphic life spent in the attainment of ethical and ceremonial purity of the soul hoped to enjoy heavenly bliss for a thousand years,[74] while the incorrigibly wicked were consigned to Tartarus. Those who occupied an intermediate position between the 'saved' and the 'damned' were punished for a millennium and then returned to earth and were given another chance to live three series of good lives on both sides of the grave, at the end of which the soul would be purged and enter a permanent paradise in a divine status.

The Orphic conception of immortality constitutes the first really serious attempt in Greece to make human destiny depend upon character and conduct in the present state of existence, with the subjective aspect of sin being given greater prominence than the objective approach. While the soul was in the body it was believed to be conscious of its defilement which was inherited from its previous incarnations, and the object of the ritual observances, mortifications and tabus—the wearing of white garments, abstention from eating eggs and beans, avoiding contact with women in childbirth or corpses, and practising chastity—and of the more ethical code of conduct, was to regain the divine life from which the soul had fallen.

The golden tablets found much later in the Orphic graves in southern Italy and in Crete show, like the Egyptian Book of the Dead, that at death those who had practised the prescribed good life were provided with careful instructions as to the route of the soul through the underworld, how its dangers were to be avoided, and the formula to be used in addressing Persephone and the other chthonian gods on arrival in Hades.[75] Having declared itself to be of the divine race, to have duly performed all the ritual purifications, 'flown out of the sorrowful wheel', and paid the penalty of unrighteous deeds, it came to Persephone to be given a place in 'the seats of the hallowed', raised to the status of god instead of mortal.

According to the Odes of Pindar, confirmed by Plato, after a threefold probation the Orphic good life attained its goal in the perpetual sunshine of the Isles of the Blest in the company of the gods and heroes, relieved of all toil and vexation, and knowing no tears.[76] In this terrestrial paradise, resembling the Egyptian Elysium in its idealized earthly conditions, the thrice-justified souls enjoyed in full measure the reward of their mundane mortifications and struggles, in contrast to the grim shadowy shades of the Homeric tradition. But unlike most similar conceptions of the culmination of the good life in eternal bliss, the Orphic hereafter was an intermediate state pending the final consummation, when the thrice-tested soul attained its divinity.

Orphism and the Homeric and Hesiodic Olympian ethical tradition
However Orphism is to be understood and evaluated, it was the

expression of a real ethical and religious need when social life was undergoing profound disturbances in the Hellenic world, and neither the Homeric aristocratic heroic virtues of strength, courage and wisdom, nor the fair dealing, temperance, industry and simplicity urged by Hesiod, met the fundamental needs of struggling humanity. The conditions that among the cultivated classes in Ionia had given rise to a profound disillusionment with life, resulted among the people in a heightened sense of sin and resort to ritual purity and asceticism as the way of salvation, based on the Orphic and Pythagorean conception of the good life. The Olympian gods and heroes of the Homeric and Hesiodic tradition had failed to gain the spiritual and ethical allegiance of Greece, because transcendentally they had little or nothing to offer, since they differed only from mankind in having greater power and knowledge, and this in degree rather than in kind. They were subject to the same ethical weaknesses and shortcomings as were mortals and they were too much involved in their own intrigues to be concerned with human affairs or cosmic processes. At its best Homeric Olympianism was a mystical idealism and a romantic heroism; a symbol of idealized qualities belonging to an age of chivalry, or in the case of Hesiod of the simpler virtues, homely wisdom and everyday requirements of the farmer and peasant.[77] In Homer the old gods retained a romantic significance as the chief actors in a heroic drama of adventure, courage and conquest, sometimes allegorized or made symbols of virtue and justice, military skill and sagacity, and fidelity between husband and wife and the master and his household, including horses and dogs.[78] But they were merely glorified men, and Xenophanes maintained that 'Homer and Hesiod have ascribed to the gods all things that among men are a shame and a reproach—theft and adultery and deceiving one another'.[79]

'This judgment, however, fails to recognize that the literature in question does not consist of theological or ethical treatises, or of historical records of past events. The *Iliad and Odyssey* are excellent tales giving a reasonably accurate picture of the life and manners that prevailed in Greece at the transition from the Bronze Age to the Iron Age, for entertainment rather than for edification and 'uplift'. It is true, as Herodotus asserted, that 'Homer and Hesiod created the generations of the gods for the Greeks; they gave the divinities their names, assigned to them their prerogatives and functions, and made their forms known'.[80] They represented their divine heroes in the semblance of men and, therefore, made them subject to the faults, failings and limitations of human beings, particularly those of warriors and capricious chieftains.[81] They never moved in ethical spheres; their actions generally were determined by motives of self-interest and self-regard, and in so far as they controlled the destinies of nations and individuals, they acted for good or ill according to their mood and passion of the moment. As guardians of justice they deliberately led men into sin and error, and were themselves prone to sensuality, envy, lying, and all the offences and transgressions they punished, or sometimes rewarded, in mortals. With the exception of the righteous king who feared the gods and upheld justice and was recompensed with a bumper harvest, prolific flocks and herds, abundance of fish and the prosperity of his people,[82] virtue seldom was rewarded in this life, still less hereafter.

It is not surprising, therefore, that when the stories about the gods were rationalized or explained away by the poets and the pre-Socratic thinkers, and dramatists like Aeschylus, Sophocles and Euripides moralized the Olympian mythology, it was to the Orphic and Pythagorean ethical doctrines that recourse was made, in spite of much that was naïve, fantastic and sometimes unedifying in their mythology and practice. Here at least was a way of life to be followed for definite and highly desirable ends, in which those who embraced it were to a considerable degree masters of their own fate, and behaviour in this world in a succession of existences was a determining factor in their final destiny. Thus, from the conviction that human error arose as a result of a failure to recognize ignorance of the truth, Socrates sought to lead those with whom he argued to knowledge that would find expression in right conduct—in justice, piety, temperance, and courage. Equating virtue with knowledge as the basis of his ethic he appears to have relied on an 'inner voice', or daemon, which spoke to him, as he maintained, from time to time, inhibiting him from a wrong course of conduct, and regarded as divine messages resulting from his special relationship with Apollo, whose servant he claimed to be.[83]

The Platonic conception of God and the Good

Here may be discerned a mystical vein arising from an Orphic influence and tendency, which Plato accepted and developed in his dualistic doctrine of the pre-existence of the soul and its reincarnation as a moral economy through which the deeds done in the body were punished or rewarded by transmigration in a lower or higher form. To this was added a realm of Ideas or Reality over and above that of sense experience to which the soul aspires and attains by the pursuit of philosophy, starting from the Socratic proposition that virtue is acquired by knowledge. But Plato went further than his master in making the desire for the possession of an eternal Good manifest itself in higher forms, passing from beautiful and good things to beautiful and good souls, and from these to that which is beautiful and good in itself, which alone can satisfy the craving of the soul.[84] It was this concept of perfect goodness, beauty and truth that made particular souls, persons and virtues good in a relative sense and its realization the goal of the good life and the end of striving.

Thus, the breaking away from the Olympian tradition of the Platonic differentiation of the visible order from the invisible world of Ideas made possible a conception of Deity as a single personal ground who was the Good in the abstract; the Ultimate Reality responsible for the orderly motions of the universe. But while the 'best soul' was the supreme Cause, it was not the only source of motion.[85] To explain the disorder and irregularity in the cosmos two or more souls were postulated. An absolute dualism, however, was ruled out, since it was nowhere suggested that a bad 'world-soul' existed, any more than in the Platonic doctrine of Forms were there two disconnected worlds, as in oriental dualisms. Nevertheless, in the thought of Plato the problem remained unsolved. The eternal pattern as the sum total of all Forms was the ideal model of what ought to be. But the idea of the Good and the doctrine of God as the highest ethical ideal developed independently in his mind, so that the conception of providential beneficence was never completely reconciled with the existence of evil.

Although God was the transcendent sanction of morality He was not the sole ultimate source of all that is. A demiurgic principle, or order and harmony, contended with recalcitrant 'necessity' from which evil was derived by the soul identifying itself with disorderly motion.[86] Thus, in matter was the origin of evil, but God was exonerated from any complicity because He was responsible only for the good motions.[87] Evil was pure negation (μὴ ὄυ), being that by which the world fell short of good,[88] but unlike Aristotle Plato never attempted to get behind the idea of God as the Supreme Soul to that of an Unmoved Mover as the ultimate source of all movement, with evil as a necessary element in the continual process of change to which matter was subject.[89] But why evil exists was not explained, and an Unmoved Mover knowing nothing of human aspirations in an imperfect world could hardly be an ethical Creator. Indeed, in maintaining a difference in kind between the two worlds Aristotle arrived at a more absolute dualism than can be attributed to Plato, while his conception of divine transcendence removed the Deity altogether from mundane affairs and the right ordering of the good life.

Unlike the Hebrew prophets neither Plato nor Socrates nor Aristotle made a determined effort to establish and vindicate an ethical monotheism in place of the traditional Olympian polytheism or that of the Graeco-oriental mystery cults. Their respect for the ancient gods may have been slight, but their worship was taken for granted and given a place in the ideal Platonic republic which was visualized as the *summum bonum* of the social order and the good life in this world. The trend towards monotheism was essentially philosophic and the development of moral ideas proceeded along intellectual lines, without religious predilections. In Israel and Iran the ethical reforms initiated respectively by the Hebrew Prophets and Zarathushtra, were based on the character of God as conceived in relation to Yahweh and Ahura Mazda. It was His absolute righteousness that was the inspiration of morality, and the chief factor in determining its demands on all who would live in accordance with His requirements, and walk in His ways, from the greatest to the least, irrespective of philosophic attainment. The Highest Good must be found not in the complete development of the soul in its communion with the eternal world of Ideas, but in union with the living God who is Himself the suprapersonal embodiment of the ethical ideal.

CHAPTER TEN

THE DEVELOPMENT AND DIFFUSION
OF NEAR EASTERN DEITIES

Western Asiatic Cradleland, rise of the Goddess cult, emergence of syncretistic Great Mother—The Sky-god and creation, solar cult in Egypt, Babylonian Great Triad, Dumuzi-Tammuz and Inanna-Ishtar—Baal, Anat and Asherah in Syria, Hadad, Storm-god and Weather-god in Anatolia, Baal and Yahweh in Israel—Hellenistic Judaism, Graeco-oriental syncretism, Mithraism, emergence of the Christian concept of Deity

The Western Asiatic Cradleland

THERE IS now every reason to regard Mesopotamia, Asia Minor, Syria, the Iranian plateau and Egypt as the cradleland of the pre-historic and proto-historic civilizations in which the antecedents of the higher living religions emerged in the Neolithic and Chalcolithic periods, not later than the fifth millennium BC, when the use of stone was gradually being supplanted by the employment of metals. Indeed, it is becoming apparent at Jericho and at Qalat Jarmo in northern Iraq that a pre-pottery Neolithic culture existed in the sixth millennium BC in Palestine and Mesopotamia, with an elaborate funerary and fertility cultus. Moreover, it is not improbable that further investigation will show that it had a much wider geographical distribution throughout the Fertile Crescent and the adjacent regions, though the original centre of dispersal is most likely to remain south-western Asia, with a greater or smaller lag in time and cultural development as the diffusion proceeded eastwards and westwards in successive migrations from what is now Syria, Palestine and northern Iraq. In the peripheral regions the beliefs and practices arising out of this expanding agricultural civilization appeared relatively later and in a derivative form. If the Nile valley, and subsequently Anatolia, the Aegean, Crete and Greece were influenced by Mesopotamia and Syria during the formative period, they never lost their distinct and independent characters and remained highly individualized centres of cultural development and of religious thought and practice.

In recent years as our knowledge of Mesopotamian, Egyptian and western Asian civilization has very considerably increased, it has become apparent that it was in an agricultural *milieu* that religion assumed its dominant position in the newly-established settled communities of mixed farmers who were engaged in the cultivation of the soil and in stock-breeding in the Near East. When subsistence depended largely on the hazards of the chase, supplemented by fishing, where this was possible, and the collection of edible fruits, roots and berries, the attention seems to have been concentrated upon the mysterious life-giving processes—fecundity, maternity, generation and birth—and their converse, the baffling phenomenon of death. A magico-religious cultus developed around these ever-present realities of everyday observation and experience, which found expression in the ritual control of these natural forces and human events interpreted in terms of supernatural powers and principles, beneficent and malevolent, constantly at work for good or ill in this precarious environment. Therefore, in the Palaeolithic background of the ancient civilizations of the Near East the religious preoccupation was mainly with fertility, the mysterious phenomena connected with birth and generation, coupled with the ever-pressing problem of subsistence and the food supply, together with the final dissolution at death and its aftermath.

The rise of the Goddess cult
This will to live, manifest in a great variety of symbolic objects and actions—female figurines, phalli, masks, disguises, mimetic rites and sacred dances—appears to have found its principal mode of representation in the figure of the life-producing mother and her various maternal organs, attributes and functions. Whether or not in Palaeolithic times this symbol was actually personified as the Mother-goddess, and when it was extended to the vegetable kingdom as Mother-earth, the womb in which the crops were sown and produced, this personification was certainly accomplished after the transition from the precarious life of hunting and food-gathering to the cultivation of the soil and the keeping of flocks and herds under the less hazardous conditions that prevailed in Neolithic society and its economy. Then with the establishment of husbandry and domestication, which must have taken place somewhere in the Fertile Crescent not later than the seventh millennium BC, the Goddess-cult doubtless began to assume a theistic guise. This is suggested by the increasing prominence of its emblems, especially in the Halafian sites in Mesopotamia. Furthermore, as the function of the male in the process of generation became more apparent and vital, probably as a result of stock-breeding, the Mother-goddess was assigned a spouse to play his part as the begetter in procreation. Eventually, in the capacity of the Sky-father, he fecundated the Earth-mother, or in Egypt

visited the queen as the Sun-god in order to beget an heir to the throne who would reign as his son.

In Egypt, however, it was the male solar deity as the heavenly father of the Pharaoh, not the Goddess, who took the initiative, because he was above all the life-giver. Consequently, both he and the king exercised their functions in their own right rather than, as in Mesopotamia, through the agency of the Goddess. Even Hathor, the Cow-goddess, appeared in the New Kingdom as the wife and mother of Horus the Elder, who in the Pyramid Texts was equated with Re.[1] But she was only one of his many wives when all the great goddesses became 'forms and attributes of Hathor worshipped under different names'. Being essentially the goddess of birth, she was originally his mother, just as Ishtar was the mother of Tammuz in Babylonia, and it was not until Horus was confused and identified with the son of Osiris (of whom Hathor was never the spouse) that she became his wife at Edfu, where the marraige was celebrated annually. Then she was equated with Isis, and as 'the throne woman' she was thought to give birth to the prototype of the living king, Horus, the avenger of his father Osiris.

Both goddesses, in fact, were closely associated with motherhood and the kingship, and their similarities of function gave rise to the confusion in their mythology and respective offices and relationships. But the role of Hathor in Ancient Egypt was that of the Great Mother in her original form, exercising her maternal offices in the suckling of the Pharaohs here and hereafter, and conferring upon them her divinity as her sons. When eventually the Goddess became the wife of the chief god who was formerly her son, the image of Hathor was taken by her priests from her temple at Denderah to visit her consort Horus at Edfu so as to engage in a sacred marriage. The queen as the 'God's Wife' in the New Kingdom was also regarded as the embodiment of Hathor, and she presided over the musician-priestesses as the royal concubines in the temple at Luxor. Her own union with Atum-Re to conceive an heir to the throne probably took place during the Theban festival of Opet when the god in all his glory was believed to visit the sanctuary for this purpose.[2] The sacred marriage is depicted in the reliefs on the walls of the temple.

In Egypt the reproduction of life was the function of the Mother-goddesses, but they were not the actual source of life as in Mesopotamia. It was the god in the person of the Pharaoh who took the initiative, whereas in Babylonia the king was invited to share the couch of the Goddess, and perhaps by so doing became divine. Similarly, creation was ascribed in Egypt solely to the male gods, Re-Atum, Ptah or

Khnum, and the goddess Nut or Hathor merely reproduced life within it. In western Asia, Mesopotamia, the Aegean and Greece, on the other hand, Mother-earth was the source of all life, and the seasonal decline in the autumn was ascribed to the bereaved Mother withdrawing her beneficence because she had lost her child. In Syria the Baal-Anat myth reflects the same agricultural ritual situation, whether as an annual event or a recurrent cycle of drought. In Crete the Goddess retained her earlier status and function, as in the Minoan civilization she was the chief divine being and object of worship, depicted either by herself or in association with her priestesses and her characteristic emblems—snakes, doves, lions, the double axe, sacral horns, trees, pillars and the mountain on which so often she was shown standing alone. Her cult predominated throughout the Aegean and the eastern Mediterranean and the virility of the sacred bull may have been poured out sacrificially to fertilize the Earth-mother on the horned altars in Minoan sanctuaries, especially at the Spring Festival. But she herself was never adorned with horns nor represented as suckling her offspring, because in Crete she did not assume the role and symbolism of the divine cow as in Egypt and elsewhere.

On the mainland Zeus took the guise of a bull to carry off Europa to Crete, where she became the mother of Minos. His wife Pasiphae in her turn concealed herself in the effigy of a cow to have intercourse with the bull with which she had become infatuated, and so conceived the Minotaur. Here there would appear to be a survival of a symbolic ritual marriage to a sacred bull and of the kind of mimetic dance portrayed in a Palaeolithic engraving of a man and woman clothed in skins with tails in the cave of Combarelles near Les Eyzies in the Dordogne.[3] The classical Moon-goddess Selene, the daughter of the Sun, with whom Pasiphae is connected by her name, was figured as a cow-goddess with horns, and in the legend the bull was the universal god of the sky and of fertility.[4] This association with the moon brings Pasiphae into line with the Goddess cult in the Near East, where the goddess of fertility was so often a lunar deity, perhaps because in arid districts like parts of Mesopotamia and western Asia the moon stimulates the dew and so promotes the growth of vegetation, just as the Earth-mother was thought to be fertilized by the rain bestowed upon her by the Sky-father. Therefore, so as to secure fertility in nature, the life-giving forces had to be made operative through a ritual re-enactment of the act of copulation between the Goddess and her spouse, symbolized by the cow and the bull, the earth and the sky, the moon and the sun.

Under this imagery the myth and ritual of the fertility and vegetation

cult in Asia Minor, Syria, Babylonia, Egypt and the eastern Mediterranean, Crete and the Aegean developed. The figures of male gods
were of very infrequent occurrence in the Minoan-Mycenaean region,
while those of goddesses abounded. Indeed, the universal Mother
appears everywhere to have lain behind the various emblems and
localizations of maternity, representing the mystery of birth and
generation in its manifold aspects and attributes in human society and
in the natural order. But the Young male god as her brother, spouse or
son, was closely associated with the Goddess and she was united with
him in a nuptial ritual in relation to the annual cycle of vegetation in
the agricultural calendrical sequence, in which the king and queen
were cast to play the leading roles, either in a divine capacity as in
Egypt, or as servants of the Goddess as in Mesopotamia.

With the concentration of creative energy on the male principle as
the begetter, the Goddess tended in some measure to lose her dominance
and prestige, but the western Asiatic cult persisted in its diffusion from
its cradleland in the Near East to Anatolia and the Aegean, and thence
to the Iberian peninsula and to north-western Europe, where it was
associated with the spread of the megalithic culture. In its easterly
extension from the Tigris to the Indus valley by way of the succession
of tells along the foothills and valleys in western Iran, the Elburz,
Makran and those of the uplands of Baluchistan to the plains of Sind
and the Punjab, the female principle (*sakti*) in the form of the Earth-
mother retained its earlier predominance. The pre-Aryan vegetation
cult persisted in the village-goddesses throughout India, in fact, along
lines parallel to those of the Goddess in western Asia, with a male deity
often assuming the functions of the Sky-father, as in the union of the
Vedic Earth-mother Prithivi with Dyaus Pitar, the Aryan Zeus and
Jupiter, as the universal progenitor of gods and men.[5]

The emergence of the syncretistic Great Mother
As the cult of the Mother-goddess spread throughout the region of the
expansion of ancient agricultural civilization from south-western Asia
to Egypt, western Europe and India, its central figure became more and
more a syncretistic deity embracing all the goddesses connected with the
various attributes of maternity, generation and fertility. This became
most apparent in the case of Isis who from being the source of vitality
as the 'throne-woman', personifying the sacred stool charged with the
mysterious power of knowledge, became the prototype of the life-giving
mother and faithful wife. It was she who taught her brother-spouse,
Osiris, the secrets of agriculture, sent him on his civilizing mission,

discovered his dismembered body after he had been slain by Seth and caused it to be reassembled and reanimated by his posthumous son, Horus, whom she had conceived from his restored body. Originally, however, she was not a Mother-goddess, for this was primarily the role of Hathor in Egypt, and it was not until Isis acquired her attributes, together with those of Nut and Neith, that she was virtually equated in the Hellenistic period with the Magna Mater of western Asia and the Graeco-Roman world. Then as 'the goddess of many names' she became the most popular of all the Egyptian divinities and was identified with the allied foreign goddesses, Silene and Io, Demeter, Aphrodite and Pelagia, while Osiris occupied a relatively subordinate position in her syncretistic mysteries.

Although she was never a tragic figure like Ishtar in Mesopotamia, her devotion to her husband-brother made a strong emotional appeal, and she captured the popular imagination of the Roman Empire as did no other deity. In spite of the official opposition of the Senate, her rites, as we have seen, attracted an ever-increasing number of votaries, as she had absorbed so many Greek and Asiatic features after her fusion with Astarte in the form of Atargatis, and shared a temple with Zeus, Hera and Kore at Oxyrhynchus. The diffusion of her worship throughout the Empire is, in fact, an outstanding example of the adaptation of a cult to a foreign and alien environment, an adaptation so complete that its original characteristics disappeared almost entirely. Equated with Demeter and Persephone and the other Hellenic goddesses, she lost her earlier Egyptian features, though her priests continued to be clad in Egyptian vestments. But she became so essentially a Hellenic figure that all her traits were transmuted into those of the environment into which she had been diffused.

Having become the Mother of the Gods in the Saite and Greek periods (i.e. from 663 BC), the local goddesses were invested with her attributes and she absorbed their features and functions until they were so merged as to be indistinguishable. She was then the prototype of all goddesses and had her own shrines in the temples of Gizeh, Philae, and her sanctuaries everywhere in the Hellenistic and Roman world, as well as in Malta, Sardinia, Phoenicia and southern Italy, making its way to the Capitoline Hill in Rome through such centres as Puteoli, Pompeii, Herculanaeum, and Ostia. She was not, however, the only Graeco-oriental syncretistic representation of the Mother of the Gods who personified the female principle in its several manifestations, symbols and attributes, absorbing first one goddess and then another wherever her cult was diffused.

In Anatolia and throughout western Asia she was primarily the personification of the productivity of the soil as the 'Lady of the land' and source of fecundity, in association with the Young god as the embodiment of generation and procreation. At first it was the self-reproduction of the universal Mother that was emphasized, but when the male partner was introduced as a satellite of the Goddess, and their joint worship was diffused from the fertile plain of Mesopotamia into Asia Minor, largely through Hittite and Hurrian influences, the youthful consort tended to become the dominant partner in the alliance. Thus, in Syria, Anat was overshadowed by the virile Baal, and she and Asherah, the consort and daughter of El, were never merged as a single syncretistic deity, and were, in fact, often rival would-be spouses of Baal.

In Greece the Mother-goddess was identified by Homer[6] and Hesiod[7] with Rhea, the wife of Kronos. From the fifth century BC she was associated with the Phrygian Magna Mater, Kybele,[8] while in Crete her affinities had been with the Minoan Goddess in her threefold aspects as an Earth-Mountain-mother and a chthonic divinity guarding the dead. If she was not actually herself the earth, she was so intimately associated with the Earth-goddesses as to be virtually indistinguishable from them. But on the mainland in Greece, although she was a syncretistic figure, her attributes were divided among so many goddesses—Hera, Aphrodite, Athena, Artemis and Demeter, each with a name and independent personality of her own—that she was never completely merged with Kybele until after the time of the Persian wars, though the assimilation began in a much earlier period going back, perhaps, to a pre-Hellenic Mother of the Gods common to both the Greeks and the Phrygians.[9] This would explain the worship of Rhea in her own sanctuaries in Arcadia and at Olympia and Athens,[10] though, as Farnell contended, Greek travellers familiar with her cult in Crete could have transferred it to the mainland either under her own name or that of the Magna Mater.[11] But in Crete, the Aegean and Asia Minor, while the Mother-goddess appeared under several names, she had so many common elements in her functions, mythology and cultus pointing to a syncretistic figure in the remote background which became differentiated in the process of diffusion in and adaptation to a changing environment.

For example, Rhea, from being a somewhat nebulous goddess, retained her identity in the Greek theogonies when she became associated with Kybele, but, nevertheless, the cymbals, drums and pipes of the orgiastic Phrygian cultus were transferred to her.[12] As the mother of the Cretan Zeus by Kronos, possibly originally a pre-Hellenic god of the harvest,[13] she stood in the same vegetation tradition as Kybele and her counterparts elsewhere. Therefore, behind both divinities lay the universal concept of the Goddess representing the ultimate source and embodiment of life and fertility personifying the female principle. But she was never a monotheistic deity. She always tended sooner or later to be blended with a son or consort, and with the goddesses she absorbed or assimilated. Moreover, in Greece she was subordinate to her illustrious offspring Zeus, who was destined to become the self-existent Creator and unifying principle of the universe. But it was in virtue of her status in the divine hierarchy that she was accredited in Cretan tradition with the dignity of having given birth to 'the father of gods and men'. It was not until much later that the ecstatic qualities which characterized Kybele-worship in Asia Minor, and caused her to be regarded as a foreign accretion in Greece, were identified with her Semitic counterpart Ishtar or Astarte,[14] and Aphrodite, beloved of Adonis, who in the Hellenistic age was said to have been killed by a boar like Attis, or castrated himself under a pine-tree and died from loss of blood.

Such a syncretistic figure incorporating so many very diverse traits, traditions and transformations, observances, developments and distinguishing features, could hardly fail to be at once highly attractive and repulsive. In popular esteem she was held in veneration and devotion as the personification of the female principle and all that this implied in its widespread emotional, ecstatic and mystical appeal to the masses in western Asia and India, the eastern Mediterranean, Crete and the Aegean, and in the Graeco-Roman world. The main purpose of the rites was to secure the union of the votary with the Great Mother in one or other of her forms, not infrequently by the aid of frenzied dancing, wild music, and sexual symbolism, in the hope of attaining communion with the source of life and vitality in a condition of ecstatic abandonment and mystical communion. Originally the ritual enactment was in the guise of a sacred marriage for the purpose of re-awakening the reproductive forces in nature after their slumber in the long dark night of winter, brought into conjunction with the death and resurrection of the sacral king symbolizing the annual decay and revival of vegetation. As these observances were the occasion of debauchery, licence and unedifying frenzies, when the cult assumed these features its diffusion in the Graeco-Roman world came under official condemnation and was branded as neither Hellenic nor Roman in its character and content, notwithstanding its long and chequered history in the region. But so deeply laid were its roots and popular appeal that eventually it had to be accepted, and in the Roman imperial period the Goddess regained her official status, though in a much more restrained and sobered form, like the worship of Dionysus in Greece.

The Sky-god and creation

If it was to the more accessible and immanent goddesses connected with maternity, fertility and domesticity that popular devotion was directed in the Ancient Near East, and wherever its influence was diffused, the more remote transcendent Sky-god in his various manifestations and attributes became no less firmly established, once attention was concentrated upon the cosmic problem of creation. From Neolithic times onwards the existence of an extra-mundane divine power was recognized as the source of universal creative activity, centred in a celestial Supreme Being who became the head of the pantheon. Thus, in ancient Egypt the concept of Deity appears to have emerged and become co-ordinated in relation to creation, generation and resurrection, expressed in symbols connected with the sky, the sun and the Nile and its inundations. The Falcon-god Horus, 'the Lord of Heaven', was represented in the Pyramid Texts as the source of life, rain, procreation, rebirth and the divinity of the Pharaoh. He was said to have been the god who 'first came into being when no other god had yet come into existence, when no name of any thing had yet been proclaimed. When thou openest thine eyes so as to see, it becomes light for everyone.'[15] So in his daily course, flying across the heavens like a falcon crowned with the solar disk, he was known as Harakhte, 'the Horus of the Horizon', who with three local Horuses constituted the Four Horuses of the eastern sky.[16]

He was primarily, however, the Sky-god, as his solar connexions were subsidiary to his celestial provenance. Indeed, the many forms in which the Sun-god was represented in the Egyptian texts were doubtless survivals of an earlier cult of the omnipresent Sky-god, brought into conjunction with the solar cultus in its many manifestations. It is true that early man was not interested in speculations about cosmic origins and processes, being occupied with the pressing and perplexing problems occasioned by the hazards of the seasonal sequence and the forces concerned with the means of subsistence. But in approaching creation from the standpoint of human experience the Egyptians interpreted the existing order as the result of a series of births in the realms of the gods beginning with either a primal pair, or a single self-existent progenitor, who proceeded from the original state of chaos deified as Nun comparable to the life-producing Inundation upon which vegetation and the well-being of the Two Lands depended.

In all probability there was behind the many forms which the Creators assumed in the Nile valley—those of Atum-Re at Heliopolis, of Ptah at Memphis, of Thoth at Hermopolis, of Amon-Re at Thebes and of Khnum at Elephantine—one Supreme Being who was regarded as the transcendent source of the creative process, summing up in himself its various aspects and responsible for the control of the weather and the seasons. Thus, it is significant, as we have seen,* that the same linguistic root connects the heavens, the clouds and the rain with the all-embracing god of the sky, and his manifestations in nature, the storm and the rain, as evidenced by Zeus or Dyaus among the Indo-Europeans, Teshub in Anatolia, and Horus, 'the Lofty One', in Egypt. But in view of the very prominent place occupied by the sun in the environmental conditions of the Nile valley, it is not surprising that the Sky-god tended to be replaced by the Sun-god as the Creator.

The solar cult in Egypt

At Heliopolis before the First Dynasty Re was conceived as the sun in the sky, manifest in the solar disk, but when in conjunction with Atum he became head of the Ennead he combined in this composite form all the forces of nature and creative activity. As the solar cult predominated after the unification of Egypt, myths and legends accumulated around him in the Pyramid Age which represented him as supreme among the gods, absolute in his control of the Nile valley, and the ally and protector of the throne. In addition to being the source of life and generation, he was a divine king and the self-created Creator, Re-Atum, the youthful god of the eastern horizon, Re-Harakhte, and eventually at Thebes Amon-Re, the 'King of the gods', worshipped with great magnificence at Karnak and Luxor (Fig. 82).

As the solar cult was diffused over the whole country from Heliopolis, every local god was identified in some way with the Sun-god, and the cultus everywhere was based on the Heliopolitan liturgy just as its Great Ennead set the pattern of the cosmic mythology and its divine genealogies. It is true that Ptah, the Great One of Memphis, retained his independence as the sole Creator of the universe of whom all the other gods were but attributes, including Atum who was his tongue and heart. But the aspects of Deity, together with those of Ptah, were in due course blended in a pluralism of divine manifestations of gods with the same nature, born at the same time from Nun. The Egyptians, there-

*Chap. VII, p. 201.

fore, arrived at a conception of a universal solar deity not very different from that of the Goddess of many names, without abandoning their polytheistic tradition except for the very short interlude in the Eighteenth Dynasty when Amenhotep IV (Ikhnaton) transferred his allegiance solely to Aton, the ancient god of air and light (Show), whom he proclaimed as the sole Creator of heaven and earth and the sustainer of all things.

This ephemeral Aton cult was the first and only attempt to reduce a pantheon of polytheistic deities to a single all-embracing heavenly Creator. Thus, Yahweh among the Hebrews was only the god of Israel, until the end of the Exile in the sixth century BC, with a local sovereignty in the land of his own choosing and among the people with whom he stood in a particular covenant relationship. Even Ikhnaton, except for the temple he erected in Nubia, never attempted to introduce the worship and jurisdiction of the Aton outside Egypt. But he went further than his predecessors, who had already recognized the universality of Amon-Re, in eliminating the syncretistic nature of Re as a blend of the deified sun, the horizon and the falcon. Nevertheless, while the Aton was proclaimed as the one and only god, for the populace, in so far as they were at all concerned with the new royal cult, it was the heavenly orb in the sky, like the falcon identified with the ancient god Show, that was regarded as the supreme object of worship, journeying daily from the eastern to the western horizon. But the Aton really was too remote to make a popular appeal. Therefore, when it was divorced from mundane affairs and the needs of mankind at large, it was destined to suffer the fate of High Gods everywhere who merely remained Supreme Beings. For practical purposes the Sky-gods and goddesses of the solar cycle had to be brought into relation with the Earth-gods of the Osiris-Isis cycle and the cult of the dead, so that the beneficence of the celestial realms might be bestowed through their agency on the soil in fruitful seasons blessed with abundance of corn and wine, destroying the forces of evil and giving immortality and resurrection to the dead.

The Babylonian Great Triad

Much the same situation recurred in Mesopotamia, except that the country was in a much less stable and secure condition than the Nile valley, and its religious development was more complex and obscure. The home of various peoples for thousands of years, its history shows a succession of upheavals very different in character from the even course of events in Egypt. When the Sumerians arrived about 3000 BC, they had already developed a highly organized pantheon under the leadership of Anu, whose name meant 'heaven' and whose function and status were similar to those of Zeus in Greece or Jupiter in Rome. Nammu, the primeval sea, the Mother-goddess who gave birth to heaven and earth having brought the universe into being, Anu lifted it out of chaos and anarchy and made it an organized whole, for he was the supreme power in the sky, the father and king of the gods, the prototype of all earthly rulers and the ultimate source of their authority and of natural law. It was his sovereignty to which Marduk in due course succeeded, when all power was bestowed upon him by the gods.

Enlil, the Storm-god and the second member of the Great Triad, who like Anu was adopted by the invading Semites from the Sumerians, was less beneficent, revealing his divine activity in hurricanes and devastating storms and floods sweeping over cities and fields, men and animals, and responsible for the catastrophes of the cosmic order and in human history, enforcing the punitive decrees of the gods, though he was represented sometimes as the creator of mankind and the guardian of 'the Tablets of Destiny'. In this dual capacity, while he was destructive in his operations and hostile to human beings, he was the upholder of the law and order instituted by Anu for the well-being of society, and he received the adoration and homage as well as the fear of foreign lands.[17]

Ea, or Enki, the 'lord of the earth and of the underworld'—the third of the divine powers in the universe—was definitely favourable to the human race. As the Sumerian god of water and wisdom, he was the personification of intelligence, knowledge and magical insight, who revealed to Ut-napishtim the intention of Enlil to destroy mankind in a destructive flood, and gave instructions for the building of the boat to act as an 'ark' to save himself and his family from the impending disaster. Ea imparted his wisdom and magical skill to his son Marduk, and so enabled him to attain the supremacy among the younger generation of the gods and to defeat Tiamat in the great cosmic struggle in which he was destined to engage, and from which creation emerged, having himself already triumphed over Apsu, the begetter of the great gods and Mummu (Tiamat). It was because of his unrivalled knowledge and wisdom and supernatural power that he became the patron of the exorcists and diviners whom, as we have seen, played such an influential part in Babylonia, and to whom men turned for help and guidance and protection, beset as they were on all sides by so many sinister and demonic forces.

Dumuzi-Tammuz and Inanna-Ishtar

The Lesser Triad of divinities, consisting of Shamash the Sun-god, Sin the Moon-god, and Adad the Storm-god, although they were Semitic in their names were also Sumerian in origin, occurring in the earlier lists as Babbar or Utu, Nannar, and Ishkur. Similarly, the cult of Tammuz and Ishtar went back to Sumerian times as its Egyptian Osirian counterpart originated in the Predynastic period. Tammuz, however, occupied a unique position in the Babylonian pantheon. He did not belong to either the Great or the Lesser Triads, but as Dumuzi, 'the faithful son of the waters which came from the earth', he was the Sumerian Shepherd-god who in one myth is represented as seeking the hand of the goddess Inanna in marriage, though in the form of a young girl rather than in that of her more familiar guise as the Sumerian Ishtar, the wife of Anu and queen of heaven. Her brother and guardian, however, was the Sun-god, Utu, who espoused her cause.[18] At the end of the third millennium BC his union with Inanna-Ishtar was celebrated annually in Isin in southern Mesopotamia at the Spring Festival enacted by the king and queen impersonating the Young virile Shepherd-god and the Mother-goddess as the source of regenerative power, to awaken the dormant earth and make it bring forth abundantly. But in this alliance she was the dominant partner, as has been demonstrated,* for when he was brought into close connexion with Ishtar in the Tammuz myth, he was her son as well as her lover and brother, and always subordinate to her as the Young god. Annually he died in the rotation of the seasons and it was by the goddess that he was rescued from the nether regions. He was dependent upon her for his resuscitation, on which the renewal of nature in its turn likewise depended, as he was instrumental in his re-creative powers only as her agent.

The Tammuz cult was undoubtedly one of the earliest and most widespread rituals in the Near East, reflecting the original agricultural conditions in which it arose and was diffused. Thus, after it gained a prominent place in the seasonal drama in the urban civilization of Babylon when Marduk assumed the role of Tammuz after his city had become the capital about 1728 BC, it retained its fertility vegetation features in the New Year Festival in the spring. After lamentations resembling those in the ancient Tammuz liturgies, dirges and a ritual combat, the king having temporarily abdicated was restored in the throne as 'the resurrected child' or servant of the Goddess, and sorrow was turned into joy and consummated by a royal sacred marriage

*cf. Chap. III, p. 79f.

enacting the Sumerian divine union, whereby re-creative potency was bestowed upon all the lands.[19] Here, again, the Goddess remained predominant, and the king in his Tammuz-Marduk role acted at her behest in the renewal of the reproductive forces, passing through a ritual death to rise again, perpetuating vitality from season to season.

Baal, Anat and Asherah in Syria

In Syria the Tammuz motif and its cultus recurred in the Baal, Anat, Mot myth with certain modifications. Anat and Asherah, however, in the Ugaritic texts, as has been shown, never attained the dominant position of Ishtar in their efforts to secure the supreme status as the consorts of the virile and all-powerful Storm-god and Weather-god, Aleyan-Baal, 'the master'. Nevertheless, when he suffered defeat at the hand of Mot, Anat, his original wife, attacked his adversary with all her strength and might, defending her beloved Baal like a cow her calf, or as a ewe her lamb, seizing Mot and splitting him open with her sickle in a sieve, burning him in the fire, grinding him like corn between the millstones and giving his scattered remains to the birds to eat. She was, therefore, quite capable of taking drastic action as and when required. Indeed, like most Mother-goddesses, she had a warlike aspect wallowing in blood, and when she was aroused her militant characteristics were efficacious. But passionate as she was in love, the leading role in the fertility cult was played by Baal, and she was content to be enjoyed rather than take the initiative.

She was, in fact, generally called the 'Virgin Goddess', though having been originally also the spouse of the earlier Supreme God El she may have been the Mother-goddess *par excellence* in the beginning before his daughter and consort Asherah became her rival for the hand of the more potent and youthful Baal, thereby leading her to assume the status of a maiden. Thus, Asherah was described as the 'creatress of the gods', a title suggesting that she was the chief goddess, and so in the first instance married to the principal deity. Hence would arise her description on a Sumerian inscription as 'the bride of Anu', the Mesopotamian god of heaven. In the fifteenth century BC she was also the chief goddess of Tyre, and before she gave her name to the sacred pole in Canaanite and Hebrew sanctuaries she must have been venerated as a female deity, identified with Astarte with whom she is so often coupled in the Old Testament. In the Ugaritic texts her advice and help are said to have been sought by Baal and Anat about the building of a temple for Baal similar to that of the other gods, and as Baal replaced El as the leading figure in the pantheon, Asherah vied with Anat to become his consort and so to retain her original status as the first goddess in the land. But she never wholly succeeded in transforming herself from the wife of El into his daughter, in order to become the spouse of Baal.

While in this respect the Syrian version of the Tammuz theme developed characteristics of its own with its two rival goddesses struggling for supremacy, it followed the Mesopotamian pattern in its essential mythical features and cultic traits. The same struggle between an older and a younger generation of gods recurred and a vegetation motif centred in the seasonal drama of nature found expression in an analogous myth and ritual with their agricultural, fertility and temple-building characteristics. Behind it lay the emotional needs of everyday life, created by the environmental conditions, in which rain was the principal necessity in the absence of an effective system of inundation and irrigation as in the Nile valley, be it an annual event or only recurrent cycles of drought. Without an adequate rainfall the land could not give her increase, and the social and religious structure of Mesopotamia and Syria was very largely determined by the need of rain and fertility. It was under these conditions that the Tammuz-Baal cult was diffused throughout the region.

Hadad

Before he was introduced into the Canaanite pantheon Baal may have been identified with Hadad, the Semitic Storm-god (i.e. the Akkadian Adad), who reigned as 'the lord' enthroned on a lofty mountain in the northern heavens like Zeus on Olympus, or Yahweh on Sinai-Horeb. His name usually occurs in a contracted form on the Ras Shamra tablets in association with Baal in such a manner as to suggest that the two were one and the same divinity, though Hadad had a wider distribution spread over the greater part of the Near East in the middle of the second millennium BC, especially among the Assyrians, the Amorites, the Syrians, and throughout Asia Minor, his worship having been fostered by Hammurabi.[20] True to type he was responsible for sending rain to replenish the earth, or withholding it when he was angry. Temples were, therefore, erected or dedicated in his honour everywhere,[21] so popular and prominent was his cultus and essential for the well-being of the vast territory over which he held sway. This included his control of fertility as the 'lord of abundance', 'the irrigator of heaven and earth', pouring down from heaven the life-giving rain in the role of the dying and rising god. But he was also feared as a Storm-god and 'the thunderer', since he released forces of destruction and caused disastrous floods.

The occurrence of his name in the Mari Letters shows that his cult was established in northern Mesopotamia, and at Arrapha he seems to have been associated with the Akitu New Year Festival.[22] The Greek writer Lucian refers to his worship in association with the Goddess Atargatis in his shrine at Hieropolis[23] to the south at Carchemish, with rites which go back to a much earlier period. He was worshipped likewise in Sam'al, in Aleppo and in Damascus, and as the Sky-god *par excellence* he was later identified with the Sun-god, assuming the role of Zeus and Jupiter in the Graeco-Roman world. In Palestine at Megiddo he appeared as the dying and reviving Storm-god and Weather-god Hadad-Rimmon,[24] and at Byblus and in Cyprus as Adonis, while a sanctuary was dedicated to him at Halab near Ugarit.

The Storm-god and Weather-god in Anatolia

In the Land of Hatti on the Anatolian plateau he was equated with Teshub, the chief god in the Hurrian pantheon, the husband of Hebat (Hepit), and his Hittite counterpart, the Weather-god of Hatti, the husband of the Sun-goddess of Arinna. His connexion with the bull indicates that his role was that of fecundity, while his son Telipinu was a vegetation deity harrowing, ploughing and irrigating the fields and making the crops flourish. Therefore, when he (Telipinu) disappeared in a rage all life was paralysed; the rivers and streams dried up and famine prevailed as in the parallel situation in the Tammuz, Adonis and Attis myth. But the Telipinu story was not apparently directly connected with a seasonal rite, and the god is represented as merely vanishing without any suggestion that he died or descended into the underworld as in the other versions, or that he was sought by the Goddess as his wife and mother.

It is by no means improbable, however, that the myth had a cultic significance, since there is a break in the narrative at the point where the goddess of healing and magic was commissioned to pacify Telipinu and bring him back. It may have been then that the prescribed ritual was performed to appease his anger, followed by the goddess engaging in a purificatory rite in which sacrifices were offered, and ointments and unguents were employed. That they were efficacious is shown by the restoration of fertility, and the king and queen having been 'provided with enduring life and vigour'.[25] Therefore, it is clearly a ritual text and it is in the Tammuz tradition centred in the vital forces in nature which decline in the winter and are revived in the spring, personified in a Weather-god who is true to type, although with certain distinctive features in the details and setting of the narrative and its ritual.

In Anatolia the relation of the Hurrian to the Hittite goddess is obscure. The Sun-goddess of Arinna was the wife of the Weather-god of Hatti, but unlike the Hurrian goddess Hebat she was a solar divinity. The Sun-god, however, seems to have been subordinate to her, her spouse being the Weather-god of Hatti, and she herself the queen of heaven and the supreme Goddess in the state. The Babylonian Ishtar was identified with the Hurrian goddess Shaushka, sister of Teshub, who combined belligerent qualities with those of love and sexuality, and had a very considerable retinue of attendants, among whom were Ninatta and Kulitta. She was worshipped at Samuha and other cities in the Taurus region, and as usual she combined beneficent and malevolent qualities, promoting fertility and bringing catastrophes and disasters upon mankind. Hebat also developed martial features in this district where later in Komana she was known as MA—the Ma Bellona of the Romans. The Anatolian equivalent of the Magna Mater, however, was Hannahanna, the 'Grandmother', whose name was written with the ideogram of the Sumerian Mother-goddess Nintud. It was she who was consulted by the Weather-god when Telipinu disappeared, and on her advice effective action was taken to bring him back and to secure the restoration of fertility.

Thus, throughout the myths and cults of Mesopotamia, Egypt, Syria and Anatolia, the principal agricultural deities—the Goddess as mother and wife of the virile Young male god, and their intimate associates—recur with very similar attributes and functions but preserving their own peculiarities and independent developments in the several regions of their diffusion. Everywhere what may be described as the 'Tammuz cult', as in its Mesopotamian area of characterization it was most clearly defined, was centred in the Goddess, who personified generation and procreation in perpetuity with her youthful male partner embodying the transitory life which arose anew every spring, matured in early summer and then withered away in the seasonal decline. This drama of nature was enacted normally by the king and queen impersonating the God and Goddess in the New Year Festival, but in the course of development and diffusion it became overlaid with accretions and modifications in accordance with local circumstances and conditions, so that it is not clear, for instance, whether in Syria the rites were held annually or septennially at times of severe drought. The names of the gods were also variable, though such generic terms as *ba'lu* or *adon*, for 'lord' or 'master', became applicable to the Storm-god and Weather-god in his several forms. Hence arose the identification of 'Baal' or 'Adonis' with Tammuz, Hadad, Aleyan and El as a recurrent composite deity who combined a number of allied creative activities in widely dispersed mythological settings and theogonies in which a creation story was generally inherent.

Baal and Yahweh in Israel

In Israel, while Yahweh was equated with Baal when he assumed the role and functions of the indigenous vegetation gods in Palestine, as the many proper names in Yahwistic circles show,[26] so deeply rooted and fundamental was the conception of the Sinaitic covenant in the desert tradition that so far from the two gods being permanently assimilated they were in violent opposition to each other. Yahweh certainly acquired and retained many of the characteristics of Baal, as has been shown, but the setting of the Carmel story presupposes a highly organized opposition to the Baal cultus by the Mono-Yahwist minority, which continued throughout the monarchy. In the earlier phases of Hebrew religion, however, there can be little doubt that the attributes of Yahweh were in many respects identical with those of Baal or Hadad elsewhere in the surrounding region, and in the northern Kingdom of Israel in particular these persisted in the period of the monarchy. Although Yahweh moved essentially on a transcendental plane in might and splendour, he was described as 'the Rider of the Clouds' like Baal in the Ugaritic texts. Similarly, he sent the rain to nourish the earth, he appeared in the lightning and spoke in the thunder, heaven was his throne, the earth his footstool, and he engaged in battle with other gods and primeval monsters, asserting his power over the primeval waters of chaos, bringing the earth into existence and establishing order and harmony in the cosmos. He triumphed over the arch-enemy Death much as Baal did in his victorious conflict with Mot, though Death was not regarded as a god as in the Ras Shamra tablets.[27]

During the period of the settlement of the Hebrew tribes in Palestine they are represented in the book of the Judges as being in a state of transition in which the local Baals were worshipped intermittently with returns to the cult of Yahweh.[28] In the song of Deborah the God of Israel is described as arising in the midst of the Storm-cloud from his mountain fastness in Seir in the southern deserts to lead his people to victory,[29] and the Mono-Yahwists continued to echo these sentiments. It is hardly surprising, therefore, if the populace, who had never ceased to recognize the vegetation functions of the local Baals, as Hosea opined,[30] still looked to them in the eighth century for their corn and wine, and, as Jeremiah lamented,[31] to the Queen of Heaven for their victuals and well-being.

Nevertheless, in spite of all their vacillations, loyalty to the national god persisted even after the catastrophe that resulted in the Exile in the sixth century BC, when the Deutero-Isaiah and Ezekiel dismissed the foreign gods of the land of their captivity as mere wood and stone, in striking contrast to Yahweh whose creative activity was the proof of his unique divine status and power, as would be revealed when he restored his people to their own land again.[32] Babylon was about to fall and the captives would be liberated, because Yahweh, the sole creator, sustainer and controller of all things, would vindicate his name and his honour, and wipe out the sins of his people, however little they might deserve his divine beneficence and mercy towards them.[33] As at the Exodus, so now Israel would be restored and Jerusalem resuscitated, because Palestine was 'the land of Yahweh' and there he and he alone must be worshipped in his central sanctuary on Mount Zion, which was destined to become the *omphalos* whither all nations would be gathered under his righteous rule.[34] But it was only through suffering, interpreted in personal terms in the Isaianic Servant saga, that a regenerated Israel could fulfil its vocation in the establishment of a universal monotheistic theocracy wherein Yahweh would be worshipped solely and perfectly in the beauty of holiness.[35]

In post-exilic Judaism the relation between Yahweh and Israel was the covenant (*berith*) in which he occupied much the same position as the king in the West Asiatic communities as the dynamic centre of the nation who had released it from its conquerors and protected it from its enemies. At long last the backsliding people had been weaned away from the rival Canaanite gods and the neighbouring cultus, whatever lapses might occur among the dispersed groups, such as those at Elephantine. He had now become not only supreme but the one and only God; 'there was none else beside Him.'[36]

Hellenistic Judaism

To prevent contamination by the surrounding foreign influences Ezra and Nehemiah adopted an intense isolationist policy along strictly 'Zionist' lines, consolidating the Judaeans as a closed community concentrated upon the Temple and its worship, embodied in the Priestly Code, the Law, the punctilious observance of the Sabbath, and the putting away of alien wives. By so doing they intensified the deeply laid 'chosen nation' concept, and cut off Judaism from its wider connexions and contacts among the surrounding countries, Iranian, Mesopotamian, Canaanite and Anatolian, while the subsequent Maccabaean revolt had a reciprocal effect in relation to Hellenism, until at length it was brought within the orbit of the Roman Empire. The result was the development of a separate people largely isolated from and independent of the rest of the contemporary culture and religion in the Near East in the centuries immediately preceding the rise of the Christian era.

Its eschatology shows, however, that it was not completely impervious to outside influences. Furthermore, its widespread dispersion throughout Asia Minor and the adjacent region brought considerable numbers of Jews into intimate contact with the Hellenistic world. But the worship of Yahweh, interpreted as the one and only Creator and Ruler of the entire universe, remained the fundamental bond, a belief that constituted the unifying centre of the People of Israel equally in their native land in and around Jerusalem, and in the wider environments of Hellenistic Judaism, where the impact was felt on the Diaspora during several centuries of intimate association with the culture of western Asia and the eastern Mediterranean. This included not only Greek thought and practice but also Iranian, Mandaean, Gnostic, Essenic and Hermetic influences mainly from the second century BC onwards.

Although comparatively little is known about these dualistic and proto-Gnostic Judaean sects, because reference to them was systematically suppressed in orthodox Judaism, it is now becoming apparent that they were much more influential than has been hitherto supposed from the casual mention of them by Josephus, Philo, and Pliny in the first century AD. In the light of recent investigations, stimulated by the discovery of the scrolls in the caves at Khirbet Qumran at the northern end of the Dead Sea in 1947, the existence of Jewish eschatological groups with Iranian, Canaanite and Aramaean affinities, seems to have been rife in Judah and the Jordan valley just before and after the beginning of the Christian era. The Essenes, for example, may have originated in Mesopotamia and made their way to Palestine in the second century BC,[37] where they functioned as an ascetic quasi-monastic Jewish community extolling celibacy, living a common life, observing rules of silence and holding esoteric doctrines which included a developed angelology, eschatology and astrology, and having a sacred literature. In place of the Judaic sacrificial system with its blood rites, they introduced elaborate sacramental meals and lustrations which may have originated in the Euphrates valley. Albright, in fact, has suggested that the Mesopotamia lustration ritual lies behind the Johannine conception of a 'fountain of water gushing forth to eternal life' in the New Testament,[38] having reached Palestine through Jewish sects, such as the Essenes and the Qumran groups, and the movement initiated by John the Baptist.[39]

BLACK SEA

Mt Olympus
Thessaly
Troy
Delphi
Eleusis
Corinth Athens
Mycenae Epidaurus
Tyrins
GREECE

ANATOLIA

ASIA MINOR

Boghaskö
Alishar
Hüyük

Mersin
Carcher

CRETE
Knossos
Messara
Phaestos

CYPRUS

Ras
Sha
SYR
Bybl
Mt.
Carmel
PALESTINE
Beth-Shan
Samari
Bethel Shechen
Gezer DEAD SE
Gaza
Lachish

MEDITERRANEAN SEA

Alexandria

Heliopolis

Memphis
Sakkarah

SYR
DESE
SINAI

FAYUM

EGYPT

Badari
Gebel el' Araq
Abydos Denderah
Negada
Karnak
Hierakonpolis Luxor

RED SEA

Elephantine

R. Nile

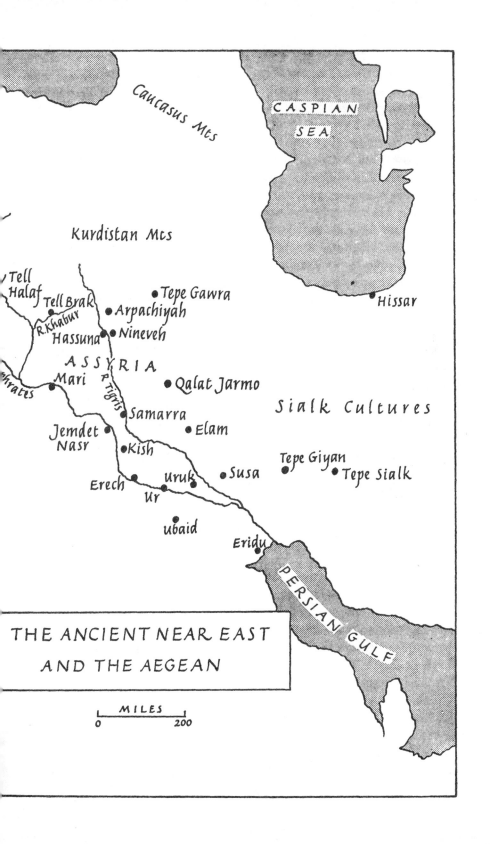

Caucasus Mts

CASPIAN
SEA

Kurdistan Mts

Tell
Halaf
Tell Brak
R. Khabur
Hassuna

Tepe Gawra
Arpachiyah
Nineveh

Hissar

ASSYRIA
Mari
R. Tigris

Qalat Jarmo

Sialk Cultures

Samarra
Jemdet
Nasr
Kish

Elam

Euphrates

Erech
Uruk
Ur

Susa

Tepe Giyan
Tepe Sialk

ubaid

Eridu

PERSIAN GULF

THE ANCIENT NEAR EAST
AND THE AEGEAN

MILES
0   200

Another oriental element in Hellenistic Judaism and the proto-Gnostic sects was the personification of 'Wisdom' (Sophia) as the first creation of Yahweh, in line with the Gnostic imagery of a lesser Sophia descending from the realms of spirit and light into the world of matter, and by a divine intervention restored to her original source in the heavens.[40] This has its antecedents in the Canaanite and Phoenician texts where El is said to have attributed wisdom (*hkmt*) to Baal together with eternal life and good fortune,[41] while in the Aramaic proverbs of Akhiqar, belonging to the sixth century BC, Wisdom is said to have 'come from the gods' to whom 'she is precious', and who have 'raised her to their kingdom in heaven'.[42] If the conception of wisdom in the book of Proverbs (viii) is hardly mythological in the Ugaritic sense, it has every appearance of having a Canaanite origin both linguistically and in its affinity to the Logos-idea in its western Asian form. It was utilitarian, like that attributed to Solomon, which was said to excel that of 'all the children of the East, and of all the wisdom of Egypt', so that 'his fame was in all the lands round about.'[43] But gradually the Hebrew concept developed wider implications and values which transcended its mercenary ends,[44] so that its first-fruits were the fear of Yahweh as a religious experience and aspiration.[45]

It was, however, regarded at the same time as a pre-existent divine element active in the creative process so that 'without it was not anything made that was made'—an attribute of Godhead not so very far removed from Plato's conception of universal Ideas in relation to Ultimate Reality, or as Ben Sirach in the second century BC poetically affirmed, a breath emanating from the mouth of the Most High and permeating all things, infusing mankind fashioned by divine wisdom in the likeness of his Creator.[46] By making wisdom the *élan vital* in man's urge to the good life, the Hebrew writers transformed the Canaanite-Aramaean mythological figure into an ethical concept in which the Ultimate Reality was divine righteousness which disclosed to mortal man the way wherein he should walk.

The Iranian influences in the apocalyptic literature were more pronounced; these, as it has been pointed out, first appeared in the book of Daniel and in the later sections of that of the Ethiopic Enoch (I. Enoch) under the pressure of events in the days of Antiochus Epiphanes at the beginning of the second century BC, when hought was centred on an eschatological vision of the future in contrast to the persecutions of the present. As the conception of the Kingdom of God took its final form in Judaism in the apocalyptic literature Iranian ideas in particular, though not to the exclusion of those from Babylonian and Egyptian sources, played a very prominent part in its development. While the inspiration was the Hebraic realization of the transcendent holiness of Yahweh, the structural outlines of the cosmic vision of the reign of God were primarily Iranian, as were the world aeons, the dualism, demonology, angelology, the resurrection of the dead, and the conception of a Primal Heavenly Man, the abodes for the righteous and the wicked in the next life and their souls hovering over the corpse for three days and three nights before passing to the place of judgment for reward or punishment.[47] This also applies to the component parts of the resurrection body and to the recognition of human likenesses and relationships after death.

The effect on later Judaism of this contact with Persian thought and imagery was to bring into greater relief the distinctive Hebrew belief in the transcendent righteousness and omnipotence of Yahweh and the divinely ordained ultimate destiny of Israel, so deeply laid in its traditional faith. Moreover, the impact occurred at a critical juncture in the history of religion in the Graeco-oriental world, when so many rival and converging cults and systems were contending or amalgamating with each other in a syncretistic age, in an attempt to arrive at some kind of synthesis. The breaking down of national barriers and the use of a common language throughout the region made possible a reciprocal exchange of ideas and universal borrowing and adaptation of religious thought and practices which could not be resisted in spite of the nationalistic isolation maintained with fanatical zeal in official Judaism. Efforts might be made to maintain the unique character of the faith of Israel, and to resist assimilation by every available means, but the process could not be prevented. It was as inevitable as it had been at the time of the settlement of the Hebrew tribes in Palestine in the days of the Judges. Then it was the vegetation Canaanite cultus that intruded upon the worship of Yahweh and the desert tradition; in the Hellenistic age it was Graeco-oriental polytheism and the mystery religions that permeated the environment in which the Jewish settlers were dispersed in the Greek cities of Asia Minor and the Fertile Crescent, from Egypt and the eastern Mediterranean littoral to Mesopotamia and Phrygia.

Graeco-oriental syncretism

In all these centres they endeavoured to render their own distinctive faith and way of life explicit, and to commend Judaism to the Gentile population among whom they lived, just as the oriental mystery rituals tried to recruit votaries among all and sundry. Thus, by mutual efforts to make proselytes, the two religions reacted on each other and this resulted in considerable syncretistic assimilation, the converts retaining and introducing into their newly adopted faith many of the beliefs and practices of their former allegiances. In the case of the Jews this was apparent in the decoration of the synagogues with the Signs of the Zodiac, solar symbols, seasonal vegetation figures, sphinxes, centaurs, winged genii, lions, eagles and pomegranates, among the many emblems of the contemporary religions.[48] Similarly, Phoenician and Aramaic literature exercised a considerable influence on Jewish thought, as is shown, for instance, in the apocryphal Tobit legend, and in the Elephantine papyri. But notwithstanding all these extraneous influences the fundamental faith of Judaism remained firmly established in spite of the syncretism and the frequent lapses both in Palestine and among the Diaspora,[49] and the heresies of the Phrygian Jews, who identified the Thracian Dionysiac god Sabazios with Yahweh.[50]

On the other hand, Judaean ethical monotheism was by no means without its influence on Graeco-oriental polytheism at a time when there was a movement in both religious and philosophical circles towards unity in the Near East and the Hellenic world. The prevailing tendency was to exalt one God as supreme above all others, be it Yahweh, Ahura Mazda, or the Sun-god, and to relate the One to the Many. This was one of the results of the diffusion of Ionian speculation, which found expression in Graeco-Roman religion in the recognition of the unity underlying the multiplicity of the manifestations of the divine, in such composite figures as 'the Goddess of many names', or in the identification of Osiris with his solar counterpart Re, and Isis with the Eleusinian Demeter and the widespread Anatolian Mother of the Gods. In this way divine names, symbols, rituals and myths were blended, a process that was made easier by the adaptability of oriental deities.

Western Asian and Egyptian gods could readily be identified with their Greek and Roman counterparts, and freed from their local restrictions could develop the characteristics and functions required by their new habitat without losing their individualities. Various expedients were adopted to relate one god with another, and to modify their systems to meet the needs of the environment in which they were diffused. In the Hellenic philosophic tradition the movement was in the direction of pantheism, based on an ultimate unifying principle which when translated into theistic terms became the many gods of Olympian polytheism resolved in one divine cosmic order interpreted physically or mentally as a First Cause. This, however, failed to satisfy the deeper spiritual needs of the human spirit, and when a period of intense intellectual inquiry and alertness was followed by one of decadence, with reason giving way to emotion, mysticism to magic, and religion to allegory and the syncretistic fusions of divine attributes, something more definite and defined was required; a more authoritative statement of belief and a guide to conduct, creditable alike to reason and morality, and capable of arousing an emotional response. The various elements, religious, philosophic and ethical, were tending towards some approach to a higher monotheism which would involve an effective relationship between god and man issuing in a standard of conduct in this life linked with rewards and punishments after death.

If all these demands were to be satisfied, a synthesis of the current faiths and systems had to be effected, so that what was best and most enduring in them could be conserved and made accessible in a disintegrating Hellenic civilization. In the background lay the Holy One of Israel, all-righteous and omnipotent; the Creator and wholly good First Cause of Plato, and the Unmoved Mover of Aristotle; together with the beneficent Wise Lord, Ahura Mazda, of Zarathushtra with the twin-spirits of good and evil in opposition to each other, and their respective forces in perpetual conflict. As these movements developed along their own lines in accordance with their own traditions and came into conjunction with each other and with the oriental mystery cults, an emergence eventually occurred which was more than a syncretism of the contemporary religions.

Mithraism

Zoroastrianism had developed into Mazdaean dualism and a Magian combination of Hellenic polytheism and oriental astrology, and Mithraism as a mystery cult which provided a link between a sacramental religion and morality had emerged out of this and passed into the Roman world by the first century AD. There it attracted a very considerable number of converts, especially in military circles, and was a powerful force which provided its initiates with an incentive to live the good life, with a supramundane theological basis. It had been diffused in Asia Minor in the Hellenistic period from Persia and before it reached Europe and spread rapidly westwards along the trade-routes, especially in the Danubian provinces, and in the military stations *en route*, it had accumulated a number of extraneous elements. Thus Mithras (Fig. 85) became associated with the Attis cult and the Kybele Taurobolium, with Chaldean astrology, the Zodiac, the *hvareno*, or nimbus dispensing its heavenly light on kings and emperors, and as the god of light was eventually identified with the sun and, like Baal, became *sol invictus* and the mediator between the celestial powers and the human race. But although in this capacity the youthful virile hero in the victorious struggle against the hosts of darkness, who never grew old or lost his vigour, inspired the devotion of those who found in his cult strength to fight successfully not only on the field of battle but also against their own passions and temptations, Mithraism was rooted in oriental polytheistic mythology and was devoid of any historical foundation in fact. Mithras in his original Indo-European form was the Vedic god of light, Mitra, and subsequently as the champion of Ormuzd was identified with the *sol invictus*, 'the invincible sun', having been equated with the Babylonian solar deity Shamash and the Hellenic Helios.

Emerging from Mazdaism, the Mithraic cosmic struggle in which man shared˙was a dualistic conflict between two opposed forces. While this supplied a strong moral motive for the initiates to engage in perpetual warfare against the powers of evil, it provided a solution for the problem of evil on a polytheistic basis only. This was doubtless of little concern for the common man who embraced the cult, but the mythological setting at a time when thought had moved in a monotheistic and monistic direction and the current Graeco-oriental cosmic polytheism was at a discount in intellectual circles, was a factor in its dissolution. At best, Mithras was but a member of the hierarchy of the ancient gods who in the cold light of reason stood revealed in his true nature, and a religion built upon these precarious foundations could not hope to conquer the civilized world at that juncture in its history. If it escaped persecution in the Empire because it found no difficulty in joining the polytheistic family of pagan gods and cults, imperial favour could not save it from extinction, owing to its own inherent weakness and decay. Therefore, as doubtless will be considered in greater detail in subsequent volumes in this series, in spite of its higher morality and spiritual standards, the 'unconquered Mithras' fell with the rest of the oriental cults in the fourth century AD in the ruins of a discredited paganism.

As the Delphic oracle and the disillusioned Julian were compelled to recognize, the ancient gods and their cultus were a spent force. They had had their day and were incapable of revival or survival. Cicero might claim with some truth that in the worship of the gods of the State religion the Romans were far superior to that of the foreign nations,[51] but they had borrowed their deities from Greece, the Aegean and western Asia, and adapted them to their own environment and its requirements. Therefore, they were doomed to extinction with the rest of the myth and ritual, except in the case of any who could be incorporated in the new Christian tradition that was in process of emergence, and which expressed its own independent faith and practice in terms of the age, and in forms which could be understood and which seemed natural in that period in the Graeco-Roman world.

The emergence of the Christian concept of Deity

Having itself arisen as a sect within Judaism when Palestine was a province of the Empire, the Christian Church based its theology on the ethical monotheism of the Hebrew prophets and the Messianic eschatology of Hellenistic Judaism, brought into relation with a highly spiritualized reinterpretation of the death and resurrection sacred drama so fundamental in Near Eastern religion from time immemorial and reassembled around the unique personality of Christ the King. Whether or not it is thought to have been a divinely ordered *praeparatio Evangelii*, the fact remains that Christianity was the heir of the ages in the sense that it fulfilled the spiritual needs and demands of the age in which it emerged. Otherwise it could not have become the consolidating dynamic in the disintegrating Empire. It succeeded where the former syncretisms had failed because it was not merely the synthetic product of diffusion and development, like its predecessors. It was rather an emergence of a genuinely new movement in the history of religion 'in the fullness of time when Greek conquered Jew and Jew conquered Greek and the world inherited the legacy of their struggle through Roman hands.'

Unlike Mithraism and the other oriental cults and the Greek philosophic systems with which it had to contend when it broke away from its Jewish moorings, its antecedents were fundamentally monotheistic. By the beginning of the era to which it has given its name polytheism had been eliminated in Judaism, and the conception of Deity had reached a stage in which divine transcendence and immanence had been brought into conjunction. He was the God who stands over and above the world, and in Him man lived and moved and had his being, for Israel claimed to be 'the sons of the living God'.[52] God was in heaven but He was also everywhere, 'nigh unto all them who call upon Him.'[53] Moreover, His Fatherhood was as firmly established as in Christian tradition. Where the Founder of Christianity broke new ground and made a genuine departure from the accepted belief of Judaism, as Dr Montefiore has recognized, was in his insistence on the constraining love of God in seeking the sinful and giving them a place in His Kingdom, not by right or merit but solely as an act of divine grace.[54] This went beyond the merciful kindness of the Lord as conceived by the Hebrew psalmist,[55] and it inaugurated a new idea of redemption as divine self-giving on behalf of sinful humanity, involving suffering and complete surrender, even of life itself, interpreted in terms of a sacrificial self-offering by God Himself, giving an assurance of salvation.[56]

This conception of the Fatherhood of God and of redemptive sacrifice raising mankind to a new status of sonship, thereby enabling the human race to gain access as never before to the inmost nature of the divine, was in line with the later developments of Jewish religious thought and practice, and was by no means unintelligible to the Gentiles acquainted with the higher and more spiritual aspects of the Mystery cults. But, nevertheless, it introduced a new era in the history of religion, because it went beyond anything envisaged in the Messianic theology of Judaism in respect of the sovereign rule of Yahweh and the status and function of the Son of Man, or of the Saoshyant in Zoroastrian eschatology. It was far removed from the polytheistic mythological setting of the pagan Mysteries and the vegetation cults in which they were grounded, in spite of the retention and reinterpretation of much of the ancient myth and ritual in Christian faith and practice. Similarly, while Graeco-Roman philosophy provided the conception of theistic thought into which Christian philosophical theology had to be fitted, the attempt to combine Platonism, Stoicism and Judaism in a composite Christian metaphysic in the Catechical school at Alexandria was largely responsible for the protracted heresies and controversies that characterized the first three centuries of the new era, when the Church was engaged in rendering its own independent faith explicit amid the vigorous currents and cross-currents of the thought and practice of the Graeco-Roman world.

Its struggle with Gnosticism, Neoplatonism and the Mysteries had to be carried on side by side with a new series of contests with the State on the one hand and with its own apologists on the other. It was because it represented an emergence rather than another syncretism that it had not only to defend itself in terms of current Greek thought, and to carry on a polemic against polytheism, but had also to vindicate its claims to be a specifically new and unique divine self-disclosure, described by Professor C. H. Dodd as 'the entry into history of a reality beyond history'.[57] How this was accomplished it remains for other volumes in this series to determine, but so far as the ancient gods in the Near East and the Graeco-Roman world were concerned, the Christian concept of Deity represented the culmination of the long process of development and diffusion, of adaptation and amalgamation, and of syncretism and emergence on which this inquiry has been concentrated.

NOTES

N.B.—The following abbreviations are used in the Notes:

AASOR	*Annual of the American Schools of Oriental Research.* New Haven.
AB	*Anat-Baal Texts.*
AJSL	*American Journal of Semitic Languages and Literature.* Chicago.
ANET	*Ancient Near Eastern Texts relating to the Old Testament.* Ed. J. B. Pritchard. 2nd edition 1955.
BSA	*Annual of the British School at Athens.*
BASOR	*Bulletin of the American Schools of Oriental Research.*
CGS	*Cult of the Greek States.* L. R. Farnell, Oxford.
ERE	*Encyclopaedia of Religion and Ethics,* edited by J. Hastings.
IPEK	*Jahrbuch für Prehistorische und Ethnographische Kunst.* Cologne.
JAOS	*Journal of the American Oriental Society.*
JEA	*Journal of Egyptian Archaeology.*
JHS	*Journal of Hellenic Studies.*
JNES	*Journal of Near Eastern Studies.*
JRAS	*Journal of the Royal Asiatic Society.*
KUB	*Keilschrifturkunden aus Boghazhoi* (Berlin).
PT	*Pyramid Texts.*
SBE	*Sacred Books of the East.*

CHAPTER I: THE RISE OF CIVILIZATION IN THE ANCIENT NEAR EAST

1. *Antiquity,* Vol. XXX. 1956, pp. 132ff.
2. Kenyon, *Digging up Jericho* (London 1957), pp. 51ff.
   Antiquity, Vol. XXX. 1956, pp. 184ff.
3. R. J. Braidwood, *Antiquity,* Vol. XXXI. 1957, pp. 73ff., for a criticism of the Jericho dating.
4. JNES, IV. 1945, pp. 262ff.
5. Oppenheim, *Tell Halaf* (Berlin 1943).
6. A. L. Perkins, *The Comparative Archaeology of Early Mesopotamia* (University of Chicago Press 1949), p. 44.
7. Fuad Safar, *Sumer* (Baghdad 1947), Vol. III. pp. 103ff.
8. T. Jacobsen, *The Sumerian King-List* (Chicago 1955), pp. 58ff., 65ff.
   Kramer, *Sumerian Mythology* (London 1944), pp. 97ff.
   ANET, 1955, pp. 42ff., 88.
9. V. G. Childe, *New Light on the Most Ancient East* (London, 3rd ed. 1952), pp. 128f.
   Antiquity, Vol. XXXI. 1957, p. 37.
10. Adam Falkenstein, *Archaische Texte aus Uruk* (Leipzig 1936).
    W. Andrae, *Antiquity,* Vol. X. 1936, pp. 137ff.
    Hooke, *Antiquity,* Vol. XI. 1937, pp. 267ff.
11. Frankfort, *Studies in Ancient Oriental Civilization,* No. 4 (Chicago University 1932), pp. 18ff.
12. D. E. McCown, *The Comparative Stratigraphy of Early Iran* (Studies in Ancient Oriental Civilization, No. 23. Chicago University Press 1942), pp. 36ff.
13. McCown, *op. cit.*
    G. Ghirshman, *Fouilles de Sialk près de Kashnan* (Paris 1938).
14. E. E. Herzfeld, *Iran in the Ancient East* (Oxford 1941), p. 7.
15. R. de Mecquenem, *Mémoires de la Mission Archéologique en Iran,* XXX (Paris 1947), pp. 177ff.
16. R. de Mecquenem, *Fouilles préhistoriques en Asie occidentale* (Paris 1934–37).
    L'Anthropologie, XLVIII, 55–71, 1938, pp. 67ff.
17. Piggott, *Antiquity,* Vol. XVII. 1943, pp. 162ff.
    R. E. M. Wheeler, *Ancient India,* Vol. I. 1945, pp. 8–26, Vol. IV. 1948, pp. 162ff.
18. Sir Aurel Stein, *An Archaeological Tour in Gedrasia* (London 1931).
    N. C. Majumdar, *Explorations in Sind* (London 1934).
    Piggott, *Prehistoric India* (London 1950), pp. 72ff.

19. Marshall, *Mohenjo-daro and the Indus Civilization* (London 1931), Vol. I. p. 15.
20. *Prehistoric India*, p. 169.
21. Mackay, *The Indus Civilization* (London 1953), pp. 53ff.
22. Marshall, *op. cit.*, p. 24.
23. *Prehistoric India*, pp. 96ff., 142ff.
24. *Mostagedda* (London 1937), pp. 26ff.
    Antiquity, Vol. III. 1929, pp. 456ff.
25. Brunton and Caton-Thompson, *The Badarian Civilization* (London 1928), pp. 40ff.
    Baumgärtel, *The Cultures of Prehistoric Egypt* (Oxford 1955), p. 20.
26. Quibell and Green, *Hierakonpolis* (London 1902), Vol. I. p. 26on.
27. Frankfort, *Studies in Early Pottery of the Near East* (London 1924), p. 122. Pl. XII.
28. *Hierakonpolis*, Vol. II. Pl. LXXV.
29. *Hierakonpolis*, Pl. XXVI. pp. 40ff.
30. *Hierakonpolis*, Pls. XXVIc. p. 41, XXIX. p. 42.
31. H. and H. A. Frankfort, J. A. Wilson, T. Jacobsen, W. A. Irwin, *The Intellectual Adventure of Ancient Man* (Chicago 1946), pp. 125ff.
32. Frankfort, *American Journal of Semitic Languages and Literatures*, LVIII. 1941, pp. 329ff.
33. R. S. Hardy, AJSL, 1941, pp. 178ff.
34. R. H. Pfeiffler and E. A. Speiser, AASOR, XVI, 1935–36, pp. 11ff.
35. AASOR, XX, 1940–41, pp. 1ff.
36. G. E. Wright, *The Pottery of Palestine to the End of the Early Bronze Age* (New Haven 1937), pp. 74ff.
37. Albright, BASOR, No. 67 (1937), pp. 26ff.; No. 77 (1940), pp. 20ff.
    G. Dossin, *Syria*, XX. 1939. pp. 97ff.
    Parrot, *Mari* (Paris 1953).
38. James, *Myth and Ritual in the Ancient East* (London 1958), pp. 58ff., 300ff.
39. BASOR, No. 73 (1939), p. 21.
    Palestine Exploration Fund, Quarterly Statement, 1936, pp. 211ff.
40. Albright, BASOR, No. 70 (1938), pp. 11ff., No. 80 (1940), pp. 11ff., No. 82 (1941), p. 24.
    H. Torczyner, *Lachish I. The Lachish Letters* (Oxford 1938), pp. 15ff.
41. Gen. xxiv. 10. cf. xi. 22–27.
42. BASOR, No. 77 (1940), pp. 32; No. 78 (1940), pp. 32ff.
43. Gen. xii. 10ff.; xxvi. 1ff.
    Albright, BASOR, No. 38 (1935), pp. 10ff.; No. 74 (1939), pp. 11ff.
    Meek, BASOR, No. 61 (1950), pp. 17ff.
    Meek, *Hebrew Origins* (New York 1950), pp. 7ff.
44. Exod. i. 11.
45. Griffiths, *The Exodus in the Light of Archaeology* (London 1923), p. 49.
    Barton, *Archaeology and the Bible* (London, 6th ed. 1939), p. 375.
    Rowley, *From Joseph to Joshua* (London 1950), pp. 24ff., 109ff.
46. Jacks, *The Date of the Exodus* (London 1925).
    T. H. Robinson, *History of Israel* (London 1932), Vol. I. pp. 71ff.
    Albright, BASOR, No. 58 (1935), pp. 16ff.
47. Rowley, *op. cit.*, p. 4.
48. Deut. vii. 12; xx. 10–17. cf. II Sam. vii. 9.
49. Joshua ix; xiv. 6–15.
50. Garstang, *Joshua-Judges* (London 1931), pp. 145ff.
51. *Digging up Jericho*, p. 262.
52. Garstang, *op. cit.*, p. 255.
    S. A. Cook, *Cambridge Ancient History* (1924), Vol. II. pp. 256ff.
    Dhorme, *La Religion des Hébreux Nomades* (Paris 1937), p. 80.
53. *Tell el Armana Texts*, 148:14; 140:19,16; 238:11.
54. Albright, BASOR, No. 58 (1935), pp. 10ff.
    Meek, *Hebrew Origins*, p. 20.
55. Joshua viii.
56. Tufnell, Inge, Harding, *Lachish II* (Oxford 1940), pp. 22ff.
57. Isa. xiv. 1. cf. xliv. 28.
58. Childe, *Prehistoric Migrations in Europe* (Oslo 1950), p. 41.

59. Hawkes, *The Prehistoric Foundations of Europe* (London 1940), p. 150.
60. A. Evans, *The Palace of Minos* (London 1922–37).
61. Ventris and Chadwick, *Documents in Mycenaean Greek* (Camb. 1956), pp. 31ff.
62. Emmett, Bennett, *The Pylos Tablets* (Princeton 1951).
63. *Antiquity*, Vol. XXVII. 1953, pp. 84ff.
64. Dikaios, *Antiquity*, Vol. XXVII. 1953, pp. 233ff.

CHAPTER II: EMERGENCE OF RELIGION IN THE ANCIENT NEAR EAST

1. Burkitt, *Eurasia Septentrionalis Antique* (Helsinki 1934), IX. pp. 113ff.
   L. Passemard, *Les Statuettes Féminines Dites Vénus Stéatopyges* (Nîmes 1938).
2. Mallowan and Cruikshank, *Iraq*, II. i. 1935, pp. 81ff.
3. E. Douglas van Buren, *Clay Figurines of Babylonia and Assyria* (New Haven 1930), pp. xlix.ff.
4. *Digging up Jericho*, pp. 59ff.
5. Mallowan, *Syria*, Vol. III. 1936, pp. 19ff.; Fig. V. 1–12, Pl. 1.
6. Tobler, *Excavations at Tepe Gawra* (Philadelphia 1950), II. pp. 163ff. Pls. LXXXI, CLIII.
7. *Iraq*, IX. 1947, pp. 156ff.
8. Van Buren, *Iraq*, XII. 1950, pp. 141ff.
   O. G. S. Crawford, *The Eye Goddess* (London 1957), pp. 25ff., 139.
9. E. F. Schmidt, *The Alisha Hüyük Seasons 1928–29* (Chicago 1932), Pt. I. p. 128. Fig. 157; p. 131. Fig. 161. *Season 1927*, Pt. II. p. 36, Fig. 27.
10. Garstang, *Prehistoric Mersin* (Oxford 1953), p. 71. Fig. 39.
11. Ghirshman, *Fouilles de Tepe-Giyan* (Paris 1933), pp. 50. Pl. vi.
    Ghirshman, *Fouilles de Sialk* (Paris 1938), Vol. I. p. 19.
    cf. E. F. Schmidt, *Excavation at Tepe Hissar* (Philadelphia 1937), p. 300.
12. Contenau, *La Déesse Nue Babylonienne* (Paris 1914), p. 59. Fig. 58. cf. p. 62. Fig. 59.
    Syria, Vol. VIII. 1927, p. 198. Figs. 2, 3.
13. *Prehistoric India*, pp. 72ff., 107ff., 126ff.
    Ancient India, No. 1. 1946, pp. 8ff.; No. 3. 1947, pp. 113ff.
14. Piggott, *Ancient India*, p. 127.
15. Stein, *Memoirs of the Archaeological Survey of India*, No. 37. 1925. Pl. tx. P. G. 17.
16. Mackay, *Further Excavations at Mohenjo-daro* (London 1937), Vol. II. Pls. LXXIII. 6; LXXII. 5, 6; LXXV. 1, 5; LXXXVI. 21, 22; LXXIII. 1, 5; LXXV. 10, 14, 17.
17. Marshall, *Mohenjo-daro and the Indus Civilization*, Vol. I. p. 339.
18. Mackay, *op. cit.*, Vol. I. pp. 335 ff.; Vol. II. Pls. LXXXVIII. 223, 235.
    Marshall, *op. cit.*, Vol. I, pp. 52ff. Pls. XII, XVII.
19. Vats, *Excavations at Harappa* (Delhi 1940), pp. 51, 53, 116, 140, 368ff.
20. *The Badarian Civilization*, pp. 29ff.
21. *Hierakonpolis* (1900), Pt. I. Pl. XI, XVIII. 3.
    Petrie, *Abydos* (London 1903), Pt. II, p. 24, Pl. II.
22. Homer, *Odyssey*, 125ff. (Henceforth referred to as *Od.*)
    Hesiod, *Theogony*, 969.
    Diodorus Siculus, V. 25ff.
23. *Palace of Minos*, Vol. I. p. 52.
24. *Palace of Minos*, Vol. I. p. 447.
25. F. E. Zeuner, *Dating the Past* (London, 3rd ed. 1953), pp. 274ff.
26. *Digging up Jericho*, Pl. 20B. p. 122; cf. Pl. 21. p. 123; Pl. 22. p. 124; Pl. 23. p. 125.
27. *Digging up Jericho*, p. 72.
28. Petrie, *Nagada and Ballas* (London 1896), p. 31.
29. Budge, *The Book of the Dead*, Chap. XLIII.
30. Budge, *Osiris and the Egyptian Resurrection* (London 1911), Vol. I, pp. 212ff.
31. M. de Morgan, *Recherches sur les Origines de l'Egypte* (Paris 1897), pp. 207, 267.
32. *The Book of the Dead*, Chap. XLIII.
33. J. Roscoe, *The Baganda* (London 1911), p. 282.
34. Junker, JEA, Vol. I. 1914, pp. 252ff.
35. W. R. Dawson, *Egyptian Mummies* (London 1924), p. 26.
36. *Excavations at Sakkara* (1907–08), p. 113; Vol. III. (1909), Pl. LV.

37. *Hierakonpolis* (1902), II. pp. 20ff.
    H. J. Kenton, JNES, III. 1944, pp. 100ff.
38. Petrie, *Royal Tombs of the First Dynasty* (London 1900), Pt. I. pp. 8ff.
    Abydos, Vol. I. 1902; Vol. II. 1903.
39. Petrie, *Pyramids and Temples at Gizeh* (London 1885).
    C. M. Firth and J. E. Quibell, *The Step Pyramid* (London 1936).
40. Blackman, JEA, Vol. III. 1916, pp. 253ff.
41. Gardiner, ERE, VIII. p. 23.
    Breasted, *Development of Religion and Thought in Ancient Egypt* (London 1914), p. 54.
42. Sethe, *Urkunden des aegyptischen Altertums* (Leipzig 1903), p. 114.
    Budge, *The Book of the Opening of the Mouth* (London 1909), Vol. I. pp. 9ff.
43. *The Book of the Opening of the Mouth*, Vol. I. p. vii.
44. Seton Lloyd, JNES, IV. October 1945, pp. 276ff. Fig. 17, 27. Pl. iii. 1, 2, 3.
45. Tobler, *Excavations at Tepe Gawra* (Philadelphia 1950), Vol. II. pp. 51ff.
46. Woolley and Hall, *Ur Excavations* (Oxford 1927), Vol. I. p. 174.
47. Mallowan and Cruikshank, *Iraq* (1930), II. p. 36.
    Frankfort, *Archaeology and the Sumerian Problem* (Chicago 1932), p. 27.
48. Woolley, *Excavations at Ur* (London 1954), p. 16.
49. *Excavations at Ur*, Vol. II. pp. 33ff.
50. Mackay, *Further Excavations at Mohenjo-daro* (1938), Vol. I. pp. 116ff., 615, 648ff.
51. Vats, *Excavations at Harappa* (New Delhi 1940), Vol. I. pp. 198ff., 161ff.
52. *The Indus Civilization*, Cambridge History of India 1953, pp. 24ff.
53. *The Indus Civilization*, pp. 48ff.
54. *Mémoires de la Mission Archéologique en Iran*, Vol. XXV. 1934. Figs. 60, 3, 12; 61, 1; 62, 1–2.
55. Dikaios, *Iraq*, Vol. VII, 1940, pp. 77ff.
56. Evans, *Proceedings of the Prehistoric Society*, XIX. 1953, pp. 41ff.
57. *Palace of Minos*, Vol. II. p. 279.
58. Sophocles, *Trachiniae*, pp. 1191ff.
    Hyginus, *Fab.*, p. 36.
59. Monier-Williams, *Brahmanism and Hinduism* (London 1887), pp. 283ff.
60. Iamblicus, *De Mysteriis*, p. 12.
61. Frazer, *Worship of Nature* (London 1926), pp. 9ff.
    Tylor, *Primitive Culture* (London, 4th ed. 1903), Vol. I. pp. 426ff.
62. Evans-Pritchard, *Nuer Religion* (Oxford 1956), pp. 2ff., 118ff., 124, 200ff.
63. Mercer, *Horus, the Royal God* (Grafton, Mass. 1942), pp. 20ff.
    G. A. Wainwright, *The Sky-Religion in Egypt* (Camb. 1938), pp. 9ff.
64. Breasted, *Development of Religion and Thought in Ancient Egypt*, p. 9.
65. PT. 1521. (UT 217) cf. 1479.
    The Book of the Dead, Chap. XVII.
66. PT. 1248.
67. Wainwright, JEA, XVI. 1930, pp. 35ff.; XVII. 1931, pp. 151, 185ff.
68. PT. 832, 865, 972, 1033, 1500.
69. Langdon, *Semitic Mythology* (Boston 1931), pp. 93ff.
70. cf. Kramer, *Lamentation over the Destruction of Ur* (Assyriological Studies No. 12) (Oriental Institute of Chicago 1940), pp. 35ff., 39ff.
71. Jacobsen, JAOS, LIX. 1939, pp. 486ff.
72. Gadd, *Ideas of Divine Rule in the Ancient East* (Oxford 1948), p. 34.
73. Frankfort, *Kingship and the Gods* (Chicago 1948), p. 228.

CHAPTER III: THE MOTHER-GODDESS AND THE YOUNG GOD

1. Langdon, *Tammuz and Ishtar* (Oxford 1914), p. 5. For a full discussion of the situation cf. James, *The Cult of the Mother Goddess*, 1959.
2. Kramer, *Sumerian Mythology* (Philadelphia 1944), pp. 56ff.
   Jacobsen, JNES, IV. 1946, pp. 149ff.
3. Kramer, *Proceedings of th American Philosophical Society*, LXXXV. 1942, pp. 293ff.
   Pls. i-x.
   ANET, pp. 52, 109ff.
   Sumerian Mythology, pp. 83ff

4. *Sumerian Mythology*, pp. 43ff.
5. Sethe, *Urgeschichte*, pp. 85ff.
   Murray, JRAI, XLV. 1915, pp. 305ff.
6. PT. 630–3.
7. Budge, *From Fetish to God in Ancient Egypt* (Oxford 1934), p. 58.
8. PT. 470.
9. Budge, *The Gods of the Egyptians* (London 1904), Vol. I. pp. 431ff.
10. Newberry, *Ancient Egypt* (London 1914), p. 155.
11. *The Gods of the Egyptians*, Vol. I. pp. 450ff.
12. *The Book of the Dead*, Chap. XLII, 11; LXVI, 2.
13. *Gods of the Egyptians*, Vol. II. p. 463.
    Mallet, *Le Culte de Neit à Sais* (Paris 1888), pp. 140, 252.
14. cf. Plutarch, *De Iside et Osiride*, ix.
    Horapollo, *Hieroglyphica*, i. 12.
    cf. Mallet, *op. cit.*, p. 191.
15. *Gods of the Egyptians*, Vol. II. pp. 103ff.
16. *Papyrus Oxyrhynchus*, XI. 1380, 71–5. (Henceforth referred to as Papyrus Oxy.).
17. *Papyrus Oxy.*, XI. 1380, 100; XII. 1449, 5.
18. Driver, *Canaanite Myths and Legends* (London 1956), p. 12.
    Ginsberg, ANET (1955), pp. 133ff.
19. Gaster, *Thespis* (New York 1950), p. 181.
    Schaeffer, *The Cuneiform Texts of Ras Shamra-Ugarit* (London 1939), p. 68.
20. *Anat-Baal Texts*, II. 39ff; 49:IV; 27.29; *Krt Text*, 125, col. iii. 1, 5ff. (Anat-Baal Texts henceforth referred to as AB)
21. AB. 51: IV: 43ff.
22. AB. II: 3ff.
23. AB. 49: 11: 5ff (IV. AB ii. 28)
24. AB. 67: VI, 8ff.
25. AB. 62: 1: 15, 18ff.
26. AB. 49: 1: 11–15, 34.
27. AB. 49: 11: 10ff.
28. Frazer, *The Golden Bough* (London 1914), Pt. VII. pp. 216ff.
    V. Jacob, *Harvard Theological Review*, 38, 1945, pp. 8off.
29. I. AB: ii, 15–20.
30. AB. 49: III. 6ff., 12.
31. AB. 51: VII: 42; 67:11, 10ff.
32. AB. 49: V. 1ff.
33. Pope, *El in the Ugaritic Texts* (Leiden 1955), pp. 32ff.
    A. S. Kapelrud, *Baal in the Ras Shamra Texts* (Copenhagen 1952), pp. 72ff.
34. 'nt. V. 35; VI:IV:8.
35. AB. 51:I:22; III: 25ff., 29ff., 34ff.; IV. 31ff.
36. AB. 75:1:26ff.
37. AB. 49: I:11–15.
38. AB. 51:IV:43ff.
39. I Kings. xviii. 19.
40. I Kings xix. 14.
41. Jer. vii. 18.
42. Jer. xliv. 15ff.
43. Jer. xliv. 2off.
44. Amos v. 4–6;
    Hos. x. 9ff.
45. Albright, *Archaeology and the Religion of Israel* (London 1946), p. 173.
46. Pritchard, *Palestine Figurines* (London 1943).
47. W. F. Bade, *Quarterly Statement of the Palestine Exploration Fund*, LXII. 1930, pp. 12ff.
48. I Sam. ii. 32.
49. Amos ii. 7ff. cf. Jer. v. 7; iv. 30.
50. I Kings xv. 12.
    Hos. iv. 14ff.
51. Deut. xxiii. 17ff.

52. Gen. xxxiv. 31 ; xxxviii. 15, 21.
    Jos. ii. 1ff.
53. Hos. ii. 16ff.
54. Garstang, *The Hittite Empire* (London 1929), pp. 95ff.
    Garstang, *The Land of the Hittites* (London 1910), pp. 211ff. Pls. lxiv-lxxi.
    Gurney, *The Hittites* (London 1954), pp. 135, 141ff.   •
    Bittel, Naumann, Otto, *Yazilikaya* (Leipzig 1941).
    Laroche, *Recherches sur les noms des Dieux Hittites* (Paris 1947), pp. 47ff.
55. *The Hittite Empire*, pp. 109ff.
    Gurney, *op. cit.*, p. 201.
56. *The Land of the Hittites*, pp. 211ff., 256ff.
57. *The Land of the Hittites*, p. 239.
    Garstang, *The Syrian Goddess* (London 1913), pp. 7ff.
    Frazer, *The Golden Bough*, Pt. V, pp. 133ff.
    Farnell, *Greece and Babylon* (London 1911), p. 264.
    Ramsay, JRAS, XV. 1885, p. 113.
58. KUB XXXVI. 97.
    Otten, *Orientalistische Literaturzeitung*, LI. 1956. Cols. 102ff. p. 113.
59. *The Hittite Empire*, pp. 116ff.
60. KUB XXI. 27.
    ANET, pp. 199ff.
    Muller, *Mitteilungen der Vorder-asiatischen Gesselschaft*, VII. 1902. No. 5. pp. 193ff.
61. KUB XXXI. 127.
    Gurney, *Annals of Archaeology and Anthropology* (Liverpool 1940), 27, pp. 10ff., 22ff.
    Laroche, *op. cit.*, p. 106.
    Journal of Cuneiform Studies, I. 1947, p. 214.
62. *Annals of Archaeology and Anthropology*, VI. No. 3, pp. 109ff.
63. *Annals of Archaeology and Anthropology*, VI. No. 3, pp. 10, 22ff.
64. KUB XXI. 27.
    Goetze, *Kleinasien* (Munich, 1957), p. 129.
65. KUB XXXI. 27.
66. Laroche, *op. cit.*, p. 96.
67. KUB XVII. 10; XXXIII. 1-12.
    Goetze, ANET, pp. 126ff.
    Gaster, *Thespis*, pp. 353ff.
68. Goetze, ANET, pp. 125ff.
69. Pausanias, VII. 17, 10-12.
    cf. Arnobius, *Adversus Nationes*, V. 5-7.
70. Servius on Virgil, *Aeneid*, IX. 115.
    Pausanias, *op. cit.*
    Scholiast on Nicander, *Alexipharmaca* 8.
71. Polybius, 22, 20.
72. Clement of Alexandria, *Protrept.* ii. 15, p. 13 (ed. Potter).
    Firmicus Maternus, *De errore profanarum religionum*, 18.
73. Prudentius, *Peristephan*, X. 1034-9.
    Firmicus Maternus, *op. cit.* 27.8.
74. Strabo, XII. II. 3.
75. *Corpus inscript. Latinarum*, VI. 490 ; IX. 3146.
76. Hesiod, *Theogony*, 453ff.
    Euripides, *Bacchae*, 119-134.
    J. Harrison, *Themis* (Camb. 1912), pp. 3ff.
    Nilsson, *Minoan-Mycenaean Religion* (Lund, 2nd ed. 1950), pp. 546ff.
77. Strabo, X. 466ff.
78. R. C. Bosanquet, BSA, XL. 1943, pp. 66ff.
79. Nilsson, *op. cit.*, p. 536.
80. *Palace of Minos*, Vol. I. p. 51.
81. *Palace of Minos*, Vol. I. pp. 500ff.
82. B. E. Williams, *Gournia* (Philadelphia 1908), pp. 47ff. Pl. X.
83. *Palace of Minos*, Vol. IV. pp. 138ff., 159.

84. A. Evans, *The Earlier Religion of Greece* (London 1913), p. 25.
85. Paribeni, *Monumenti Antichi*, XIX. 1909, pp. 1ff.
    Nilsson, *op. cit.*, pp. 428ff.
    Picard, *Les Religions Préhelléniques* (Paris 1948), pp. 168ff.
86. A. Evans, *Tree and Pillar Cult* (London 1904), pp. 7ff.
    Nilsson, *op. cit.*, pp. 212ff.
87. Nilsson, *op. cit.*, pp. 58, 62, 518ff.
    Od., xix. 188.
    Strabo, x. 476.
88. *Palace of Minos*, Vol. I. p. 159ff.
89. *Palace of Minos*, Vol. I. pp. 161ff.
90. *Palace of Minos*, Vol. II. pp. 838ff.
91. Nilsson, *op. cit.*, p. 267.
92. Evans, *Archaeologia*, XV. 1914, pp. 10ff. Fig. 16.
93. *Tree and Pillar Cult*, p. 78. Fig. 52.
    cf. Tsoundas, *Ephemeris archaiologike* (Athens 1890), p. 170.
    Persson, *Religion of Greece in Prehistoric Times* (London 1942), pp. 36ff.
94. *Tree and Pillar Cult*, p. 79. Fig. 53.
95. *Palace of Minos*, Vol. I. pp. 430ff.
96. Nilsson, *op. cit.*, p. 275. cf. p. 163.
97. Evans, BSA, IX, 1902–03, pp. 59ff. Figs. 37, 38.
98. *Palace of Minos*, Vol. VII. 1900–01, pp. 28ff. Fig. 9.
99. *Tree and Pillar Cult*, p. 3. Fig. 1; p. 19. Figs. 12–14; pp. 66ff. Figs. 44–46.
    Nilsson, *op. cit.*, p. 356.
100. *Palace of Minos*, Vol. IV. p. 467.
101. *Tree and Pillar Cult*, p. 77. Fig. 51.
    Palace of Minos, Vol. III. pp. 143, 438ff.
102. *Palace of Minos*, Vol. III. pp. 471ff. Fig. 328.
103. Tsountas, *Ephemeris archaiologike* (Athens, 1887), pp.x,3.
    Rodenwaldt, *Athenische Mitteilungen*, 37. 1912, pp. 129ff. Pl. VIII.
104. *Palace of Minos*, Vol. II. p. 277.
    Marinatos, *Ephemeria Archaiologika* (Athens 1937), p. 290.
    Persson, *op. cit.*, p. 123.
    Farnell, *Essays to Sir A. Evans* (London 1927), pp. 11ff.
    Wace, *Mycenae* (London 1949), p. 113.
105. Nilsson, *op. cit.*, pp. 392ff.
    History of Greek Religion (London 1925), p. 18.
106. Evans, *The Earlier Religion of Greece in the Light of Cretan Discoveries*, p. 41.
107. *Palace of Minos*, Vol. II. p. 277.

CHAPTER IV: THE SACRAL KINGSHIP

1. *The Book of the Dead*, Chap. XVII.
   Sethe, *Urkunden des aegyptischen Altertums* (Leipzig 1903), Vol. VI.
2. Frankfort, *Kingship and the Gods*, pp. 151ff.
3. Breasted, *Ancient Records of Egypt* (Chicago 1907), III. p. 400.
4. PT. 3–5, 8; Ut. 219; PT. 632, Ut. 373; PT. 1194–5, 1833.
5. N. de Garis Davies, *The Tomb of Rekh-mi-Re at Thebes* (New York 1943), Pl. xi. 18.
   A. H. Gardiner, *Zeitschrift für aegyptische Sprache* (Leipzig 1925), 60. p. 69.
6. Sethe, *op. cit.*, Vol. IV. 1074.
   Armarna-Poem, III. 29.
   J. M. A. Janssen, *Mens en Dier* (Amsterdam 1954), pp. 71ff.
7. cf. N. de Garis Davies, JEA, IX. 1923, pp. 134ff.
8. Sethe, *op. cit.*, Vol. IV. pp. 219–21.
9. Naville, *Deir el-Bahari* (London 1894), Pt. II. pp. 12ff.
10. Naville, *op. cit.*, Pt. II. Pl. XLVII.
    Moret, *Du caractère Religieux de la Royauté Pharaonique* (Paris 1902), pp. 49ff. 72.
11. Naville, *op. cit.*, Pt. II. pp. 15ff.
    Sethe, *op. cit.*, Vol. IV. p. 227.

12. Naville, *op. cit.*, Pt. II. Pl. LI–LIII.
    Moret, *op. cit.*, pp. 53ff.
    Sethe, *op. cit.*, Vol. IV. pp. 244ff.
13. Naville, *op. cit.*, Pt. III. Pl. LVII.
14. Naville, *op. cit.*, Pt. III. Pl. LXI.
    Moret, *op. cit.*, pp. 79ff.
15. Gardiner, JEA, II. 1915, pp. 122ff.; XXXI. 1945, p. 24; XXXIX. 1953, p. 23.
    Frankfort, *op. cit.*, pp. 101ff.
16. Sethe, *Dramatische Texte zu altaegyptischen Mysterienspielen* (Leipzig 1928), i–ii.
17. Moret, *op. cit.*, pp. 75ff.
    Sethe, *Urgeschichte*, pp. 180ff.
    Sethe, *Untersuchungen*, III. pp. 133ff.
18. Moret, *op. cit.*, pp. 77ff.
    Breasted, *op. cit.*, II. p. 99.
    Blackman, *Proceedings of the Society of Biblical Archaeology*, XL. 1918, p. 90.
    Blackman, ERE, Vol. X. p. 478.
    Sethe, *Urkunden*, IV. p. 262n.b.
19. Blackman, *Journal of the Manchester Egyptian and Oriental Society*, 1918–19, pp. 51ff.
20. Blackman, *Journal of the Manchester Egyptian and Oriental Society*, 1918–19, p. 30.
    Blackman, ERE, Vol. XII. 1921, pp. 777ff.; Vol. V. 1918, pp. 162ff.
    Blackman, *Recueil de Travaux*, XXIX, 1920, pp. 44ff.
    Moret, *Le Rituel du Culte Divin Journalier en Egypte* (Paris 1902), pp. 9–66.
21. Moret, *op. cit.*, pp. 235ff.
    Breasted, *Development of Religion and Thought in Ancient Egypt*, p. 39.
    M. Murray, *Ancient Egypt*, II. 1912, pp. 33ff.; 1932, pp. 70ff.
22. von Bissing-Kees, *Das Re Heiligtum des Konigs Ne.Waser-Re* (Munchen 1922).
    B. van de Walle, *La Nouvelle Clio*, VI. 1954, pp. 283ff.
23. *Acta Orientalia*, XXIII. 1956, pp. 383ff.
24. A. Fakhry, *Annales du Service des Antiquités de l'Egypte*, XLII. 1943, pp. 449ff.
25. A. H. Gardiner, JEA, II. 1925, p. 124.
    Frankfort, *op. cit.*, p. 79.
26. Moret, *op. cit.*, p. 105, Fig. 21.
27. Murray, *op. cit.*, 1926. Pt. I. p. 34.
28. Moret, *op. cit.*, p. 256.
29. H. Gauthier, *Les Fêtes du Dieu Min* (Cairo 1931).
    Frankfort, *op. cit.*, pp. 188ff.
    Wilson and Allen, *Medinet Habu* (Chicago 1940), IV. Pls. 196–217.
30. JEA, II. 1915, p. 125.
31. Moret, *op. cit.*, pp. 283ff.
    Transactions of the Third International Congress of the History of Religions (Oxford 1908), pp. 216ff.
32. Erman, *Handbook of Egyptian Religion* (London 1907), pp. 37ff.
33. *Medinet Habu*, III. Pl. 140; II. 55ff.
34. Nelson, JNES, Vol. I. 1942, pp. 145, 150ff.
35. Nelson, JNES, Vol. VIII. 1949, pp. 201ff.
36. Frankfort, *op. cit.*, p. 221.
37. Thureau-Dangin, *Les Inscriptions de Sumer et Akkad* (Paris 1905), pp. 47, 49.
38. Langdon, *The Legend of Etana and the Eagle* (Paris 1932), p. 9, 1.20.
39. Jacobsen, *The Sumerian King-List* (Chicago 1939), pp. 169ff.
    JAOS, LIX. 1939, pp. 86ff.
    Thureau-Dangin, *Sumerische und Akkadische Koniginschiften* (Leipzig 1907), pp. 156ff.
    Labat, *Caractère Religieux de la Royauté Assyro-Babylonienne* (Paris 1939), pp. 63ff.
40. Thureau-Dangin, *Sumerische und Akkadische Koniginschiften*, p. 219.
41. Barton, *The Royal Inscriptions of Sumer and Akkad* (New Haven 1929), p. 275.
42. Harper, *Code of Hammurabi* (London 1904), p. 3.
43. S. Smith, JEA, VIII. 1922, pp. 41ff.
44. *The Sumerian King-List*, pp. 38ff.
45. Frankfort, *op. cit.*, p. 297.
46. Frankfort, *op. cit.*

Zimmern, *Berichte über die Vervandlungen der kgl. Sachischen Gesellschaft der Wissenschaften Phil-hist. Klasse.* 68. 1916.

47. Chiera, *Sumerian Religious Texts*, No. 1. col. V. II, 18ff.
Langdon, JRAS, 1926, pp. 35ff.
Lambert and Tourney, *Revue Biblique*, 1948, pp. 408ff.
Revue d'Assyriologie, 1949, pp. 128ff.

48. AB. 11. 65ff., 146ff.

49. Virolleaud, *La Légende Phénicienne de Danel* (Paris 1950), p. 145.
Virolleaud, *Les Poèmes de Ras Shamra* (Paris 1939), pp. 10ff.

50. I. AB. ii. 1–6.
II. AB. iv. 68.
III. AB.

51. Gaster, *Thespis*, pp. 115ff.
Gordon, *Ugaritic Literature* (Rome 1949), pp. 9ff.
Driver, *Canaanite Myths and Legends* (London 1956), pp. 73ff.
AB. 67, II: 3ff.; VI. 8ff. 62: I: 11–15, 34.

52. Gordon, *op. cit.*, p. 4.

53. Engnell, *Studies in Divine Kingship in the Ancient Near East* (Uppsala 1943), pp. 173ff.
Gaster, *Thespis*, pp. 119ff.
J. de Fraine, *Analecta Biblica* (Rome 1954), pp. 43ff. (1956), pp. 59ff.

54. Ezek. xxviii. 12–14.
Widengren, *Revue Biblique*, II. 1943, pp. 71, 74.

55. Albright, *Archaeology and the History of Israel* (Baltimore 1946), p. 90.

56. Ginsberg, BASOR, Supplementary Studies, 2/3, 1946, pp. 6ff.

57. Ginsberg, *op. cit.*, p. 8.

58. J. Gray, *The Krt Text in the Literature of Ras Shamra* (Leiden 1955), p. 2.
Avan Selms, *Marriage and Family Life in Ugaritic Literature* (London 1954), p. 141.
Driver, *op. cit.*, p. 5.

59. Krt, A., 171ff.
Gordon, *Ugaritic Handbook*, 125, 17ff.; 128, iii, 13–15.

60. *Ugaritic Handbook*, 126. iii.

61. Gray, *op. cit.*, pp. 5ff.

62. Judges viii. 27.

63. Judges vi. 25ff.

64. Judges v.

65. I Kings xii. 28.
II Chron. xi. 15; xiii. 8.

66. II Sam. vi. 17.

67. I Kings xi. 36.
Ps. lxxxix. 3ff.

68. II Sam. vi. 14.

69. I Kings ix. 25.

70. Hos. ii. 3–5; x. 9; xiii. 9–11.

71. I Sam. viii. 7; x. 17, 19. cf. xii, xv.

72. Ps. lxxxix. 26ff.
Test. Judah xxiv. i.

73. I Macc. xiv. 35.

74. Test. Levi viii. 14; xviii. 2–14.

75. Ps. cx. 4.
Gen. xiv. 18ff.
Heb. vii. 13.
Johnson, *Sacral Kingship in Ancient Israel* (Cardiff 1955), pp. 32, 46ff.

76. Snaith, *The Jewish New Year Festival* (London 1947), p. 218.

77. cf. Widengren, *Sakrales Koenigtum in Alten Testament und in Judentum* (Stuttgart 1955), p. 44ff.

78. Ezek. xxxiv. 24; xxxvii 25.
cf. Mic. v. 2.
Zech. vi. 9ff.
Haggai ii. 23.

79. Zech. i; ii. 4ff; vi. 9ff.
    Ezra iii. 1–6.
    Haggai i-ii.
80. R. S. Hardy, *American Journal of Semitic Languages*, LVIII. 1941, pp. 182ff.
81. Goetze, ANET, pp. 394ff.
    Gurney, *Hittite Prayers of Mursili II* (Liverpool 1940).
82. ANET, p. 393.
83. Garstang, *The Hittite Empire*, pp. 116ff.
    Garstang, *The Syrian Goddess* (London 1912), pp. 7ff.
84. *Keilschriftexte aus Boghazköi*, II, 5, iii. 38ff.
85. Goetze, *Language*, XXVII, 1951, p. 467.
    Otten, *Orientalistische Literaturzeitung*, LI. 1956. cols. 102–5.
    KUB XXXVI. 95.
86. *Keilschriftexte aus Boghazköi*, III. 4, i. 16–18.
    Goetze, *Die Annalen des Mursilis* (Leipzig 1933), p. 20.
87. KUB XXV. 14. i. 10ff.
88. Goetze, *Kleinasiatische Forschungen* (Weimar 1930), I. pp. 161ff.
    cf. ANET, pp. 394ff.
89. KUB XXIX. i. 17ff.
    Goetze, *Journal of Cuneiform Studies*, I. 1947, p. 91.
90. Goetze, ANET, 195.
    Güterbock, JAOS, Supplement 17. 1954, pp. 17ff.
91. Gurney, in *Myth, Ritual and Kingship* (Oxford 1958), p. 118.
92. *Palace of Minos*, Vol. I. p. 5; Vol. IV. pp. 907ff.
93. Apollodoros, III. 2ff.
94. Wace, *Mycenae* (Princeton 1949), pp. 86ff.
95. Wace, *Archaeologia*, LXXXII, 1932, pp. 146ff.
    Evans, *The Prehistoric Tombs of Knossos* (London 1906), pp. 165, 170ff.
    Evans, *The Shaft-graves and Beehive Tombs of Mycenae* (London 1929), pp. 6off.
    C. E. Mylonas, *Ancient Mycenae* (London 1957), pp. 85ff.
96. G. Kato, *Die Schachtgraber von Mykenai* (Munich 1930–33), pp. 342.
    H. J. Kantor, *Journal of American Archaeology*, LI. No. 1. 1947, pp. 5off.
    Blegen and Wace, *Klio*, 1939, pp. 131ff.
97. Wace, BSA, XXV. 1921–22, pp. 224ff.
98. Nilsson, *Minoan-Mycenaean Religion*, pp. 468, 558.
    Persson, *Religion of Greece in Prehistoric Times*, pp. 149ff.
99. Aristotle, *Athen. Pol.* 57.
100. Wace, *Mycenae*, 1949, p. 86.
101. Nilsson, *op. cit.*, p. xxiv.
102. Aristotle, *Athen. Pol.* 3.
103. *Iliad*, XIV, 346f.

CHAPTER V: THE SEASONAL FESTIVALS

1. Brugsch, *Zeitschrift für aegyptische Sprache und Alterthumskunde*, XIX. 1881, pp. 71ff.
   M. A. Murray, *The Osireion at Abydos* (London 1902), pp. 27ff.
2. Budge, *The Gods of the Egyptians* (London 1904), Vol. II. pp. 131ff.
3. Brugsch, *Thesaurus*, V. 1891. p. 1190.
4. Murray, *op. cit.*, p. 28.
5. Brugsch, *Matériaux pour servir à la reconstruction du calendrier*, Pl. 9.
   Recueil de Travaux relatifs, Vol. IV. 1882, pp. 32ff.
6. PT. 1751.
   Moret, *The Nile and Egyptian Civilization* (London 1927), p. 181.
7. Sethe, *Urkunden des aegyptischen Altertums* (Leipzig 1908), Vol. IV. pp. 134ff.
8. Gardiner and Davies, *The Tomb of Amenemhet* (London 1915), p. 115.
9. Frankfort, *Kingship and the Gods*, pp. 123ff.
10. Blackman, *Analecta Orientalia*, XVII. 1938, p. 2.
11. Wainwright, JEA, XVII. 1931, pp. 185ff.

12. Gauthier, *Les Fêtes du Dieu Min* (Paris 1913), pp. 194, 235.
    Petrie, *The Making of Egypt* (London 1939), p. 46.
13. Wilson and Allen, *Medinet Habu*, IV.
14. Frankfort, *op. cit.*, p. 188.
15. Gardiner, JEA, II. 1915, p. 125.
16. Moret, *Du Caractère Religieux de la Royauté Pharaonique*, pp. 104ff.
17. Thureau-Dangin, *Rituels accadiens* (Paris 1921), pp. 127–154.
    A Sachs, ANET, pp. 531ff.
18. Frankfort, *Cylinder Seals* (London 1939), pp. 117ff. Pl. XXI. a-d.
19. Langdon, *Tammuz and Ishtar* (Oxford 1914), pp. 10ff.
20. *Vorderasiatische Abteilung* (VAT) 9555, Berlin Museum, K.3476.
    Pallis, *The Babylonian Akitu Festival* (London 1926), pp. 252ff.
21. Zimmern, *Der alte Orient*, XXV. 1926, p. 18.
22. Pallis, *op. cit.*, pp. 124ff.
    Delitzsch, *Mitteilungen der deutschen Orient Gesselschaft*, No. 33. 1907, p. 34; No. 38. 1908,
    p. 19.
23. Thureau-Dangin, *op. cit.*, pp. 86ff.
    Pallis, *op. cit.*, pp, 19ff.
24. cf. Virolleaud, *Syria*, XV. 1935, pp. 29–45; XVII. 1936, pp. 150ff.
25. Gordon, *Orientalia*, XXII. 1953, pp. 79ff.
26. I Kings xvii.
    Gen. xii. 10; xli. 1ff., 57.
    Ruth i.
27. *Legend of Aqht*, I. 44–46.
28. cf. Joel ii. 25.
29. AB. 49 : 8–VI. 31.
30. II. AB. VI : 45.
31. cf. BASOR, 1936. No. 63, p. 29, n. 36; No. 71. 1938, p. 39, n. 38.
    Virolleaud, *La Déesse 'Anat* (Paris 1938), p. 97.
32. Exod. iii. 13–15.
    Rowley, *From Joseph to Joshua* (1950), pp. 149ff.
    cf. Meek, *Hebrew Origins* (1950), pp. 93ff.
33. *The Golden Bough*, Pt. IV. pp. 176ff.
34. Exod. xii. 12ff.; xvi. 1–8.
35. Exod. xiii. 15ff.
36. Robertson Smith, *Religion of the Semites* (London 1927), p. 345.
37. Exod. ii. 22ff.
    Curtiss, *Primitive Semitic Religion Today* (London 1902), pp. 226ff.
38. Exod. xii. 21ff.; xi. 4.
39. Exod. xii. 13, 23, 27; xi. 4.
40. Buchanan Gray, *Sacrifice in the Old Testament* (London 1925), p. 364.
41. Exod. xiii. 15ff.; xxiv. 18.
    Lev. xxiii. 10.
    Deut. xvi. 9.
42. Nielsson, *Handbuch der altar-bischen Altertumskunde* (Leipzig 1927), I. p. 213ff.
43. Exod. xiii. 15ff.; xiii. 4; xxiv. 18; xxiii. 15ff.
    Lev. xxiii. 10f.
44. Lev. xxiii. 17.
45. Exod. xii. 26; xiii. 14.
46. *Pesahim*, 10.
47. I Kings xxiii. 21ff.
48. Exod. xii. 1–20.
    Lev. xxiii.
    Num. ix. 1–14; xxviii, xxix.
49. Exod. xxiii. 16; xxxiv. 22.
50. Exod. xii.
51. Exod. xxiii. 16 (E); xxiv. 22 (J).
    Num. xxix. 1.
    Lev. xxiii. 24.

52. Exod. xii. 2ff.
53. Zech. xiv. 16ff.
54. Moscati, *L'epigrafia ebraica antica 1935-1950* (Rome 1951), pp. 8ff.
55. Ps. xlvii; lxviii. 9.
56. Ps. xciii, xcv–xcix.
57. Mowinckel, *Psalmenstudien* (Kristiana 1922), II. pp. 102ff.
    P. Volz, *Das Neujahrsfest Jahwas* (Tübingen 1912), p. 15.
    Johnson, *Sacral Kingship in Ancient Israel* (Cardiff 1955), pp. 53ff.
    Snaith, *The Jewish New Year Festival*, pp. 195ff.
    Oesterley, *Myth and Ritual* (London 1933), pp. 125ff.
58. Ps. xciii. cf. xxix.
59. Mowinckel, *op. cit.*, p. 301.
    H. Schmidt, *Die Thronfahrt Jahves am Fest der Jahreswunde im alten Israel* (Tübingen 1927).
60. Snaith, *op. cit.*, p. 102ff.
    Johnson, *op. cit.*, p. 61, no. 2.
61. II Sam. vi. 133ff.
62. *Sukkah*, v. 3, 4.
    Tos Suk, iv. 4ff.
    Middoth, ii. 6.
    cf. Ps. lxviii.
63. Ezek. viii. 16.
    Thackeray, *The Septuagint and Jewish Worship* (London 1921), p. 64ff.
    Ps. xxiv. 7ff.; lxxxvi. 1.
64. Hooke, *The Origins of Early Semitic Ritual* (London 1938), p. 54. (S. Smith, JRAS 1928, pp. 849ff.
65. Jer. ii. 2.
    Ezek. xvi. 8.
    Hos. ii. 14–20.
66. *Sukkah*, iv. 9, 10.
    Rosh hashana, 16, 9.
67. Hvidberg, *Graad og Latter i det Gamle Testamente* (Copenhagen 1938), pp. 85ff., 115ff.
    Gressman, *The Expositor* (London 1925), Series IX.3, p. 422.
68. Ezek. viii. 14–16.
69. Widengren, *Sakrales Königtum im Alten Testament und im Judentum* (Stuttgart 1955), p. 63ff.
    cf. Neh. viii–ix.
70. Ezek. xlv. 13, 20.
71. Lev. xvi. cf. xvii. 2.
72. Lev. viii. 14ff.; xxvii. 11.
    Deut. xii. 23.
73. Lev. xiv. 4.
    Zech. v. 5, 11.
74. Isa. lv. 6, 7; xliv. 22.
    Ps. xlv. 6, 8–14; li. 16ff.; lxix. 30ff.
75. *Yoma*, viii. 8.
    cf. Lev. xvi. 30.
    Shabbat Shabbaton.
    Lev. xxiii. 32.
76. *Keilschrifttexte aus Boghazköi*, ii. 5, iii. 38ff.
77. KUB XXX. 42. i. 5–7.
78. Goetze, ANET, pp. 125ff.
    KUB XII. 66, XVII. 5, 6.
79. Gaster, *Thespis*, pp. 317ff.
80. O. R. Gurney, *The Hittites*, pp. 153ff.
81. KUB XVII. 95, III. 9–17.
82. KUB XXXVI. 97.
83. J. Freiderich, in *Mitteilungen der Alterorientalischen Gesellschaft*, LV. 1928–29, pp. 46ff.
84. Goetze, *Kleinasien*, p. 155.
85. Aristotle, *Ethica Nicomachea*, VIII. p. 1160a.

86. J. E. Harrison, *Prolegomena to the Study of Greek Religion* (Camb. 1903), pp. 120ff.
    Farnell, CGS, Vol. III. pp. 75ff.
    Nilsson, *Griechische Feste von religiöer, Bedeuntung, mit Ausschluss der Attischen* (Leipzig 1906), pp. 106ff.
    Deubner, *Attische Feste* (Berlin 1932), pp. 179ff.
87. Nilsson, *Greek Popular Religion* (Columbia Press 1940), pp. 51ff.
88. *Palace of Minos* (1928), Vol. II. pp. 578ff.
89. Hesiod, *Theogony*, 970.
90. T. W. Allen, E. E. Sykes, T. W. Halliday, *The Homeric Hymn* (Oxford, 3rd ed. 1936), pp. 10ff.
91. Farnell, CGS, Vol. III. pp. 177, 183.
92. Hippolytus, *Refutatio omnium haeresium*, V. 8.
93. Cicero, *De legibus*, II. 63.
    Plutarch, *De facie in orbe lunae*, p. 943b.
94. Proclus, *ad Plato, Timaeus* (Lobeck), p. 293.
95. Farnell, CGS, Vol. III. p. 185.
96. Julian, *Adversus Christianos*, i. pp. 167ff.
    Pindar, *Frag.* i. 35 (Bergk), p. 127.
    Plato, *Laws*, 70c.
    Plato, *Phaedo*, 70c.
    Origen, *Contra Celsum*, iv. 17.
97. *Pausanias*, I. iv. 1, 2.
    Aristophanes, *Frogs.* 353ff.
98. Livy, 8–19.

CHAPTER VI: THE CULT OF THE DEAD

1. Elliot Smith, JEA, 1914, p. 192.
2. Blackman, JEA, V. 1918, pp. 118ff.
3. J. A. Wilson, JNES, III. 1944, p. 208.
    The Mastaba of Mereruka, Vol. II. Chicago Oriental Institute Proceedings XXXIX. 1.130.
4. J. A. Wilson, JNES, III. 1944, pp. 205ff.
5. PT. 383, 467, 756, 891, 913.
6. PT. *Ut*, 273, PT. 484, 1118ff.
7. PT. 812f.
8. Breasted, *The Dawn of Conscience* (London 1934), pp. 21ff., 125ff.
9. TR. 37; Rec. 30: 189.
10. *Coffin Texts*, I. 181.
11. *The Papyrus of Ani*, Ed. Budge, p. 26.
12. *The Book of the Dead*, Chap. VI.
13. PT. *Ut.* 467; PT. 364, 390, 482, 891, 913, 1090, 1118ff.
14. Thureau-Dangin, *Hilprecht Anniversary Volume* (Leipzig 1909), p. 161.
    Watchin, *Kish* (Paris 1934), Vol. IV. pp. 17ff.
15. Kramer, ANET, p. 50.
16. Kramer, ANET, p. 90.
17. Kramer, ANET, pp. 42ff.
    cf. Kramer, *Sumerian Mythology* (Philadelphia 1944), p. 97ff.
18. ANET, p. 87.
19. ANET, p. 96.
20. A. Heidel, *The Gilgamesh Epic and Old Testament Parallels* (Chicago 1946), pp. 1ff.
    Speiser, ANET, pp. 72ff.
21. Speiser, ANET, pp. 101ff.
    Heidel, *The Babylonian Genesis* (Chicago 2nd ed. 1951), pp. 148ff.
22. Heidel, *op. cit.*, p. 123.
23. ANET, p. 103.
    Heidel, *op. cit.*, p. 153.
24. I. AB. 1–62. (ANET, pp. 139ff.)
25. *Aqht* C(i), 38ff.; ANET, p. 153ff.
26. ANET, 134–147.
27. AB, 67.VI.8–25.

28. AB, 62.9–18.
29. Ezek. viii. 14.
    Zech. xii. 11.
30. Judges xi. 37–40.
31. II Sam. xii. 20.
32. II Sam. xii. 15ff.
33. II Sam. xiii. 19.
34. Vincent, *Revue Biblique*, 1925, pp. 161ff.
    Dussaud, *Syria*, V. 1924, pp. 135ff.
35. Tobit iv. 17.
36. D. Mackenzie, *Palestine Exploration Fund Annual*, II. 1912–13, pp. 58, 67.
    Macalister, *Excavations at Gezer* (London 1912), Vol. I. pp. 300ff.
    E. Grant, *Beth Shemesh* (Haverford 1929), pp. 56ff.
37. Kenyon, *Digging up Jericho*, pp. 195, 212ff., 235ff.
38. Mackenzie, *op. cit.*, p. 83.
39. I Sam. xxv. i. cf. xxviii. 3.
40. I Kings i. 34.
41. II Sam. ii. 32.
42. II Sam. xvii. 23.
43. I Kings ii. 10.
44. I Kings xi. 43; xiv. 31; xv. 8, 24 etc.
45. II Chron. xxxii. 33.
46. II Kings xxi. 18, 26. cf. xxiii. 30.
    II Chron. xxxv. 24.
47. Gen. xxiii. 17ff.; xxv. 9; xlix. 31.
48. Gen. xxxv. 19ff.
    I Sam. x. 2.
49. Gen. xxxv. 8.
50. Jos. xix. 32.
51. Exod. xiii. 19.
52. I Sam. xxviii. 3.
53. I Sam. xxviii. 7ff.
54. Lev. xix. 31.
    Deut. xviii. 11.
55. Isa. viii. 19; xxix. 4.
    Deut. xviii. 11ff.
    Lev. xx. 6, 27.
56. Ps. lxxxviii. 11ff.; xciv. 17; cxv. 17.
    Job xxvi. 6; xxviii. 22.
    Isa. xiv. 9ff.
    Prov. ii. 18ff.; ix. 18.
57. Job xiv. 21.
    Eccles. ix. 2, 5.
58. Isa. xxvi. 14; xxxviii. 18.
    Ps. vi. 5; xxx. 9; cxv. 17.
59. Lods, *La Croyance à la Vie Future et le Culte des Morts dans l'antiquité Israélite* (Paris 1906),
    pp. 108ff.
60. Gen. xiv. 5; xv. 20.
    Deut. iii. 11, 13.
    Jos. xii. 4; xiii. 12; xvii. 15.
61. Gen. vi. 1–7.
    cf. Lagrange, *Etudes sur les Religions Semitiques* (Paris 1905), pp. 318ff.
62. Gen. ii. 7.
    Job x. 10ff.
    Ps. cxxxix. 13ff.
    Eccles. xi. 5; xii. 7.
    Ezek. xxxvii. 1ff.
63. Eccles. xii. 7.
64. Deut. xxv. 5ff.

65. Ecclus. xli. 1-4.
66. Ecclus. xlvi. 12.
    cf. Ezek. xxxvii. 1-14.
67. Ezek. xxxii. 27.
68. I Sam. xvii. 5; xxxi. 9ff.
    II Sam. iv. 12.
    Job iii. 15.
69. Jer. xxxi. 15.
70. Ps. lxxiii. 24ff.
    Wisdom iii. 1-9; iv. 17-19; v. 5.
    Isa. xxvi. 19.
    Dan. xii. 2.
71. Job xix. 25-27.
72. Dan. xii. 2ff.
73. Job xiv. 14.
74. II Macc. vii. 9-11; xii. 43ff.; xiv. 36, 46.
75. I Enoch xxii. 2.
76. II Macc. iii. 39.
    I Enoch i. 2; vi. 2; ix. 3.
77. I Enoch xviii. 2ff.; ix. 2; xxxiii. 1ff.
78. II Enoch iii-xxi.
    II (IV) Esdras vvi. 81-98.
    III Baruch ii-xi.
79. Parables of Enoch xxxix. 3ff.; xli. 2; lxxi.
80. Apoc. Mosis xxxv.1; xxxviii. 4; xli. 2.
    cf. II Enoch viii. 1, 5.
81. II Cor. xii. 2ff.
82. Ascension of Isaiah ix. 7.
83. I Enoch lxxxvii. 3, 4; lxxxix. 3, 4.
84. I Enoch xx. 7; lx. 8; xxvii. 21.
    Testament of Levi xviii. 10.
85. II Kings xvi. 3.
    II Chron. xxviii. 3; xxxiii. 6.
    Jer. vii. 31; xxxii. 35.
86. I Enoch xxii. 11; xxvii. 2; liii. 2-5; liv. 1, 2.
    Psalms of Solomon xiv. 61; xv. 11. cf. xvi. 1ff.
87. II Enoch x. 1ff; xl. 12ff.
    Apoc. of Abraham xiv.
    cf. I Enoch x. 4.
88. Sibylline Oracles iv. 43, 185ff.
89. II(IV) Esdras vii. 36.
    II Enoch viii. 3; ix. 1.
90. II Enoch xlii. 36.
91. II Enoch xl. 12ff.
92. II Baruch xxx. 4; xliv. 12ff.; xlviii. 39, 43; lxiv. 7; lxxxv. 13.
93. cf. St Matthew xiii. 42; xviii. 8; xxv. 41. (Henceforth referred to as St Mt.)
    St Mark ix. 43.
94. St Mark iii. 28.
    St Mt. v. 20; xii. 31ff.
    St Luke xii. 10; 47ff.; xvi. 19-31.
95. St John iii. 15ff.; v. 26; vi. 54ff.; x. 28; xvii. 3.
96. St John v. 24ff.; vi. 40; xiv. 2ff.
97. St John v. 28ff.
    cf. Charles, *Eschatology* (London 1913), p. 429.
98. St John iii. 36.
99. Dussaud, *Revue de l'histoire des religions*, LVIII. 1908, p. 368.
    Picard, *Les Origines du Polythéisme Hellénique* (Paris 1930), p. 123.
    Nilsson, *Minoan-Mycenaean Religion*, p. 438.
    Webster, *From Mycenae to Homer* (London 1958), Pl. 6.

100. Mylonas and J. K. Papademetriou, *Archaeology*, Vol. V. 1952, pp. 194ff.
     Wace, BSA, XLVIII. 1953, pp. 7ff.
101. Blegen and Wace, *Symbolae Osloenses*, Fasc. IX. 1930, pp. 28ff.
     A. W. Persson, *New Tombs at Dendra near Midea* (Lund 1945), p. 23.
102. Nilsson, *op. cit.*, pp. 587ff.
103. Wace and Blegen, *Klio*, 1939, p. 147.
     Persson, *op. cit.*, pp. 146, 164ff.
     Mylonas, *Studies Presented to David M. Robinson* (St Louis 1951), Vol. I. pp. 100ff.
     Matinatos, *Studies Presented to David M. Robinson*, Vol. I. p. 127.
104. *Palace of Minos*, Vol. II. pp. 39ff.
105. Homer, *Iliad*, XVI. 456, 674; XXIII. 50. (Henceforth referred to as *Il.*)
106. *Il.* XXIII. 171ff.
107. Nilsson, *Homer and Mycenae* (London 1933), pp. 155ff.
     Persson, *op. cit.*, pp. 12, 69ff.
108. *Il.* XXXIII. 43ff.
109. *Il.* XXIV. 664, 710ff.
110. *Il.* XXIV. 237, 245ff.
111. *Il.* XXIII. 104.
     Od. XI. 51.
112. *Od.* XI. 140ff.
113. *Od.* X. 494.
114. *Od.* IV. 561ff.; V. 135ff.; 209ff.; XXIII. 335ff.
115. *Od.* XI. 488 ff.
116. *Od.* XI. 29ff.
117. Rhode, *Psyche* (London 1925), p. 55.
118. Plutarch, *De anima*, Frags. Vol. VIII. p. 23.
     Stobaeus, Ed. Meineke, Vol. IV. p. 107.
119. Pindar, *Olympia*, II. 53.
     Pindar, *Frags.* 131, 133. (Bergk).
     cf. Plato, *Phaedrus*, 249A.
120. Pindar, *Frags.* 129, 137. (Schroeder ed.)
121. Plato, *Philebus*, 30C.
     Plato, *Timaeus*, 46B, 69A–70C.
     Phaedrus, 245, 248C–249.
     Plato, *Phaedo*, 72E–81.
     Plato, *Meno*, 81ff.
     cf. A. E. Taylor, *Plato and his Works* (London 1929), p. 308, n.1.
122. Plato, *Republic*, 500D, 540B, 613A.
     Phaedrus, 248ff.

CHAPTER VII: COSMOLOGY

1. Sethe, *Dramatische Texte zu altaegyptischen Mysterienspielen* (Leipzig 1928), pp. 47ff.
2. Sethe, *op. cit.*, Vol. I. pp. 53ff.
   Sethe, *Zeitschrift für aegyptische Sprache und Altertumskunde* (Leipzig 1901), XXXIX.
   pp. 39ff.
3. ANET, p. 5.
4. Breasted, *Development of Religion and Thought in Ancient Egypt*, p. 47.
   Breasted, *Dawn of Conscience*, p. 37.
5. PT. 1479, 1521.
6. Frankfort, *The Birth of Civilization in the Near East* (London 1951), pp. 82ff.
   Frankfort, *Kingship and the Gods*, p. 19.
7. Wilson, *The Burden of Egypt* (Chicago 1951), pp. 17, 45ff.
8. PT. 1594a.
9. Wilson, ANET, p. 431.
   Wilson, *The Burden of Egypt*, pp. 142ff.
   Frankfort, *Ancient Egyptian Religion* (New York 1948), p. 43.
10. PT. 1992–2001.
11. PT. 265b–c.

12. Sethe, *Amun und die acht Urgötter von Hermopolis* (Berlin 1929).
    G. Roeder, *Urkunden zur Religion des alten Aegypten* (Leipzig 1915), pp. 13ff.
13. Wilson, ANET, p. 251.
14. Frankfort, *Kingship and the Gods*, p. 51.
    Sethe, *Die altaegyptischen Pyramidentexte* (Leipzig 1908–22), 1775.
15. Badawi, *Der Gott Chnum* (Glückstadt 1937), pp. 56ff.
    Budge, *From Fetish to God in Ancient Egypt* (London 1934), p. 256.
16. R. V. Lanzone, *Dizionario di mitologia egiziana*, 1881–6. Pl. 336.4.
17. PT. 819C., 632.
18. Kees, *Totenglauben und Jenseitsvorstellungen der alten Aegypter* (Leipzig 1926), pp. 209ff.
    Plutarch, *De Iside et Osiride*, pp. 39, 43.
19. Nelson, *Ramses III's Temple* (London 1928), Pt. I. Pl. 54.
20. Heidel, *The Babylonian Genesis* (Chicago 1951), Tablet I, pp. 18ff.
21. Heidel, *op. cit.*, Tablets IV and V, pp. 37ff.
22. Heidel, *op. cit.*, Tablet VI, pp. 49ff.
    ANET, pp. 68ff.
23. cf. Jacobsen, *The Intellectual Adventure of Ancient Man*, pp. 180, 200.
24. *Textes religieux sumériens du Louvre* (Paris 1930), 10, 36ff., 72.
25. Chiera, *Sumerian Religious Texts* (Upland 1924), pp. 28ff.
26. Chiera, *Sumerian Epics and Myths* (Chicago 1934), p. 116.
    Langdon, *Sumerian Liturgies and Psalms* (Philadelphia 1919), p. 14.
    Kramer, *Sumerian Mythology*, pp. 53ff., 69ff., 72ff.
27. Kramer, ANET, p. 164.
28. Thureau-Dangin, *Les Inscriptions de Sumer et d'Akkad* (Paris 1905), p. 219.
29. Barton, *The Royal Inscriptions of Sumer and Akkad* (New Haven 1929), p. 275.
30. Otten, *Die Uberlieferungen des Telipinu-Mythus* (*Mitteilungen der Vorderasiatische-aegyptischen Gesellschaft* [Leipzig 1942]), 46.1.
    KUB XXXIII.
    ANET, pp. 126ff.
31. J. A. Montgomery, JAOS, LIII. 1933, pp. 102ff.
    Albright, *Journal of Biblical Literature*, 1940, p. 106.
    Albright, *Archaeology and the Religion of Israel* (London 1953), p. 72.
32. Gaster, *Thespis*, p. 171.
    Albright, *American Journal of Semitic Languages and Literature*, XXXV (1919–20), pp. 161ff.
33. Gen. ii. 10–14.
    Albright, *American Journal of Semitic Languages and Literature*, XXXIX (1922), pp. 15ff.
34. AB. 51 : VII, 14ff.; 49: IV, 27, 29; 67: V. 14ff.
35. Schaeffer, *The Cuneiform Texts of Ras Shamra-Ugarit* (London 1939), p. 8.
36. Ps. xcv. 3; xcvi. 4ff.; xcvii. 7. cf. lxxiii. 3, 8; lxxxii. 8.
37. Ps. xciii. 1; xcv. 5; xcvi. 10.
    cf. I Sam. ii. 8.
    cf. Isa. xxxvii. 16.
38. Gen. i. 14–18.
39. cf. Gunkel, *Schöpfung und Chaos willzeit und Endzeit* (Göttingen 1895).
40. Isa. li. 9ff. cf. xxx. 7.
    Ezra xxix. 3; xxxii. 2ff.
41. Isa. li. 9.
42. Gen. i. 21.
    Ps. cxlviii. 7.
    Job xxvi. 12.
43. Isa. xxvii. 1.
44. Job xl. 25–41.
45. Job iii. 8.
46. Ps. lxxiv. 13ff.
    Gen. i. 9ff.
47. Ps. xxiv, xxxiii. 6ff.; lxv; xcv. 4; xcvii. 7; civ.
    cf. Job xxviii. 23ff.; xxxvii ff.
48. Isa. lx. 1ff.; xl. 22.
    Ps. civ. 3ff.

x

49. Ps. civ. 3, 32ff.
50. Isa. xlii. 8; xlviii. 11.
51. Ps. xix. 2; civ. 31.
52. Job xxxviii.
    Jer. xxxiii. 20, 25.
53. Gen. i. 1–26.
54. Babylonian Tablet VII. 2.
    Kramer, *Sumerian Mythology*, p. 39.
    King, *The Seven Tablets of Creation* (London 1902), p. 123.
55. Humbert, *Revue d'histoire et de philosophie religieuses*, XV. 1935, pp. 1, 27.
56. Ps. lxxiv. 12–14; civ; cxxxvi.
    Isa. li. 9.
57. Gunkel, *Genesis* (Göttingen 1910), pp. 25ff.
58. Ezek. xxviii. 12–14.
59. Gen. iii.
60. cf. Heidel, *The Babylonian Genesis*, pp. 125ff.
61. Gen. x. 19. cf. xiv.
62. *Il.* XV. 192.
63. *Il.* XV. 197ff.
64. Güterbrock, *American Journal of Archaeology*, 1948 pp. 123ff.
    Goetze, ANET, pp. 121ff.
65. Speiser, JAOS, 62. 1942, pp. 98ff.
66. cf. J. Adams, *Stob.* i. i. 12, in *Vitality of Platonism*, Essay IV (London 1911), pp. 105ff.
67. *Il.* XIV. 201, 241.
68. *Od.* XI. 315.
69. *Il.* XVII. 425.
    Od. III. 2; XI. 315.
70. G. Murray, *The Five Stages of Greek Religion* (Oxford 1925), pp. 66ff.
71. Hesiod, *Theogony*, 116ff.
72. Orpheus, *Frags.* 210ff. (Kern).
    Guthrie, *Orpheus and Greek Religion* (London 1952), pp. 107ff.
73. Guthrie, *op. cit.*, p. 128.
74. Diogenes, L., *Prooem.* 3.
75. Guthrie, *op. cit.*, p. 75.
76. Xenophanes, *Frag.* ii. 23, 30.
    cf. W. Jaeger, *The Theology of the Early Greek Philosophers* (Oxford 1947), p. 45.
77. Heraclitus, *Frag.* 20, 22, 28, 65, 67.
78. Parmenides, *Frag.* B. 8.
79. Parmenides, *Frag.* B. 12.
80. Parmenides, *Frag.* B. 5, 12.
81. Plato, *Timaeus*, 30A.
82. *Timaeus*, 41A.
83. Aristotle, *Metaphysics*, I. 1, 990, 996ff.; VI. 1, 8; XIII. 5.
84. *Metaphysics*, XI.
    Aristotle, *Physics*, VIII. 6, 2586, 10ff.
85. *Metaphysics, Met.* I. 983b. 6.

CHAPTER VIII: DIVINATION, ASTROLOGY AND PROPHECY

1. cf. Malinowski, *Magic, Science and Religion*, ed. R. Redfield (London 1948), p. 249.
   C. K. Ogden and I. A. Richards, *The Meaning of Meaning* (London 1936), p. 315.
   G. N. Mead, *The Philosophy of the Act* (Chicago 1938), pp. 518, 547.
2. Num. xxii. 38.
3. *Rig-Veda*, i. 14, 163, 179; ii. 2, 10; vi. 5, 7, 19; viii. 3, 9.
   Aitareya Brahmana, vii. 18.
4. Acts ii. 4, 17; x. 46; xix. 6.
   I Cor. xii. 10, 30.
5. cf. R. A. Knox, *Enthusiasm* (Oxford 1950).
6. Eph. v. 18ff.

7. Zimmern, *Beiträge zur Kenntnis der Babylonischen Religion* (Leipzig 1901), p. 116. No. 24. lines 1, 23.
8. J. Nougayrol, *Ecole pratique des Hautes Etudes, Annuaire*, 1944–45, p. 8. No. 14.
9. Dhorme, *La Religion Assyro-Babylonienne* (Paris 1910), p. 298.
10. Zimmern, *op. cit.*, p. 86.
    Dhorme, *op. cit.*, p. 197.
    F. Wetzel, *Zeitschrift für Assyriologie und verwandte Gebiete*, XXX. 1915, pp. 16ff., 101ff.
11. Jastrow, *Zeitschrift für Assyriologie und verwandte Gebiete*, XX. 1907, pp. 118ff.
    Jastrow, *Die Religion Babyloniens und Assyriens* (Giessen 1912), II. pp. 213ff.
12. Lam. ii. 11.
    Prov. vii. 23.
13. Tobit vi. 4–16.
14. Ezek. xxi. 21.
15. Thulin, *Religionsgeschichtliche Versuche und Verarbeiten* (Geissen 1906), III.
16. Meissner, *Babylonien und Assyrien* (Heidelberg 1925), Vol. II. p. 258.
17. R. Campbell Thompson, *Assyrian Medical Texts from the Originals in the British Museum* (Oxford 1923).
18. Campbell Thompson, *Devils and Evil Spirits of Babylonia* (London 1904–05).
19. Campbell Thompson, *op. cit.*, Vol. I. pp. 16ff.; Vol. II. pp. 152ff.
    Campbell Thompson, *Semitic Magic* (London 1908), pp. 7ff.
20. *Western Asiatic Inscriptions*, II. 51B, line 1ff.
    Utukku series, Tablet III. I. 204.
21. Utukku series, Tablet N, col. iii. lines 37ff.
22. Langdon, *Expository Times*, XXIV. 1912, pp. 11ff.
23. Surpu series, Tablet VII.
24. Surpu series, Tablet T, lines 50ff.
25. Zimmern, *Beiträge zur Kenntnis der Babylonischen Religion*, Vol. II. p. 33.
26. *Ebers Papyrus*, 46.
    Oefele, *Vorhippokratische Medizin*, 64.
27. *Papyrus Turin*, 131, 1–8.
    Metternich Stele, 3–8.
28. *Papyrus Turin*, 136, 8–9.
    Papyrus Leyden, 347, 4, 11ff.
29. *Papyrus Turin*, 131, 7.
    Papyrus Leyden, 348, 3, 4.
30. Chabes, *Bibl. Egyptol.* XII. 127–335.
    Budge, *Egyptian Magic* (London 1899), pp. 224ff.
31. *Papyrus med. Berlin*, 8, 10.
    Papyrus med. London, 8, 12.
    Petersburg, 1116B, recto. 9.
    The Ebers Papyrus, 99, 2.
32. *Papyrus med. Berlin*, 3027 (I. 9–11, 6).
    Papyrus Magical Harris, 6, 10.
33. Dittenberger, *Syllage Inscriptionum Graecarum*, 1168. (Henceforth referred to as Syll.)
    Pausanias, II. 3, 118; III, 237.
    Aristophanes, *Plutus*, 733.
34. Spencer and Gillen, *Native Tribes of Central Australia* (London 1938), pp. 522ff.
35. Livy, X. 47.
    Ovid, *Metamorphoses*, XV. 622ff.
    cf. Warde Fowler, *The Religious Experience of the Roman People* (London 1911), p. 260.
36. Virgil, *Aeneid*, VII. 81ff.
    cf. Ovid, *Fasti*, IV. 649ff.
37. R. Heinzey, *Vergil's epische Technik* (Leipzig 1908), p. 174. n. 2.
    Flavian, *Corpus Inscrip. Latinarum*, VI. 8, 14.
38. Aeschylus, *Eumenides*, 1ff.
    Pausanias, II; XXXIII. 2.
    Strabo, VIIIc.
    Homeric Hymn to Apollo, 214ff.

39. *Homeric Hymn to Apollo*, 124 ff.
40. Plutarch, 389C.
41. Pliny, *Nat. Hist.* II. 208.
    Livy, I. lvi. 10.
    Cicero, *de Div.* I. xxxvi. 79.
    Strabo, *Geog.* ix. 419.
    Pausanias, X. v. 7, 12.
42. Stutzle, in *Programm der Kon. Gymnasiums zu Ellwangen*, p. 14.
    Bousquet, *Bulletin de Correspondance Hellénique*, LXIV–LXV. p. 228.
43. Courby, *Fouilles de Delphés*, II. 1915-17, pp. 58ff.
44. Plutarch, III, 405C, 414B.
45. Latte, *Harvard Theological Review*, XXXIII. 1940. pp. 9ff.
46. Guthrie, *The Greeks and Their Gods*, pp. 78ff.
47. Pausanias, X. 6, 24.
48. Dem. Macart. 1072.
49. Cratylus, 414C.
    Plato, *Phaedo*, 64, 66.
    Plato, *Phaedrus*, 247ff.
50. Plutarch, III. 404D., 511B.
51. Demosthenes, XLVII, 68.
    Plato, *Laws*, XI. 919C.
52. H. M. Parke and D. E. W. Wormell, *The Delphic Oracle* (Oxford 1956), Vol. I.
    pp. 49ff.
53. Plato, *Apol.* 19A.
54. Dittenberger, *Syll.* 697e, line 9.
    F. Jacoby, *Atthis* (Oxford 1949), pp. 29ff.
55. Plato, *Laws*, 759C,D, 828A, 865B,D, 916C, 958D, 988A.
56. Plutarch, *Demosthenes*, 20.
    Cicero, *de Div*, ii. 57, 118.
57. Diodorus Siculus, XVI. xxvi. 6.
58. Cicero, *de Div.* I. xxxvii. 81.
    Diodorus Siculus, XXII. frag. ix. 5.
59. Pausanias, X. xxii. 12–xxiv.
60. Diodorus Siculus, XXII. ix. 4.
    Strabo, IV.C. 188.
    Livy, xxxviii. 2, 9, 48.
    Homeric Hymn to Apollo, 23ff.
61. Flacelière, *Etudes d'Archéologie Grecque* (Ghent 1938), pp. 125ff.
62. Diodorus Siculus, XXXV. xiii.
63. Livy, xxix.
64. Tacitus, *Annals*, III. 63.
65. Tacitus, *Hist.* IV. lxxxiii.
    Plutarch, *Moralia*, 984A.
66. *Bulletin de Correspondance Hellénique*, VI. p. 451.
67. *Bulletin de Correspondance Hellénique*, XX. pp. 719, 128.
68. Prudentius, *Apotheosis*, 438ff.
69. Julian, *Contra Galilaeos*, 198 C.
    Pauly-Wissowa, *Real-Encyclopadie*, 'Delphoi', 2583.
70. Origen, *Contra Celsum*, VII. Chaps. iii. iv.
    Justin Martyr, *Apologia*, XVIII.
71. Hermas, *Vis*, ii. 4.
    Justin Martyr, *Quaest. et resp. ad Orthodoxes*, 74.
    Justin Martyr, *Apologia*, I. 20, 59.
    Origen, *op. cit.*, VII. 56.
72. Warde Fowler, *Religious Experience of the Roman People*, p. 257.
    C. Bailey, *Phases in the Religion of Ancient Rome* (Oxford 1932), p. 122
73. Pauly-Wissowa, *Religion und Kultur der Römer* (Munich 1912), pp. 297ff.
74. Livy, xxii. 27.
75. *Sibylline Books*, III. 97–294, 491ff.

76. *Sibylline Books*, I, II, VIII. 217–501.
77. *Sibylline Books*, XI–XIV.
78. C. Alexandre, *Oracula Sybyllina* (Paris 1841–56), ET by M. S. Terry, *The Sibylline Oracles* (New York 1890).
79. Lucian, *Sibyllines*, I. 140ff., 326–31.
    Origen, *Contra Celsum*, VII. 56.
80. Eusebius, *Orat. Constantine*, XVIII. p. 574ff.
81. St Augustine, *De Civitate Dei*, xviii. 23.
82. Gen. xii. 6ff.
83. Gen. xxviii. 1–22.
84. Gen. xxviii. 16.
85. Exod. iii. 2–5.
    Deut. xxxiii. 16.
86. Exod. xix. 19; xxxiii. 11.
    I Kings xix. 9, 13.
87. Num. xii. 6ff.
88. Exod. xxv. 22; xxxiii. 7.
    Deut. xxiii. 15.
    Num. v. 3; vii. 89; xi. 25ff.; xii. 5.
89. Num. xi. 25.
90. Exod. iii, 10ff.; iv. 2, 16.
    Deut. xviii. 15.
91. Deut. xii. 2ff.
92. Num. xi. 25ff.; xii. 5.
93. Judges, ix. 37.
94. Gen. xii. 8; xxxv. 4.
95. Joshua xxiv. 26.
    Deut. xi. 30.
96. II Sam. v. 24.
97. Joshua vii. 16ff.
    II Sam. iv. 5, 8; x. 20ff.
    Prov. xiv. 33.
98. I Sam. x. 5ff.
    I Kings xviii. 20ff.; xxii. 11ff.
99. C. Bezold, *Babylonisch-assyrisches Glossar* (Heidelberg 1926), p. 167.
    Langdon, JRAS, 1932, p. 392.
100. Meek, *Hebrew Origins*, pp. 148ff.
101. I Sam. x. 5ff; xix. 18ff.
102. I Sam. xvi. 13ff.
103. I Sam. ix. 12ff.; xi. 15; xiii. 7ff.
104. I Sam. i. 20.
105. I Sam. xiii. 9ff.
106. I Sam. xiv. 35.
107. I Kings ix. 25.
108. I Sam. ix. 6, 9, 15.
109. I Sam. xxviii.
110. I Sam. i. 24ff.; ii. 18; iii. 1.
111. I Sam. iii. 8.
112. Jepsen, *Nabi* (Munich 1934), pp. 111ff.
113. I Kings xix. 19ff.
    cf. II Kings i; ii; iv. 33, 38; vi. 32; viii. 12.
114. R. Temple, *Jubilee Congress of the Folklore Society*, 1928 (London 1930), pp. 21ff.
115. I Kings xviii. 46.
116. I Kings xvii. 4–17.
117. I Kings xviii.
118. cf. II Kings viii. 7–15; ix. 1–6.
119. I Kings xviii. 31ff.; xix. 10.
120. I Kings xviii. 33ff.
121. I Kings xxii. 6ff.

122. Amos i. 1; vii. 12–15.
123. Jer. xv. 19; xxiii. 31.
 Isa. i. 20; iv. 10ff.
 Ezek. xii. 21–28.
124. Haggai i. 13.
 Mal. ii. 7; iii. 1.
125. Johnson, *The One and the Many in the Israelite Conception of God* (Cardiff 1941), p. 37.
126. Hos. xiii. 15.
 Job ix. 9.
 I Sam. x. 6, 10.
127. Jer. xxiii. 16ff.
128. Jer. xxviii. 6, 11.
129. Jer. xxviii. 8, 9, 12ff.
130. Isa. lvi. i.
 Amos v. 4.
131. Amos vii. 15.
132. Jer. xxiii. 18, 22.
133. Isa. vi. 1–8.
134. Isa. v. 9; xxii. 14.
135. Ezek. viii–xi.
136. Jer. xxiii. 26ff.

CHAPTER IX: THE GODS AND THE GOOD LIFE

1. Bleeker, *De beteekenis van de Egyptische godin Maat* (Leiden 1929), p. 33.
 Frankfort, *Ancient Egyptian Religion* (Columbia Univ. Press), pp. 54ff.
2. J. A. Wilson, ANET, p. 251.
3. Erman and Blackman, *The Literature of the Ancient Egyptians* (London 1927), p. 57.
4. Breasted, *Ancient Records*, 1906. Vol. II. p. 299.
5. Erman and Blackman, *op. cit.*, p. 57.
6. Sethe, *Urkunden des Aegypt. Altertums* (Leipzig 1908), IV. p. 913ff.
7. Erman and Blackman, *op. cit.*, p. 109.
8. Erman and Blackman, *op. cit.*, p. 57.
 Amenemope, VI. 1–12; XXII. 1–18; XXIII. 11.
9. Sethe, *Urkunden des Aegypt. Altertums*, IV. p. 993.
10. Amenemope, XXII. 1–18.
 cf. Wilson, *The Intellectual Adventure of Ancient Man*, p. 115.
11. Breasted, *The Dawn of Conscience*, pp. 129ff.
12. Breasted, *Development of Religion and Thought in Ancient Egypt*, p. 142.
13. Breasted, *Ancient Egyptian Religion*, p. 64.
14. *The Book of the Dead*, Chap. CXXV.
 Breasted, *Ancient Records*, Vol. II. pp. 343, 768.
 Mercer, 'The Wisdom of Amenemope' in *Egyptian Religion* (New York 1934), II. 1934.
15. A. H. Gardiner, *Zeitschrift für aegypt. sprache und Altertumswissenschaft*, XLV. 1908,
 p. 125.
16. Budge, *The Teaching of Amen-em-apt* (London 1924), pp. 93ff.
 Mercer, 'The Wisdom of Amenemope' in *Egyptian Religion*, pp. 93ff.
17. Mercer, XXIV. 4. line 473.
18. Mercer, XXIV. 4. lines 409, 418ff.
19. Jastrow, *Religion of Babylonia and Assyria* (London 1898), p. 291.
20. Stephens, ANET, p. 385.
 L. W. King, *The Seven Tablets of Creation*, Vol. I. pp. 233–37.
21. Zimmern, *Bab. Busspsalmen*, IV. pp. 100–106.
 Langdon, *Babylonian Penitential Psalms* (Paris 1927), pp. 43ff.
 Stephens, ANET, p. 392.
22. Jastrow, *Aspects of Religious Belief and Practice in Babylonia and Assyria* (London 1911),
 pp. 319ff.
23. Langdon, *Babylonian Penitential Psalms*, pp. 40–47.

24. Zimmern, *Die Keilinschriftliche und Das A.T.* (Leipzig 1903), pp. 609ff.
Zimmern, *Der alte Orient* (Leipzig 1903), VII. 3. pp. 27ff.
ANET, pp. 434ff.
Langdon, *Babylonian Wisdom* (London 1923), pp. 35ff.
25. ANET, pp. 437ff.
Langdon, *op. cit.* pp. 67ff.
26. Harper, *Code of Hammurabi*, Prologue, Col. I. 8.
cf. Driver and Miles, *The Babylonian Laws* (Oxford 1955), Vol. II. p. 13.
Code of Hammurabi, p. 3.
27. *Code of Hammurabi*, v.a. 6–9; xxiv.b. 49–52; iv. a. 11–16, 29–30.
28. *Code of Hammurabi*, ii.a. 214; v.a. 10–12; i.a. 16–19; iv.a. 55–62.
29. *Code of Hammurabi*, v.a. 14–24.
30. A. Alt, *Die Ursprunge des israelitischen Rechts* (Leipzig 1934).
31. Num. vi. 8.
32. I Sam. vi. 10.
Isa. ii. 6–21.
33. Isa. i. 4; vi. 10.
Amos iv. 2.
34. Deut. xxv. 15.
Ps. liii. 3; xxiii. 3.
35. Isa. lvi. 4; v. 4.
36. Zech. viii. 16.
Rabbi Simeon, *Abot.* i. 2, 18.
37. Amos v. 13.
38. Hos. ix. 10.
39. Amos iv. 4.
40. Mic. vi. 6–8.
41. St Mt. xxiii. 2f.
42. Gen. vi. 5.
Ecclus. xv. 11.
Kiddushim, 30b.
43. Isa. xlv. 7.
44. II Sam. xxiv.
45. I Chron. xxi. 1.
46. Job i. 6ff.
Zech. iii. 1ff.
47. I Enoch xix. 1ff. cf. 5, 7.
Jubilees x. 10–13; xi. 4ff; xii. 20.
Testament of the Twelve Patriarchs.
Reuben iii. 3–6.
Simeon iv. 8, 9.
48. Gen. i. 31.
49. Dan. viii. 16; ix. 21, 23; x. 13, 21; xii. 1.
50. Dan. x. 5ff.; 20ff.
51. Dan. ii. 18ff., 44; vi 26; vii. 16; viii. 16; ix. 4,22.
52. Gen. vi. 4.
53. Gen. iii.
54. Ecclus. xv. 11–17.
55. Ecclus. xxv. 24.
56. II Esdras iii. 21ff.; iv. 30ff.; vii. 118.
57. Wisdom of Solomon ii. 23ff.
58. Ecclus. xv. 14ff.; xxxiii. 14ff.; xxxvii. 3.
Bereshith Rabba, xxvii.
Kiddushim, 30b.
59. *Vendidah*, i. 1ff.
Yasht, x. 97; xiii. 77.
Yasna, ix. 15.
Bundahish, i. 1–28.
60. *Yasna*, xliv. 5; xlvii. 2–3.

61. *Vendidah*, iii. 1–4, 24ff., 31ff.
62. M. Burrow, *The Dead Sea Scrolls* (New York 1955), pp. 374ff.
    T. H. Gaster, *The Scriptures of the Dead Sea Sect* (London 1957), pp. 53ff.
63. Zaehner, *Zurvan, A Zoroastrian Dilemma* (Oxford 1955), pp. 70, 157.
64. St John ii. 15ff.; v. 19.
    I John i. 5; v. 19.
65. I Cor. xv. 45ff.
    Rom. v. 14ff.; xii. 1.
    I Cor. v. 19.
    II Cor. iv. 16.
66. Zaehner, *op. cit.*, p. 79.
    Widengren, *Zeitschrift für Religions und Geistesgeschichte*, 1952, Heft. 2.
67. F. M. Cornford, *From Religion to Philosophy* (London 1912), p. 176.
68. Empedocles, B.18, 8 and B.26, 6.
69. Anaxagoras, B.11, 12.
70. Democritus, *Frag.* 191, 215.
    cf. Plato, *Republic*, ix. 583B.
71. cf. I. M. Linforth, *The Arts of Orpheus* (California 1941).
    Nilsson, *Harvard Theological Review*, XXVIII. 1935, pp. 181ff.
72. Plato, *Republic*, X. 600B.
73. Plato, *Phaedo*, 69C.
74. *Republic*, X. 615A, B.
75. J. E. Harrison, *Prolegomena to the Study of Greek Religion*, Appendix.
76. Pindar, *Frag.* 29, 130.
77. Hesiod, *Works and Days*, 311, 350, 287ff.
78. *Od.* VI. 182ff.; XVII. 292ff.
79. Xenophanes, *Frag.* xi. 15, 16 (Diels).
80. *Herodotus*, II. 53.
81. *Il.* VIII.
82. *Od.* XIX. 109ff.
83. Plato, *Phaedrus*, 84E ff.
84. Plato, *Symposium*, 211.
85. Plato, *Laws*, 896E–898D.
86. Plato, *Theaetetus*, 176A.
87. Plato, *Timaeus*, 42.
88. *Republic*, V. 477A.
89. Aristotle, *Metaphysics*, XII. ix. 1074B.

CHAPTER X: DEVELOPMENT AND DIFFUSION OF NEAR EASTERN DEITIES

1. PT. 1125.
2. Blackman, JEA, XI. 1925, p. 250.
3. Capitan, *Les Combarelles aux Eyzies* (Paris 1924), Pl. vi.
   Picard, *Revue de Philologie*, 1923, pp. 344ff.
4. Malton, *Archaeologisches Jahrbuch*, 1928, pp. 90ff.
5. *Rig-veda*, I. 106, 3; 159, 1; 185, 4; IV. 56, 2.
6. *Il.* XV. 187.
7. Hesiod, *Theogony*, 634.
8. Euripides, *Bacchae*, 58ff., 127ff.
9. Rapp and Roscher, *Lex. der Gr. und Rom. Mythologie*, 1882, ii, 16660.
10. Pausanias, I. xviii. 7; VIII. xxxvi. 2.
11. CGS, Vol. III. p. 296.
12. Rapp and Roscher, *op. cit.*, II. p. 1659; IV. 91ff.
    Hymn. Homer, xiv; xxx. 17.
13. Nilsson, *Minoan-Mycenaean Religion*, p. 464.
14. Lucian, *De Dea Syria*, 15.
15. Moret, *Le Rituel du Culte Divin Journalier en Egypte*, p. 129.

16. PT. 1105.
17. Langdon, *Cuneiform Inscriptions* (Oxford 1923), I. p. 50.
18. Kramer, *Cuneiform Inscriptions*, pp. 101ff.
19. Chiera, *Sumerian Ritual Texts* (London 1924), I. v. 14ff.
20. *Code of Hammurabi*, epilogue, rev. XXVII. 64ff.; prologue, III. 56ff.
    Meek, ANET, 179 (6180).
21. *Mitteilungen der altorientalischen Gesellschaft*, I. 3. 1925, pp. 15ff.
22. de Genouillac, *Revue d'assyriologie et d'archéologie orientale*, VII. 1910, pp. 151ff.
23. Strong and Garstang, *The Syrian Goddess* (London 1913), pp. 25ff.
24. Zech. xii. 11.
25. Goetze, ANET, pp. 126ff.
26. Judges vi. 32; vii.
    II Sam. ii. 2–4; v. 16; xi. 21.
    I Chron. vii. 33; ix. 39ff.; xiv. 7.
27. Ps. xlviii. 14; xviii. 4ff.
28. Judges ii. 6–iii. 6.
29. Judges v. 4ff., 23.
30. Hos. ii. 8.
31. Jer. xliv. 17.
32. Isa. xl. 12ff.; xli; xlv. 20; xli. 1ff., 5–8.
33. Isa. xliii. 22–xliv. 5; xlviii. 9, 11; lii. 5ff.
34. Isa. lii; lvi. 3, 6–8.
35. Isa. xlii. 6; xlix. 1–7; 7, 7ff.; liii.
36. Isa. xlvii. 8.
37. Albright, *American Journal of Semitic Languages*, XXXVI. 1920, p. 293.
38. St John iv. 14, 38.
39. Albright, *Harvard Theological Review*, XVII. 1924, pp. 190ff.
40. Prov. vii, ix.
41. Albright, *Journal of Palestine Oriental Society*, XIV. p. 122.
42. Albright, AJSL, XXXVI. p. 285.
43. I Kings iv. 30ff.
44. Prov. iii. 13–15.
45. Ps. cxi. 10.
    Prov. i. 7.
    Job xxviii. 28.
46. Ecclus. xxiv. 3ff.
    Wisdom of Solomon vii. 25.
47. *Yasht*, XXII. 2ff.
48. S. A. Cook, *The Religion of Palestine in the Light of Archaeology* (London 1930), pp. 206ff.
    E. L. Sukenik, *Ancient Synagogues in Palestine and Greece* (London 1934), pp. 29, 34, 65ff., 86.
49. I Macc. i. 11–15, 34–37.
    II Macc. iv. 7–10.
50. Oesterley, *The Labyrinth* (London 1935), pp. 130ff.
51. Cicero, *de Natura Deorum*, ii. 3. 8.
52. Hos. i. 10.
53. Ps. cxlv. 18.
54. Montefiore, *Some Elements in the Religious Teaching of Jesus* (London 1919), pp. 97ff.
    Montefiore, *The Synoptic Gospels* (London 1927), Vol. I. p. cxviii.
55. Ps. ciii.
56. St Mark xiv. 24ff.; x. 45.
    cf. St Luke xii. 50.
    St John xiv. 13; xii. 24.
    Rom. v. 8, 15.
    Heb. viii. 6; ix. 15; xii. 24.
    II Cor. v. 19.
57. C. H. Dodd, *History and the Gospel* (London 1938), p. 181.

BIBLIOGRAPHY

For the general reader the books (mostly in English) listed in this selected bibliography will be useful for further study of the topics discussed in the chapters in this volume. The source material and more technical publications are given in the references in the text. Except where otherwise stated the books are all published in London. English translations are indicated by the letters ET.

CHAPTER I

New Light on the Most Ancient East by V. G. Childe New edition 1952, is the most comprehensive investigation of the prehistoric and proto-historic evidence in the Ancient East from Egypt to the Indus valley, brought up to date in the fourth edition in 1952.

The Birth of Civilization in the Ancient Near East by H. Frankfort, 1951, gives concisely an account of the rise of civilization in Egypt and Mesopotamia, and of the social and political innovations which became manifest in the process.

For a more detailed study of the several regions the following may be consulted:

Excavations at Ur by Sir Leonard Woolley, 1954, summarizes the author's much larger and more technical two volumes, *Ur Excavations* (OUP 1934), in which a full description of the Royal Cemetery and its contents will be found with plates.

Everyday Life in Babylonia and Assyria by G. Contenau, 1954 (ET), surveys life in Mesopotamia from the third millennium BC until the invasion of Alexander the Great in 330 BC in the light of the knowledge obtained from the excavations and the decipherment of the tablets. For the earlier period, *From the Tablets of Sumer* by S. N. Kramer (Colorado 1957) might be consulted.

Everyday Life in Ancient Egypt by A. W. Shorter, 1932, provides a similar introduction to the ancient civilization in the Nile valley, and *Everyday Life in Egypt* by P. Montet (ET 1958) concentrates on the New Kingdom in the Nineteenth Dynasty.

The Splendour That Was Egypt by M. A. Murray, 1949, gives a general survey of Egyptian culture from prehistoric times onwards.

Iran by G. Ghirshman (Pelican 1954) was written in the ancient city of Susa while the author was directing excavations there, to give an overall picture of the region from the earliest times to the end of the Iranian civilization and the Islamic invasion. This may be supplemented by E. Herzfeld's Schweich Lectures in 1934 entitled *An Archaeological History of Iran* (OUP 1935), and his larger volume *Iran in the Ancient East* (OUP 1941) containing a full account of the discoveries and their interpretation.

The Archaeology of Palestine by W. F. Albright (Pelican 1954) and the companion archaeological books in the Penguin series—those of Ghirshman on Iran, O. R. Gurney on *The Hittites* (1954), and S. Piggott on *Prehistoric India to 1000 BC* (1950)—afford a very valuable background for the study of Near Eastern Religion.

Digging Up Jericho by K. M. Kenyon, 1957, gives an illuminating account of Miss Kenyon's excavations at this important site since 1952. This has been supplemented by Lady Wheeler's *Walls of Jericho* (1956), describing her own impressions of the 'dig'.

The Palace of Minos at Knossos by Sir Arthur Evans in four volumes (1921–35) will always remain the standard pioneer work of reference on his excavations in Crete.

The Archaeology of Crete by J. D. S. Pendlebury is a good introduction to the Minoan civilization.

Biblical Archaeology by G. E. Wright, 1957, summarizes the recent archaeological discoveries which have thrown so much light on biblical history. For a fully documented account of the early period *From Joseph to Joshua* by H. H. Rowley (1950) should be consulted. In the new introduction to the Doubleday Anchor Book edition of *From the Stone Age to Christianity* by W. F. Albright (1957) the most important advances in knowledge in this field since the Second World War are described. *Ancient History of Western Asia, India and Crete* by B. Hroznay (Prague, E.T. 1953) surveys the entire region very adequately.

The Cuneiform Texts of Ras-Shamra-Ugarit by C. F. A. Schaeffer, 1939, and the more recent volume (in French), *Les Textes de Ras Shamra-Ugarit* by R. de Langhe (Paris 1944–45), afford a convenient survey of the very considerable Ugaritic literature and its contents since the discovery of the Ras Shamra tablets in and after 1930. The literature of Greece and the Aegean is so vast that it must suffice to mention only the latest addition to it—the volume *From Mycenae to Homer* by T. B. L. Webster, 1958—which is relevant for the present inquiry.

CHAPTER II

The Intellectual Adventure of Ancient Man by H. and H. A. Frankfort, J. A. Wilson, Th. Jacobsen and W. A. Irwin (Chicago 1946), and reprinted in part as a Pelican book under the title *Before Philosophy* (1949), is a stimulating introduction to the study of Near Eastern Religion by a group of scholars for the purpose of distinguishing between the mythopoeic thought of the Ancient Near East and the critical thought of modern times, in three sections dealing respectively with Egypt, Mesopotamia and the Hebrews, to which Frankfort has contributed an introduction on Myth and Reality, and a conclusion on The Emancipation of Thought from Myth. In his important work *The Kingship and the Gods* (Chicago 1948) he has defined the essential beliefs and practices in Mesopotamia and the Nile valley, and devoted a separate volume to *Ancient Egyptian Religion* (Columbia 1948) along the same lines. Among earlier books on Egyptian religion *A Handbook of Egyptian Religion* by A. Erman (1905, ET 1907) represents a pioneer volume written from a knowledge of the texts, and *Development of Religion and Thought in Ancient Egypt* by J. H. Breasted (1914) gives from the evolutionary standpoint a brilliant account of Egyptian belief and practice from Predynastic times to the final period of decadence based on the texts. More recently *The Religion of Ancient Egypt* by S. A. B. Mercer (1949) and *Ancient Egyptian Religion* by J. Cerny (1952) provide very useful sketches of the subject by Egyptologists of repute.

Very little has been written in English on Assyro-Babylonian religion at all comparable to *Les Religions de Babylonie et d'Assyrie* by E. Dhorme (Paris 1945) or *La Religione Babylonienne e Assire* by Giuseppe Furlani (Bologna 19282–9) in two volumes. *Babylonian and Assyrian Religion* by S. H. Hooke, 1953, is the most recent general account, based on the original cuneiform texts, while reference is made in their proper places to a number of works dealing with particular aspects of Babylonian belief and practice. *Religion of Ancient Palestine in the Light of Archaeology* by S. A. Cook, 1930, *Archaeology and the Religion of Israel* by W. F. Albright (Baltimore, 3rd ed. 1953), and *Israel, Its Life and Culture* by J. Pedersen (ET 1926) place Hebrew religion against its archaeological and cultural background in the Ancient Near East. A very useful compendium entitled *Forgotten Religions*, edited by V. Ferm and published by The Philosophical Library, New York, in 1950, contains in addition to essays on Egyptian, Sumerian and Babylonian and Assyrian religion, a lucid account of Hittite Religion, with references, by H. G. Güterbock. This may be read in conjunction with the appropriate sections of *The Hittites* by O. R. Gurney (1954), where a full bibliography of the literature will be found. *Religions of the Ancient Near East*, edited by I. Mendelsohn (New York 1955), provides translations of a number of Sumerian, Akkadian and Ugaritic epics, rituals, hymns, prayers and incantation texts, and in *Thespis* by T. H. Gaster (New York 1950) the author's translations of the Ras Shamra and other myths are discussed in relation to the sacred drama in its cultural setting. *Ugaritic Mythology* by J. Obermann (New Haven 1948) contains the leading motifs of the Ugaritic texts though in some cases they are open to criticism (cf.Review by Gaster, JNES VII 1948, pp. 184ff.). The most comprehensive and important translation of *Ancient Near East Texts Relating to the Old Testaments* (ANET), edited by J. B. Pritchard (Princeton 2nd ed. 1955) which is the principal source-book on the subject. *Myth and Ritual in the Ancient Near East* by E. O. James (1958) gives a fully documented general account of Near Eastern mythology and cultus based on the new material now available against the prehistoric background given in *Prehistoric Religion* by the same author (1957) and in the first volume of this series by Maringer.

CHAPTER III

Tammuz and Ishtar by S. Langdon (Oxford 1914) contains extracts from the Mesopotamian Tammuz liturgies and an account of the cult. For the earlier Sumerian versions *Sumerian Mythology* by S. N. Kramer (Philadelphia 1944) should be consulted in the light of a critical review by Th. Jacobsen in JNES, V. 1946, pp. 128ff., and the Sumerian myths in ANET. *La Déesse Nue Babylonienne* by G. Contenau (Paris 1914) is a comparative study of the iconography of the Babylonian Mother-goddess in which the female figurines, described in detail by E. Douglas van Buren in *Clay Figurines of Babylonia and Assyria* (Yale Press 1930), are examined. Similar terracotta figurines and plaques of a nude goddess in Palestine are investigated by J. B. Pritchard in *Palestinian Figurines in Relation to Certain Goddesses in Literature* (New Haven 1943), while the diffusion of the cult from Brak in eastern Syria has been traced in connexion with 'face-idols' with large eyes by O. G. S. Crawford in *The Eye Goddess* (1957). *The Syrian Goddess* by J. Garstang and H. A. Strong (1913) describes the cult of the goddess of northern Syria, Atargatis, in a translation of Lucian's 'De Dea Syria' with an introduction. *Le Culte de Cybele* by H. Graillot (Paris 1912) gives an account of the Phrygian Great Mother in Rome and throughout the Empire. In Crete the various forms and aspects of the Minoan Mother are discussed by Arthur Evans in *The Palace of Minos* (see Index. Vol. V. 1936) and by M. P. Nilsson in *Minoan-Mycenaean Religion* (Lund 2nd ed. 1950). Her Greek counterparts are considered by J. E. Harrison in *Prolegomena to the Study of Greek Religion* (Cambridge 1903) and in *Themis* (Cambridge 1912), and by L. R. Farnell in *Cult of the Greek States*, Vol. III (Oxford 1907). Various aspects of the cult are interpreted in an interesting manner by G. R. Levy in *The Gate of Horn* (1948), and the evidence now available is brought together concerning the nature, position and function of the Goddess in the Ancient Near East and the eastern Mediterranean in *The Cult of the Mother Goddess* by E. O. James (1959).

CHAPTER IV

Kingship and the Gods by H. Frankfort (Chicago 1948) is the most exhaustive study of the sacral kingship in Egypt and Mesopotamia. *Ideas of Divine Rule in the Ancient East* by C. Gadd (1948) contains the Schweich Lectures on this subject delivered in 1945. On the same Foundation S. H. Hooke in 1935 discussed *The Origins of Early Semitic Ritual* (1938) in which he elaborated his outline in *Myth and Ritual* (Oxford 1933), a compendium of lectures on this theme given in Oxford and London in 1932. A new edition under the title of *Myth, Ritual and Kingship* has now been issued (1958) in which the hypothesis has been reviewed in the light of further knowledge by a fresh team of contributors, but still edited by S. H. Hooke. Among older volumes attention may be called to *Du Caractère Religieux de la Royauté Assyro-Babylonienne* by R. Labat (Paris 1939), and to its Egyptian counterpart (where the divinity of the reigning Pharaoh was most firmly established) *Du Caractère Religieux de la Royauté Pharaonique* (Paris 1902) by A. Moret, and to *Le Rituel du Culte Divin Journalier en Egypte* (Paris 1902) by the same author. *Studies in Divine Kingship in the Ancient Near East* by Ivan Engnell (Uppsala 1945) is a comprehensive investigation of the subject, while the bearing of the myths in the Ugaritic texts on this theme is discussed in Gaster's *Thespis* (1950), in *Baal in the Ras Shamra Texts* by A. S. Kapelrud (Copenhagen 1952), in *Canaanite Myths and Legends* by G. R. Driver (Edinburgh 1956) and in *Ugaritic Literature* by C. H. Gordon (Rome 1949). In Israel the situation is described by A. R. Johnson in *Sacral Kingship in Ancient Israel* (Cardiff 1956) against the background of the Canaanite vegetation cultus and the enthronement psalms, while the nature and function of the Anatolian priest-kings are considered by O. R. Gurney in his article in *Myth, Ritual and Kingship* (new edition 1958) and by J. Garstang in *The Hittite Empire* (1929). The setting of the Minoan sacral kingship is vividly displayed in the several volumes of *The Palace of Minos* by Arthur Evans, and that of the Mycenaean kings on the mainland in *Mycenae* by A. J. B. Wace (Princeton 1949) and in *Ancient Mycenae* by C. E. Mylonas (1957).

CHAPTER V

Les Fêtes du Dieu Min by H. Gauthier (Cairo 1931) gives an account of the Harvest Festival in Egypt. The great autumnal festival Khoiak described in a lengthy inscription on the walls of the temple at Denderah is very briefly summarized by J. G. Frazer in *The Golden Bough* (3rd ed. 1914, Pt. IV. Vol. II) and by A. M. Blackman in *Myth and Ritual* (1933). The complete inscription has been published by H. Brugsch, *Zeitschrift für Aegyptische Sprache und Altertumskunde* (XIX, 1881) and by V. Loret, *Recueil de Travaux* (iii. 1882, pp. 43ff.; iv. 1883, pp. 21ff.; v. 1884, pp. 77ff.). For the Coronation Drama see *Dramatische Texte zu*

Altaegyptischen Mysterienspielen by K. Sethe (Leipzig 1928). The New Year Festival as cele-brated at Babylon has been described by S. A. Pallis in *The Babylonian Akitu Festival* (Copenhagen 1926), but it now requires some modification in respect of the enactment of the death of the god. For a later treatment Frankfort's *Kingship and the Gods* (1948), Chap. 22, and Sidney Smith's contribution to *Myth, Ritual and Kingship* (1958 edition) should be consulted. The connexion between the Festival and the Epic of Creation is considered by A. J. L. Wensinck in *Acta Orientalia* (Vol. I, 1923), by Thureau-Dangin in *Rituels Accadiens* (Paris 1921) and by C. J. Gadd in *Myth and Ritual* (1933). Reference also should be made to *The Babylonian, Epic of Creation* by S. Langdon (1932) and to his *Tammuz and Ishtar* (Oxford 1914).

The similar cult rituals in the Ugaritic texts have been described and discussed by A. S. Kapelrud in *Baal in the Ras Shamra Texts* (Copenhagen 1952), Engnell in *Studies in Divine Kingship in the Ancient East* (Uppsala 1943), and by T. H. Gaster in *Thespis* (New York 1950) who maintains that the sacred drama everywhere has taken its origin in seasonal rituals representing the rhythm of nature through the medium of myth. *The Jewish New Year Festival* has been investigated by N. H. Snaith (1947), by H. Schmidt in *Die Thronfahrt Jahres am Fest der Jahreswunde im Alten Israel* (Leipzig 1927), and by A. R. Johnson in *Sacred Kingship in Ancient Israel* (Cardiff 1955), who like S. Mowinckel in *Psalmenstudien* (Kristiania 1921, 1923) is mainly concerned with the cultic setting of many of the psalms.

Greek Popular Religion by M. P. Nilsson (Columbia 1940) describes the rural seasonal festival in Greece, and against this background the public cult dramas and mystery rituals have to be set, as is shown by J. E. Harrison in *Prolegomena to the Study of Greek Religion* (Cambridge 1903), *Themis* (1912) and *Ancient Art and Ritual* (1913). Reference should also be made to *Cult of the Greek States* by L. R. Farnell (Vol. III) and to *The Religion of Greece in Prehistoric Times* by A. W. Persson (California 1942). In *Modern Greek Folklore and Ancient Greek Religion* by J. C. Lawson (Cambridge 1910) a good deal of light is thrown on the ancient festivals as well as on many other aspects of Greek religion by the popular observances still in vogue.

CHAPTER VI

The two major sources of first-hand information about mortuary beliefs and customs in Egypt are *The Pyramid Texts*, translated with a Commentary by S. A. B. Mercer in 4 vols., 1952, and *The Book of the Dead*, translated by E. A. W. Budge—the Theban recension, 'The Chapters of Coming Forth by Day' in 1898, 1910, and a new edition in 1951, and 'The Papyrus of Ani' in 1913. In addition to these volumes Budge has produced the Egyptian texts with English translations of *The Book of the Opening of the Mouth* (1909); 'The Book Am-Tuat', and 'The Book of Gates' under the title *The Egyptian Heaven and Hell* (1906), and *The Liturgy of Funerary Offerings* (1909). In his *Osiris and the Egyptian Resurrection* (1911) in 2 vols., he endeavoured to elucidate the Egyptian beliefs about Osiris and the hope of resurrection by the evidence afforded by the adjacent Nilotic African tribes. Frankfort has considered the Egyptian preoccupation with death and survival in his *Ancient Egyptian Religion* (Columbia Press 1948), as has Breasted in *Development of Religion and Thought in Ancient Egypt* (1914) from their respective standpoints. For the elaborate process of mummification see *Egyptian Mummies* by G. Elliot Smith and W. R. Dawson (1924).

The Mesopotamian mortuary literature is relatively small because the immortality of the individual caused little concern in this region. The names of the underworld are discussed by K. Tallquist in *Sumerisch-Akkadische Namen der Totenwelt* (Helsingfors, 1934). The withholding of the boon to mankind by the gods is explained in *The Gilgamesh Epic and Old Testament Parallels* by A. Heidel (Chicago 1946) and in ANET by E. A. Speiser. Apart from a very slight and out-of-date book on *The Babylonian Conception of Heaven and Hell* by A. Jeremias in 1902, only passing references to the subject occur in the standard works. The importance of proper interment is stressed in the Ugaritic *Aqht Text* in ANET (pp. 153ff.), and as is explained with references this also recurs in the canonical Hebrew scriptures. For the disposal of the body in early times see *The Religion of Ancient Palestine in the Light of Archaeology* by S. A. Cook (1930), *The Excavation of Gezer* by R. A. S. Macalister (1921), *Digging Up Jericho* by K. M. Kenyon (1957), and the publications of the Palestine Exploration Fund. A. Lods gives a fuller account of the idea of immortality in *La Croyance à la Vie Future et Le Culte des Morts dans l'Antiquité Israélite* (Paris 1906), and the subject is discussed by J. Pedersen in

Israel (1947), Vol. 2. The prophetic and post-exilic conceptions of the afterlife are described and contrasted by W. O. E. Osterley in *Immortality and the Unseen World* (1921), while the later eschatological developments are investigated by R. H. Charles in *A Critical History of the Doctrine of a Future Life* (Edinburgh 1913).

For Aegean burial customs and beliefs Nilsson's *Minoan-Mycenaean Religion* (1950) and his *Homer and Mycenae* (1933) should be consulted, together with *From Mycenae to Homer* by T. B. L. Webster (1958), *New Tombs at Dendra near Midea* by A. W. Persson (1942), and the *Palace of Minos* by Arthur Evans. The literature concerning the various and varied avenues of approach to the Greek conception of immortality and the soul is very large. The most comprehensive study for our present purpose is *Psyche* by E. Rhode (ET 1925). *The Idea of Immortality* by A. Seth Pringle-Pattison (Oxford 1922) and *The Socratic Doctrine of the Soul* by J. Burnet (1916) might also be consulted.

CHAPTER VII

The Intellectual Adventure of Ancient Man (Chicago 1946) contains a general conspectus of the Egyptian view of the physical universe and this is further discussed by J. A. Wilson in *The Burden of Egypt* (Chicago 1951). The part played by the gods in the creative process is considered by Frankfort in *Ancient Egyptian Religion* (1948) and in *Kingship and the Gods* (1948), and in the mystery play performed at the accession of Senusert I, translated by K. Sethe, *Dramatische Texte* (Leipzig 1928). For the creation stories see J. A. Wilson in ANET.

The prominent roles played by the Mesopotamian gods in creation are set forth in the epics translated and discussed in *The Babylonian Genesis* by A. Heidel (Chicago 2nd ed. 1951), *The Seven Tablets of Creation* by W. L. King (1902) and 'The Creation Epic' by E. A. Speiser in ANET and *The Babylonian Epic of Creation* by S. Langdon (1923). The Sumerian myths of origin occur in *Sumerian Mythology* by S. N. Kramer (1944), *Sumerian Liturgies and Psalms* (Philad. 1919) by S. Langdon, and in *Sumerian Epics and Myths* by E. Chiera (Chicago 1934). The relation of the Mesopotamian stories to those current among the Hebrews is considered by Heidel in *The Babylonian Genesis*, by W. A. Irwin in *The Intellectual Adventure of Ancient Man* and by Widengren in *Myth, Ritual and Kingship* (1958 ed.). For the conflict with mythical primeval monsters see *Schopfung und Chaos Willzeit und Endzeit* by H. Gunkel (Göttingen 1895) and the relevant chapters in Pedersen's *Israel, Its Life and Culture*.

The Greek cosmological literature is very widespread as usual. For a concise statement the article by I. F. Burne in ERE (Vol. IV) 'Cosmogony and Cosmology (Greek)' might be consulted. For more detailed information about the Orphic cosmogonies see *Orpheus and Greek Religion* by W. K. C. Guthrie (1952), for the pre-Socratic period *The Theology of the Early Greek Philosophers* by W. Jaeger (Oxford 1947), and for the entire range of speculation *The Religious Teachers of Greece* by J. Adams (1908), *The Development of Greek Philosophy* by R. Adamson (1908), and *Principium Sapientiae* by F. M. Cornford (Cambridge 1952).

CHAPTER VIII

The Religion of Babylonia and Assyria by M. Jastrow (1898) and *La Religion Assyro-Babylonienne* by P. E. Dhorme (Paris 1910) give a general account of divination in Babylonia brought up to date by S. H. Hooke in *Babylonian and Assyrian Religion* (1953). The translations of the cuneiform incantation texts will be found in *The Devils and Evil Spirits of Babylonia* in 2 vols. 1904–05, by R. Campbell Thompson, and in his later volume *Assyrian Medical Texts from the Originals in the British Museum* (Oxford 1923), the therapeutic texts are given. Their Egyptian equivalents are considered in *Magician and Leech* by W. R. Dawson (1929).

The mantic tradition in Greece is surveyed in *Greek Divination* by W. R. Halliday (1913) and Roman augury in *The Religious Experience of the Roman People* by W. Warde Fowler (1912) and in *Phases in the Religion of Ancient Rome* by C. Bailey (Oxford 1932). The most comprehensive treatment of the subject is in *Histoire de la Divination dans l'Antiquité* in 4 vols. by A. Bouche-Leclercq (1879–82). A short account of astrology was produced by F. Cumont in 1912 in a volume entitled *Astrology and Religion among the Greeks and Romans* in which he expanded what he had said in *Oriental Religions on Roman Paganism* (ET, Chicago 1911) where a full bibliography is given. *The Royal Art of Astrology* by R. Eisler (1947) is a more recent addition to the literature. *The Delphic Oracle* by H. M. Parke and D. F. W. Wormell (Oxford 1956) in 2 vols. is the latest and most exhaustive treatment of this aspect of the subject with bibliographical details. *Delphi* by F. Poulson (ET 1920) gives a less elaborate account of the shrine. For the Sibyls and the Sibylline Oracles see M. S. Terry *The Sibylline Oracles* (New York 1890) and the above volumes by Warde Fowler and C. Bailey. The article on the Oracles in the *ERE* Vol. XI has a very full bibliography.

Prophecy and Divination by A. Guillaume (1938) deals very adequately with cultic theophany and prophecy in Hebrew and Semitic tradition, and the Hebrew aspect is elaborated in *Nabi, Saziologische Studien Zur Altestamentlichen Literatur und Religiongeschichte* (Munich 1934) by A. Jepsen, in *The Cultic Prophet in Ancient Israel* by A. R. Johnson (Cardiff 1944), and in *Associations of Cultic Prophets among the Ancient Semites* by P. Haldar (Uppsala 1945). The subsequent developments of Hebrew prophecy are discussed in their earlier context by A. Welch, in *Prophet and Priest in Old Israel* (Oxford 1953), by S. H. Hooke in *Prophets and Priests* (1938), by E. O. James in *The Nature and Function of Priesthood* (1955) and by J. Skinner in *Prophecy and Religion* (Cambridge 1922).

CHAPTER IX

The movement towards ethical ideals has been considered by J. H. Breasted in his *Development of Religion and Thought in Ancient Egypt* and rather overstated in his *Dawn of Conscience* (1934). Against this treatment of the subject should be set that of Frankfort in *Ancient Egyptian Religion* and *Kingship and the Gods*, and that of J. A. Wilson in *The Intellectual Adventure of Ancient Man*, together with the magical aspect of the mortuary ritual in *The Book of the Dead* and in *The Teaching of Amen-En-Apt* by E. A. W. Budge (1924) and *The Wisdom of Amenemope* by S. A. B. Mercer in *Egyptian Religion* (New York 1934). The Babylonian conception of sin and transgression is treated by M. Jastrow in *Religion of Babylonia and Assyria* (1898) and later in his *Aspects of Religious Belief and Practice in Babylonia and Assyria* (1911), by S. H. Hooke in *Babylonian and Assyrian Religion* (1953), and S. Langdon in *Babylonian Penitential Psalms* (Paris 1927). The legal side has been very fully described and discussed by G. R. Driver and J. C. Miles in their volumes on *The Assyrian Laws* (1935) and *The Babylonian Laws* (1955), which contains the text and translation of the Code of Hammurabi, published in Chicago by R. F. Harper in 1904. The closely related Hebrew legislation is considered by S. A. Cook in *The Laws of Moses and the Code of Hammurabi* (1903) and by C. F. Kent in *Israel's Laws and Legal Precedents* (1907), and J. M. Powis Smith, *The Origin and History of Hebrew Law* (Chicago 1946). For ethical monotheism of the prophetic movement *The Prophets and Their Times* (Chicago 1941) also by J. M. Powis Smith, and T. H. Robinson, *Prophecy and the Prophets in Ancient Israel* (1923). B. Davidson's *Old Testament Prophecy* (Edinburgh 1903) remains a standard work on the subject.

The Zoroastrian ethic is briefly described in *The Religion of the Good Life* (1938) by R. P. Masani, himself a Parsi, and by J. H. Moulton in *Early Zoroastrianism* (1913) which is still a useful work. *The Western Response to Zoroaster* by J. Duchesne-Guillemin (Oxford 1958) is the latest estimate of the influence exercised by Zoroastrianism on the development of Greek and Hebrew thought and practice. For more detailed study of the later phases of Zoroastrianism *Zurvan, A Zoroastrian Dilemma* by R. C. Zaehner (Oxford 1955) should be consulted. Among the vast literature that in recent years has developed on the Qumran sect *The Dead Sea Scrolls* by M. Burrows (1956) gives an objective account of these contentious manuscripts. *From Religion to Philosophy* by F. M. Cornford (1912) and *The Theology of the Early Greek Philosophers* by W. Jaeger (1947) deal with the pre-Socratic Hellenic ethical concepts, and the Orphic life is discussed in *Orpheus and Greek Religion* by W. K. C. Guthrie (1935), by M. P. Nilsson in 'Early Orphism and Kindred Religious Movements', *Harvard Theological Review*, XXVIII. 1935, and by I. M. Linforth, *The Arts of Orpheus* (California 1941).

CHAPTER X

The rise, development and diffusion of the ancient gods in the region under review in this volume have to be set against the background briefly sketched in the opening chapters and studied in the literature that has been indicated, and in the sources mentioned in the references in this chapter. Particular attention should be paid at this stage in the inquiry to the later phases in Graeco-oriental theistic development and syncretism. In this connexion among many books that might be suggested, the following are very relevant to the investigation pursued in this volume—*The Cult of the Greek States* by L. R. Farnell in 5 vols. (Oxford 1896–1909) is the most complete account of the Greek gods, while *Zeus* by A. B. Cook (3 vols. Cambridge 1914–40) is the fullest treatment of the Sky-god cult, if some of the interpretations are open to question. *The Greeks and Their Gods* by W. K. C. Guthrie (1950) is a very useful general survey, as is *Higher Aspects of Greek Religion* by L. R. Farnell (1912), *The Gods of the Greeks* by C. Kerényi (1951), and *Ancient Greek Religion* by H. J. Rose (1946). *Religious Thought of the Greeks* by C. H. Moore (Cambridge, Mass. 2nd ed. 1925) is a well-informed account of the progress of religious thought from Homer to the Christian era. For the Hellenistic Age, *Phases in the Religion of Ancient Rome* by C. Bailey (Oxford 1932), *Hellenistic Religions* by F. C. Grant (Liberal Arts Press, New York 1953) and his *Ancient Roman Religion* (1957) describe very adequately the development and nature of the cults and beliefs in the Empire. *The Pagan Background of Christianity* by W. R. Halliday (1925) remains a standard work. The Hellenistic impact on Judaism is considered in great detail in eight volumes by E. R. Goodenough under the title *Jewish Symbols in the Graeco-Roman Period* (Pantheon Books, 1953–58), and in his study of Philo in *By Light, Light: The Mystic Gospel of Hellenistic Judaism* (Yale Press 1935). For the Egyptian amalgam see *Cults and Creeds in Graeco-Roman Egypt* by H. Idris Bell (Liverpool University Press 1953). For Mithraism the two outstanding volumes are still *Mystères de Mithra* (Paris 1913, ET 2nd ed. 1910) by F. Cumont, and *Eine Mithrasliturgie* by A. Dieterich (Leipzig 1910). *Primitive Christianity in Its Contemporary Setting* by R. Bultmann (ET 1956)—although the last chapter should not be read uncritically, the description of the Hellenistic and Palestinian environment in which Christianity arose is illuminating. *Conversion* by A. D. Nock (Oxford 1933) is quite one of the best concise expositions of the religious situation in the Roman Empire from the time of Alexander the Great to that of St Augustine, and of what adhesion to Christianity involved for pagans living in this environment.

INDEX

Eumolpidae, the, 133, 166
Euphrates, the, 19ff., 28, 62, 77, 117, 134, 220, 266
Euripides, 289, 344
Evans, Sir Arthur, 41, 54, 100, 104ff., 130, 323ff., 348
Evans-Pritchard, E. E., 69, 324
Evil, the problem of, 276ff., 290, 318
Exile, the, 126, 190, 277
Exodus, the, 36ff., 149, 151, 219
Exorcism, 237ff., 239
Expiation rites, 156ff.
Eye-goddess, the, 48
Ezekiel, 258ff., 310
Ezra, 310

Fall of man, the, 221ff., 278
Farnell, L. R., 165, 298, 326ff., 333, 348, 352
Ferm, V., 347
Fertile Crescent, the, 28, 43, 70, 292ff.
Fertility cults, 46ff., 293, see Figurines, Corn cultus, Vegetation ritual
Festivals: Sed, the, 110ff., 114ff.
    Seasonal, 91, 94, 112, 115ff., 117, 122, 128ff., 134ff., 308
    in Anatolia, 128ff., 157
    in Egypt, 110ff., 134ff.
    in Greece, 160ff.
    in Israel, 147ff.
    in Mesopotamia, 140ff.
    in Syria, 146
Figurines, female, in:
    Anatolia, 49
    Baluchistan, 51ff.
    Crete, 53ff., 101
    Eastern Mediterranean, 53ff.
    Egypt, 53ff.
    Indus valley, 52
    Neolithic, 47ff.
    Palaeolithic, 46
    Transcaspia, 50
First-fruits, the offering of, 150, 162
Firstlings, 149
Flood, the Hebrew, 219, 222, 278; Mesopotamian, 74, 118, 303
Fractional burials, 63, 66
Frankfort, H., 121, 204, 264, 322, 327, 331, 347ff., 349, 351
Frazer, Sir J. G., 149, 324ff., 326, 348
Funerary ritual in:
    Egypt, 171ff.
    Greece, 195
    Israel, 186ff.
    Mesopotamian, 62ff., 178
    Mycenaean, 193ff.
    Syrian, 182ff.

Gadd, C., 348, 349

Gaia, 225ff.
Gardiner, A. H., 116, 327ff., 330, 342
Garstang, J., 36, 38, 94, 322ff., 326, 348
Gaster, T. H., 158, 325ff., 332, 337, 344, 347ff.
Gauthier, H., 331, 348
Gawra Tepe, 48, 63
Geb, 71, 81, 85, 169, 177, 225
Gebel el Arak, knife handle scene, 30
Gehenna, 192
Gerzean period, 29, 71, 139; cemetery, 59
Ghirshman, G., 321, 323, 346
Gideon, 124
Gigunu, the, 144, 154
Gilgal, 252ff.
Gilgamesh epic, the, 119, 180ff., 221
Ginsberg, H. L., 325
Glossolaly, 231
Gnostic dualism, 282, 311
God, see Deity, Earth-goddess, Mother-goddess, Sky-god
    fatherhood of, 320; suffering god, 78, 320, see Adonis, Attis, Tammuz
    the Young, 77, 81ff., 87, 90, 97, 104ff., 143, 296, 298, 304, 306
Goetze, A., 326, 330, 332
Good, the, 290, see Plato
Good and evil, conception of in:
    Babylonia, 266ff.
    Egypt, 260ff.
    Greece, 283ff.
    Israel, 272ff.
    Zoroastrianism, 279ff.
Goodenough, E. R., 352
Gordon, C. H., 122, 146, 329, 331, 348
Graillot, H., 348
Grave-goods, 59, 64, 66, 184, 194ff.
Gray, B., 149, 331
Gray, J., 124, 329
Greece, rise of civilization in, 40ff.; city-states in, 43; language, 43
Gudea, 73, 208, 271
Guillaume, A., 351
Gunkel, H., 350
Gurney, O. R., 326, 330, 332, 347ff.
Güterbock, 330, 338, 347
Guthrie, W. K. C., 226, 244, 338, 340, 350ff., 352

Habiru, the, 38ff.
Hadad, 122, 214, 306
Hades, 195ff., 223, 287
Hagia Triada, sarcophagus, 55, 68, 100
Halafian culture, the, 19, 34ff., 47, 67, 293
Halliday, W. R., 350, 352
Hammurabi, 35, 75, 119, 121, 212, 271, 306; code of, 271ff.
Hannahanna, 96, 308
Harakhte, 71, 300ff.